EXPLORIN␣ FAMILY THEORIES

Bron B. Ingoldsby
Brigham Young University

Suzanne R. Smith
Washington State University Vancouver

J. Elizabeth Miller
Northern Illinois University

Roxbury Publishing Company
Los Angeles, California

Library of Congress Cataloging-in-Publication Data

Ingoldsby, Bron B.
Exploring family theories / Bron B. Ingoldsby, Suzanne R. Smith, J. Elizabeth Miller.
p. cm.
Includes bibliographical references and index.
ISBN 1-931719-17-9
1. Family—Research. 2. Interpersonal conflict—Research. 3. Interpersonal communication—Research. 4. Symbolic interactionism. I. Smith, Suzanne R., 1968– II. Miller, J. Elizabeth, 1958– III. Title.
HQ519.I54 2004
305.85—072—dc21   2003043189
                                                            CIP

Exploring Family Theories

Publisher: Claude Teweles
Managing Editor: Dawn VanDercreek
Production Editor: Monica K. Gomez
Copy Editor: Pauline Piekarz
Cover Design: Marnie Kenney
Typography: SDS Design, info@sds-design.com

Printed on acid-free paper in the United States of America. This book meets the standards of recycling of the Environmental Protection Agency.

ISBN 1-931719-17-9

ROXBURY PUBLISHING COMPANY
P.O. Box 491044
Los Angeles, California 90049-9044
Voice: (310) 473-3312 • Fax: (310) 473-4490
E-mail: roxbury@roxbury.net
Website: www.roxbury.net

To our own families,
with whom family life is not a theory,
but a wonderful reality.

Acknowledgments

The authors would like to acknowledge each other as equal collaborators in this endeavor. We have been colleagues and friends for our entire careers, yet we still learned from each other's expertise, knowledge, and teaching styles while working on this project.

We would like to collectively thank Claude Teweles, Stephanie Trkay, and Monica Gomez at Roxbury Publishing Company for guiding us through this process. In addition, thanks to the many colleagues who graciously gave of their time and expertise in reviewing the prospectus and the final product: Maureen Blankemeyer (Kent State University), Mary Bold (Texas Woman's University), Lillian Chenoweth (Texas Woman's University), J. Kenneth Davidson, Sr. (University of Wisconsin–Eau Claire), Deborah Gentry (Illinois State University), Richard Glotzer (University of Akron), Charles B. Hennon (Miami University), Patrick McKenry (Ohio State University), Walter Schumm (Kansas State University), Bahira Sherif (University of Delaware), and Elizabeth Thompson (Miami University).

We would also like to thank our departments for their support throughout this project. Specifically, we would like to thank the School of Family Life at Brigham Young University, the Human Development Department at Washington State University Vancouver, and the School of Family, Consumer, and Nutrition Sciences at Northern Illinois University. We also acknowledge the earlier efforts of the faculty in the Department of Child and Family Development at the University of Georgia who taught the importance of integrating theory, research, and application, thus producing three alumni in three different cohorts who are all committed enough to those ideals to write this book together.

A personal note of appreciation from Beth Miller goes to Gary Gray for his diligent and loving editorial support, to Anchal Khanna for her work on the original market analysis, and to the Graduate School of Northern Illinois University for its support of this project.

Finally, we pay tribute to the originators of the theories themselves, many of whose works are included in this text. We acknowledge the important contributions of today's family researchers that continue to enhance our understanding of family theories, and recognize that their scholarship will expand our knowledge of families and further our ability to apply that knowledge in its proper theoretical context. Finally, we recognize those students reading this book who will one day write their own text on family theories based on the ideals of those before them, but enlightened by their own educational and research experiences. ✦

Contents

Sample Reading:

Chapter Two
Family Developmental Theory

Sample Reading:

Chapter Three
Exchange Theory

Chapter Four
Symbolic Interactionism Theory 81

Chapter Five
Conflict Theory

Chapter Six
Family Stress Theory

Sample Reading:

About the Authors

Bron B. Ingoldsby is an Associate Professor of Family Life at Brigham Young University in Provo, Utah. He earned his Ph.D. from the University of Georgia. Dr. Ingoldsby is a recognized scholar in the area of cross-cultural family relationships, and an active member of the National Council on Family Relations.

Suzanne R. Smith is an Associate Professor of Human Development at Washington State University Vancouver. She earned her Ph.D. from the University of Georgia. Dr. Smith's primary area of research is parent-child relationships. She has served as president of both the North West Council on Family Relations and the Teaching Family Science Association.

J. Elizabeth Miller is an Associate Professor of Family and Child Studies at Northern Illinois University. She has also served as director of Teaching Assistant Training and Development in the Graduate School. She earned her Ph.D. from the University of Georgia. Her primary research is in the area of family policy and education. Dr. Miller is active in the National Council on Family Relations and the American Association of Higher Education. ✦

of discrete objects—matter (such as protons, neutrons, and electrons) and energy (such as electricity and heat). Things were described as "absolutes," and the speed of light was "absolutely" the fastest speed that anything could reach. Einstein looked at this theory and asked the question "What if I were traveling in a rocket at the speed of light?" This question led him to develop his theory of relativity ($e = mc^2$), which stated that matter and energy were two forms of the same thing, linked together by the speed of light, and that time was relative, depending on how fast you could travel in relation to the speed of light.

Where Do Theories Come From?

Theories generally don't emerge fully formed all at once. Instead, they build slowly over time, as scholars gather data through observation and analysis of evidence, relating concepts together in different ways. This type of reasoning, moving from specific bits of information toward a general idea, is known as *inductive reasoning*. Once the theory exists, scholars use the general ideas of the theory to generate more specific questions, often in the form of research questions, thereby moving in the opposite direction. Taking a general idea from a theory and testing it out to tease the details is known as *deductive reasoning*. Both

kinds of thinking patterns are common in theory construction and development, and demonstrate the linkage between research and theory once again.

Theories are not stagnant, however. Theories give rise to research, which generates data. The data filter back into the cycle, contributing to our knowledge of and refining our understanding of the theory. As our understanding changes, so then do our research questions. It is also important to remember that theories do not exist in a cultural vacuum, but are the product of humans and their experiences. As humans redefine their values, their theories are influenced by those changes. This is particularly evident in theories of social science, but can be seen in natural science as well. After all, it was once believed that the world was flat, and that the earth was the center of the universe.

Radical changes or shifts in scientific views are known as "paradigm shifts" (Kuhn 1970). These shifts occur after significant data have been gathered that do not fit the current theory. Thus, a new theory is needed to explain the data. According to Kuhn, in the natural sciences, paradigm shifts change science dramatically, as did Einstein's theory of relativity

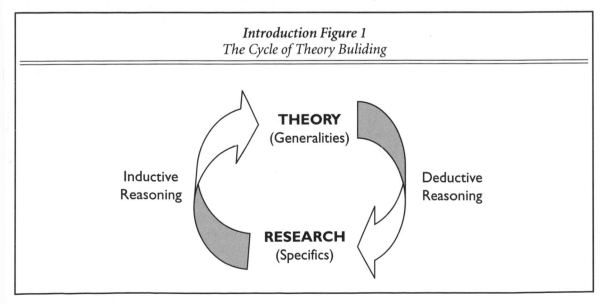

Introduction Figure 1
The Cycle of Theory Buliding

THEORY
(Generalities)

Inductive
Reasoning

Deductive
Reasoning

RESEARCH
(Specifics)

Introduction

"The fascination of sociology lies in the fact that its perspective makes us see in a new light the very world in which we have lived all our lives. This also constitutes a transformation of consciousness."

—P. L. Berger, *Invitation to Sociology: A Humanistic Perspective*

"Why do you do that? Why do you behave that way?" Questions about people's behavior are the essence of social science inquiry. The focus may be on individuals, families, social groups, communities, or cultures. In order to engage in the process of social science inquiry, you need two things: research and theory. Before we enter into a discussion of social science theory, and specifically family theory, we first need to have a general discussion about theory.

WHAT IS THEORY?

A theory is a tool used to understand and describe the world. More specifically, a theory is a general framework of ideas and how they relate to each other that can be used to answer questions about the world. The usefulness of a theory is measured by its ability to describe or predict some event or behavior.

You probably are familiar with many theories already, such as the theory of evolution, the theory of relativity, the theory of the big bang,

and the theory of plate tectonics. There are a[l] theories that describe human activities, such music theory, economic theory, and the theo[ry] of language. The theory of plate tectonics, f[or] example, describes the earth's surface as hu[ge] sections of the earth's solid crust floating o[n] molten, liquid inner core. It predicts *where* v[ol]canoes and earthquakes will most likely occ[ur] that is, where these sections of crust r[ub] against or bump into each other. It does n[ot,] however, predict *when* volcanoes will erupt [or] earthquakes will happen. But earth scienti[sts] can use the theory as a basis for research a[nd] data collection so that they can someday pr[e]dict when earthquakes will occur.

The degree to which a theory helps us ge[n]erate questions—its *heuristic* value—is al[so] important. A theory can help us decide what [to] research, and the results of that research c[an] lead to the development of new theories, wh[ich] again leads to new research. Such a benefic[ial] relationship is called a *symbiotic* relationsh[ip.] Research poses questions and then tries to a[n]swer them by making observations and c[ol]lecting data. When enough data have been c[ol]lected, patterns emerge, and a theory [is] developed to try to explain the patterns t[hat] are observed. Thus, the theory helps us *expl*[ain] "what's going on" and can allow us to *pre*[dict] "what's going to happen" when certain con[di]tions are present.

A theory can also change the way we v[iew] and understand the world. Take, as an exa[m]ple, Einstein's theory of relativity. Before E[in]stein, the world was viewed as being made [up] or the fact that Columbus did not, in fact, fall off the end of the earth.

In the social sciences, paradigm shifts are not as obvious because we do not evaluate our theories from the standpoint of truth, but rather on how useful they are. We as scholars cannot define what is true for all humans or families, so neither can our theoretical perspectives. At times significant changes in culture or human experience can change theoretical perspectives in radical ways. However, generally social theories are not discarded as they are in natural science, but instead are used to explain more specific social phenomena from different perspectives.

Many of the world's greatest minds, those whose ideas literally changed the way we understand the world, were theoreticians. For example, we live in a post-Freudian world: Freud's theories revolutionized our understanding of the mind, sexuality, and how we deal with stress. Karl Marx suggested that communism was an alternative to social injustice and oppression, and a method by which all humans could achieve a humane and equitable life. Freud and Marx brought about significant shifts in the way we thought about issues in society and human behavior that are still valued today, although we do not believe every aspect of Freudian psychology, and Marx's Communist Manifesto had its limitations. Similarly, Piaget brought about another paradigm shift in the area of cognitive development with his insight that children think in ways that are qualitatively different from adult processes. His theory has undergone modifications, and many still use his work as a basis for their research, but some have also gone beyond his work and expanded it. In this way, we evaluate theories based on the aspects of those theories that are useful.

How Are Theories Developed?

Theories are abstractions of the mind. They are not the data themselves, but rather the ideas that make sense of the data. They are intellectual constructs. Nevertheless, they have identifiable components that make up their structure. *Assumptions* are the beliefs that are taken for granted or believed to be true. They form the foundation underlying the theory. *Concepts* are the terms and specific ideas used in building the theory. *Propositions* are statements that demonstrate how concepts fit together in a context. They are the relationships between the concepts, the "glue" holding the theory together. Thus, a theory is based on assumptions and should be composed of clearly defined concepts that fit together in the form of propositions. To be useful, these propositions should be specific enough to lead scholars to be able to describe, explain, and predict phenomena, and to be able to ask questions that would guide their research in deductive ways. The theories should also be flexible enough to be able to grow and change so that new information can feed back into the theory, causing the theory to adapt and change in an inductive feedback loop. But the theory also needs to be general enough to apply to a wide variety of specific cases. In short, the usefulness of a theory is determined by its ability to describe more, rather than less, detail; to predict with more, rather than less, accuracy; and to apply to a broader, rather than a more narrow, range of specific cases.

It is also true that theories have a certain point of view, or lens. Depending on our emphasis, the perspective may be more broad (macro) or more narrow (micro). The lens we choose is often a function of the question we are asking, and so, again, a theory's usefulness depends on the subject at hand. In the social sciences, human situations are complex, and it is difficult to find one theory that can explain or predict every emotion, behavior, interaction, process, and event. Because of this, social theories are those lenses that we can use to help us to interpret or focus on the components of human interactions, and which allow us to do so in conceptual ways.

Although theories are abstract, they do serve important purposes in our understanding of social phenomena. Theories provide a general framework for understanding data in an organized way, as well as showing us how to intervene (Burr 1995). In social sciences, it is rare to find anyone who believes that there is only one way to understand social phenomena, particularly those as complicated as individuals and families. Thus, the frustrating but truthful response to many questions in social science is "It depends." Indeed it does depend on one's point of view, but that is not the same as one's opinion. For example, someone may believe that divorce sets a bad example for children. As scholars, we know that divorce is far more complex than "good or bad" and that a question about the effects of divorce on children cannot be easily answered. We need more complex ideas to analyze such situations, and we need to consider multiple elements within families to study aspects of divorce, its development, and its effects. To decide which theory to turn to, we consider the usefulness of the theory, or how well it enables us to answer the questions at hand. "How well" a theory does in explaining a situation depends on the researcher's point of view, or lens. Thus, two social scientists may each choose a different theory to explain the same situation.

Each theory allows us to look at different aspects of family life. One theory might suggest that we focus on the roles that people play, whereas another suggests that we focus more on the individual's gains and losses. Taking on the lens of the theory enables us to see how the world looks from that perspective. Each theory has underlying basic assumptions that focus the lens, just as each has concepts and propositions that guide what we analyze. Each theory was also developed within a historical context, and has asked different questions, and thus has a different research history. Because of this, each theory can give us a different answer to our question. Thus, "it depends."

THEORY IN HISTORICAL PERSPECTIVE

It can be interesting to trace the evolution of theory building and see how theories have become more sophisticated and accurate over time. Some of the earliest scientific writings of the western world come from the golden age of Greek civilization. Thinkers such as Aristotle were what we call "armchair philosophers." That is, they simply presumed that their ideas, if logical or rational, had to be true. Therefore, no effort was made to test them empirically. As a result, many of their ideas were later found to be incorrect. It was Galileo, for instance, who centuries later tested Aristotle's beliefs concerning weights and gravity. He, like many others, found that the truth is sometimes counterintuitive. Some of Aristotle's other ideas cannot even be called rational. For example, it is reported that he believed a woman could increase her chances of having a male child if she conceived it under a full moon and north wind after drinking lion's blood!

During the Renaissance, a number of key philosophers developed theories about the nature of children. John Calvin, a Protestant minister, felt that they were born evil and therefore needed to be forced into acting appropriately. Jean-Jacques Rousseau took the opposite position: that they were born good and therefore needed very little adult intervention. John Locke stood in the middle with his view that children are born as "blank slates," neither good nor bad, but empty vessels to be filled by proper environmental training. Most modern parenting theories and approaches derive from these basic theoretical frameworks.

A number of very important human development theories emerged in the late 1800s and early 1900s from the works of men that we will call "intuitive geniuses." We have the theory of evolution by Darwin, which has resulted in a dramatic paradigm shift in biology and related fields. Freud and his followers, such as Erik Erickson, took their clinical data and extrapolated elaborate theories of the mind that transformed psychology. Jean Piaget's careful observations and questions revolutionized our understanding of how we think. Each of these scholars built upon the data available to him or her with original and imaginative thinking.

By 1900, positivism was the dominant approach to science and theory building. It is based on the belief that "reality," or "truth," can be measured and understood independent of the observer. Behaviorism and most of the theories in this book are built on the tradition of careful measurement of empirical data. Newtonian physics makes the same assumptions. The idea is that there are repetitive and predictable patterns of behavior or action that can be found, measured, and explained in an organized way.

In recent years, we have seen the rise of postmodernism. Social scientists have drawn on Einstein's theory of relativity and on chaos theory, which developed from quantum mechanics. In this view, there is no reality independent of the observer and individual actions cannot be predicted. However, general patterns can be discerned.

Many of the ideas of former theoreticians, including some presented in this text, have become so well known as to seem mundane. As a result, there may be a temptation to say "Well, that is just common sense. Everyone knows that or could think of it on his or her own." Generally, that is the case because hardworking scholars have developed those very ideas, and they are so good that the public has come to know and accept them. As a result, we are changed and enriched by the contributions of the theoreticians.

FAMILY THEORY

Why study family theory? The family is certainly the most important and enduring of all human social groupings. What, then, could be more fascinating than the attempt to understand family dynamics? Nothing impacts our personality and happiness more than our family relationships. Why is kinship always the center of any human society? How do these interactions work, and why are they so influential in our lives?

Because there are so many perspectives to consider, it is not a simple thing to develop a coherent theory of family interaction. Social science is made even more difficult because we are attempting to understand ourselves. Whereas in the natural sciences we are examining objects and life forms that are less complex than we are, in human development we do not have the advantage of a higher intelligence than the subject in order to get a good *metaperspective*. With groups like families, there is the added complexity of looking beyond the individual to the relationships between individuals. All of this makes family theory development difficult at best.

We are also hindered by the difficulty in even having a good and commonly accepted definition of the term "family." Anthropologist George Murdock (1949) surveyed the world's cultures and came up with this definition: "The family is a social group characterized by common residence, economic cooperation, and reproduction. It includes adults of both sexes, at least two of whom maintain a socially approved sexual relationship, and one or more children, own or adopted, of the sexually cohabitating adults" (p. 1). His work (described in greater detail in our chapter on structural/functionalism) has generated a half century of ongoing scientific and political debate on what we mean when we say "family." As we will see, each theory has its own variation on the definition.

This is also a good example of why we need more than one family theory. First, there is more than one type of and definition of family. Second, even if you agree on how to define the family, you may disagree on which particular aspect of their interactions or behaviors you should focus your attention. Finally, each theory offers an insight the others cannot provide because of their different lenses.

The purpose of this text is to provide a basic introduction to the major theories pertaining to the family among professionals today. Each addresses different aspects of family life and answers different questions. Humans are extremely complex, and it is difficult to analyze ourselves; therefore, every theory will be imperfect. But each one brings us closer to understanding and being able to make positive change where needed in family life. Each theory has its own basic assumptions and concepts, and is a product of its own historical context as well. Each is used in answering specific research questions that other theories may not answer, or may answer differently. It will be up to you to try on the lens of each theory and determine how well you think it explains human and family behavior.

TEXT ORGANIZATION

We will discuss nine theories about the family that have been widely used and accepted over the last half century. We present them in rough chronological order. It is difficult to be precise, as most of them experienced a gradual emergence and some have long histories as general social theories before focusing on the family. Our order of placement is determined by the time in which significant publications discussing the theory from a family perspective appeared.

Shortly after World War II, three theories took center stage in the infancy of family theory building. Structural/functionalism, which comes from sociology and anthropology, takes a "macro" view of the family within culture. It looks at the family through the lens of asking what the family does to justify its existence in society.

Family developmental theory applies basic stage theory from psychology to families. It considers how families change over time in response to normative family events. Although its widespread use comes later, family stress theory, which looks at how the family as a system deals with challenging situations or events, was developed while studying family reactions to the depression, and later to wartime.

In the late 1950s and early 1960s, another trio of theories began to gain prominence. Each theory took more of an inside look at family communication and interaction. First, exchange theory takes its inspiration from behaviorism and economics in analyzing family decision-making as a rational process of choosing between rewards and costs. Next, symbolic interaction stems from the pragmatic philosophers of the early 1900s and is based on the belief that we construct our own realities. Events take on different meanings based on an individual's perceptions and the context of a situation. Finally, family systems theory derives from communication and clinical work. It makes a "micro" analysis of how family members relate to each other in a complex world of multi-causality.

Our final three theoretical approaches began to receive significant notice in the 1970s. First, conflict theory comes from a sociological perspective and focuses on how people and families create stability and instability in their relationships due to differences in status. Next, feminist theorists began their investigations with the perspective that womens' experiences are central to our understanding of families, and focus on the influences of social situations and politics. Finally, the biosocial perspective has its roots in the work of Charles Darwin. The general premise is that humans are driven by innate structures, but that the family and cultural environment influence those behaviors.

Each chapter begins with a fictional vignette to introduce a way of using that particular theory for understanding an aspect of family life. It is followed by a brief history of the development of the theory, and then an explanation of the basic assumptions that undergird the theory. The primary terms and concepts used in understanding the theory are provided. The usefulness of each theory is highlighted by examples of research and application within the particular framework. Every theory is critiqued, with its principle problems and strong points. Finally, the reader is provided with a series of questions and exercises designed to relate the implications of the theory to the vignette, and to the personal and family life of the student.

A highlight of this book is the integration of research with theory. After each chapter a professional research article has been included. Each research article illustrates how new information about families is gained when researchers used theories to guide their effort. The Epilogue links the chapters together, using a conceptual model for comparing and contrasting the theories. This model indicates how each can be useful for understanding and guiding intervention for particular situations from its viewpoint.

Once again, anyone can collect facts, but being a scholar requires understanding them in a way that allows for research, testing, comprehension, and practical application. In order to be useful, data must be ordered within a theoretical framework. Which will you enjoy the most and find the most useful? There is only one way to find out! ✦

References

Berger, P. L. (1973). *Invitation to Sociology: A Humanistic Perspective.* Woodstock, NY: Overlook.

Burr, W. R. (1995). Using theories in family science. In R. D. Day, K. R. Gilbert, B. H. Settles, and W. R. Burr (eds.), *Research and Theory in Family Science* (pp. 73–88). Pacific Grove, CA: Brooks-Cole.

Kuhn, T. S. (1970). *The Structure of Scientific Revolutions* (2nd ed.). Chicago: University of Chicago Press.

Murdock, G. P. (1949). *Social Structure.* New York: Free Press. ✦

Chapter One
Structural/ Functionalism Theory

Ralph and Alice have been married for about 20 years. Ralph feels that they have a good thing going. He works in construction and is able to provide well for his family. He was able to offer Alice this sense of security when they got married. He is also handy around the house, fixing things as they break or wear out and keeping the place looking nice.

Alice is attractive and a good sexual partner. Rather than working outside the home, she has kept the house clean and meals prepared, and focused her time on the rearing of their four beautiful children. The kids have always appreciated her help with schoolwork and her ability to attend and support their various activities. They have been representative of the traditional, nuclear Western family.

Recently, Alice has grown restless and less satisfied. She would like to get a part-time job in order to have some spending money that she could control. And she would like Ralph to spend more time talking with her instead of working on some project in the garage. Ralph feels that things are just fine the way they are—why do they have to change?

But things are changing. With the children growing up and moving out, the family structure is reverting back to that of a couple. Alice has more free time than she had in the past and would like to focus on some of her own interests. Ralph can see the point of using some of his salary to hire someone to make home repairs—but in order to give him more time to watch sports on TV, not to use it for the womanly tasks of shopping and talking about feelings!

Ralph wants both of them to do what they are supposed to do: He works as the provider and she takes care of him. Alice feels that it makes more sense for them both to provide and nurture.

HISTORY

Functional theory, as it is often called, is based on the "organic analogy." This is the idea, developed by early social philosophers such as Comte and Durkheim, that society is like the human body. Just as the body is made up of various parts that need to function together and properly for it to be healthy, so is society. Each part needs to be in a state of *equilibrium*, or balance. Just as the human body has evolved over time, so has society. Comte introduced "positivism"—the view that social science should be based on empirical observations—into social thought. He focused on terms that later became popular in functional theory—solidarity and consensus, which refer to the interconnectedness of social life and the source of its unity. Durkheim was also concerned with how social systems are integrated and hold themselves together (Kingsbury and Scanzoni 1993).

The writings of social anthropologist Alfred Radcliffe-Brown (1952) were pivotal in establishing a field of comparative sociology, with structural functionalism as its most important tool. His essay on understanding the role of the mother's brother in certain societies helped to supplant social Darwinism with the new and, at the time, relatively sophisticated framework of structural/functionalism.

The leading thinker of functionalism in America was Talcott Parsons (1951), who believed that behavior was driven by our efforts to conform to the moral code of society. The purpose of such codes is to constrain human behavior in ways that promote the common good. The purpose of an organism is to survive. In order for a society to survive, the subsystems (the family and other institutions) must function in ways that promote the maintenance of society as a whole. This is similar to how a person's organs must function in interrelated ways in order to maintain a healthy body.

For Parsons, the key to societal survival was the shared norms and values held by its individual members. Deviation from those norms leads to disorganization, which threatens the survival of the system. Since the family is the key system in society, divorce, teen rebellion, non-marital sex, and single parenthood all threaten the structure or the functions of the family and therefore need to be avoided.

By the 1950s functionalism had become the dominant paradigm in sociology, and it has had a tremendous impact on family studies. Family research since the 1930s has adopted the organic model, with its many studies on marital quality and adjustment. Family stability is assumed to be critical to childhood outcomes, and since marital satisfaction is central to that stability, it must be one of the most important research questions in the field. The existence of any social structure, such as the family, is explained by the functions it carries out for the greater society (Kingsbury and Scanzoni 1993).

The social upheaval of the 1960s led many to criticize functionalism for its inability to deal with change. Parsons did not see deviant behavior as contributing to positive change, whereas others, such as Merton (1957), did recognize the role of conflict in maintaining equilibrium or leading to a new relationship status. Other writers (Goode 1969) strove to raise the level of theoretical rigor in the discipline. Parsons ignored these ideas, feeling that change always came from the outside (such as industrialization leading to the pre-eminence of the nuclear family) and that children only learned culturally approved values in the family. He also called on Freudian ideas to support his claim that there were biologically driven roles (instrumental and expressive) that men and women should fulfill within the ideal structure of the nuclear family.

As a result, structural/functionalism fell into disfavor with scientists after the 1970s. Holman and Burr (1980) declared it to be a "peripheral"

theory with very little to contribute to contemporary thinking. Nevertheless, its organic model and the concept of the family needing to stay in balance are important assumptions in more modern family theories, such as stress and systems (Kingsbury and Scanzoni 1993).

In addition, the case has been made (White, Marshall, and Wood 2002) that a considerable amount of present-day family research uses family structure without explicitly recognizing it as a key variable. They concluded, using Canadian data on childhood outcomes, that parenting processes are more important than family structure. There are contemporary scholars, such as Wallerstein and Blakeslee (1989) and Popenoe (1996), who argue that the intact nuclear family is still an important component in healthy child rearing.

Perhaps more important is the fact that family structure continues to play a role in political decision making. White et al. (2002) indicate that politicians, in making decisions about single parents and welfare, for instance, often overestimate the importance of family structure in creating their policies.

BASIC ASSUMPTIONS

The function of families is to procreate and socialize children. Structural/functionalism is basically a theory of social survival. Its key idea is that families perform the critical functions of procreation and socializing of children so that they will fit into the overall society. Theorists ask themselves what is needed for a society to maintain itself and then what institutions or subgroups within that society are providing them. They conclude that the intact nuclear family of husband, wife, and their children is the ideal structure. This is the configuration of individuals in the modern world that works best in meeting the needs of its members, as well as those of the larger society. That is, it *functions* best.

All systems have functions. Theoretical work has focused principally on the functions carried out by the family and what these functions accomplish. Although other functions are mentioned, the procreation and socialization of children are central. The main function of any social system, including the family, is simply to maintain its basic structure.

Parsons concluded that the best way to do this was for husbands and wives to play certain roles. Males need to be *instrumental,* which means that they are the ones who provide for the family. Because of this, their abilities should be focused on meeting the physical needs of the members in terms of food, shelter, education, and income. In contrast, females are to be *expressive,* meaning that they meet the emotional needs of family members by being nurturing and smoothing out problems in relationships. According to this theory, the biological imperatives of motherhood predispose women for this "indoor" work, whereas the greater physical strength of men leads them naturally into the provider role (Winton 1995).

PRIMARY TERMS AND CONCEPTS

STRUCTURE

The structure refers to the composition of the family, or what members make up the family institution within a particular society. Is it a nuclear or single-parent family? Is the marriage intact, or has there been a death or divorce?

FUNCTION

What are the services the family provides to society? The family exists for the functions that it serves which enhance the survival of the larger group. We best understand the purpose of any organization by examining what it does, or its functions.

INSTRUMENTAL

Tasks that need to be performed within a family to ensure its physical survival are instrumental in nature. The focus is placed on providing the material needs of the family members, and it is often assumed from historical analysis that males are best suited for these tasks. This would include earning a family income, paying the rent, and providing for transportation and clothing.

EXPRESSIVE

The human relationship interactions necessary for the psychological satisfaction of the family members are expressive in nature. They include love, communication, and support and are generally assumed, due to biology, to be tasks best suited for females. Thus, mothers are often thought to better meet the emotional needs of children than fathers.

EQUILIBRIUM

The assumption here is that any human system will resist change. Change comes gradually, but in general, family members function best when things are in balance. Parsons felt that this is best achieved when the members share the same values and goals and when they carry out differentiated roles—that is, each spouse fulfilling a different role, such as an instrumental husband and an expressive wife (Winton 1995).

✦THE BENCHMARK FAMILY✦

The benchmark family refers to the traditional intact nuclear family of a husband, wife, and their children, with the husband as breadwinner and the wife as homemaker. (Yes, Ward, June, Wally, and Beaver Cleaver may come to mind here!) Many Americans consider most relationship patterns that differ from this ideal as less desirable, or even deviant, by comparison (Kingsbury and Scanzoni 1993).

DEVIANT BEHAVIOR

Merton (1957) developed a typology of deviant behavior. The purpose here is to go beyond the initial development of the theory and show how behaviors that deviate from the social norms can play a useful role in the theory. The examples are drawn from Kingsbury and Scanzoni (1993) but could also be made for a wife/mother or children in their respective roles.

CONFORMITY

Non-deviance is the same as conformity. For instance, a husband/father is a good provider and does so in the approved manner of hard work and achievement. In this case, he has conformed to the social norm of being the family breadwinner.

INNOVATION

In the category of innovation, the man accepts the goal of material success but attains it in an illegal or otherwise socially unacceptable manner. He is therefore both conforming and deviant. An example of this would be the corporate lawyer who uses privileged information for his own economic gain.

RITUALISM

Ritualism refers to a man who gives up on success but still works hard. Therefore, no matter how hard he tries, he will not meet his wife's expectations of him as a provider. Why does he continue to try? Because that is his nature, or his ritual.

RETREATISM

Retreatism refers to the husband who rejects both the normative goals and the means to obtain them. Drug addicts and homeless people are examples of individuals who might fall into this category. They avoid both the rewards of society and the frustrations that come with trying to attain them. In other words, they retreat from cultural norms.

REBELLION

Rebellious individuals are like those in the previous category, except that they also attempt to create a new social structure. They might argue that material success is corrupting and that we should focus on spiritual or other goals instead. This last category in particular allows functionalism to deal with change in ways that Parsons could not.

COMMON AREAS OF RESEARCH AND APPLICATION

Structural/functionalism has been most useful in guiding comparative research about the family, chiefly as it is carried out by anthropologists and sociologists who were searching for any universalities in family life as well as cultural variations. This research has provided the foundation upon which much of modern family science is built. Below are some of the key areas of knowledge attained, thanks to the structural/functionalism framework.

FAMILY STRUCTURE

George Murdock (1949) surveyed 250 societies described in the Human Relations Area Files, an immense collection of ethnographic field notes on cultures around the world. From this, he concluded that what he called the "nuclear family" was the basic social structure for humans everywhere. It consists of a husband, wife, and their children. This was the minimal structure, and it was the norm in one-fourth of the societies surveyed. The others were either polygamous or extended but had a nuclear family at the core.

FAMILY FUNCTIONS

Historical analysis demonstrates that, across time, the family has provided many important functions for society. In modern times many of these functions—religion, health care, protection, education, and entertainment—have been taken over by other institutions. Today we have churches, the medical establishment, the police, public and private schools, movies, and other entities to meet these needs. As these kinds of changes occur, the family adapts and focuses on what it does best (Ingoldsby and Smith 1995).

Murdock (1949) concluded that there were four essential functions that the family provides for all societies. The first is *sexual*. All societies have found that this powerful impulse must be restrained in order to avoid chaos. However, it must not be overregulated or personality problems and an insufficient population would result. The compromise found everywhere is marriage. Although sexual relations do occur outside of marriage, most sexual expression occurs in marriage, and it is the one context in which sexual behavior is always socially acceptable.

The second function is *reproduction*. This follows naturally from the fact that marriage is the primary sexual relationship in all societies. While many children are born out of wedlock, the majority are born according to society's preference, which is within the family. Such children are usually privileged in terms of acceptance, inheritance, and other factors.

The third function is *socialization*. In addition to producing children, the family must care for them physically and train them to perform adult tasks and adopt the values deemed appropriate by their particular culture. As Lee (1982) points out, this is much more than just learning occupational skills. It involves language skills and the transmission of culture as well. All societies depend on the family to love and nurture their children so that they will become civilized.

The final function is *economic*. This does not mean that the family is the economic unit of production, although it has been in many times and places. Here Murdock (1949) was referring to the division of labor by gender. "By virtue of their primary sex differences, a man and a woman make an exceptionally efficient cooperating unit. . . . All known human societies have developed specialization and cooperation between the sexes roughly along this biologically determined line" (p. 7). In other words, since males have greater physical strength and females bear the children, marital pairs have found that their survival is enhanced if they divide responsibilities according to their capacities.

In addition, the functions of rituals and behaviors within the family are also analyzed. Each culture has its own approaches to birthing, parenting, sexual taboos, and other matters. A productive way of understanding these family rules is to investigate what functions they each serve for the family and the society at large.

Origin of the Family

The questions of how and when the family originated among humans is presently considered to be beyond the reach of science. How-

ever, there have been many philosophical and theoretical speculations, and the large majority of them have come to the same basic conclusion: The structure of the family developed as the result of the economic division of labor. Social and technological changes have reduced this traditional (expressive/instrumental) division of labor proposed by the functionalists (Ingoldsby and Smith 1995), but the argument that economic efficiency and sexual attraction are the basis for marriage and family life is still a powerful one. As Lee (1982) explains, "the family originated among human beings because a certain division of labor between the sexes was found to be convenient or efficient and maximized the probability of survival for individuals and groups . . . the logic here implies that the origin of sex roles . . . coincided with the origin of the family" (p. 54).

Family Universality

Functionalists have wanted to determine if the family exists everywhere as a social institution. If it does, then it can be said that the family may be necessary for the survival of human society. However, if it can be demonstrated that there exists even one culture without the family as we define it, then it must be concluded that although the family unit is common, there are viable alternatives. Murdock's (1949) research convinced him that the nuclear family is universal and necessary for human social life. "No society, in short, has succeeded in finding an adequate substitute for the nuclear family, to which to transfer these functions. It is highly doubtful whether any society ever will succeed in such an attempt, utopian proposals for the abolition of the family to the contrary notwithstanding" (p. 11).

Stephens (1963) describes the work of Edith Clarke in Jamaica, and Melford Spiro with the Israeli kibbutz, which tells a different story. Clarke argued that fathers are missing from lower-class Jamaican families and that therefore the structure is mother-child rather than the father-mother-child triangle of the nuclear family. Similarly, Spiro's work gives the impression that the socialization and economic functions are not provided by the family in the kibbutz. Despite these studies, careful review by scholars has rejected these arguments and found in favor of Murdock's ideas instead.

However, Lee (1982) demonstrates that there are a few stable societies, such as the Nayar of India, in which biological fathers do not live with or provide for their families or help socialize their children. Mother-child dyads, typically with help from other male relatives, do exist as the norm in a few places, and function much like single-parent families do in the modern western world. Divorce can be said to provide the important function of enabling adults to escape from difficult relationships, and single parenting may become a necessary adaptation to that situation. In these other societies, however, mother-only parenting is the preferred family structure, even though the couple remains married.

A case could also be made that there are other functions beyond Murdock's four that are emerging as important family contributions to society. The principal one would be providing companionship and emotional support to its members. While love is not yet found to be essential for marriages everywhere, it is playing an ever greater role in urban, industrialized societies (Ingoldsby and Smith 1995).

MARITAL STRUCTURE

Students are often surprised to learn that historically polygyny (plural wives) is the preferred marital structure in over three-fourths of all societies. This is the case in spite of the fact that the relatively balanced sex ratio results in most people practicing monogamy. The temptation has always been to blame polygyny on the male sex drive, although functionalists make a very convincing case that it is actually about economics. Societies that engage in light agriculture and animal husbandry tend to prefer polygyny because the labor of women and children creates wealth, and therefore these families are better off than monogamous ones. In contrast, polyandrous (multiple husbands) unions, which are very rare, appear to be adaptations to economic poverty due to living in a

harsh environment (Ingoldsby and Smith 1995).

WORKING WOMEN

Early functionalists found working mothers to be destabilizing and therefore a threat to quality child rearing. Political conservatives who continue to take that position blame uncaring and greedy mothers in a materialistic society. However, structural/functionalism tends to look to outside forces, particularly economics, to explain change—for example, the rise in the number of working mothers since the 1960s has resulted from the shift in the United States from a manufacturing to a service economy. Since these new salaries are much lower than those paid for skilled factory work, couples have found it necessary for both of them to work outside the home in order to maintain a middle-class lifestyle. In this way, many valued supports for their children, such as music lessons and sports activities, can continue to be provided. This theory always encourages us to look to larger societal forces to explain changes in the family as it adapts to other changes.

FAMILY DEFINITION

There is considerable public debate today over what structures make up a family and what they need to do in order to qualify. Are single parents or gay/lesbian couples a family? These questions matter not only because of public acceptance but also because many government programs and privileges are connected to how the term *family* is defined. Basically, this issue is evaluated through the lens of structural/functionalism. Current scholarly debate over the impact of divorce, and the decline or adaptability of the family, is also informed to some degree by this framework.

CRITIQUE

A number of problems have contributed to the general decline in the acceptance and use of structural functionalism. The main ones are listed below. See Kingsbury and Scanzoni

(1993) and Winton (1995) for a more detailed description.

First, very few scientific ideas can be completely free of the dominant values of society, and structural/functionalism is no exception. Historically, it developed in a conservative time and therefore values traits that were popular at the time, such as structure, stability, and unity. As political views and cultural values have changed, support of the theory has waned.

At a deeper level, the theory is criticized for confusing "function" with "cause." Even though it may be possible to demonstrate that families perform certain functions that are necessary to society, it does not necessarily serve as a causal explanation for why families exist. The theory does not do a good job of explaining the historical process of how family types come to exist in a given society.

Functionalism also focuses on a macro-analysis of large social systems and assumes that maintaining a steady state is important. Many other theorists feel that understanding the interpersonal struggles that go on in family life are critical, and that disagreement must be assumed to be intrinsic to family life.

Finally, some theorists have made the mistake of assuming that just because something is functional, it deserves to be maintained. Feminists in particular have been offended by the notion that women should always perform expressive tasks, since this is seen as hurting their status in the system. Therefore, the status quo is dysfunctional for women, even if it has been functional for the rest of the family or the overall society in some times and places. This has been the most damaging critique of the theory.

However, structural/functionalism has a number of strengths that result in its usefulness in family studies today. As mentioned previously, the organic analogy is still used in other more current theoretical approaches. Family systems theory takes the basic concepts of equilibrium and roles and successfully applies them to a micro-analysis of family relationships.

As the research examples in the chapter demonstrate, the theory is very useful for cross-cultural scholarship. No other framework has been as successful in providing us with an understanding of different family forms and why they work at various times and in various places. An example would be the relationship between marital structure (monogamy, polygyny, and so forth) and economy (Lee 1982).

Finally, as Pittman (1993) explains, "the presumed moralism allegedly undergirding functionalism with a conservative, consensus-based, status quo bias, is almost certainly the product of the period of theory development (1940s and 1950s) rather than inherent to the theory itself" (p. 221). For example, the theory itself does not demand that all families need to be nuclear, with the husband acting instrumentally and the wife expressively. Researchers using this framework have simply noted the historical and comparative success of this approach in many societies. As times and circumstances—such as social views and economic structures—change, other structures or functions may prove to be more useful. Equilibrium can change and therefore be understood as dynamic. The basic theory is neutral in that it looks at stability but does not necessarily value it as superior to other possible forms. More modern interpretations of the theory have attempted to integrate conflict and change into the paradigm.

APPLICATION

1. Think about the couple described at the beginning of the chapter. How much can we learn about a family just by analyzing its structure and the functions that are performed?

2. Write a short paper listing every member of your own family of origin. What was its basic structure? Who performed the instrumental and expressive tasks? Were there other roles necessary to a calm functioning of the family, and if so, who carried them out?

3. Think back to a time of family crisis. What changes were taking place, and was a new and different equilibrium reached? Did anyone play a rebellious role in the crisis, and if so, how did that turn out? How strong were societal forces for things to remain the same?

4. How typical are the families that you know? What percentage do you think meet the criteria for being a benchmark family as described earlier in the chapter? How well, in comparison, do you feel the less traditional families function?

5. After reading the following article on love, discuss how dating and mate selection behaviors were handled in your family as you were growing up. In what ways did your parents try to control love?

SAMPLE READING

This chapter concludes with a copy of the classic article by William Goode, "The Theoretical Importance of Love." Goode takes a historical and cross-cultural look at love and analyzes its function in society and family life. He concludes that it must generally be controlled, to varying degrees, in the interest of mate selection processes that contribute to societal goals of chastity, social and kinship structure, and economics.

References

Goode, W. J. (1969). The theoretical importance of love. *American Sociological Review* 34: 38–47.

Holman, T., and Burr, W. (1980). Beyond the beyond: The growth of family theories in the 1970's. *Journal of Marriage and the Family* 42: 729–742.

Ingoldsby, B., and Smith, S. (1995). *Families in Multicultural Perspective.* New York: Guilford.

Kingsbury, N., and Scanzoni, J. (1993). Structural-functionalism. In P. G. Boss, W. J. Doherty, R. LaRossa, W. R. Schumm, and S. K. Steinmetz (eds.), *Sourcebook of Family Theories and Methods: A Contextual Approach* (pp. 195–217). New York: Plenum.

Lee, G. (1982). *Family Structure and Interaction: A Comparative Analysis.* Minneapolis, MN: University of Minnesota Press.

Merton, R. K. (1957). *Social Theory and Social Structure.* Glencoe, IL: Free Press.

Murdock, G. P. (1949). *Social Structure.* New York: Free Press.

Parsons, T. (1951). *The Social System.* New York: Free Press.

Pittman, J. (1993). Functionalism may be down, but it is not out: Another point of view for family therapists and policy analysts. In P. G. Boss, W. J. Doherty, R. LaRossa, W. R. Schumm, and S. K. Steinmetz (eds.), *Sourcebook of Family Theories and Methods: A Contextual Approach* (pp. 218–221). New York: Plenum.

Popenoe, D. (1996). *Life Without Father.* New York: Free Press.

Radcliffe-Brown, A. (1952). *Structures and Function in Primitive Society.* Glencoe, IL: Free Press.

Stephens, W. (1963). *The Family in Cross-Cultural Perspective.* New York: Holt, Rinehart & Winston.

Wallerstein, J., and Blakeslee, S. (1989). *Second Chances: Men, Women and Children a Decade After Divorce.* New York: Ticknor and Fields.

White, J., Marshall, S., and Wood, J. (2002). Confusing family structures: The role of family structure in relation to child well-being. Paper presented at the North West Council on Family Relations, Vancouver, British Columbia.

Winton, C. (1995). *Frameworks for Studying Families.* Guilford, CT: Duskin Publishing Group. ✦

The Theoretical Importance of Love

William J. Goode

Love is analyzed as an element of social action and therefore of social structure. Although the romantic complex is rare, a "love pattern" is found in a wide range of societies. Since love is potentially disruptive of lineages and class strata, it must be controlled. Since its meaning is different within different social structures, it is controlled by various measures. The five principal types of "love control" are described. Disruptions are more important to the upper social strata, who possess the means for control. Therefore these strata achieve a higher degree of control over both the occurrence of love relationships and the influence of love upon action.

Because love often determines the intensity of an attraction[1] toward or away from an intimate relationship with another person, it can become one element in a decision or action.[2] Nevertheless, serious sociological attention has only infrequently been given to love. Moreover, analyses of love generally have been confined to mate choice in the Western World,, while the structural importance of love has been for the most part ignored. The present paper, views love in a broad perspective, focusing on the structural patterns by which societies keep in check the potentially disruptive effect of love relationships on mate choice and stratification systems.

TYPES OF LITERATURE ON LOVE

For obvious reasons, the printed material on love is immense. For our present purposes, it may be classified as follows:

1. Poetic, humanistic, literary, erotic, pornographic: By far the largest body of all literature on love views it as a sweeping experience. The poet arouses our sympathy and empathy. The essayist enjoys, and asks the reader to enjoy, the interplay of people in love. The storyteller—Bocaccio, Chaucer, Dante—pulls back the curtain of human souls and lets the reader watch the intimate lives of others caught in an emotion we all know. Others—Vatsyayana, Ovid, William IX Count of Poitiers and Duke of Aquitaine, Marie de France, Andreas Capellanus—have written how-to-do-it books, that is, how to conduct oneself in love relations, to persuade others to succumb to one's love wishes, or to excite and satisfy one's sex partner.[3]

2. Marital counseling: Many modern sociologists have commented on the importance of romantic love in America and its lesser importance in other societies and have disparaged it as a poor basis for marriage, or as immaturity. Perhaps the best known of these arguments are those of Ernest R. Mowrer, Ernest W. Burgess, Mabel A. Elliott, Andrew G. Truxal, Francis E. Merrill, and Ernest R. Groves.[4] The antithesis of romantic love, in such analyses, is "conjugal" love; the love between a settled, domestic couple.

   A few sociologists, remaining within this same evaluative context, have instead claimed that love also has salutary effects in our society. Thus, for example, William L. Kolb[5] has tried to demonstrate that the marital counselors who attack romantic love are really attacking some fundamental values of our larger society, such as individualism, freedom, and personality growth. Beigel[6] has argued that if the female is sexually repressed, only the psychotherapist or love can help her overcome her inhibitions. He claims further that one influence of love in our society is that it extenuates illicit sexual relations; he goes on to assert: "Seen in proper perspective, [love] has not only done no harm as a prerequisite to marriage, but it has mitigated the impact that a too-fast-moving and unorganized conversion to new socio-economic constellations has had upon our whole culture and it has saved monogamous marriage from complete disorganization."

In addition, there is widespread comment among marriage analysts, that in a rootless society, with few common bases for companionship, romantic love holds a couple together long enough to allow them to begin marriage. That is, it functions to attract people powerfully together, and to hold them through the difficult first months of the marriage, when their different backgrounds would otherwise make an adjustment troublesome.

3. Although the writers cited above concede the structural importance of love implicitly, since they are arguing that it is either harmful or helpful to various values and goals of our society, a third group has given explicit if unsystematic attention to its structural importance. Here, most of the available propositions point to the functions of love, but a few deal with the conditions under which love relationships occur. They include:

(1) An implicit or assumed descriptive proposition is that love as a common prelude to and basis of marriage is rare, perhaps to be found as a pattern only in the United States.

(2) Most explanations of the conditions which create love are psychological, stemming from Freud's notion that love is "aim-inhibited sex."[7] This idea is expressed, for example, by Waller who says that love is an idealized passion which develops from the frustration of sex.[8] This proposition, although rather crudely stated and incorrect as a general explanation, is widely accepted.

(3) Of course, a predisposition to love is created by the socialization experience. Thus some textbooks on the family devote extended discussion to the ways in which our society socializes for love. The child, for example, is told that he or she will grow up to fall in love with some one, and early attempts are made to pair the child with children of the opposite sex. There is much joshing of children about falling in love; myths and stories about love and courtship are heard by children; and so on.

(4) A further proposition (the source of which I have not been able to locate) is that, in a society in which a very close attachment between parent and child prevails, a love complex is necessary, in order to motivate the child to free him from his attachment to his parents.

(5) Love is also described as one final or crystallizing element in the decision to marry, which is otherwise structured by factors such as class, ethnic origin, religion, education, and residence.

(6) Parsons has suggested three factors which "underlie the prominence of the romantic context in our culture": (a) the youth culture frees the individual from family attachments, thus permitting him to fall in love; (b) love is a substitute for the interlocking of kinship roles found in other societies, and thus motivates the individual to conform to proper marital role behavior; and (c) the structural isolation of the family so frees

the married partners' affective inclinations that they are able to love one another.[9]

(7) Robert F. Winch has developed a theory of "complementary needs" which essentially states that the underlying dynamic in the process of falling in love is an interaction between (a) the perceived psychological attributes of one individual and (b) the complementary psychological attributes of the person falling in love, such that the needs of the latter are felt to be met by the perceived attributes of the former and *vice versa.* These needs are derived from Murray's list of personality characteristics. Winch thus does not attempt to solve the problem of why our society has a love complex, but how it is that specific individuals fall in love with each other rather than with someone else.[10]

(8) Winch and others have also analyzed the effect of love upon various institutions or social patterns: Love themes are prominently displayed in the media of entertainment and communication, in consumption patterns, and so on.[11]

4. Finally, there is the cross-cultural work of anthropologists, who in the main have ignored love as a factor of importance in kinship patterns. The implicit understanding seems to be that love as a pattern is found only in the United States, although of course individual cases of love are sometimes recorded. The term "love" is practically never found in indexes of anthropological monographs on specific societies or in general anthropology textbooks. It is perhaps not an exaggeration to say that Lowie's comment of a generation ago would still be accepted by a substantial number of anthropologists:

> But of love among savages? . . . Passion, of course, is taken for granted; affection, which many travelers vouch for, might be conceded; but Love? Well, the romantic sentiment, occurs in simpler conditions, as with us—in fiction. . . . So Love exists for the savage as it does for ourselves—in adolescence, in fiction, among the poetically minded.[12]

A still more skeptical opinion is Linton's scathing sneer:

> All societies recognize that there are occasional violent, emotional attachments between persons of opposite sex, but our present American culture is practically the only one which has attempted to capitalize these, and make them the basis for marriage. . . . The hero of the modern American movie is always a romantic lover, just as the hero of the old Arab epic is always an epileptic. A cynic may suspect that in any ordinary population the percentage of individuals with a capacity for romantic love of the Hollywood type was about as large as that of persons able to throw genuine epileptic fits.[13]

In Murdock's book on kinship and marriage, there is almost no mention, if any, of love.[14] Should we therefore conclude that, cross-culturally, love is not important, and thus cannot be of great importance structurally? If there is only one significant case, perhaps it is safe to view love as generally unimportant in social structure and to concentrate rather on the nature and functions of romantic love within the Western societies in which love is obviously prevalent. As brought out below, however, many anthropologists have in fact described love *patterns.* And one of them, Max Gluckman,[15] has recently subsumed a wide range of observations under the broad principle that love relationships between husband and wife estrange the couple from their kin, who therefore try in various ways to undermine that love. This principle is applicable to many more societies (for example, China and India) than Gluckman himself discusses.

THE PROBLEM AND ITS CONCEPTUAL CLARIFICATION

The preceding propositions (except those denying that love is distributed widely) can be grouped under two main questions: What are the consequences of romantic love in the United States? How is the emotion of love aroused or created in our society? The present paper deals with the first question. For theoretical purposes both questions must be reformulated, however, since they implicitly refer only to our peculiar system of romantic love. Thus: (1) In what ways do various love patterns fit into the social structure, especially into the systems of mate choice and stratification? (2) What are the structural conditions under which a range of love patterns occurs in various societies? These are overlapping questions, but their starting point and assumptions are different. The first assumes that love relationships are a universal psychosocial possibility and that different social systems make different adjustments to their potential disruptiveness. The second does not take love for granted, and supposes rather that such relationships will be rare unless certain structural factors are present. Since in both cases the analysis need not depend upon the correctness of the assumption, the problem may be chosen arbitrarily. Let us begin with the first.[16]

We face at once the problem of defining "love." Here, love is defined as a strong emotional attachment, a cathexis, between adolescents or adults of opposite sexes, with at least the components of sex desire and tenderness. Verbal definitions of this emotional relationship are notoriously open to attack; this one is no more likely to satisfy critics than others. Agreement is made difficult by value judgments: one critic would exclude anything but "true" love, another casts out "infatuation," another objects to "puppy love," while others would separate sex desire from love because sex presumably is degrading. Nevertheless, most of us have had the experience of love, just as we have been greedy, or melancholy, or moved by hate (defining "true" hate seems not to be a problem). The experience can be referred to without great ambiguity, and a refined measure of various degrees of intensity or purity of love is unnecessary for the aims of the present analysis.

Since love may be related in diverse ways to the social structure, it is necessary to forego the dichotomy of "romantic love–no romantic love" in favor of a continuum or range between polar types. At one pole, a strong love attraction is socially viewed as a laughable or tragic aberration; at the other, it is mildly shameful to marry without being in love with one's intended spouse. This is a gradation from negative sanction to positive approval, ranging at the same time from low or almost nonexistent institutionalization of love to high institutionalization.

The urban middle classes of contemporary Western society, especially in the United States, are found toward the latter pole. Japan and China, in spite of the important movement toward European patterns, fall toward the pole of low institutionalization. Village and urban India is farther toward the center, for there the ideal relationship has been one which at least generated love after marriage, and sometimes after betrothal, in contrast with the mere respect owed between Japanese and Chinese spouses.[17] Greece after Alexander, Rome of the Empire, and perhaps the later period of the Roman Republic as well, are near the center, but somewhat toward the pole of institutionalization, for love matches appear to have increased in frequency—a trend denounced by moralists.[18]

This conceptual continuum helps to clarify our problem and to interpret the propositions reviewed above. Thus it may be noted, first, that individual love relationships may occur even in societies in which love is viewed as irrelevant to mate choice and excluded from the decision to marry. As Linton conceded, some violent love attachments may be found in any society. In our own, the Song of Solomon, Jacob's love of Rachel, and Michal's love for David are classic tales. The Mahabharata, the great Indian epic, includes love themes. Romantic love appears early in Japanese literature, and the use of Mt. Fuji as a locale for the suicide of star crossed lovers is not a myth invented by editors of tabloids. There is the familiar tragic Chinese story to be found on the traditional "willowplate," with its lovers transformed into doves. And so it goes—individual love relationships seem to occur everywhere. But this fact does not change the position of a society on the continuum.

Second, reading both Linton's and Lowie's comments in this new conceptual context reduces their theoretical importance, for they are both merely saying that people do not *live by* the romantic complex, here or anywhere else. Some few couples in love will brave social pressures, physical dangers, or the gods themselves, but nowhere is this usual. Violent, self-sufficient love is not common anywhere. In this respect, of course, the U.S. is not set apart from other systems.

Third, we can separate a *love pattern* from the romantic love *complex*. Under the former, love is a permissible, expected prelude to marriage, and a usual element of courtship—thus, at about the center of the continuum, but toward the pole of institutionalization. The romantic love complex (one pole of the continuum) includes, in addition, an ideological prescription that falling in love is a highly desirable basis of courtship and marriage; love is strongly institutionalized.[19] In contemporary United States, many individuals would even claim that entering marriage without being in love requires some such rationalization as asserting that one is too old for such romances or that one must "think of practical matters like money." To be sure, both anthropologists and sociologists often exaggerate the American commitment to romance;[20] nevertheless, a behavioral and value complex of this type is found here.

But this complex is rare. Perhaps only the following cultures possess the romantic love value complex: modern urban United States, Northwestern Europe, Polynesia, and the European nobility of the eleventh and twelfth centuries.[21] Certainly, it is to be found in no other major civilization. On the other hand, the *love pattern,* which views love as a basis for the final decision to marry, may be relatively common.

WHY LOVE MUST BE CONTROLLED

Since strong love attachments apparently can occur in any society and since (as we shall show) love is frequently a basis for and prelude to marriage, it must be controlled or channeled in some way. More specifically, the stratification and lineage patterns would be weakened greatly if love's potentially disruptive effects were not kept in check. The importance of this situation may be seen most clearly by considering one of the major functions of the family, status placement which in every society links the structures of stratification, kinship lines, and mate choice. (To show how the very similar comments which have been made about sex are not quite correct would take us too far afield; in any event, to the extent that they are correct, the succeeding analysis applies equally to the control of sex.)

Both the child's placement in the social structure and choice of mates are socially important because both placement and choice link two kinship lines together. Courtship or mate choice, therefore, cannot be ignored by either family or society. To permit random mating would mean radical change in the existing social structure. If the family as a unit of society is important, then mate choice is too.

Kinfolk or immediate family can disregard the question of who marries whom, only if a marriage is not seen as a link between kin lines, only if no property, power, lineage honor, totemic relationships, and the like are believed to flow from the kin lines through the spouses to their offspring. Universally, however, these are believed to follow kin lines. Mate choice thus has consequences for social structure. But love may affect mate choice. Both mate choice and love, therefore, are too important to be left to children.

THE CONTROL OF LOVE

Since considerable energy and resources may be required to push youngsters who are in love into proper role behavior, love must be controlled *before* it appears. Love relationships must either be kept to a small number or they must be so directed that they do not run counter to the approved kinship linkages. There are only a few institutional patterns by which this control is achieved.

1. Certainly the simplest, and perhaps the most widely used, structural pattern for coping with this problem is child marriage. If the child is betrothed, married, or both before he has had any opportunity to interact intimately as an adolescent with other children, then he has no resources with which to oppose the marriage. He cannot earn a living, he is physically weak, and is socially dominated by his elders. Moreover, strong love attachments occur only rarely before puberty. An example of this pattern was to be found in India, where the young bride went to live with her husband in a marriage which was not physically consummated until much later, within his father's household.[22]

2. Often, child marriage is linked with a second structural pattern, in which the kinship rules define rather closely a class of eligible future spouses. The marriage is determined by birth within narrow limits. Here, the major decision, which is made by elders, is *when* the marriage is to occur. Thus, among the Murngin, *galle,* the father's sister's child, is scheduled to marry *due,* the mother's brother's child.[23] In the case of the "four-class" double-descent system, each individual is a member of *both* a matri-moiety and a patri-moiety and must marry someone who belongs to neither; the four-classes are (1) ego's own class, (2) those whose matri-moiety is the same as ego's but whose patri-moiety is different, (3) those who are in ego's patri-moiety but not in his matri-moiety, and

(4) those who are in neither of ego's moieties, that is, who are in the cell diagonally from his own.[24] Problems arise at times under these systems if the appropriate kinship cell—for example, parallel cousin or cross-cousin—is empty.[25] But nowhere, apparently, is the definition so rigid as to exclude some choice and, therefore, some dickering, wrangling, and haggling between the elders of the two families.

3. A society can prevent widespread development of adolescent love relationships by socially isolating young people from potential mates, whether eligible or ineligible as spouses. Under such a pattern, elders can arrange the marriages of either children or adolescents with little likelihood that their plans will be disrupted by love attachments. Obviously, this arrangement cannot operate effectively in most primitive societies, where youngsters see one another rather frequently.[26]

    Not only is this pattern more common in civilizations than in primitive societies, but is found more frequently in the upper social strata. *Social* segregation is difficult unless it is supported by physical segregation—the harem of Islam, the zenana of India[27]—or by a large household system with individuals whose duty it is to supervise nubile girls. Social segregation is thus expensive. Perhaps the best known example of simple social segregation was found in China, where youthful marriages took place between young people who had not previously met because they lived in different villages; they could not marry fellow-villagers since ideally almost all inhabitants belonged to the same *tsu.*[28]

    It should be emphasized that the primary function of physical or social isolation in these cases is to minimize informal or intimate social interaction. Limited social contacts of a highly ritualized of formal type in the presence of elders, as in Japan, have a similar, if less extreme, result.[29]

4. A fourth type of pattern seems to exist, although it is not clear cut; and specific cases shade off toward types three and five. Here, there is close supervision by duennas or close relatives, but not actual social segregation. A high value is placed on female chastity (which perhaps is the case in every major civilization until its "decadence") viewed either as the product of self-restraint, as among the 17th Century Puritans, or as a marketable commodity. Thus love as play is not developed; marriage is supposed to be considered by the young as a duty and a possible family alliance. This pattern falls between types three and five because love is permitted before marriage, but only between eligibles. Ideally, it occurs only between a betrothed couple, and, except as marital love, there is no encouragement for it to appear at all. Family elders largely make the specific choice of mate, whether or not intermediaries carry out the arrangements. In the preliminary stages youngsters engage in courtship under supervision, with the understanding that this will permit the development of affection prior to marriage.

I do not believe that the empirical data show where this pattern is prevalent, outside of Western Civilization. The West is a special case, because of its peculiar relationship to Christianity, in which from its earliest days in Rome there has been a complex tension between asceticism and love. This type of limited love marked French, English, and Italian upper class family life from the 11th to the 14th Centuries, as well as 17th Century Puritanism in England and New England.[30]

5. The fifth type of pattern permits or actually encourages love relationships, and love is a commonly expected element in mate choice. Choice in this system is *formally* free. In their 'teens youngsters begin their love play, with or without consummating sexual intercourse, within a group of peers. They may at times choose love partners who they and others do not consider suitable spouses. Gradually, however, their range of choice is narrowed and eventually their affections center on one individual. This person is likely to be more eligible as a mate according to general social norms, and as judged by peers and parents, than the average individual with whom the youngster formerly indulged in love play.

For reasons that are not yet clear, this pattern is nearly always associated with a strong development of an adolescent peer group system, although the latter may occur without the love pattern. One source of social control, then, is the individual's own teen age companions, who persistently rate the present and probable future accomplishments of each individual.[31]

Another source of control lies with the parents of both boy and girl. In our society, parents threaten, cajole, wheedle, bribe, and persuade their children to "go with the right people," during both the early love play and later courtship phases.[32] Primarily, they seek to control love relationships by influencing the informal social contacts of their children: moving to appropriate neighborhoods and schools, giving parties and helping to make out invitation lists, by making their children aware that certain individuals have ineligibility traits (race, religion, manners, tastes, clothing, and so on). Since youngsters fall in love with those with whom they associate, control over informal relationships also controls substantially the focus of affection. The results of such control are well known and are documented in the more than one hundred studies of homogamy in this country: most marriages take place between couples in the same class, religious, racial, and educational levels.

As Robert Wilkman has shown in a generally unfamiliar (in the United States) but superb investigation, this pattern was found among 18th Century Swedish farmer adolescents, was widely distributed in other Germanic areas, and extends in time from the 19th Century back to almost certainly the late Middle Ages.[33] In these cases, sexual intercourse was taken for granted, social contact was closely supervised by the peer group, and final consent to marriage was withheld or granted by the parents who owned the land.

Such cases are not confined to Western society. Polynesia exhibits a similar pattern, with some variation from society to society, the best known examples of which are perhaps Mead's Manu'ans and Firth's Tikopia.[34] Probably the most familiar Melanesian cases are the Trobriands and Dobu,[35] where the systems resemble those of the Kiwai Papuans of the Trans-Fly and the Siuai Papuans of the Solomon Islands.[36] Linton found this pattern among the Tanala.[37] Although Radcliffe-Brown holds that the pattern is not common in Africa, it is clearly found among the Nuer, the Kgatla (Tswana-speaking), and the Bavenda (here, without sanctioned sexual intercourse).[38]

A more complete classification, making use of the distinctions suggested in this paper, would show, I believe, that a large minority of known societies exhibit this pattern. I would suggest, moreover, that such a study would reveal that the degree to which love is a usual, expected prelude to marriage is correlated with (1) the degree of free choice of mate permitted in the society and (2) the degree to which husband-wife solidarity is the strategic solidarity of the kinship structure.[39]

LOVE CONTROL AND CLASS

These sociostructural explanations of how love is controlled lead to a subsidiary but important hypothesis: From one society to an-

other, and from one *class* to another within the same society, the sociostructural importance of maintaining kinship lines according to rule will be rated differently by the families within them. Consequently, the degree to which control over mate choice, and therefore over the prevalence of a love pattern among adolescents, will also vary. Since, within any stratified society, this concern with the maintenance of intact and acceptable kin lines will be greater in the upper strata, it follows that noble or upper strata will maintain stricter control over love and courtship behavior than lower strata. The two correlations suggested in the preceding paragraph also apply: husband-wife solidarity is less strategic relative to clan solidarity in the upper than in the lower strata, and there is less free choice of mate.

Thus it is that, although in Polynesia generally most youngsters indulged in considerable love play, princesses were supervised strictly. 40 Similarly, in China lower class youngsters often met their spouses before marriage. 41 In our own society, the "upper upper" class maintains much greater control than the lower strata over the informal social contacts of their nubile young. Even among the Dobu, where there are few controls and little stratification, differences in control exist at the extremes: a child betrothal may be arranged between outstanding gardening families, who try to prevent their youngsters from being entangled with wastrel families.[42] In answer to my query about this pattern among the Nuer, Evans Pritchard writes:

> You are probably right that a wealthy man has more control over his son's affairs than a poor man. A man with several wives has a more authoritarian position in his home. Also, a man with many cattle is in a position to permit or refuse a son to marry, whereas a lad whose father is poor may have to depend on the support of kinsmen. In general, I would say that a Nuer father is not interested in the personal side of things. His son is free to marry any girl he likes and the father does not consider the

selection to be his affair until the point is reached when cattle have to be discussed.[43]

The upper strata have much more at stake in the maintenance of the social structure and thus are more strongly motivated to control the courtship and marriage decisions of their young. Correspondingly, their young have much more to lose than lower strata youth, so that upper strata elders can wield more power.

CONCLUSION

In this analysis I have attempted to show the integration of love with various types of social structures. As against considerable contemporary opinion among both sociologists and anthropologists, I suggest that love is a universal psychological potential, which is controlled by a range of five structural patterns, all of which are attempts to see to it that youngsters do not make entirely free choices of their future spouses. Only if kin lines are unimportant, and this condition is found in no society as a whole, will entirely free choice be permitted. Some structural arrangements seek to prevent entirely the outbreak of love, while others harness it. Since the kin lines of the upper strata are of greater social importance to them than those of lower strata are to the lower strata members, the former exercise a more effective control over this choice. Even where there is almost a formally free choice of mate—and I have suggested that this pattern is widespread, to be found among a substantial segment of the earth's societies—this choice is guided by peer group and parents toward a mate who will be acceptable to the kin and friend groupings. The theoretical importance of love is thus to be seen in the sociostructural patterns which are developed to keep it from disrupting existing social arrangements.

Endnotes

1. On the psychological level, the motivational power of both love and sex is intensified by this curious fact: (which I have not seen remarked on elsewhere) Love is the most projective of emotions, as sex is the most projective of drives; only with great difficulty can the attracted person believe that the object of his love or passion does not and will not reciprocate the feeling at all. Thus, the persona may carry his action quite far, before accepting a rejection as genuine.

2. I have treated decision analysis extensively in an unpublished paper by that title.

3. Vatsyayana, *The Kama Sutra,* Delhi: Rajkamal, 1948; Ovid, "The Lovers," and "Remedies of Love," in *The Art of Love,* Cambridge, Mass.: Harvard University Press, 1939; Andreas Capelanus, The Art of Courtly Love, translated by John J. Parry, New York: Columbia University Press, 1941; Paul Tuffrau, editor, *Marie de France: Les Lais de Marie de France,* Paris: L'edition d'art, 1925; see also Julian Harris, *Marie de France,* New York: Institute of French Studies, 1930, esp. Chapter 3. All authors but the first *also* had the goal of writing literature.

4. Ernest R. Mowrer, *Family Disorganization,* Chicago: The University of Chicago Press, 1927, pp. 158–165; Ernest W. Burgess and Harvey J. Locke, *The Family,* New York: American Book, 1953, pp. 436–437; Mabel A. Elliott and Francis E. Merrill, *Social Disorganization,* New York: Harper, 1950, pp. 366–384; Andrew G. Truxal and Francis E. Merrill, *The Family in American Culture,* New York: Prentice-Hall, 1947, pp. 120–124, 507–509; Ernest R. Groves and Gladys Hoagland Groves, *The Contemporary American Family,* New York: Lippincott, 1947, pp. 321–324.

5. William L. Kolb, "Sociologically Established Norms and Democratic Values," *Social Forces,* 26 (May, 1948), pp. 451–456.

6. Hugo G. Beigel, "Romantic Love," *American Sociological Review,* 16 (June, 1951), pp. 326–334.

7. Sigmund Freud, *Group Psychology and the Analysis of the Ego,* London: Hogarth, 1922, p. 72.

8. Willard Waller, *The Family,* New York: Dryden, 1938, pp. 189–192.

9. Talcott Parsons, *Essays in Sociological Theory,* Glencoe, Ill.: Free Press, 1949, pp. 187–189.

10. Robert F. Winch, *Mate Selection.* New York: Harper, 1958.

11. See, e.g., Robert F. Winch, *The Modern Family.* New York: Holt, 1952, Chapter 14.

12. Robert H. Lowie, "Sex and Marriage," in John F. McDermott, editor, *The Sex Problem in Modern Society.* New York: Modern Library, 1931, p. 146.

13. Ralph Linton, *The Study of Man.* New York: Appleton-Century, 1936, p. 175.

14. George Peter Murdock, *Social Structure.* New York: Macmillan, 1949.

15. Max Gluckman, *Custom and Conflict in Africa.* Oxford: Basil Blackwell, 1955, Chapter 3.

16. I hope to deal with the second problem in another paper.

17. Tribal India, of course, is too heterogeneous to place in any one position on such a continuum. The question would have to be answered for each tribe. Obviously it is of less importance here whether China and Japan, in recent decades, have moved "two points over" toward the opposite pole of high approval of love relationships as a basis for marriage than that both systems as classically described viewed love as generally a tragedy; and love was supposed to be irrelevant to marriage, i.e., noninstitutionalized. The continuum permits us to place a system at some position, once we have the descriptive data.

18. See Ludwig Friedländer, *Roman Life and Manners under the Early Empire* (Seventh Edition), translated by A. Magnus, New York: Dutton, 1908, Vol. 1 Chapter 5, "The Position of Women."

19. For a discussion of the relation between behavior patterns and the process of institutionalization, see my *After Divorce,* Glencoe, Ill.: Free Press, 1956, Chapter 15.

20. See Ernest W. Burgess and Paul W. Wallin, *Engagement and Marriage,* New York: Lippincott, 1953, Chapter 7 for the extent to which even the engaged are not blind to the defects of their beloveds. No one has ascertained the degree to which various age and sex groups in our society actually believe in some form of the ideology.

   Similarly, Margaret Mead in *Coming of Age in Samoa,* New York: Modern Library, 1953, rates Manu'an love as shallow, and though these Samoans give much attention to love-making, she asserts that they laughed with incredulous contempt at Romeo and Juliet (pp. 155–156). Though the individual sufferer showed jealousy and anger, the Manu'ans believed that a new love would quickly cure a betrayed love (pp. 105–108). It is possible that Mead failed to understand the shallowness of love in our own society: Romantic love is, "in our civilization, inextricably bound up with ideas of monogamy, exclusiveness, jealousy, and undeviating fidelity" (p. 105). But these are *ideas* and ideology; behavior is rather different.

21. I am preparing an analysis of this case. The relation of "courtly love" to social structure is complicated.

22. Frieda M. Das, *Purdah,* New York: Vanguard, 1932; Kingsley Davis, *The Population of India and Pakistan,* Princeton: Princeton University Press, 1951, p. 112. There was a widespread custom of taking one's bride from a village other than one's own.

23. W. Lloyd Warner, *Black Civilization,* New York: Harper, 1937, pp. 82–84. They may also become "sweethearts" at puberty; see pp. 86–89.

24. See Murdock, *op. cit.,* pp. 53 ff. *et passim* for discussions of double-descent.

25. One adjustment in Australia was for the individuals to leave the tribe for a while, usually eloping, and then to return "reborn" under a different and now appropriate kinship designation. In any event, these marital prescriptions did not prevent love entirely. As Malinowski shows in his early summary of the Australian family systems, although everyone of the tribes used the technique of infant betrothal (and close prescription of mate), no tribe was free of elopements, between either the unmarried, and the "motive of sexual love" was always to be found in marriages by elopement, B. Malinowski. *The Family Among the Australian Aborigines,* London: University of London Press, 1913, p. 83.

26. This pattern was apparently achieved in Manus, where on first menstruation the girl was removed from her playmates and kept at "home"—on stilts over a lagoon—under the close supervision of elders. The Manus were prudish, and love occurred rarely or never. Margaret Mead, *Growing Up in New Guinea,* in *From the South Seas,* New York: Morrow, 1939, pp. 163–166, 208.

27. See Das, *op. cit.*

28. For the activities of the tsu, see Hsien Chin Hu, *The Common Descent Group in China and Its*

Functions, New York: Viking Fund Studies in Anthropology, 10 (1948). For the marriage process, see Marion J. Levy, *The Family Revolution in Modern China,* Cambridge: Harvard University Press, 1949, pp. 87–107. See also Olga Lang, *Chinese Family and Society,* New Haven: Yale University Press, 1946, for comparisons between the old and new systems. In one-half of 62 villages in Ting Hsien Experimental District in Hopei, the largest clan included 50 percent of the families; in 25 percent of the villages, the two largest clans held over 90 percent of the families; I am indebted to Robert M. Marsh who has been carrying out a study of Ching mobility partly under my direction for this reference: F. C. H. Lee, *Ting Hsien. She-hui K'ai-K'uang t'iao-ch'a,* Peiping: Chuung-hua p'ing-min Chiao-yu ts'u-chin hui, 1932, p. 54. See also Sidney Gamble, *Ting Hsien: A North China Rural Community,* New York: International Secretariat of the Institute of Pacific Relations, 1954.

29. For Japan, see Shidzué Ishimoto, *Facing Two Ways,* New York: Farrar and Rinehart, 1935, Chapters 6, 8; John F. Embree, *Suye Mura,* Chicago: University of Chicago Press, 1950, Chapters 3, 6.

30. I do not mean, of course, to restrict this pattern to these times and places, but I am more certain of these. For the Puritans, see Edmund S. Morgan, *The Puritan Family,* Boston: Public Library, 1944. For the somewhat different practices in New York, see Charles E. Ironside, *The Family in Colonial New York,* New York: Columbia University Press, 1942. See also: A. Abram, *English Life and Manners in the Later Middle Ages,* New York: Dutton, 1913, Chapters 4, 10; Emily J. Putnam, *The Lady,* New York: Sturgis and Walton, 1910, Chapter 4; James Gairdner, editor, *The Paston Letters, 1422–1509,* 4 vols., London: Arber, 1872–1875; Eileen Power, "The Position of Women," in C. G. Crump and E. F. Jacobs, editors, *The Legacy of the Middle Ages,* Oxford: Clarendon, 1926, pp. 414–416.

31. For those who believe that the young in the United States are totally deluded by love, or believe that love outranks every other consideration, see: Ernest W. Burgess and Paul W. Wallin, *Engagement and Marriage,* New York: Lippincott, 1953, pp. 217–238. Note Karl Robert V. Wilkman, *Die Einleitung Der Ehe. Acta Academiae Aboensis (Humaniora),* 11 (1937), pp. 127 ff. Not only are reputations known because of close association among peers, but songs and poetry are sometimes composed about the girl or boy. Cf., for the Tikopia, Raymond Firth, *We, the Tikopia,* New York: American Book, 1936, pp. 468 ff.; for the Siuai, Douglas L. Oliver, *Solomon Island Society,* Cambridge: Harvard University Press, 1955, pp. 146 ff. The Manu'ans made love in groups of three or four couples; cf. Mead, *Coming of Age in Samoa, op. cit.,* p. 92.

32. Marvin B. Sussman, "Parental Participation in Mate Selection and Its Effect upon Family Continuity," *Social Forces,* 32 (October, 1953), pp. 76–81.

33. Wilkman, *op. cit.*

34. Mead, *Coming of Age in Samoa, op. cit.,* pp. 97–108; and Firth, *op. cit.,* pp. 520 ff.

35. Thus Malinowski notes in his "Introduction" to Reo F. Fortune's *The Sorcerers of Dobu,* London: Routledge, 1932, p. xxiii, that the Dobu have similar patterns, the same type of courtship by trial and error, with a gradually tightening union.

36. Gunnar Landtman, *Kiwai Papuans of the Trans-Fly,* London: Macmillan, 1927, pp. 243 ff.; Oliver, *op. cit.,* pp. 153 ff.

37. The pattern apparently existed among the Marquesans as well, but since Linton never published a complete description of this Polynesian society, I omit it here. His fullest analysis, cluttered with secondary interpretations, is in Abram Kardiner, *Psychological Frontiers of Society,* New York: Columbia University Press, 1945. For the Tanala, see Ralph Linton, *The Tanala,* Chicago: Field Museum, 1933, pp. 300–303.

38. Thus, Radcliffe-Brown: "The African does not think of marriage as a union based on romantic love, although beauty as well as character and health are sought in the choice of a wife," in his "Introduction" to A. R. Radcliffe-Brown and W. C. Daryll Ford, editors, *African Systems of Kinship and Marriage,* London: Oxford University Press, 1950, p. 46. For the Nuer, see E. E. Evans-Pritchard, *Kinship and Marriage Among the Nuer,* Oxford: Clarendon, 1951, pp. 49–58. For the Kgatla, see I. Schapera, *Married Life in an African Tribe,* New York: Sheridan, 1941, pp. 55 ff. For the Bavenda, although the report

seems incomplete, see Hugh, A. Stayt, *The Bavenda,* London: Oxford University Press, 1931, pp. 111 ff., 145 ff., 154.

39. The second correlation is developed from Marion J. Levy, *The Family Revolution in China,* Cambridge, Harvard University Press, 1949, p. 179. Levy's formulation ties "romantic love" to that solidarity, and is of little use because there is only one case, the Western culture complex. As he states it, it is almost so by definition.

40. E.g., Mead, *Coming of Age in Samoa, op. cit.,* pp. 79, 92, 97–109. Cf. also Firth, *op. cit.,* pp. 520 ff.

41. Although one must be cautious about China, this inference seems to be allowable from such comments as the following: "But the old men of China did not succeed in eliminating love from the life of the young women. . . . Poor and middle-class families could not afford to keep men and women in separate quarters, and Chinese also met their cousins. . . . Girls . . . sometimes even served customers in their parents' shops." Olga Lang, *op. cit.,* p. 33. According to Fried, farm girls would work in the fields, and farm girls of ten years and older were sent to the market to sell produce. They were also sent to towns and cities as servants. The peasant or pauper woman was not confined to the home and its immediate environs. Morton H. Fried, *Fabric of Chinese Society,* New York: Praeger, 1953, pp. 59–60. Also, Levy (*op. cit.,* p. 111): "Among peasant girls and among servant girls in gentry households some premarital experience was not uncommon, though certainly frowned upon. The methods of preventing such contact were isolation and chaperonage, both of which, in the 'traditional' picture, were more likely to break down in the two cases named than elsewhere."

42. Fortune, *op. cit.,* p. 30

43. Personal letter, dated January 9, 1953. However, the Nuer father can still refuse if he believes the demands of the girl's people are unreasonable. In turn, the girl can cajole her parents to demand less.

Chapter Two
Family Developmental Theory

John and Natasha Morrison were looking forward to their retirement in a few years. Their eldest daughter, Tamara, was just finishing law school and was pregnant with her first child. John Jr., their only son, was doing well in college and planning a career in communications. Their youngest daughter, Kamika, would soon be graduating from high school. With her college tuition safely tucked away in an education IRA, they were hoping to take retirement in their early sixties. As a couple with active professional careers and three children, they had often dreamed of an extended vacation but had been too busy to take one. They planned to take a grand world tour when they retired.

Natasha's parents, who lived nearby and saw the family regularly, came to visit for Father's Day. The family sat around the picnic table out back and reminisced about the changes in their lives over the years. When the children were young, they all had the same kinds of activities and friends. Now it was as if they were all in their own separate worlds. It was difficult to find time together because each person was so busy and focused on his or her own life. John and Natasha were worried about John's father, who lived 500 miles away and was in poor health. Tamara and her husband were busy getting ready for their first child and establishing their professional careers. Johnny was beginning to show signs of seriousness about a girlfriend for the first time in his life. Kamika was hardly ever at home anymore, staying busy with her friends and after-school activities. She was particularly interested in dance and recently had made a new friend, Matt, who also wanted to be a dancer.

Everyone gathered around the table to watch John open his Father's Day presents. Kamika seemed very excited. "Daddy, I have the greatest surprise for you! You'll be so excited! I'm so very sure! I'm going to go to New York to be a dancer! I've been accepted into a little company in New York where they will train me, and Matt and I are moving there in a month! Isn't that just great?"

HISTORY

Family developmental theory emerged in the late 1940s, corresponding with the development of the field of family science. It was one of the first family-focused theories, with a separate identity from psychology or sociology. Psychology-based theories, with their narrower emphasis on individuals, did not fully explain what happened in families with competing individual needs. Sociology-based theories, focused on society and culture, were too broad in their analysis. Thus, family developmental theory developed from the critiques of these two perspectives.

In 1948, Evelyn Duvall and Ruben Hill pointed out that families were social groups that were influenced by developmental processes, in the same way that individuals were. Like individuals, families experienced life cycles, with clearly delineated stages. But families needed to be studied as a dynamic unit, not as a collection of individuals. According to family developmental theorists, the family life cycle had two major stages—expansion and contraction. During expansion, children are born and raised, whereas during contraction, children leave the family home. This "cycle" of expansion and contraction gave rise to the term "family life cycle" (Duvall 1957).

In 1948 Duvall and Hill first presented their version of the family life cycle, in which they identified tasks that would be accomplished by both parents and children. These tasks were grouped into eight stages of development across the family life cycle. Duvall and Hill proposed that, like individuals, families passed through developmental stages delineated by the accomplishments of specific tasks within each stage. Later versions of the theory went beyond the demarcation of stages and tasks and began to focus on changes within the family over time, including transitions and social roles. Duvall later codified these in a textbook, *Family Development,* first published in 1957. Updated and republished many times, this was one of the most widely used textbooks on the subject for the next 30 years. Thus, Duvall's eight stages of the family life cycle are the best-known stages of the family developmental theory.

Other theorists, building on the foundation laid by Duvall and Hill, worked to expand these concepts. In 1964, Roy Rodgers developed a version of the theory with 24 different stages, but its complexity overshadowed its usefulness. Rodgers (1973) further expanded the concept of family interaction by focusing on three dynamics across the family career. He emphasized that families were influenced by institutional norms, by the expectations that arise from the family itself, and by the expectations that arise from the individuals within the family. In contrast, Joan Aldous (1978) suggested that family development should be considered in only four stages, since families are often in several stages of parenting at the same time. She further suggested the term *family career,* rather than *family life cycle,* should be used, since families did not return to the way they had been at the beginning of their lives (1978, 1996).

In the 1970s and 1980s, some family scholars criticized family development theory because it lacked scientific testability. In 1973, Wesley Burr, a renowned theorist and researcher, reviewed many of the major issues in family studies, including the family life cycle. In his book Burr wrote: "It has not yet been proved that the family life cycle will turn out to be a very useful concept in deductive theories" (p. 219). His concern with the theory was that the concepts and variables were not well defined and so could not be properly tested in empirical research. Addressing these concerns, James

White published a book in 1991 entitled *Dynamics of Family Development: A Theoretical Perspective,* in which he outlined specific testable propositions and variables for family developmental theory. White is considered one of the major proponents of family development theory today.

At about the same time, a new variant of family development theory—life course perspective—was being described. The life course perspective went beyond the life cycle view by including additional variables such as multiple views of time (ontogenetic, generational, and historical), micro- and macro-social contexts, and increasing diversity over time (Bengtson and Allen 1993).

Basic Assumptions

Families undergo stages of development, just like individuals. Family developmental theory focuses on the developmental stages of the family as well as the individual. Transitions from one stage to the next are usually related to changes in individual development. For example, newly married couples, couples with preschoolers, couples with teenagers, and couples whose children have moved out of the home clearly are in different stages of development and have different tasks to accomplish.

There are tasks associated with each stage of development. This concept is taken from psychologically based developmental theories (for example, Havighurst 1948). Tasks are defined on the basis of normative expectations. Each stage is delineated by a set of tasks that must be accomplished to prepare adequately for the next stage of development. Failure to complete a task does not necessarily preclude moving to the next stage of development but may limit a family's optimal functioning at the next level. For example, parents who pay too much attention to raising their children and not enough to their own relationship may find that they encounter problems with their relationship after the children leave home.

Development is reciprocal. The individual development of each family member influences other family members, as well as the overall development of the family. The family's development influences the critical periods of individual development as well. Because there is reciprocity in the interaction of the family and individual development, it is necessary to consider them in concert.

Families must be viewed in multiple levels of analysis. Family developmental theory requires that family life be considered in the multiple contexts of the society, the family, and the individual. The social context influences both the processes within the family and the developmental issues of each individual within the family.

Families should be viewed over time. Family developmental theory takes as its core assumption that families are not static but change over time. This "change over time" is the primary focus of the theory. How and when families change, what they accomplish at different points of time, and why they change can be known only if one studies families over time.

PRIMARY TERMS AND CONCEPTS

FAMILY

Duvall proposed that the family is composed of "interacting persons related by ties of marriage, birth, or adoption, whose central purpose is to create and maintain a common culture which promotes the physical, mental, emotional, and social development of each of its members" (Duvall 1977, 5). The dynamics of the family may change over time, dependent on the needs of the individuals, the relationships between them, and the impact of society on the family. These variables determine the components of the developmental tasks and are dependent on the family "tempos and rhythms."

NORMATIVE EVENTS

Rather than focusing on crises in families, family developmental theorists focus on the things that happen more normatively, such as marriages, childbirth, developmental and educational milestones, and the passage of time.

STAGES

Probably the most unique aspect of family developmental theory is its focus on the stages of the family life cycle. These stages are periods of "relative equilibrium in which consensus about the allocation of roles and rules of procedure is high" (Hill 1986, 21). In the model developed by Duvall and Hill, stages are the result of major changes in family size, changes in the developmental age of the oldest child, or changes in the work status of the breadwinner (Hill 1986).

Each stage of development is related to behaviors or tasks that would normally be expected to occur during that stage. Norms govern both group and individual behavior, often defining the roles that people play. It is important to note that these norms are socially defined and change over time as cultural mores change.

TASKS

The concept of tasks in family developmental theory is derived from a similar concept of tasks (as defined by Havighurst 1948, 1953) in individual developmental theory. According to Havighurst, developmental tasks occur at particular points in development in response to either physical maturation or cultural changes. The individual must respond by developing new abilities, roles, or relationships. If the challenge of development is met positively, then the individual will be happier and have more success with later stages of development. If not, then, as with other stage theories of development (for example, Erikson and Piaget), we would predict that the individual would be less successful.

Using this model, Duvall and Hill incorporated specific tasks for each of the eight stages of the family life cycle. These tasks focus on what the family, as a unit, must accomplish, while taking into account the individual needs of the parents and children. For example, Duvall (1957, 1977) outlined the tasks (as an individual) that a child would have to achieve to develop optimally. She further linked those individual tasks to the tasks that the family must achieve as it assimilates the individual child into its unit. Thus, when a newborn moves into the toddler stage, the family must create a safe physical environment for the toddler to explore. Later, when a young adult enters into the launching phase, the family's task is to provide a secure base but recognize that the young adult's reliance on the family may be more economic than physical. Each stage of development requires the family to change and accommodate the needs of the children as they age (Duvall 1977).

TIMING

When something happens in family life has an impact on family life. In other words, it makes a difference to the family when a child is born, or when someone retires, or when someone moves out of the house. This is particularly apparent when there are multiple events occurring at or near the same time.

The life course perspective theorists introduced the concept of different qualities of time into family developmental theory. *Ontogenetic time* refers to the time one recognizes as one grows and changes through one's own lifetime (one's personal awareness of time—like an "internal clock"). *Generational time* refers to how one's time is experienced within one's social group (as in one's family or in a cohort). *Historical time* refers to how time is experienced in the social context or greater historical period (for example, living during the Great Depression in contrast to being a Baby Boomer) (Bengtson and Allen 1993). Thus, one can experience one's adolescent period as a unique stage in one's developmental history (ontogenetic). But it might matter whether that adolescence was experienced during the turbulent Vietnam era or the late 1990s (historical). Similarly, it might make some difference if one becomes a first-time parent at the age of 17 or at the age of 44 (generational).

CHANGE

Something changes when it undergoes a transformation from one state to another. (For example, a caterpillar changes into a butterfly;

ice changes into water.) Family developmental theory proposes that family relationships are not static but rather change over time. Catalysts for change can be either internal (such as biological growth) or external (through interaction with the environment). The nature of this interaction is reciprocal—that is, the organism both elicits and responds to stimuli in its environment.

Change comes with varying levels of acknowledgment and acceptance by family members. Individual changes become the catalyst for family change, causing shifts from one family stage to another. Changes in personal roles within the family are often the result of individual changes and transitions from one stage to the next.

TRANSITIONS

One cannot study change without studying transitions. Transitions are the process(es) that form a bridge between the different states when something changes. (For example, the process of metamorphosis changes the caterpillar into a butterfly; the process of thawing changes ice into water.) In family developmental theory, transitions are the shifts in roles and identities encountered with changes in developmental stages (Hagestad 1988). Ease of transition is dependent on the resolution of the stages beforehand, or the degree to which the stage is perceived to be a crisis. As families shift from one stage to the next, their roles, behaviors, and tasks are reallocated in accordance with their new stage. Some families move easily from one stage to the next and some do not. Depending upon how prepared they are for the new stage, families will respond to the change as either a crisis or as an opportunity (Rapoport 1963). Some developmental transitions, such as when one's child begins school, are easy to recognize. Other transitions, such as identifying exactly when a child becomes an adolescent, are more difficult for the family to pinpoint and to accommodate. Furthermore, crises can create critical transitions—that is, those that occur in addition to normally expected transitions, such as an unexpected pregnancy. Focusing on transitions helps us to understand what families go through as they move from stage to stage (Duvall 1988).

COMMON AREAS OF RESEARCH AND APPLICATION

THE FAMILY LIFE CYCLE

Evelyn Duvall's eight-stage model is the most well known version of the family developmental theory. As with all stage theories, there are specific tasks associated with each stage. The chart provided by Duvall and Miller

(1985)[1] provides a delineation of those eight stages.

Stage One: Establishment phase—courtship and marriage. Stage one is known as the *establishment phase* because couples are focused on establishing their home base. There are many tasks associated with the establishment phase of relationships, and as in individual developmental models (for example, Piaget and Erikson), the accomplishment of future tasks relies heavily on the successful negotiation of the previous stage's tasks. If couples can blend their individual needs and desires, find workable solutions to conflicts, and maintain good

---

Table 2.1
Stage-Sensitive Family Developmental Tasks Through the Family Life Cycle

Stages of the family life cycle	Positions in the family	Stage-sensitive family developmental tasks
1. Married couple	Wife Husband	Establishing a mutually satisfying marriage Adjusting to pregnancy and the promise of parenthood Fitting into the kin network
2. Childbearing	Wife-mother Husband-father Infant daughter or son or both	Having, adjusting to, and encouraging the development of infants Establishing a satisfying home for both parents and infant(s)
3. Preschool-age	Wife-mother Husband-father Daughter-sister Son-brother	Adapting to the critical needs and interests of preschool children in stimulating, growth-promoting ways Coping with energy depletion and lack of privacy as parents
4. School-age	Wife-mother Husband-father Daughter-sister Son-brother	Fitting into the community of school-age families in constructive ways Encouraging children's educational achievement
5. Teenage	Wife-mother Husband-father Daughter-sister Son-brother	Balancing freedom with responsibility as teenagers mature and emancipate themselves Establishing postparental interests and careers as growing parents
6. Launching center	Wife-mother-grandmother Husband-father-grandfather Daughter-sister-aunt Son-brother-uncle	Releasing young adults into work, military service, college, marriage, and so on with appropriate rituals and assistance Maintaining a supportive home base
7. Middle-aged parents	Wife-mother-grandmother Husband-father-grandfather	Refocusing on the marriage relationship Maintaining kin ties with older and younger generations
8. Aging family members	Widow or widower Wife-mother-grandmother Husband-father-grandfather	Coping with bereavement and living alone Closing the family home or adapting it to aging Adjusting to retirement

Source: Duvall, Evelyn Millis & Miller, Brent C. (1985) *Marriage and Family Development,* 6th ed. Published by Allyn and Bacon, Boston, MA. Copyright © 1985 by Pearson Education. Reprinted by permission of the publisher.

communication and intimacy patterns, then they are better able to handle the tasks associated with the next stages.

In the United States, the establishment phase generally begins with some form of courtship. Courtship is the personal preparation for marriage, consisting of three general tasks. Duvall (1977) lists these tasks as (1) readying oneself for the roles of husband or wife, (2) disengaging from close relationships that might compete with the marriage, and (3) reprioritizing so the couple's interests are more important than those of the individual. The degree to which one is successful at addressing these tasks during courtship predicts success during marriage.

Individuals thinking about forming a couple need to learn about each other's desires, dreams, expectations, and style of living. They need to find out more about each other's habits and hobbies, ways of interacting with their friends and families, and likes and dislikes, from foods to movies to household decorations. In addition to these pragmatic considerations, couples also have to develop intellectual and emotional communication patterns, patterns of behaviors and preferences, and a jointly workable philosophy of life and set of values. Some couples, frequently encouraged by clergy or marriage counselors, sit down with a list of "things to discuss before marriage" in order to be certain that the most important issues have been discussed.

Once these things are discussed, the marriage ceremony is an outward and clearly demarcated symbol of status change for couples. It receives both legal sanction and public recognition and, in many instances, religious validation. Before cohabitation became more common, the marriage ceremony also signaled the end of individuals living separately.

The new marital tasks for the couple include developing systems for acquiring and spending money, establishing daily routines, and creating a satisfying sex life. Both partners must also create new and appropriate relationships with relatives and old friends while establishing new friendships as a couple.

Many of the tasks associated with early marriage focus on the establishment of a home suitable for children. Some of these tasks include developing family-planning strategies, agreeing on the timing of pregnancy, arranging for the care of the baby, acquiring knowledge regarding parenthood, and adapting the home to accommodate children. It used to be that couples did not have much control over when they became pregnant. Today, however, couples can use contraceptives to choose the "best" time to become pregnant. But with this choice comes the responsibility for the couple to determine, and to agree, when the "best" time is.

Stage Two: Childbearing families—families with infants. The arrival of an infant brings about a new set of tasks for the family to face. The family must expand both physically and emotionally. New roles of "father" and "mother" appear. The couple must now negotiate how they will share the new responsibilities of caring for the child and must reallocate previously assigned household responsibilities.

Infants are completely dependent on their parents for food, clothing, shelter, and medical care. Parents are also responsible for nurturing their infant's cognitive and emotional needs. Infants require a safe and stimulating environment, which can include car seats, diapers, cribs, and toys. The couple might have to expand their household space by moving to a new home or rearranging their current space and how they use it.

All of this, of course, costs money, which places an additional financial demand on the family. These stressors can be damaging to the couple's relationship, so the couple must continue to practice effective communication strategies to maintain a strong bond. They should remember to pay attention to their own relationship while they attend to their infant's needs.

Stage Three: Families with preschool children. In families with more than one child, it is not uncommon for the firstborn to be only a few years old when the next child is born

(Glick 1977). In addition to adapting to the even greater physical needs of two (or more) children, the family must also adjust to the individual differences and temperaments of the children. Preschoolers need structure in their play and activities, and they benefit from intensive parental involvement. Infants also need a lot of physical attention, with diaper changes and feedings, as well as emotional and cognitive nurturing.

Just as in Stage Two, there are the issues of additional physical space and additional financial demands. The more children there are, the more difficult it becomes for the couple to meet their own developmental needs and continue to grow as a couple. Despite the demands on the resources of time, energy, and money, the couple still needs to spend time together, such as dining out once a week or twice-yearly weekends away. Regardless of the activity, it is just as important to the relationship to spend some time focusing only on their marriage as it is to focus on their roles as parents.

Stage four: Families with school-aged children. School is the first public social system that children encounter outside the immediate family. This is significant because families give up some authority over their children to the school. Their parenting skills and their children's behaviors are judged in this public forum. School represents an expansion of the family to other social systems that influence the family in significant ways.

The child's individual development drives the family at this stage. Trying out new activities is a major task of the school-aged child. Families with school-aged children must provide for their children's activities outside of school, which often include sports, music, and religious and social interactions. Parents must work to develop relationships with teachers, religious leaders, and parents of other children. They must develop strategies for accomplishing tasks around the home, particularly if schedules require the parents and children to be away from home more frequently (for example, evening ball games and weekend birthday parties) and find ways to appropriately delegate family tasks to various family members. Parents must also determine what the appropriate expectations are for their children (who may be at different developmental stages) for helping around the house, developing responsible behavior, watching television, or listening to music. While it is relatively easy to recognize appropriate music for a preschooler, it is more difficult to figure that out for a 10-year-old. And 10-year-olds bring additional issues to the families because they are influenced by their friends and by television. Because these issues require parental decisions, R-rated movies may be prohibited in one 10-year-old's household but may be allowed at her friend's house. One reason for this may be that as their children's physical autonomy increases, many parents increase their level of parental monitoring.

Stage Five: Families with adolescents. As in Stage Four, individual development drives the family in Stage Five. Adolescence is a time of rapid physical (sexual), cognitive, and psychosocial change. According to Erik Erikson, adolescents need to achieve their own identities separate from their families, and they do so by "trying on" different identities until they find one that "fits" (identity achievement). If identity is not achieved, then the adolescent will remain in a confused state without a clear sense of self (role diffusion). Parents must allow adolescents to establish their own separate identities, which sometimes may be in conflict with the family's values and ideas. Duvall states that open communication helps parents and adolescents learn from each other and helps to bridge the generation gap.

The adolescent may express a need for more space, both physical and emotional, more freedom to choose activities, and more activities to do, along with the need for more money to do those things. Additionally, many adolescents and their parents have concerns about their futures, including the cost of tuition for college or technical training.

Adolescents are able to share more of the responsibilities of family living, perhaps cooking meals, making repairs around the house, or looking after younger children. This enables many parents to work longer hours and earn more money without having to spend money on child care for the younger children. Thus, families can find ways to develop cooperative and symbiotic interactions.

Stage Six: Families with young adults—the Launching Stage. When we look at the Launching Stage, we see the beginning of the cycle of contraction of the nuclear family—that is, when family size begins to shrink as the children grow up and move out of the home. This stage begins when the oldest child leaves home and ends when the last child has left. Obviously, this may take some time if there are many children or if the children are widely spaced.

Whenever one member leaves the family, the family must adapt, and that includes reallocating responsibilities, duties, and roles among the family members who remain at home. At times there is a reallocation of physical facilities and resources, such as when bedrooms are shifted after the oldest child moves away. More frequently, there is a reallocation of financial resources, since the oldest child's move may entail tuition, room and board at a university, a large wedding, or supplementing the oldest child's finances until he or she "gets situated."

As the children leave the physical home, communication patterns change. Daily casual communication around the dinner table gives way to a phone call once a week. The nature of the communication also changes. It moves from conversation about everyday events to crisis management and questions about how to cope with being on one's own. When good communication patterns have been established in previous stages between parents and children, young adults can rely on their parents to support them during the launching stage.

With launching comes an ever-widening family circle, where friends and new family members enter into the family setting. From a roommate who visits on Thanksgiving to a potential life partner, young adults' relationships bring a new dimension into the family structure. Similarly, their new interactions may also bring divergent life philosophies into the family. Reconciling these differences can bring about major family changes.

Stage Seven: The middle years. The middle years refers to the time after all the children have launched but before the parents retire. In the 1950s, when this theory was first developed, couples generally had their children in their early twenties, and those children were launched by the time the parents were in their middle to late forties. The couple had about 10 or 15 years to accomplish the tasks of the middle years.

One of those tasks is ensuring security for later years by increasing retirement accounts. The couple must reallocate household responsibilities once again, as now they are no longer serving as "shuttle services" for their busy teens. They need to work to maintain a comfortable home but may look for a smaller one that requires less maintenance and space, given that their children have moved out. Although the children are not physically there, emotional ties still exist, of course, so parents must develop new methods of extended family contacts, which can include increased phone contact, e-mail, or visits. Their children begin to have children during this stage, and now the couple can begin to develop relationships with their grandchildren.

So what is a couple to do when they stop being caretakers of their children? For many couples, this is a major transition. They have just lost the job of parenting that they had for 20 to 25 years, and it comes at a time when, as individuals, they are approaching middle age. Many couples look to this time as an opportunity to become more involved in community life by pursuing political office, volunteer work, or mission work. They may also simply indulge themselves, for example, by eating out more frequently, since it is "just the two of them."

Most importantly, the couple must work to maintain their own communication. This is a time, however, that couples report a great deal of stress in their marriages. While many couples spent their energies raising and supporting a family, their marriages fell by the wayside. When the children are gone, they realize that they are no longer really acquainted with their partner. From an individual developmental perspective, middle age is accompanied by a re-examination of one's life, frequently referred to as a "midlife crisis." The primary issue for middle-aged persons is that, instead of considering their lives since birth, they begin to consider their lives from a perspective of death. "I only have twenty more years until I retire—do I want to be stuck in this job forever?" "I want to be with someone who shares my dream of sailing around the world, and my spouse wants to just stay at home." A commitment to become reacquainted is important to the survival of the couple. Otherwise, the couple may find that their relationship is no longer meaningful.

Stage Eight: Aging family members. According to Duvall (1977), this last stage "begins with the man's retirement, goes through the loss of the first spouse, and ends with the death of the second" (p. 385). This stage includes the task of adjusting to retirement, including the reduced income that retirement frequently brings. If there is illness or physical limitation, couples may seek a new home arrangement that is more satisfying or safe, such as a retirement village, nursing home, or moving in with one of their children. All such transitions require a shift in household routines.

Aging adults continue to spend time with their adult children and their grandchildren. Some of these couples may need to care for their elderly relatives as well their grandchildren. The "sandwich generation" faces many challenges as they deal with their multiple responsibilities.

As the couple ages, they encounter death of family and friends more frequently. Older relatives die, and then friends of their own generation whom they may have known for years or even decades begin to die. As they face bereavement, the couple must write their wills and put their financial affairs in order, preparing for their own death and the death of their partner. The family cycle is complete when the last partner dies.

The Family Career

Aldous (1978, 1996) built on the concept of the family life cycle but noted that not all families followed the cycle from beginning to end, as in the case of divorced or remarried families. She preferred the term "family careers" to indicate that families followed stages that were somewhat predictable but not cyclical in nature. Moreover, she combined Duvall's stages of parenting into one, since parents often were in several stages of parenting at the same time (depending upon the ages of their children). Thus, Aldous's family career had only four stages—the establishment of the marital relationship, the parental role, the return to the couple relationship, and the aging couple.

Aldous's model did not focus exclusively on the family, however, but went further to include dimensions of family interdependency and social networks. For example, in addition to her analysis of the family career, she also considered the parent-child career and the sibling career, and how these interactions changed over the life span of the family. Expanding on the sibling career, Cicerelli (1994) indicated that the sibling relationship was, for many individuals, likely to be the longest bond experienced in their lifetime.

The Dynamics of Family Development

White (1991) and his colleagues (Rodgers and White 1993; Watt and White 1999) have expanded the family development theory to provide a more contextualized perspective. The stages of family development are driven not only by the ontogenetic development of the individuals but also by the contexts in which the development occurs. These changing contexts make the family development stages dynamic rather than static. This perspective still takes into account stages over time but recognizes that, in this social context, all families do not follow the exact same path at the exact same time (White 1991). Understanding the family as a dynamic process encourages researchers to see fluidity and interrelationships between the process of development, the individual, and the context of the development (Fuller and Fincham 1994).

Interestingly, Watt and White (1999) found that the family development perspective created a structure for analyzing how computer technology pervades family life. Through each family developmental stage, computers serve as inexpensive tools for education, recreation, and communication. For example, computers impact mate selections by creating a "space" for cyber-dating. Computers assist newly married couples with financial planning and career enhancement. When children leave the home, computers can help parents fill the "empty nest" with e-mail or allow them to pursue educational and occupational interests.

It is not enough, according to White, to simply note that computers are used differently in each stage, but use must also be studied based on the context. For example, are boys more likely to use computers than girls? Does this create a hierarchical status in the family? What might be the effect of spending long hours on the computer? How is family life affected? And—more to the point of developmental theory—does it matter to the family *when* those hours are spent? Is there a different effect if a young adult, early in his or her married career, spends hours on the computer, compared with an older retired adult? These are all interesting questions to consider.

THE LIFE COURSE PERSPECTIVE

Bengtson and Allen (1993) expanded the theory with the "life course perspective," which addressed some of the issues not addressed in the "life cycle perspective." The life course perspective incorporated changes over time (and over the life course), identified three different "kinds" of time (ontogenetic, generational, and historical), and included the social context in which the changes occurred. They also highlighted an additional component—the meanings that individuals attach to the changes throughout their life course.

The life course perspective has a number of advantages over the family life cycle perspective, primarily in that it takes into account the complexity of family and individual change over time. Each element of the theory adds richness to our understanding of how families exist in time, space, context, and process. It enhances our understanding of the social meanings that people give to their own developmental and family life (Bengtson and Allen 1993).

Let us look at widowhood as an example. As individuals, we mourn the deaths of those we love in a multitude of ways, but it frequently follows a number of stages as outlined by Elizabeth Kübler-Ross (1969). Thus, we have an *individual response* to death. Now let's put it into a *time context*. Is the death of a spouse experienced differently depending on how old one is? Is grieving affected by our age? (Some people believe that as one ages, death is easier to accept, although it is difficult to gather hard data on that fact.) What about *family context*? Is the death of a spouse processed differently if the children are grown? Is the death processed differently if the spouses spent most of their time together (as in a family-run business) versus less time together? Next, let's consider the *social context*. Is the death processed differently if both partners worked and neither was totally dependent on the other for family income? Finally, let's consider the *meaning* associated with death. Is the death processed differently if the death is the result of a long illness? Is it different for those who ascribe religious meanings to death and "eternal life"?

Following the life course perspective encourages us to consider the multiple social contexts of family development, just as we know that many social contexts influence us individually. Although our families are our primary socialization agent, we are also influenced by our peers, our schooling, our faith systems, our government, and our culture. The diversity of that culture also should be included in any analysis of the life course, as the differences of our ethnic, racial, geographic, and religious heritage play out in our families and in our lives (Bengtson and Allen 1993).

CARTER AND MCGOLDRICK MODEL

Recently, family developmental theory has found new support in family therapy. Carter and McGoldrick (1999) analyze the individual, from a therapy perspective, in terms of his or her place in the larger context of the family life cycle. Their model is based upon developmental stages, but it also encompasses different levels—the individual, family, and social context—within those stages. As a therapeutically focused model, the emphasis includes how anxiety and its symptoms develop in individuals and families over time, particularly in response to major life transitions.

At the individual level, it includes a focus on individual temperament and genetic makeup as well as change over time. The family level of analysis might include an exploration of family secrets, expectations, role shifts, and renegotiations of power. Both the individual and the family issues are always considered in the cultural and social history, and how these change over time.

Carter and McGoldrick provide an example. The birth of a child is naturally a taxing event on a couple, producing "the normal stresses of a system expanding its boundaries at the present time" (p. 7). If there was anxiety in the family of origin for one or both of the parents, then there might be heightened anxiety for the couple as new parents. Heightened anxiety might also arise if there is a mismatch between the temperaments of the parents and the new child. Finally, additional stresses might be introduced if the child is born during a time of political upheaval, such as when the parents might be refugees living outside their own country.

The model is useful in exploring life-cycle stressors and how these interact with family stories, themes, triangles, and roles over time. It further emphasizes a balance between connectedness and separateness, as individual identity is understood in relation to significant people and relationships.

THE SYSTEMIC FAMILY DEVELOPMENT MODEL

Most recently, a new model has been proposed that incorporates aspects of family systems theory, family stress theory, and a multigenerational perspective of family development theory (Laszloffy 2002). The systemic family development (SFD) model proposes, just like other developmental theories, that families experience transitions and shifts in family roles. Unlike other theories, though, which attempt to generalize patterns of family development over time, SFD states that each family's pattern is unique. An analysis of a family must account for the combination, specific to the family being analyzed, of all of the factors influencing the family, including socioeconomic status, race, religion, gender, sexual orientation, politics, and sociocultural values. Laszloffy describes the family as a layer cake, with each layer representing a generation within the family. Each layer is at a different stage within the family cycle (aged adults, parents, adolescents, preschoolers, and others), having to deal with its own issues and developmental tasks. To fully describe the family, she argues, means studying the interrelationships between the layers and describing the complexities that result.

From a systems perspective, all change causes stress to the family. Therefore, even normative developmental transitions (within the family's social contexts) cause stress. The family's response to its stressors will vary according to its resources, as predicted by stress theory. The more difficult the transition is, the more intense the stress. If the family has many resources, and the developmental transition is normative (and therefore expected), it will be easier to handle the transition. When the family successfully negotiates the transition, stress is relieved, and the family returns to stability.

The SFD model provides a way for family scholars to view the family in multiple developmental cycles concurrently while respecting the various social contexts (for example, race, ethnicity, and socioeconomic status) that influence development. It allows us to investigate the influences across generations, as well as within generations. It may also prove to be an important research tool because scholars can use the same theory to explain a family both at a point in time (a cross-sectional view, or the vertical slice of the cake) and over a span of time (a longitudinal view, or a layer of the cake).

CRITIQUE

Developmental theory was first clearly delineated in the 1950s, a time when social norms ensured that most families consisted of a two-parent family and when childbearing was both normative and early in the marital career. Obviously, in the intervening years, social norms have changed, and so some of the "predictability value" of the theory has been lost. For example, launching comes later in life and is less complete than when Duvall first described these stages (Qualls 1997). Obviously, not all families fit the stages and tasks associated with the family life cycle as outlined by researchers in the 1950s. Many of the social issues that families face changed significantly in the 1960s and 1970s as women entered the workforce, as birth control became more readily available, and as social mores changed to accept divorce, nonmarital cohabitation, and stepfamilies.

Family developmental theory was criticized by many as being only descriptive but not heuristic (research-generating). Critics said it lacked a sense of usefulness as a theory because it had little predictive power. It described only one particular kind of family (middle-class, heterosexual, lifelong couples and their children), and it did not provide much insight into what governed their patterns of behavior (Bengtson and Allen 1993; Burr 1973; Falicov 1988). In fact, in the early 1980s, some researchers pronounced it a "minor" theory (Holman and Burr 1980). Because of these criticisms, White (1991) worked to formalize the theory in a more scientific way, with testable propositions that could be used to predict family functioning.

Mattessich and Hill (1987) worked to expand the theoretical structure, but it was still deemed too descriptive and broad (Aldous 1990). In other words, the theory suffered from trying to explain too much and so could only explain things simply so as to avoid being overwhelmingly complex. Further, while family developmental theory described the stages of the family life cycle, it did not describe the relationship between the stages or how they formed a total pattern of the family's development (Breunlin 1988).

For example, Duvall's eight-stage model was based on a nuclear family, assumed an intact marriage throughout the life cycle of the family, and was based on the oldest child's developmental needs. It did not take into account divorce, death of a spouse, remarriage, nonmarried parents, childless couples, or cohabiting couples. Her stage approach did not allow for understanding fluidity of roles when families did not follow stages in an orderly and predictable manner. It was criticized as being highly descriptive, but it could not help researchers understand the nature of the relationships between family members over time.

Family developmental theory failed to include family identity factors such as race, socioeconomic status, ethnicity, and family structure (Bennett, Wolin, and McAvity 1988; Dilworth-Anderson and Burton 1996). Bengtson and Allen's (1993) development of the life course perspective specifically includes these factors and lends itself to testable hypotheses. Carter and McGoldrick's (1999) family therapy perspective actually includes even more family identity structures (for example, stepfamilies, divorcing families, never-married families, multigenerational families) and ethnic and racial differences. Laszloffy's systemic family development model broadens the theory's scope to include not only families of different structure, race, ethnicity, and sexuality but also multiple generations of families at the same time. Despite these improvements, however, family developmental theory is generally considered a highly descriptive analysis.

Endnote

1. The edition that Duvall edited with Brent Miller was the last edition of Duvall's *Family Development* textbook. She died in 1998.

APPLICATION

1. Identify the different life cycle stages represented by the Morrison family. Note the different tasks that each must accomplish.

2. Identify the assumptions in the scenario.

3. Analyze the tasks that each family member must accomplish in terms of different social and personal constraints. Can some tasks be avoided altogether? Must some tasks be addressed within a limited time frame?

4. Indicate how the concept of change can be seen in this vignette. How do you think the family might cope with these changes?

5. Indicate how this family provides examples of the effect of social changes.

6. Think of an intimate relationship either you or people close to you have been in. How has being in the intimate relationship changed this person? What kinds of changes have you noticed? What kinds of changes are noticed by your family and friends? Can you identify any of the establishment tasks in this relationship?

7. Based on the reading by Schnittger and Bird, in what ways did life cycle influence the coping style of dual-career couples in this article?

SAMPLE READING

Schnittger, M. H., and Bird, G. W. (1990). Coping among dual-career men and women across the family life cycle. *Family Relations* 39: 199–205.

This study demonstrates differences in coping among dual-career women and men. It also differentiates how individuals choose different styles of coping at different life cycle stages.

References

Aldous, J. (1978). *Family Careers: Developmental Change in Families.* New York: Wiley.

——. (1990). Family development and the life course: Two perspectives on family change. *Journal of Marriage and the Family* 52: 571–583.

——. (1996). *Family Careers: Rethinking the Developmental Perspective.* Thousand Oaks, CA: Sage.

Bengtson, V. I., and Allen, K. R. (1993). The life course perspective applied to families over time. In P. G. Boss, W. J. Doherty, R. LaRossa, W. J. Schumm, and S. K. Steinmetz (eds.), *Sourcebook of Family Theories and Methods: A Contextual Approach* (pp. 469–499). New York: Plenum.

Bennett, L. A., Wolin, S. J., and McAvity, K. J. (1988). Family identity, ritual and myth: A cultural perspective on life cycle transitions. In C. J. Falicov (ed.), *Family Transitions: Continuity and Change Over the Life Cycle* (pp. 211–234). New York: Guilford.

Breunlin, D. C. (1988). Oscillation theory and family development. In C. J. Falicov (ed.), *Family Transitions: Continuity and Change Over the Life Cycle* (pp. 133–155). New York: Guilford.

Burr, W. R. (1973). *Theory Construction and the Sociology of the Family.* New York: Wiley.

Carter, B., and McGoldrick, M. (1999). *The Expanded Family Life Cycle: Individual, Family and Social Perspectives* (3rd ed.). Needham Heights, MA: Allyn and Bacon.

Cicerelli, V. (1994). The sibling life cycle. In L. L' Abate (ed.), *Handbook of Developmental Family Psychology and Psychopathology* (pp. 44–59). New York: Wiley.

Dilworth-Anderson, P., and Burton, L. M. (1996). Rethinking family development theory. *Journal of Social and Personal Relationships* 13: 325–334.

Duvall, E. M. (1957 and the revised editions 1962, 1967, 1971, 1977). *Family Development.* New York: Lippincott.

——. (1988). Family development's first forty years. *Family Relations* 37: 127–134.

Duvall, E. M., and Hill, R. L. (1948). *Reports of the committee on the dynamics of family interaction.* Washington, DC: National Conference on Family Life.

Duvall, E. M., and Miller, B. C. (1985). *Marriage and Family Development* (6th ed.). New York: Harper and Row.

Falicov, C. J. (1988). Family sociology and family therapy contributions to the family developmental framework: A comparative analysis and thoughts on future trends. In C. J. Falicov (ed.), *Family Transitions: Continuity and Change Over the Life Cycle* (pp. 3–51). New York: Guilford.

Fuller, T. L., and Fincham, F. D. (1994). The marital life cycle: A developmental approach to the study of marital change. In L. L'Abate (ed.), *Handbook of Developmental Family Psychology and Psychopathology* (pp. 60–82). New York: Wiley.

Glick, P. C. (1977). Updating the life cycle of the family. *Journal of Marriage and the Family* 39: 5–13.

Hagestad, G. (1988). Demographic change and the life course: Some emerging trends in the family realm. *Family Relations* 37: 405–410.

Havighurst, R. J. (1948). *Developmental Tasks and Education.* Chicago: University of Chicago.

——. (1953). *Human Development and Education.* New York: Longmans and Green.

Hill, R. (1986). Life cycle stages for types of single parent families: Of family development theory. *Family Relations* 35: 19–30.

Holman, T. B., and Burr, W. R. (1980). Beyond the beyond: The growth of family theories in the 1970s. *Journal of Marriage and the Family* 42: 729–742.

Kübler-Ross, E. (1969). *On Death and Dying.* New York: Macmillan.

Laszloffy, T. A. (2002). Rethinking family development theory: Teaching with the systemic family development (SFD) model. *Family Relations* 51: 206–214.

Mattessich, P., and Hill, R. (1987). Life cycle and family development. In M. B. Sussman and S. K. Steinmetz (eds.), *Handbook of Marriage and the Family* (pp. 437–469). New York: Plenum.

Qualls, S. H. (1997). Transitions in autonomy: The essential caregiving challenge. *Family Relations* 46: 41–46.

Rapoport, R. (1963). Normal crises, family structure and mental health. *Family Process* 2: 68–80.

Rodgers, R. (1964). Toward a theory of family development. *Journal of Marriage and the Family* 26: 262–270.

——. (1973). *Family Interaction and Transaction: The Developmental Approach.* Englewood Cliffs, NJ: Prentice-Hall.

Rodgers, R. H., and White, J. M. (1993). Family developmental theory. In P. G. Boss, W. J. Doherty, R. LaRossa, W. R. Schumm, and S. K. Steinmetz (eds.), *Sourcebook of Family Theories and Methods: A Contextual Approach* (pp. 225–254). New York: Plenum.

Watt, D., and White, J. M. (1999). Computers and the family life: A family development perspective. *Journal of Comparative Family Studies* 30: 1–15.

White, J. M. (1991). *Dynamics of Family Development: A Theoretical Perspective.* New York: Guilford. ✦

Coping Among Dual-Career Men and Women Across the Family Life Cycle

Maureen H. Schnittger
Gloria W. Bird

Differences in coping across five family life cycle stages are identified using responses from 329 dual-career women and men. Coping strategy use differs significantly by gender and life cycle stage. Women utilize the coping strategies of Cognitive Restructuring, Delegating, Limiting Avocational Activities, and Using Social Support significantly more often than do men. Dual-career men and women without children at home use Compartmentalizing significantly less frequently than men and women with children. Respondents whose oldest child is under age 6 reported less use of Delegating than those with an oldest child age 13–18. Limiting Avocational Activities is used less often by participants with children under age 6 than by those with older children. The results are discussed from a family life cycle perspective.

Past research using samples of dual-career respondents delineates the various coping strategies used to alleviate role strain in dual-career families (Bird & Bird, 1986; Elman & Gilbert, 1984; Johnson & Johnson, 1977; Rapoport & Rapoport, 1976). Although these and other studies have determined that dual-career parents with young children experience significantly greater role strain and have identified coping strategies used by these parents (Heckman, Bryson, & Bryson, 1977; Holahan & Gilbert, 1979), less attention has been focused on whether differences exist in how dual-career men and women cope and none of the reviewed literature examines coping from a life cycle perspective.

The purpose of this study is to further the understanding of coping in dual-career families by asking: (a) Does use of coping strategies differ by stage in the family life cycle? and (b) Are there differences in the way dual-career women and men cope with stressful life circumstances? The findings presented lead to some suggestions and recommendations having implications for therapists, educators, policy-makers, and employers. Research implications are also discussed.

PREVIOUS LITERATURE

The structural constraints and incentives of the work environment in early career stages usually result in high career commitment and long hours spent on career-related tasks (Betz & Fitzgerald, 1987; Kanter, 1977). These early years of career establishment appear to create minimal role strain for childless couples (Rapoport & Rapoport, 1976). However, adding the parental role to career and marital roles, elicits feelings of satisfaction as well as feelings of overload and interrole conflict (Barnett & Baruch, 1987). Career plans may be altered as work and family demands compete for personal and family resources (Faver, 1984). Dual-career couples with young children report significantly more role strain and stress than other dual-career parents, with women indicating higher strain than men (Bird & Ford, 1985; Heckman, Bryson, & Bryson, 1977).

Addition of the parent role provides increased conflict with other life roles (Holahan & Gilbert, 1979). Research shows that conflicts between professional and family roles are especially stressful for dual-career mothers and fathers (Gilbert, 1985; Heckman et al., 1977; Holahan & Gilbert, 1979). For example, Nicola (1980) found that men say career interests intrude on fathering roles while women state that parenting interferes with career roles. Women also report that parental roles and career roles conflict with marital roles. As the number of children and importance of parental role increases, so does the degree of role strain for dual-career women (Bird & Ford, 1985; Holmstrom, 1973; Rapoport & Rapoport, 1976; Voydanoff & Kelly, 1984). Dual-career men indicate experiencing interrole conflict centered around wanting to support their spouse's career, be involved in family and home care, yet at the same time, wanting to prioritize personal goals (Gilbert, 1985).

Dual-career women and men utilize a variety of coping strategies to prevent or minimize role demands and conflicts among them (Elman & Gilbert, 1984; Guelzow & Bird, 1986). Using a typology proposed by Hall (1972) coping strategies can be classified into three major types. Type I coping, structural role redefinition, refers to attempts to alter external, structurally imposed expectations. It involves dealing with the objective reality of the situation instead of subjective perception or feelings. Type I coping typically reduces experienced overload and conflict between the individual and others. Behaviors included in this style of coping are: utilizing social support and integrating and eliminating some role activities. Type II coping, personal role redefinition, involves changing one's perceptions and expectations of behavior relative to a given role. Examples include setting priorities, changing attitudes toward roles, and eliminating roles (Voydanoff, 1987).

[Type] III coping, reactive role behavior is an attempt to meet all role expectations simultaneously, assuming that the demands are unchangeable and must be met. This style of coping implies a passive manner of dealing with conflict and "would probably represent considerable strain on a person's energies, since they involve attempting to do everything demanded" (Hall, 1972, p. 480). Behaviors indicating a Type III style of coping are working harder or attempting to plan and organize better. Although Hall's concepts were first used to describe college-educated women who managed multiple roles, his descriptions of coping behavior remain applicable to dual-career families (Sekaran, 1986; Voydanoff, 1987).

Some past research, though not specific to life cycle stages, provides evidence of methods of adaptation in dual-career families. Poloma (1972) outlined four coping strategies used by dual-career women, (a) defining dual-career patterns as favorable, (b) establishing priorities among roles, (c) compartmentalizing work and family roles, and (d) compromising career aspirations. Harrison and Minor (1978) reported that structural role definition was the coping strategy used to deal with conflicts between marital and worker roles, and personal role redefinition was used when the conflicts were between the roles of parent and worker. Elman and Gilbert (1984), using reports from a sample of women with preschool children, found increased role behavior to be the most widely used coping strategy. This behavior "involves efforts by the individual to do it all, by working harder and more efficiently" (Elman & Gilbert, 1984, p. 324).

Other studies show that dual-career women also manage strain within the family by using such coping strategies as prioritizing, compartmentalizing and compromising (Amaka & Cross, 1983; Betz & Fitzgerald, 1987; Bird & Bird, 1986; Bird, Bird, & Scruggs, 1983; Holmstrom, 1973; Poloma, 1972). For example, some women consciously leave work problems at the office to separate or compartmentalize work and family roles. Others prioritize needs and compromise standards to reduce strain at home. Many manage by negotiating increased sharing of the weekly household tasks (Bird & Bird, 1987; Rapoport & Rapoport, 1976; Skinner, 1980).

Bird, Bird, and Scruggs (1983) examined coping strategies of dual-earner couples and found that men used organization more often to cope with role strain while women chose the strategy compartmentalization to a greater extent. Skinner and McCubbin (1982) found, in their sample of dual-employed families, that men utilized coping patterns that allowed them to maintain a positive perspective on the lifestyle and reduce tensions. The pattern included behaviors that attended to personal needs (i.e., planning time to exercise). Gilbert (1985) found that dual-career men used increased role behavior more often than other coping strategies. These men, especially if they were in the early stages of the career and family life cycle, did not view structural or societal changes as an option. Men married over 10 years reported frequent use of strategies that alter or change the source of conflict (i.e., personal role redefinition). Instead of arguing with wives about division of household tasks, they viewed task sharing as a part of the dual-career lifestyle.

Conflicts between personal and societal norms are minimized when dual-career couple members are supportive of and empathetic toward each other (Bird & Bird, 1986; Kater, 1985). This supportive relationship extends to friends and other couples living a similar lifestyle. Dual-career couples form friendships with other dual-career couples perhaps as a means of validating their life-style (Rapoport & Rapoport, 1976; Skinner, 1980). Bird and Bird (1986) suggest that friendships with others in a dual-career lifestyle serve to insulate dual-career couples from some societal expectations.

Although studies have identified the pre-school years as a time when both women and men feel the greatest role strain and have attempted to identify efficacious coping attempts by gender, there has been no close examination of differences in coping strategy utilization across life-cycle stages. Life-cycle stages provide a means to categorize families that are experiencing similar events, facing similar crises, and attempting to accomplish similar developmental tasks (Duvall & Miller, 1985; Mattessich & Hill, 1987). Rodgers (1973) explains that the focus of this developmental analysis is on process rather than chronological time. He states "These periods are identified not because they occur during the same chronological era in all families, but because they have a distinctive role structure which separates them from other periods in the family career" (p. 48). Each stage represents a point when the family must also initiate different behavior patterns (Trost, 1974). During the life of the typical family, important changes occur not only in the composition but also in other measurable characteristics of the group. Family life-cycle variables provide a way to map the impact of the supply and demand of both stressors and coping resources in the family (Voydanoff & Kelly, 1984).

Proponents of family life cycle theory differ in the number of stages identified as necessary to adequately describe the family life cycle; yet, "most methods for determining life cycle stages use the age of the oldest child for the operational purpose of demarcating stages" (Mattessich & Hill, 1987, p. 444).

The present study uses the following five life cycle stages, based on the early work of Duvall and Hill and most recently refined by Hill (1986) to categorize the data: Stage 1—Establishment (childless); Stage 2—New Parents (oldest child 1 day–5 years); Stage 3—Family with School-Age Child (oldest child 6–12 years); Stage 4—Family with Adolescents (oldest child 13–18 years); Stage 5—Family with Young Adults (oldest child over 18, not living at home).

METHODS

SAMPLE

Data used in this study were collected from a purposive sample of dual-career couples, drawn from a mid-Atlantic state. Initial contacts were made through professional organizations and personal networks of the five-member research team. Individuals who were contacted initially provided the names of other dual-career couples. This process continued until a sample of 310 dual-career couples were located. Responses were received from 70% of the sample after three follow-up contacts. Data from the 329 women and men who reported being employed at least 40 hours per week in professional and managerial positions and who were married to spouses in similar positions were used for the present study; 48% (158) were males, and 52% (171) were females. Examples of career positions held by those in the sample included: lawyer, professor, architect, teacher, hospital administrator, social worker, bank manager, sales manager, counselor, registered nurse, and dentist. All respondents and their spouses had earned at least a bachelor's degree. Mean individual income was $35,000.

The mean age of the men and women sampled was 40 years. Forty-two percent of the sample had been married 10 years or less; 37% were married between 10 and 20 years. The average number of children in these families was two. Twenty percent of the sample had no children; 22% had one child; 42% had two children; 14% had three or four children. Of the children living at home, 24% were less than 5 years old; 21% were 6–12 years old; 21% were 13–18 years of age. Fourteen percent of the children were over 18 years old and not living at home. Seventy-four percent had been employed 10 years or less in their present position.

Measurement and Data Analysis

Respondents were asked to consider their own experiences in a two-career family and indicate on a 7-point response scale how often they used each coping item described to manage the dual responsibilities of employment and family life. Coping strategies were assessed by items adapted from the Dual-Employed Coping Scales (DECS) (Skinner & McCubbin, 1982) supplemented with other items identified from a review of the literature concerned with coping styles of dual-career men and women (Bird & Bird, 1986; Elman & Gilbert, 1984; Gilbert, 1985; Poloma, 1972; Rapoport & Rapoport, 1976). Ratings of the 44 coping items were subjected to principal components factor analysis with varimax rotation. The in-

tent of this procedure was data reduction and strategy identification. Only items loading .40 and above on each factor were retained. Seven coping strategies were identified: Cognitive Restructuring, Delegating, Limiting Avocational Activities, Subordinating Career, Compartmentalizing, Avoiding Responsibility, and Using Social Support. Each coping strategy with sample items and factor loadings is presented in Table 1. A 2 (gender) × 5 (life cycle stages) MANOVA was conducted to test for differences in the dependent measure coping strategies.

Results

Table 2 reports the descriptive statistics for the coping strategy variable by gender and life-cycle stages. The MANOVA associated with these data is summarized in Table 3. The interaction effect is not significant, however the multivariate F tests for gender and life-cycle stages are significant ($p < .01$). The univariate tests indicate that use of the coping strategies Cognitive Restructuring, Delegating, Limiting Avocational Activities, and Using Social Support differ significantly by gender. Use of the coping strategies Subordinating Career, Delegating, and Limiting Avocational Activities differ significantly by family life-cycle stage.

Table 2 shows the following total mean score differences: Cognitive Restructuring (5.13 males, 5.46 females); Delegating (5.19 males, 5.66 females); Limiting Avocational Activities (4.83 males, 5.24 females); and Using Social Support (4.06 males, 4.65 females). With one exception (Cognitive Restructuring use by males in Stage 3), females report greater use of the significant coping strategies in every family life cycle stage.

Discussion

Differences by Gender

Women in this study, compared to men, cope significantly more often by Delegating, Using Social Support, Cognitive Restructuring, and Limiting Avocational Activities.

Table 1
Coping Factors with Sample Items and Factor Loadings

Item	Loading
Cognitive Restructuring	
Believing that our family life is better because both of us are employed.	.74
Believing there are more advantages than disadvantages to our lifestyle.	.72
Believing that my career has made me a better wife/husband than I otherwise would be.	.71
Delegating	
Encouraging our child(ren) to help out whenever possible.	.77
Encouraging our child(ren) to be more self-sufficient.	.70
Delegating tasks to other family members.	.64
Limiting Avocational Activities	
Eliminating certain community activities.	.74
Cutting down on the amount of "outside activities" in which I can be involved.	.66
Cutting back on leisure activities.	.60
Changing standards of how well household tasks must be done.	.47
Subordinating Career	
Limiting my involvement on the job; saying "no" to some of the things I could be doing.	.54
Reducing the time I spend at work.	.50
Planning career changes around family needs.	.48
Compartmentalizing	
Planning ahead so that major changes at home will not disturb my career goals.	.74
Making better use of time at work.	.73
Separating my work life from family life so I can concentrate my effort on one area at a time.	.49
Avoiding Responsibility	
Postponing certain tasks until the pressure to do them subsides.	.73
Finding legitimate excuses to keep from fulfilling obligations I dislike.	.69
Using family responsibilities to justify not accepting more job responsibilities.	.57
Using Social Support	
Arranging for child care so my husband/wife and I can spend time together.	.58
Relying on extended family members for support and encouragement.	.51
Making friends with other two-career couples.	.50

Delegating and Using Social Support are examples of structural role redefinition that reduces overload and conflict between the individual and those around him/her (Voydanoff, 1987). Delegating responsibilities, such as household tasks and child care, is consistently reported to be an efficacious strategy for managing role overload in dual-career families (Bird & Bird, 1986; Johnson & Johnson, 1977; Rapoport & Rapoport, 1976). Delegation is the most frequently used strategy for both men and women, but women use it significantly more often. This finding is probably best explained by data that show women still take the primary responsibility for family tasks (Bird, Bird, & Scruggs, 1984; Pleck, 1985). The actual labor involved in task accomplishment is shared to a greater extent within dual-career families; however, it is the women who most often implement the sharing—remember when tasks need to be done, assign tasks, and check on task progress (Ventre, 1988).

Using Social Support includes relying on family members for encouragement and making friends with other two-career couples. This pattern of coping involves obtaining both emotional and instrumental support. Because the dual-career lifestyle challenges traditional role assumptions about normative family functioning, spouse and friend support can be crucial to effective coping (Gilbert & Rachlin, 1987). That men in this study report relying on social support less often than women substantiates findings of other researchers (Bird &

Table 2
Means and Standard Deviations of Coping Strategies by Life Cycle Stages and Gender

| | Life Cycle Stages | | | | | |
| | 1 | 2 | 3 | 4 | 5 | |
Men (*n* = 158)	(*n* = 30)	(*n* = 35)	(*n* = 33)	(*n* = 34)	(*n* = 23)	Total
Subordinating Career						
Mean	3.91	4.76	4.76	4.81	3.98	4.49
Standard Deviation	1.15	.93	.96	.97	.84	1.04
Cognitive Restructuring						
Mean	4.90	5.05	5.35	5.12	5.25	5.13
Standard Deviation	.81	.86	.65	.91	.75	.81
Delegating						
Mean	4.92	4.88	5.29	5.43	5.47	5.19
Standard Deviation	.92	.85	.88	.70	.96	.88
Limiting Avocational Activities						
Mean	4.75	4.80	4.80	4.88	5.03	4.83
Standard Deviation	.91	.72	1.08	.80	.92	.88
Compartmentalizing						
Mean	4.50	5.02	4.57	4.97	5.13	4.83
Standard Deviation	.97	.91	.98	.76	.93	.93
Avoiding Responsibility						
Mean	4.00	3.73	3.73	3.56	3.66	3.72
Standard Deviation	.68	.84	.95	1.20	.87	.93
Using Social Support						
Mean	4.11	4.23	4.20	3.87	3.74	4.06
Standard Deviation	1.16	1.00	.96	1.11	1.08	1.06
Women (*n* = 171)	(*n* = 34)	(*n* = 40)	(*n* = 35)	(*n* = 36)	(*n* = 22)	Total
Subordinating Career						
Mean	4.50	5.08	5.05	4.70	3.97	4.72
Standard Deviation	.98	1.14	.80	.87	1.06	1.04
Cognitive Restructuring						
Mean	5.31	5.53	5.29	5.64	5.53	5.46
Standard Deviation	.98	.87	.88	.89	.92	.90
Delegating						
Mean	5.73	5.49	5.62	5.87	5.55	5.66
Standard Deviation	.72	.84	.91	.66	.96	.83
Limiting Avocational Activities						
Mean	4.86	5.29	5.02	5.63	5.52	5.24
Standard Deviation	.95	1.15	1.09	.81	.80	1.02
Compartmentalizing						
Mean	5.01	5.13	4.87	4.84	5.18	5.02
Standard Deviation	.91	1.08	1.02	.95	.90	.98
Avoiding Responsibility						
Mean	3.75	3.80	3.52	3.87	3.76	3.73
Standard Deviation	1.14	1.24	1.09	1.18	1.00	1.13
Using Social Support						
Mean	4.83	4.60	4.72	4.52	4.50	4.65
Standard Deviation	.85	1.06	.78	.93	1.14	.94

Bird, 1986; Rapoport & Rapoport, 1976). For example, women report being more likely to arrange for a sitter to allow the spouses time alone and to enlist kin and friend support.

Table 3

Summary of Multivariate and Univariate F Tests Associated with the Coping Factorial Design

Source	df	F
Multivariate Tests		
Gender	1	6.83*
Life Cycle Stages	4	3.83*
Interaction	4	1.15
Univariate *F* Tests		
Gender		
Subordinating Career	1	3.52
Cognitive Restructuring	1	11.96*
Delegating	1	24.34*
Limiting Avocational Activities	1	13.86*
Compartmentalizing	1	2.72
Avoiding Responsibility	1	.00
Using Social Support	1	25.98*
Life Cycle Stages		
Subordinating Career	4	10.16*
Cognitive Restructuring	4	.82
Delegating	4	3.09*
Limiting Avocational Activities	4	4.03*
Compartmentalizing	4	2.68
Avoiding Responsibility	4	.42
Using Social Support	4	1.54
Interaction		
Subordinating Career	4	.42
Cognitive Restructing	4	1.31
Delegating	4	1.70
Limiting Avocational Activities	4	1.30
Compartmentalizing	4	1.22
Avoiding Responsibility	4	.79
Using Social Support	4	.35

*$p < .01$

Cognitive Restructuring and Limiting Avocational Activities are examples of personal role redefinition which involves changing attitudes toward and perceptions of role expectations (Hall, 1972). Women and men using Cognitive Restructuring define situations and events unique to the dual-career family pattern as being favorable compared to other alternatives. They believe that the benefits of their lifestyle outweigh the costs. Cogni-

tive Restructuring allows for validation of the dual-career lifestyle. For example, dual-career women who receive conflictual messages about working full-time while being a parent most likely use this coping strategy as a means of reinterpreting the situation by focusing on the positive aspects of balancing work and family roles. In effect, these women shield themselves and their families by controlling the meaning of the problem (Folkman, Lazarus, Dunkel-Schetter, DeLongis, & Gruen, 1986; Pearlin & Schooler, 1978). Once a problem is assessed as more of a challenge than a threat, problem focused coping can more easily be implemented (Folkman, 1984).

That women limit avocational activities more often than men is consistent with the finding that they experience greater personal role strain; women are attempting to manage role overload by limiting involvement in the community, cutting back on leisure activities, and changing household standards. It is more socially acceptable to cut back on community activities or leisure time rather than to reduce time in child care or for spousal support.

It is interesting to note that this sample of dual-career women and men do not differ significantly in how often they cope by subordinating career goals in favor of meeting family needs, compartmentalizing work and family roles, or avoiding certain responsibilities by use of tactics such as postponing tasks and using legitimate excuses to limit task involvement. This finding is important because it provides some evidence of change within dual-career marriages. Previous research conducted in the 1970s found that women more often subordinated careers and compartmentalized roles to cope with role strain while men were more likely to use avoidance tactics (Holmstrom, 1973; Poloma, 1972; Rapoport & Rapoport, 1971, 1976). This study does not lend support to those findings.

In addition, though there are significant differences in use of particular coping strategies, with women indicating greater use compared to men, both report similar patterns of usage across strategies. The most used strategy for women as well as men is Delegating (encouraging children to help out and be more self-sufficient). Both also report that Cognitive Restructuring is the second most used coping strategy (focusing on advantages of the lifestyle). Similarities also exist in strategies used third and fourth in frequency: women use Compartmentalizing and Limiting Avocational Activities; men use Limiting Avocational Activities and Compartmentalizing. This is another indication of some change in dual-career families with men taking on more family responsibilities than their 1970s counterparts. Why would men indicate using these four coping strategies most heavily if their lives were following traditional career paths with expectations that wives assume almost total responsibility for meshing work and family role demands?

DIFFERENCES BY LIFE-CYCLE STAGE

Coping strategy use differed by life-cycle stage as well as by gender. Dual-career men and women without children in the home or whose oldest child had left home (Stages 1 & 5) cope by Subordinating Careers significantly less often than do men and women in other stages of the life cycle. During Stages 1 and 5, dual-career couples are usually negotiating or renegotiating spousal and professional roles. When families are childfree or when most or all of the children have left home there is less need to limit career involvement and reduced pressure to plan career changes around family needs. At each of these points in the life cycle, job flexibility is also less urgent. Prior to the birth of the first child (Stage 1) and again after children have been reared and have left home (Stage 5), couples usually initiate a more equal division of household work that includes a higher proportion of shared tasks (Hood, 1983). Feelings of overload are less often expressed.

As couples become parents, some reallocation of tasks and time typically occur (Bohen & Viveros-Long, 1981). For this sample of dual-career women and men, coping by Subordinating Career was significantly different for every stage that included children under 18 years old. This finding validates that across the fam-

ily life cycle couples must continually integrate changing demands and reestablish career and family priorities (Faver, 1984).

Participants in Stage 2 (oldest child under age 6) of the family life cycle report significantly less use of Delegating compared to respondents in Stage 4 (oldest child 13–18 years). Delegation involves asking another person to carry out various role activities. Typically, wives attempt to delegate some of the household responsibilities or child care to other family members, usually the husband or older children (Bird & Bird, 1986; Hall, 1972; Rapoport & Rapoport, 1976). Not only are there more individuals in the home during Stage 4 to share the work but given the age of the oldest child (13 to 18), more responsibility for complex tasks can be delegated (White & Brinkeroff, 1981).

Dual-career respondents in Stage 1 of the life cycle indicate Limiting Avocational Activities significantly less often than those in Stages 4 or 5. This type of coping, a Type II or personal role redefinition style of coping, involves establishing priorities and eliminating roles (Hall, 1972). Not having the role of parent, probably allows those in Stage 1 more time to concentrate on spousal and professional roles with less need to reduce role responsibility. Women and men in Stage 4 may reduce involvement in community activities and leisure pursuits as a means of having more time with the family. At this stage the oldest child is an adolescent and there is most likely one or more younger children at home as well. Adolescents, ambivalent about issues such as independence, may verbally express dissatisfaction with active parental careers that put the chauffering and advising roles of parents at risk. It may not be that they want parents at home all the time, rather that they want them available. In turn, parents may express a desire to spend more time with adolescents before they leave home.

Individuals in Stage 5 may sense that there is no longer as much need to be competitive in career roles and there is now more freedom to limit other responsibilities as well (Baruch &

Brooks-Gunn, 1984). These women and men, at mid-life, are probably established in professions and may now choose to realign how free time is spent. In addition, they may have the economic flexibility to purchase additional resources or support services.

Summary and Conclusion

This research represents a beginning in the process of identifying coping strategies used by women and men in dual-career families by life-cycle stage. The study uses cross-sectional data to compare responses of dual-career women and men of different age groups at the same point in time. Thus, while examining coping across five life-cycle stages, changes that may occur as these individuals move through future family life-cycle stages cannot be addressed or predicted. However, some inferences can be made regarding differences among the men and women in this sample.

Women indicate using the coping strategies Cognitive Restructuring, Delegating, Limiting Avocational Activities, and Using Social Support significantly more frequently than do men. This finding provides evidence that, contrary to past research on employed women in general (Barnett & Baruch, 1987), the dual-career women in this study appear to evaluate their life circumstances as more challenging than threatening and as a result cope by relying on active problem-solving approaches. These women seem to rely on Cognitive Restructuring to facilitate a positive appraisal of the chronic stressors in their daily lives and concomitantly to initiate problem focused behaviors that represent both structural and personal redefinition styles of coping.

Men report a pattern of coping similar to women, which suggests that they are more involved in family roles than were their counterparts in the 1970s. In addition, men are just as likely as women to cope with work and family demands by subordinating their careers, compartmentalizing work and family roles, and avoiding some responsibilities altogether. These results add credence to past research

which found that implementing a variety of coping strategies to alleviate strain and stress is more effective than relying on one or two strategies exclusively (Gilbert & Rachlin, 1987; Lazarus & Folkman, 1984; Pearlin & Schooler, 1978).

Use of coping strategies also differs by stage in the family life cycle. Childfree respondents are significantly less likely to cope by Subordinating Careers than are respondents with children. Women and men with an oldest child between the ages of 13 and 18 use Delegation more frequently than those with an oldest child under age 6. Limiting Avocational Activities is used significantly more frequently by men and women whose oldest child is an adolescent or young adult than by those who are childfree. These findings suggest that a key factor to studying successful adaptation to work and family roles may be a better understanding of how family members individually and collectively alter the use of coping strategies to fit the ever changing nature of family demands and responsibilities across the life cycle.

Implications for Practice

The findings presented have potential implications for family life educators, therapists, policymakers, employers, and researchers. Family life educators can help dual-career families by disseminating information about which coping strategies are used more often by women and men across life cycle stages. They can emphasize the importance of utilizing a number of coping strategies and, in addition, discuss the benefits of Cognitive Restructuring. Educators can explain how focusing on the positive aspects of the dual-career lifestyle most likely reduces emotional responses such as guilt, anxiety, and frustration and allows attention to be directed toward problem solving.

Family life educators might also identify the changes that have taken place in family life over the last two decades. They need to praise men and women for the progress they have made toward role sharing while pointing out that women are still assuming more of the responsibility for integrating work and family life. Educators can discuss how cultural expectations and the structure of the work environment have much to do with how work/family issues are handled. Yet, despite these constraints, women and men still develop ways of coping that enhance well-being and reduce stress for both of the couple. Such coping usually involves less traditional task allocation and greater flexibility in marital and parental roles.

Therapists might encourage dual-career couples to develop a network of family and friends that offer instrumental and emotional support in times of stress. Findings indicate a sense of belongingness from knowing other dual-career families experience similar situations; each can learn and benefit from the others' experiences. Information about use of coping strategies by life-cycle stage can be used as a preventive measure to guide individuals in one stage to prepare for future stages. For example, families with young children may realize a sense of hope from observing that others in similar situations have coped; that "it can be done." Therapists could also be alert to the role changes taking place in some dual-career families and help couples understand the normalcy of heightened physical and emotional stress during the process of change. They might point to this and other research that show some movement toward role sharing.

Policymakers need to continue their support of workplace policies that allow a range of alternatives for parental and kin caregiving including flexibility of work hours. Attention should be focused on ways of enhancing the planning and problem-solving abilities of employees as they balance work and family commitments. Work policies that increase opportunities for men's involvement in family life should be encouraged. At the same time, recognition is needed that for women to participate more fully in their careers, overload at home must be reduced. A repertoire of coping strategies is useful, but will have limited effects on stress if the larger work structure remains unchanged.

Employers might consider implementing career track models that offer greater flexibility in professional advancement for both women and men. The traditional model that encourages long hours and work behavior that excludes attention to family matters could be revised to more readily accommodate the increasing number of families where both of the couple wish to commit time to marital, parental, and employment roles. If employers recognize that career goals may be modified at certain stages in the family life cycle only to increase in importance during other stages, perhaps the demands on early professionals with young children could be lessened with the knowledge that benefits in productive work will be delayed rather than lost. Such attention to the realities of family life could affect morale, productivity, and job satisfaction.

Employers who scrutinize applicant's resumes for community involvement when making hiring decisions or who evaluate present employees from that perspective should be encouraged to adjust expectations based on stage in the family life cycle. Limiting Avocational Activities is a coping strategy used more frequently by families with middle-school and adolescent children, when community involvement is not as high a priority as balancing career and family goals. Another goal for employers could be facilitating the establishment of support or self-help groups at the work site. Perhaps interested individuals could meet over lunch.

For researchers, continued work from a family life-cycle/gender perspective seems justified given the results of this study. Additional research with broader samples of randomly selected employed women and men is needed to verify and expand the findings reported here. Longitudinal designs would allow more precise identification of the process of change in coping strategies across stages of the life cycle. Research models based on additional variables such as role strain, stress, and their antecedents are needed to further the study of the linkages between work and family.

References

Amaka, E., & Cross, E. Q. (1983). Coupling and careers: A workshop for dual career couples at the launching stage. *Personnel and Guidance Journal, 62,* 48–52.

Barnett, R., & Baruch, G. (1987). Social roles, gender, and psychological distress. In R. C. Barnett, L. Blener, & G. K. Baruch (Eds.), *Gender and stress* (pp. 122–143). New York: Free Press.

Baruch, G., & Brooks-Gunn, J. (Eds.). (1984). *Women in midlife.* New York: Plenum.

Betz, N., & Fitzgerald, L. (1987). *The career psychology of women.* New York: Academic Press.

Bird, G. W., & Bird, G. A. (1986). Strategies for reducing role strain in dual-career families. *International Journal of Sociology of the Family, 16,* 83–94.

———. (1987). In pursuit of academic careers: Observations and reflections of a dual-career couple. *Family Relations, 36,* 97–100.

Bird, G. A., Bird, G. W., & Scruggs, M. (1983). Role management strategies used by husbands and wives in two-earner families. *Home Economics Research Journal, 12,* 63–70.

———. (1984). Determinants of family task sharing: A study of husbands and wives. *Journal of Marriage and the Family, 46,* 345–355.

Bird, G. W., & Ford, R. (1985). Sources of role strain among dual-career couples. *Home Economics Research Journal, 14,* 187–194.

Bohen, H., & Viveros-Long, A. (1981). *Balancing jobs and family life.* Philadelphia: Temple University Press.

Duvall, E. M., & Miller, F. (1985). *Family development* (6th ed.). Philadelphia: J. B. Lippincott.

Elman, M. R., & Gilbert, L. A. (1984). Coping strategies for role conflict in married professional women with careers. *Family Relations, 33,* 317–322.

Faver, C. A. (1984). *Women in transition: Career, family, and life satisfaction in three cohorts.* New York: Praeger.

Folkman, S. (1984). Personal control and stress and coping processes: A theoretical analysis. *Journal of Personality and Social Psychology, 46,* 839–852.

Folkman, S., Lazarus, R. S., Dunkel-Schetter, C., Delongis, A., & Gruen, D. (1986). Dynamics of a stressful encounter: Cognitive appraisal, coping, and encounter outcomes. *Journal of Personality and Social Psychology, 50,* 992–1003.

Gilbert, L. A. (1985). *Men in dual-career families: Current realities and future prospects.* Hillsdale, NJ: Lawrence Erlbaum Associates.

Gilbert, L. A., & Rachlin, V. (1987). Mental health and psychological functioning of dual-career families. *The Counseling Psychologist, 15,* 7–49.

Guelzow, M., & Bird, G. (1986, November). *Dual-career women: The influences of coping responses and psychological resources on emotional and physical stress.* Paper presented at the annual conference of the National Council on Family Relations, Philadelphia, PA.

Hall, D. T. (1972). A model of coping with role conflict: The role behavior of college educated women. *Administrative Science Quarterly, 17,* 471–486.

Harrison, A., & Minor, J. (1978). Interrole conflict, coping strategies and satisfaction among black working wives. *Journal of Marriage and the Family, 40,* 799–805.

Heckman, H. A., Bryson, R., & Bryson, J. B. (1977). Problems of professional couples: A content analysis. *Journal of Marriage and the Family, 39,* 323–330.

Hill, R. (1986). Life cycle stages for types of single parent families: Of family development theory. *Family Relations, 35,* 19–29.

Holahan, C. K., & Gilbert, L. A. (1979). Conflict between major life roles: Women and men in dual-career couples. *Human Relations, 32,* 451–467.

Holmstrom, L. L. (1973). *The two-career family.* Cambridge, MA: Schenkman.

Hood, J. C. (1983). *Becoming a two-job family.* New York: Praeger.

Johnson, C. L., & Johnson, F. A. (1977). Attitudes toward parenting in dual-career families. *American Journal of Psychiatry, 134,* 391–395.

Kanter, R. M. (1977). *Men and women of the corporation.* New York: Basic Books.

Kater, D. (1985). Management strategies for dual-career couples. *Journal of Career Development, 12,* 75–79.

Lazarus, R. S., & Folkman, S. (1984). *Stress, appraisal and coping.* New York: Springer.

Mattessich, P., & Hill, R. (1987). Life cycle and family development. In M. Sussman & S. Steinmetz (eds.), *Handbook of marriage and the family* (pp. 437–469). New York: Plenum Press.

Nicola, J. S. (1980). *Career and family roles of dual-career couples: Women in academia and their husbands.* Ann Arbor, MI: University Microfilms International.

Pearlin, L. S., & Schooler, C. (1978). The structure of coping. *Journal of Health and Social Behavior,* 19, 2–21.

Pleck, J. H. (1985). *Working wives/working husbands.* Beverly Hills: Sage.

Poloma, M. M. (1972). Role conflict and the married professional woman. In C. Safilios-Rothschild (Ed.), *Toward a sociology of women* (pp. 187–197). Lexington, MA: Xerox.

Rapoport, R., & Rapoport, R. N. (1971). *Dual-career families.* Harmondsworth, England: Penguin.

———. (1976). *Dual-career families re-examined.* London: Martin Robinson.

Rodgers, R. H. (1973). *Family interaction and transaction: The developmental approach.* Englewood Cliffs, NJ: Prentice-Hall.

Sekaran, U. (1986). *Dual-career families.* San Francisco: Jossey-Bass.

Skinner, D. A. (1980). Dual-career family stress and coping: A literature review. *Family Relations,* 29, 473–480.

Skinner, D. A., & McCubbin, H. I. (1982). *Coping in dual-employed families: Spousal differences.* Paper presented at the annual conference of the National Council on Family Relations, Washington, DC.

Trost, J. (1974). This family life cycle—An impossible concept? *International Journal of Sociology of the Family,* 4, 37–47.

Ventre, M. T. (1988). *An ethnographic study of eight dual-career families: Their responsibility for and performance and negotiations of household and childcare tasks.* Unpublished doctoral dissertation, Virginia Polytechnic Institute and State University, Blacksburg, VA.

Voydanoff, P. (1987). *Work and family life.* Beverly Hills: Sage.

Voydanoff, P., & Kelly, R. (1984). Determinants of work related family problems among employed parents. *Journal of Marriage and the Family,* 46, 881–892.

White, L. K., & Brinkeroff, D. B. (1981). Children's work in the family: Its significance and meaning. *Journal of Marriage and the Family,* 43, 789–798.

Reprinted from: Maureen Schnittger and Gloria W. Bird, "Coping Among Dual-Career Men and Women Across the Family Life Cycle." In *Family Relations* 39, pp. 199–205. Copyright © 1990 by The National Council on Family Relations. Reprinted with permission. ✦

Chapter Three
Exchange Theory

Richard and Jane have been dating for about a year—exclusively for the last eight months or so. They are both juniors in college and have been thinking about whether or not they should get married. Jane frequently discusses the possibility with her roommates, and they debate the pros and cons. "He is so handsome and nice to me, and we are totally in love," says Jane. However, she wishes that he were majoring in something more substantial than history—business or law, perhaps. And she knows that he will want them to move back to his rural hometown in the West, which bothers her since she is a city girl. On the other hand, her friends point out, he is nice to children and (they have been told) is a great kisser. But is she really ready to give up dating and settle down?

For Richard it is a more private process, but he is also trying to decide. He loves Jane and wants to be with her all the time. Their physical relationship is wonderful, and he enjoys her intellect. He is afraid he might not be good enough for her, and that if she knew what he is really like, she might figure she can do better. He has no solid job or income to offer and needs to be in school for at least two more years. She gets upset when he doesn't want to talk about his feelings, and he worries about having to endure that pressure forever. And with the divorce rate as high as it is, is marriage even worth the effort?

Both of them are trying to be logical about this most important life decision, but it is hard to do. Feelings of love and hormonal urges get in the way. Isn't it too calculating to look for the negatives? Won't that just kill the romance? Can they even know what the most important considerations are in advance of living the actual relationship?

HISTORY

Philosophers have been discussing the ideas relevant to modern exchange theory for the last two centuries. The basic concept is that human social relationships can be understood as revolving around the exchange of resources valued by the participants. Utilitarian writers such as Adam Smith taught that people tend to act rationally in ways designed to maximize their profit economically. In the early twentieth century, anthropologists such as Bronislaw Malinowski and Claude Lévi-Strauss demonstrated how many cultures engage in the exchange of various goods and services as a central aspect of their social life. The latter took the collectivist position that one's behavior in social relationships tends to be a function of the social system of which one is a part (Ekeh 1974).

These early anthropologists explored the relationship between social norms and individual behavior. Frazer (1919) concluded that many social structures result from the economic needs of the individuals within the system. He was investigating the tendency of Australian aborigines to marry cross rather than parallel cousins and concluded that since the men were too poor to provide a bride price, they would trade a sister or other female relative for their bride.

Sociologists began to seriously consider the exchange model in the context of human societies and families with the groundbreaking writings of Thibaut and Kelley (1959), Homans (1961), and Blau (1964). These writers took us beyond the concepts of economic exchanges and into the more complex world of the social marketplace. In addition to trading such things as food, money, and other services, humans in relationships make exchanges that are harder to quantify, such as status, attractiveness, and love. Even though each had a somewhat different emphasis, they all agreed that what people want and need can be obtained only through exchanges with others, and that we will try to get those things at the lowest possible cost to ourselves (Turner 1991).

George Homans is probably the most influential scholar in bringing exchange theory to general sociology. Essentially adapting the principles of behaviorism, he held that reinforcement and punishment were the driving forces in human behavior, and that sociology should pay more attention to those dynamics instead of social structure. In his own study of cross-cousin marriages (Homans and Schneider 1955), he rejected the collectivist orientation of Lévi-Strauss. He took the position that societal norms result from the needs of the individuals, rather than that society regulates interpersonal behavior.

Finally, Ivan Nye (1978, 1979) summarized the concepts of the exchange model and showed how they could be applied to a large number of research questions in family science. His work completed the evolution of exchange from economic to sociological to family science theory. It has been a widely used framework in analyzing family issues since the publication of his chapter in *Contemporary Theories About the Family*.

BASIC ASSUMPTIONS

We will now examine the basic assumptions that undergird exchange theory. We will draw from the writings of Sabatelli and Shehan (1993) as well as Klein and White (1996) for this section. Although exchange theory is built upon the principles of behaviorism and economics, it goes beyond just explaining individual behavior. Its focus is on the dynamics of relationships and how they are formed, maintained, and dissolved. As a result, there are assumptions about the nature of both individuals and relationships that are embedded in the framework.

People are motivated by self-interest. The first assumption is that people are motivated by self-interest. This means that we seek those things and relationships that are beneficial to ourselves. Another way of saying this is that we seek rewards and avoid punishments or costs. Thus, we are most likely to engage in interactions we find rewarding while avoiding those we do not like.

Individuals are constrained by their choices. Second, individuals are constrained by their choices, and it is within that range of possible choices that we strive to understand one's motivations. Nye (1979), in fact, concluded that the theory is more about choice than exchange. Social structure leads us to conclude that family life is rewarding to most individuals because this is a choice most people make.

In interacting with others, individuals will seek to maximize their profits while minimizing costs. Since the actual outcome of an interaction cannot always be known, humans will use their expectations in making their decisions. This means we enter into situations we believe will be rewarding, based on our past experiences.

Humans are rational beings. Another important assumption is that humans are rational beings. This means that we have the analytical ability to calculate the ratio of rewards to costs. We consider the alternatives before acting and choose the outcome that carries the least cost. Exchange theorists also accept the fact that how rewards and costs are evaluated varies from one person to another, as well as across time. Thus, what Richard finds rewarding Jane may not, and what Jason finds rewarding ten years from now may not be the same as what is rewarding to him today.

Social relationships are also characterized by interdependence. This means that, in order to gain a profit in an exchange, we must provide the other person with rewards as well. All parties must expect some rewards in order to continue the relationship or interaction. And finally, social exchanges are regulated by the expectations or norms of reciprocity and fairness. Thus, we expect others to meet our needs if we attempt to meet their needs, and to do so based on what is right or fair.

PRIMARY TERMS AND CONCEPTS

The principal concepts used in exchange theory are listed by Nye (1979), who draws heavily from Thibaut and Kelley (1959).

REWARDS

All of the things in a person's physical, social, and psychological world that are experienced as pleasurable are considered rewards. A reward can be any satisfaction or gratification, status or relationship that one enjoys and therefore would like to experience with greater frequency. It includes anything that the individual would choose in the absence of added costs. What is rewarding will vary from one person to the next.

COSTS

In contrast, any status, relationship, or feeling that the individual does not like is considered a cost. A cost is a factor that would deter an activity, and it can be classified into two categories. The first category is anything that the individual dislikes or finds repugnant, such as some onerous duty or demeaning status; the second consists of those rewarding feelings or positions that must be given up when selecting some competing alternative. This could be giving up money for a good or service, such as a weekly housekeeper, or marrying an intelligent person who isn't all that attractive.

PROFIT

Profit refers to the outcome in terms of rewards and costs. People strive to gain the most rewards with the fewest costs. When they do so, they have profited. We all try to maximize profits and minimize costs in our relationships and interactions. Generally, most rewarding outcomes have some costs attached to them which must therefore be weighed and considered.

COMPARISON LEVEL

The evaluation of our profit against what we feel we deserve is our comparison level—that is, we compare the rewards and costs we are experiencing and judge our feelings about them based on our ideas of what should be the fair outcome for us. We might also look at how well we think others in similar positions, such as other newly marrieds or nice people, are doing in comparison to what we are experiencing. We expect our rewards to be similar to those of others in comparable situations.

LEVEL OF ALTERNATIVES

Individuals will compare their outcomes with alternative relationships, statuses, and so forth that may be out there. For instance, one could be very happy in his or her job until it is discovered that those in other similar companies are making much more money. If your personal outcome is below this comparison level, then the theory predicts that you will attempt to leave your situation for the better one. Here it is assumed that the new relationship is sufficiently superior to compensate for any costs incurred in moving from one relationship to the other, or in this case one company to another. Let us say that Adam is satisfied in his marriage until he decides that others he knows seem to be considerably happier than he is. Then he meets another woman who is more physically attractive than his present wife. Since divorce and changing locations and families usually involves considerable expense, Adam may decide that leaving his marriage to be with the beautiful new woman is not worth the cost after all.

RECIPROCITY

The social expectation that people should help those who have helped them, and that they should not injure those who have helped them, is reciprocity. This is an important norm because an effective ongoing society cannot function without it. For social interactions, including but not limited to those found in family life, to take place and continue, they must be rewarding to all of the individuals involved. Others will typically not allow us to reward ourselves at their expense, so to gain rewards we must give rewards to others. As the saying goes, "You scratch my back and I'll scratch yours."

DISTRIBUTIVE JUSTICE, FAIRNESS, AND EQUITY

Homans (1961) and Blau (1964) worked with concepts similar to reciprocity. These relate to the idea that a relationship between two people needs to be roughly equal. If one person is receiving most of the rewards while the other pays the costs, then the latter individual will feel taken advantage of and may try to end the exchange. While who gives the most may change back and forth between partners across time, both partners must feel that overall the balance of give-and-take is equal for exchange relationships to be successful.

The following general sources of rewards and costs have been identified by exchange theorists:

(1) *Social approval*—all humans desire a life that includes such things as love, respect, prestige, and admiration.

(2) *Autonomy*—this refers to the ability to control your life so as to choose activities and relationships that are high on reward and low on cost.

(3) *Ambiguity*—humans fear the unknown but do not want to be overly bored by predictability either (this, then, is a curvilinear relationship in which we seek freedom from too much ambiguity in our lives while also straying from that which is known).

(4) *Security*—we seek a life that provides economic security and therefore freedom from want. The greater our security level, however, the less value any more security would have. A millionaire will not give up much, for instance, in terms of time with his or her family, for another car. But the less we have, the greater its worth.

(5) *Money*—this is a general reinforcer because it can be used to purchase most types of security.

(6) *Value, opinion, and belief*—we all find it rewarding to have others agree with us on the issues that we feel are important. This is related to social approval.

(7) *Equality*—research consistently finds higher levels of interaction (exchange) between equals. Each has about the same to offer the other, so rejection is less likely

and negative exchanges are too costly on both sides to continue.

COMMON AREAS OF RESEARCH AND APPLICATION

Exchange has been especially useful in analyzing the mate selection process, divorce, and a few other family dynamics. The concept of the "marriage market," which is used commonly in regular conversation today, comes from exchange thinking. It is the idea that people are making choices for a companion based on what that other person has to offer them that will lead to their happiness. It also implies that the first person must have some things to offer as well. Therefore, single people list what rewards they want from a relationship, what costs they are willing to incur, and what they have to offer a possible mate.

ROMANTIC ISSUES

Winton (1995) explains how exchange thinking is used in a number of related areas. First, romantic love is seen as resulting when one feels that he or she is getting a high ratio of rewards with little cost. That is, the reward/cost ratio affects how we feel about other people. We come to like or love those whose interactions with us are rewarding. Being in love itself is a very rewarding state of being that can even have addictive qualities (Brown 1990). Similarly, we fall out of love with those who cost us too much of ourselves.

Mate selection is another topic studied using exchange principles. It assumes Adam comes to the marriage market with a certain value, which is the sum of what he has to offer in terms of family status, physical appearance, intelligence, and other factors. He will seek someone who is similar to him, since he would lose interest in someone of lesser value and fear being rejected by someone of greater value. Over the years, considerable research has been conducted attempting to identify and rank the various traits that are important to couple formation. There is an implication that partners, like material objects, will tend to be discarded when they are no longer of sufficient value to the individual. Cross-cultural research (Ingoldsby, Schvaneveldt, and Uribe 2003) indicates that there are many apparent universals. Women tend to prefer a man who is older, taller, and with good income potential, whereas men value youth and beauty in a mate. Everyone desires positive traits, such as kindness and intelligence, and seeks to avoid ending up with a partner who is violent or has drug addictions.

Why married people take the risks of being involved in extramarital sex is also studied using an exchange perspective. The theory accounts for affairs by making the assumption that the short-term rewards are seen as more powerful than the potential long-term costs of the activity. This may not turn out to be the case, of course, but decisions are based on perception rather than the actual ultimate outcome. Perhaps if people could anticipate all the possible negative outcomes, or costs, there would be fewer affairs.

RELATIONSHIP ISSUES

Many societies assume that parents will make up for the costs of bearing and rearing children (time, money, worry, and other costs) when they are elderly and their children take care of them. If this does not occur, then the elderly parents may come to feel that justice has been violated. However, there are many rewards for rearing children at the time that must be considered. They may include loving relationships with children and pride in their accomplishments.

Another family issue frequently studied using an exchange perspective is spousal abuse. Here we would look at the rewards the abuser receives, such as power over the partner and the emotional rush that may come from the behavior. Typically the costs are found to be minimal for the abuser and would need to be increased in order to provide an escape for the abused spouse (Gelles and Straus 1988). If the abused partner stays with or returns to the abuser, then we would look for what it is that he or she is getting out of the relationship that

makes it worth while to remain. Possible rewards include economic security, shelter, and perceived love.

As time goes by in a marriage, many couples reduce the number of rewarding exchanges that were typical during courtship. Behaviors that they had not paid attention to in the beginning become irritating, and therefore the costs of being in the relationship increase. As a spouse compares profits relative to other marriages, he or she may come to feel deprived. Should the level of satisfaction get low enough, a decision to separate or divorce could be made. However, many very unhappy couples stay together, especially as the length of the marriage increases. This would be explained by the many costs that are related to divorce: alimony, child support, social disapproval, role loss, loss of custody, religious concerns, and so on (White and Booth 1991).

GENDER DIFFERENCES IN SEXUAL BEHAVIOR

Klein and White (1996) draw on the work of Nye (1979) to argue the case that males are more likely to exchange rewards (money and marriage in particular) for sexual access. Assuming that the biological drive is equal for the two genders, the theory would posit that sex is more profitable for males than it is for females. This is because pregnancy is more costly for women than it is for men and males achieve orgasm more consistently than do females. As a result, males must make sexual relations more profitable for females by offering them additional rewards.

Nye (1979), in his seminal summary of the theory, formulates 120 propositions that he feels follow from the research within the context of the theory. They are in the areas of maternal employment, marital timing and parenthood, sexual behavior, communication, marital dissolution, social networks, intergenerational relations, men's work, family violence, social class, and parental behavior. Many of his hypotheses have yet to be adequately tested.

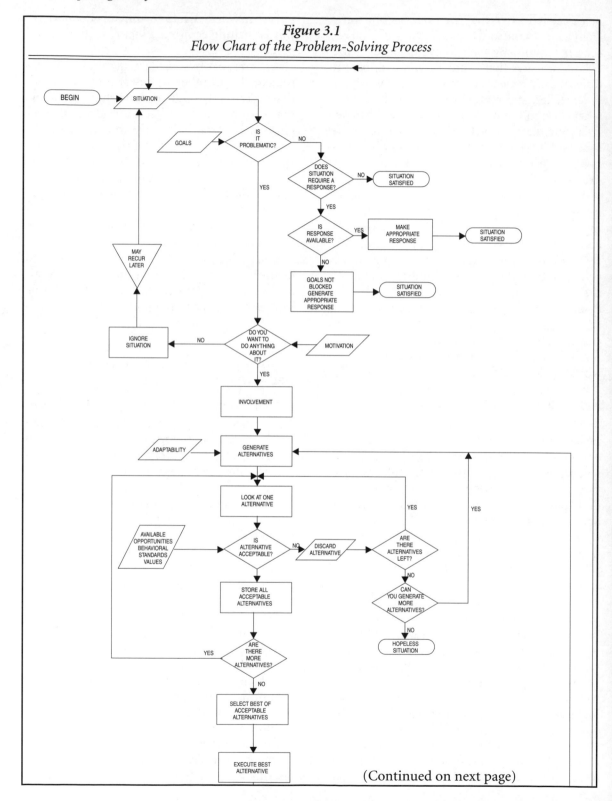

Figure 3.1
Flow Chart of the Problem-Solving Process

(Continued on next page)

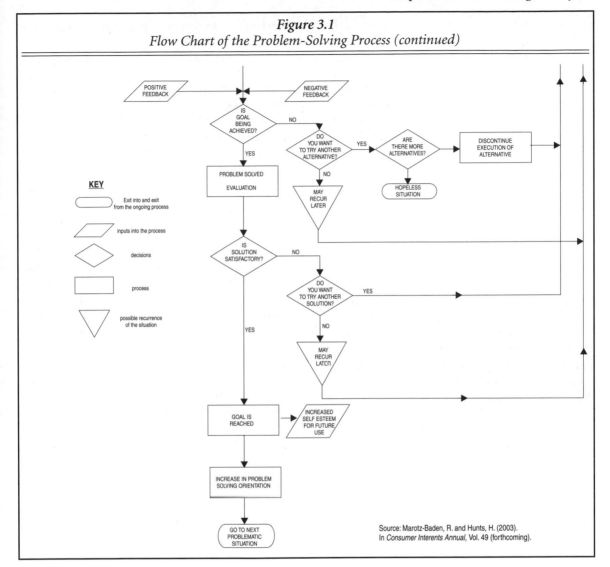

Figure 3.1
Flow Chart of the Problem-Solving Process (continued)

Source: Marotz-Baden, R. and Hunts, H. (2003).
In *Consumer Interents Annual*, Vol. 49 (forthcoming).

DECISION MAKING

One final area of utility for the theory is decision making (see Kieren, Henton, and Marotz 1975). The exchange perspective can make the logic of the process followed in important family-related decisions explicit. Using an organized approach that highlights the pros and cons of each alternative should increase the likelihood of coming to a rational conclusion with greater final profit. Marotz-Baden, Osborne, and Hunts (2001) have developed the flow chart in Figure 3.1 for this process.

In their example, a young woman is trying to decide whether or not to accept a marriage proposal. She loves the young man but is concerned because he does not approve of her career decision. With the help of concerned classmates, she goes through the steps of considering each alternative. What would it be like to be married to him and give up her career? Can she talk him into changing his mind? What would it be like to discontinue the relationship? At certain stages, activities are tried and then evaluated. Sometimes it may be realized that the particular situation is hopeless without new resources, and at other times the goals are reached.

By recognizing that life is about social exchanges, with their resultant rewards and costs, one can take the time to carefully and clearly evaluate one's logic and decision making. In this way, the theory goes beyond just analyzing what we do and helps us to make good decisions. Any time you have made a list, either physically or mentally, of the pros and cons of a decision, you have utilized the principles of exchange theory.

CRITIQUE

The exchange model does an impressive job of providing a context for predicting and explaining a great deal of human behavior in social contexts. It is just one way of looking at families, but it has a straightforward methodology that is appealing to many scholars. It is clear and relatively easy to "get a handle on," compared with some of the other approaches. Much of its power comes from its emergence from behaviorism. However, that individualistic focus also results in certain limitations.

The assumption that the family is just a collection of individuals is too simplistic for many theorists. For some, the family has too many unique and long-lasting aspects to be reduced basically to an economic system with interchangeable characters (Klein and White 1996).

Additionally, the key assumption that humans act rationally in decision making is criticized by many. Since Freud's time, practitioners and other scholars have made the case that humans are emotional beings who rarely act in ways that could be classified as truly rational and objective. Family life in particular is an emotional world where many decisions do not seem to make sense rationally. The case can be made (Beutler, Burr, and Bahr 1989) that the rational focus of the theory makes it impossible for it to deal with love and the other emotional elements that make up family life. Nye (1979) responds to this criticism by stating that people act in accordance with the best information available to them. Since such information is of-

ten lacking, they may appear to be less rational than they actually are.

It is also said that exchange theory, like some other theories, suffers from a tautology, in which terms are defined by each other and thus make it impossible to scientifically disprove conclusions. For example, we cannot find a situation in which one's behavior is not a function of rewards because the definition of a reward is the behaviors that one chooses (Turner 1991).

Feminist theorists also point out a masculine bias in exchange theory, which seems to assume a "separate" rather than a "connected" self. As a result, the theory is less capable of understanding behaviors that support the group over the individual. The assumption of maximizing profit ignores altruistic behavior, for instance. It elevates the traditionally masculine and modern western notion that autonomy and independence are more functional than caring and sharing (England 1989). Exchange theorists respond that individuals do engage in group supportive behaviors because the social approval is rewarding.

Exchange theory has been used considerably by family scholars over the last quarter century. Researchers, however, have perhaps been slow to move beyond the basics of reward and cost. Future work would benefit from a focus on the importance of interdependence in families—that is, the model could be used to better clarify joint, rather than individual, profit.

APPLICATION

1. In a small group, play out the roles of Richard and Jane with the situation at the beginning of the chapter. Weigh the pros and cons of the relationship and decide if the two should get married, and why. What important ways of viewing the relationship are missed by just focusing on the rational aspects?

2. Analyze a relationship within your own immediate family with which you are at least somewhat uncomfortable. What are

the rewards you are exchanging? Remember that this includes such intangibles as kindness and humor, in addition to goods (buying clothes) and services (fixing dinner). Now, what does it cost you to be in this relationship? After you make this list of irritating traits in the other person, can you identify the costs that he or she must endure to be with you? Now, are there ways that the relationship could be made more equitable and therefore more rewarding for both of you?

3. Divide into small groups within your class and use the problem-solving model found in the chapter. Take a real problem from one of the members and use the process to see if a solution to the relationship difficulty can be reached.

4. Have you ever been in a romantic relationship where you felt exploited? Or were you the exploiter? Use exchange theory concepts to write up an understanding of the dynamics of that relationship and what could have been done to make it fair. What aspects of the relationship are ignored by just looking at it through the lens of exchange theory?

Sample Reading

Buss, D., Shackelford, T., Kirkpatrick, L., and Larsen, R. (2001). A half century of mate preferences: The cultural evolution of values. *Journal of Marriage and the Family* 63: 491–503.

This chapter ends with the article "A Half Century of Mate Preferences: The Cultural Evolution of Values" by Buss, Shackelford, Kirkpatrick, and Larsen. It presents the major exchange traits that have been studied in the United States in reference to mate selection preferences and explains how those preferences have changed over time.

References

Beutler, I., Burr, W., and Bahr, K. (1989). The family realm: Theoretical contributions for understanding its uniqueness. *Journal of Marriage and the Family* 51: 805–816.

Blau, P. (1964). *Exchange and Power in Social Life.* New York: John Wiley.

Brown, E. (1990). *Patterns of Infidelity and Their Treatment.* New York: Brunner/Mazel.

Ekeh, P. (1974). *Social Exchange: The Two Traditions.* Cambridge, MA: Harvard University Press.

England, P. (1989). A feminist critique of rational choice theories: Implications for sociology. *The American Sociologist* 20: 14–28.

Frazer, J. (1919). *Folklore of the Old Testament.* New York: Macmillan.

Gelles, R., and Straus, M. (1988). *Intimate Violence.* New York: Simon and Schuster.

Homans, G. (1961, revised 1974). *Social Behavior: Its Elementary Forms.* New York: Harcourt, Brace & Jovanovich.

Homans, G., and Schneider, D. (1955). *Marriage, Authority, and Final Causes: A Study of Unilateral Cross-Cousin Marriage.* New York: Free Press.

Ingoldsby, B., Schvaneveldt, P., and Uribe, C. (2003). Perceptions of acceptable mate attributes in Ecuador. *Journal of Comparative Family Studies* 34. Forthcoming.

Kieren, D., Henton, J., and Marotz, R. (1975). *Hers and His: A Problem Solving Approach to Marriage.* Hinsdale, IL: Dryden Press.

Klein, D., and White, J. (1996). *Family Theories: An Introduction.* Thousand Oaks, CA: Sage.

Marotz-Baden, R., Osborne, S., and Hunts, H. (2001). Problem solving as a foundation of family science education. Paper presented at the meeting of the Teaching Family Science Association, Lewes, DE.

Nye, I. (1978). Is choice and exchange theory the key? *Journal of Marriage and the Family* 40: 219–233.

—— (1979). Choice, exchange, and the family. In W. R. Burr, R. Hill, F. I. Nye, and I. L. Reiss (eds.), *Contemporary Theories About the Family* (vol. 2, pp. 1–41). New York: Free Press.

Sabatelli, R., and Shehan, C. (1993) Exchange and resource theories. In P. G. Boss, W. J. Doherty, R. LaRossa, W. R. Schumm, and S. K. Steinmetz (eds.), *Sourcebook of Family Theories and Methods: A Contextual Approach* (pp. 385–417). New York: Plenum.

Thibaut, J., and Kelley, H. (1959). *The Social Psychology of Groups.* New York: Wiley.

Turner, J. (1991). *The Structure of Sociological Theory* (5th ed.). Belmont, CA: Wadsworth.

Waller, W. (1938). *The Family: A Dynamic Interpretation* (revised by R. Hill, 1951). New York: Holt, Rinehart and Winston.

White, L., and Booth, A. (1991). Divorce over the life course: The role of marital happiness. *Journal of Family Issues* 12: 5–21.

Winton, C. (1995). *Frameworks for Studying Families.* Guilford, CT: Duskin Publishing Group. ✦

A Half Century of Mate Preferences

The Cultural Evolution of Values

David M. Buss

Todd K. Shackelford

Lee A. Kirkpatrick

Randy J. Larsen

The qualities people believe are important in selecting a marriage partner afford one domain for assessing human values. We examined the cultural evolution of these values over more than half a century. Building on existing data on mate preferences collected in 1939 (N = 628), 1956 (N = 120), 1967 (N = 566), and 1977 (N = 316), we collected data using the same instrument in 1984/1985 (N = 1,496) and in 1996 (N = 607) at geographically diverse locations. Several changes in values were documented across the 57-year span. Both sexes increased the importance they attach to physical attractiveness in a mate. Both sexes, but especially men, increased the importance they attach to mates with good financial prospects. Domestic skills in a partner plummeted in importance for men. Mutual attraction and love climbed in importance for both sexes. The sexes converged in the ordering of the importance of different mate qualities, showing maximum similarity in 1996. Discussion speculates about causes of the cultural evolution of values.

The 20th century has witnessed changes more radical and irretrievable than any previous century in the history of the human species. Cars became commonplace during the first half of the century, and computers became commonplace during the second half. Internet dating, virtual sex, and the specter of AIDS altered the landscape of human mating. Women have entered the work force at levels and scales unprecedented, perhaps changing forever the nature of the work environment. Heightened awareness of sexual harassment, date rape, wife battering, and dozens of more subtle forms of sexism have forced people to reevaluate assumptions about men and women. In the context of these cultural changes, a core question for social psychology is: Have human values—the things we consider to be important—changed and, if so, in what ways? Have we witnessed the cultural evolution of values?

Values in human mating offer one arena within which these questions can be posed, and several considerations suggest that it would be astonishing if mate preferences had remained impervious to cultural changes. One clear example pertains to the widespread use of birth control, and particularly oral contraceptives. Birth control reduces one important risk of sex—unwanted or untimely pregnancy. On this basis alone, we might predict that the importance of chastity in a potential partner might diminish, relative to the importance of other traits. On the other hand, the widespread fear of AIDS, emerging in the mid-to-late 1980s, should have the opposite effect of increasing the relative value people place on a chaste potential partner. Precisely how these conflicting forces affect the cultural evolution of values surrounding chastity is best resolved empirically.

A second change pertains to the influx of women into the work force, with the consequence of greater personal access to economic resources. It has been well documented that women more than men value economic resources in a long-term romantic partner, an apparent universal across cultures (Buss, 1989). According to the "structural powerlessness" hypothesis (Buss & Barnes, 1986), the importance women place on a man's economic resources should diminish as women gain greater personal access to such resources. The value women place on a potential mate's financial prospects, on this hypothesis, occurs because marriage has traditionally been the primary means by which women can secure access to resources. As women's personal access to resources increases as a result of their own labors, according to this hypothesis, the relative importance they attach to a mate's resources should diminish commensurably. Recent research conducted at a single time period with a single sample in the United States failed to support the structural powerlessness hypothesis (Buss, 1994; Wiederman & Allgeier, 1992), but a cross-cultural study, also conducted at a single time period, found some support for the hypothesis (Kasser & Sharma, 1999).

A third change pertains to the bombardment of images featuring physically attractive models and actors. In the 20th century in the United States, consumers moved from a reliance on radio to a pervasive use of television, movies, and, more recently, Internet images. Intense exposure to images of attractive models produces decrements in men's commitment to their regular partner (Kenrick & Gutierres, 1980; Kenrick, Neuberg, Zierk, & Krones, 1994). From an evolutionary psychological perspective, such images may "trick" our evolved mating mechanisms, deluding us into believing that we are surrounded by hundreds of attractive partners, as well as hundreds of potential intrasexual competitors. Might this bombardment of visual images elevate the value we place on physical attractiveness, relative to other traits?

The only research design that can address these issues is a cross-generational design. Only when we have the same measures of values, administered to comparable samples across generations, can we hope to gain a sensible assay of these changes. In a rare and unprecedented research opportunity, we discovered and exploited one such design. In the 1930s, an 18-item instrument was developed to assess the value placed on a wide variety of characteristics in a potential long-term mate or marriage partner. It was first administered to a college sample in 1939 (Hill, 1945). In succeeding decades, it was administered to college samples in 1956 (McGinnis, 1958), 1967 (Hudson & Henze, 1969), and 1977 (Hoyt & Hudson, 1981). In the mid-1980s, we resurrected this instrument and administered it to four different college populations, widely varying in geographic location within the United States ($N = 1,496$). Then again in 1996, we administered it to three different college populations ($N = 607$), two of which were included in the mid-1980s sample. In sum, we have six temporally spaced value assessments from 1939 to 1996, spanning more than half a century.

The research was designed to answer the following questions: (a) Which values in a mate, if any, have changed over this 57-year period? (b) Which values have remained constant, impervious to the other changes in society? (c) Have the sex differences, particularly in the relative value placed on economic resources, diminished over time as women gained greater personal access to economic resources? (d) Are there regional cultural differences within the same generation that might reflect differing degrees of cultural shifts?

STUDY 1: MATE PREFERENCES IN 1984/1985

METHOD

Participants. During 1984 and 1985, four convenience samples of undergraduates participated in this study from four different geographic regions of the United States: Harvard University in Cambridge ($n = 230$), the University of Texas at Austin ($n = 554$), the University of California at Berkeley ($n = 453$), and the University of Michigan at Ann Arbor ($n = 259$). The total sample consisted of 1,496 undergraduates, 642 men and 854 women. Table 1 provides all available demographic information for each sample and for the total sample. Participants voluntarily completed the mate preferences survey during introductory psychology classes and during separate group

Table 1
Demographic Information for the 1984/1985 and 1996 Samples

	Male Age				Female Age				Total Age			
Sample	*M*	*SD*	*n*	% single	*M*	*SD*	*n*	% single	*M*	*SD*	*n*	% single
1984/1985												
Massachusetts	21.2	5.5	92	97.8	23.3	7.7	138	88.3	22.5	7.0	230	92.0
Texas	19.5	1.9	227	98.7	19.2	2.1	327	97.8	19.3	2.0	554	98.2
California	19.4	1.6	231	99.1	19.0	1.4	222	98.9	19.2	1.5	453	99.6
Michigan	20.0	1.6	92	98.9	20.1	1.5	167	99.4	20.0	1.6	259	99.2
Total	19.8	2.7	642	98.7	20.0	3.8	854	97.2	19.9	3.4	1496	97.8
1996												
Texas	19.2	3.9	136	98.5	18.6	1.3	190	99.5	18.9	2.7	326	99.1
Virginia	19.0	1.2	65	100	18.7	2.0	111	100	18.8	1.8	176	100
Michigan	20.6	2.2	25	100	20.8	3.0	80	96.3	20.8	2.8	105	97.1
Total	19.3	3.2	226	99.1	19.1	2.1	381	99.0	19.2	2.6	607	99.0

testing sessions for which they received course credit.

Mate selection survey. The survey used to assess mate selection criteria was developed by Hill (1945). In this survey, participants rate the importance of 18 mate characteristics: good cook and housekeeper, pleasing disposition, sociability, similar educational background, refinement and neatness, good financial prospect, chastity (no previous experience in sexual intercourse), dependable character, emotional stability and maturity, desire for home and children, favorable social status or rating, good looks, similar religious background, ambition and industriousness, similar political background, mutual attraction and love, good health, and education and intelligence. The 18 characteristics are rated on the following 4-point scale: 3 points = *indispensable,* 2 = *important,* 1 = *desirable, but not very important,* and 0 = *irrelevant or unimportant.*

This instrument contains several potential flaws. First, the 4-point rating scale may not permit as many discriminations as participants typically make in evaluating a potential mate. Second, many of the characteristics are conjunctions such as "education and intelligence" and "desire for home and children." It would be preferable to unconfound responses and to present each element separately for evaluation. Third, several of the items are ambiguously worded, such as "favorable social status or rating," the referent for which may be unclear. Despite these potential drawbacks, it was judged essential to replicate the prior studies *exactly* to facilitate cross-generational comparisons.

RESULTS

Tables 2 and 3 show the preference means, standard deviations, and rank orderings for the 18 characteristics for the four samples separately, and for men and women, respectively. A multivariate analysis of variance (MANOVA) on mean values for the 18 mate preferences by participant sex (male, female) and sample (Massachusetts, Texas, California, Michigan) revealed overall effects for both independent variables, $F(1,18) = 62.52$ and $F(3,54) = 6.64$, respectively (both $ps < .001$). To identify within-sex, between-sample differences, we conducted a one-way analysis of variance (ANOVA) on each of the 18 preference means by sample, for men and women separately. Significant ($p < .05$) main effects were followed by all possible post hoc comparisons. To control for increased Type I error rate, a Bonferroni correction for alpha inflation was employed. By the Bonferroni procedure, statistical significance was reduced from .05 to .008 (.05/6), two-tailed. Significant between-sample differences are

Table 2

Descriptive Statistics for Preferences of Male College Students in 1984/1985, by Sample Location

Characteristic	Massachusetts			Texas			California			Michigan			Average		
	M	SD	Rank	M	SD	Rank	M	SD	Rank	M	SD	Rank	M	SD	Rank
Good cook, housekeeper^a	1.35	0.76	13	1.73*	0.77	12	1.38	0.71	13	1.33	0.70	13	1.45*	0.74	13
Pleasing disposition	2.64	0.55	3	2.58	0.57	2	2.47	0.62	4	2.43	0.65	4	2.53*	0.60	4
Sociability	2.04*	0.70	8	2.14*	0.61	9	2.06*	0.73	7	2.14	0.62	6	2.10*	0.67	7
Similar education background	1.76	0.75	11	1.58*	0.82	13	1.67*	0.80	12	1.67*	0.84	12	1.67*	0.80	12
Refinement, neatness^b	1.88	0.72	10	2.10	0.69	10	1.80	0.76	10	1.70	0.72	11	1.87	0.72	10
Good financial prospect^a	0.80*	0.82	17	1.28*	0.88	16	1.04*	0.89	15	0.95*	0.78	16	1.02*	0.84	16
Chastity^a	0.55	0.83	18	1.13*	1.05	17	0.70*	0.88	17	0.81*	0.87	17	0.80*	0.91	18
Dependable character	2.62	0.55	4	2.56*	0.56	3	2.52*	0.65	3	2.58*	0.56	2	2.57*	0.58	3
Emotional stability, maturity	2.71	0.50	2	2.56	0.55	4	2.56*	0.58	2	2.53*	0.54	3	2.59*	0.54	2
Desire for home, children	2.00	0.98	9	2.17*	0.88	8	2.04*	0.87	8	2.11	0.87	8	2.08*	0.90	9
Favorable social status^c,d	0.85*	0.88	16	1.39*	0.87	15	1.10*	0.83	14	1.25	0.85	14	1.15*	0.86	14
Good looks	2.09*	0.74	7	2.18*	0.69	7	2.04*	0.66	8	2.09*	0.69	9	2.10*	0.70	7
Similar religious background^c,e	0.99	1.05	14	1.49	1.06	14	0.75*	0.94	16	1.24	1.10	15	1.12*	1.04	15
Ambition, industriousness^c	1.64*	0.81	12	1.98*	0.71	11	1.75*	0.81	11	1.93*	0.63	10	1.83*	0.74	11
Similar political background	0.95	0.93	15	0.85*	0.89	18	0.68*	0.79	18	0.77	0.81	18	0.81*	0.86	17
Mutual attraction, love	2.96	0.21	1	2.92	0.36	1	2.91	0.41	1	2.98	0.15	1	2.94*	0.28	1
Good health	2.10	0.70	6	2.22	0.68	6	2.16	0.66	6	2.13	0.68	7	2.15	0.68	6
Education, intelligence	2.42	0.60	5	2.24*	0.66	5	2.24*	0.69	5	2.15*	0.66	5	2.26*	0.65	5

Note: The following note applies to Tables 2 through 5. An asterisk indicates a within-sample sex difference in the mean preference, $p \leq .003$ (two tailed), as per independent means t-tests with Bonferroni correction for alpha inflation. Sex differences in mean preferences across the four samples also are indicated with an asterisk and are shown in the column labled "Average." Degrees of freedom for these tests are equal to 2 less than the sum total number of men and women in the relevant sample. Between-sample differences identified by superscript letters were detected by post hoc contrasts following one-way analysis of variance and are significant at $p \leq .008$ (two-tailed) after Bonferroni correction for alpha inflation. Degrees of freedom for these tests are equal to 2 less than the sum total number of participants in the two samples.

^a Mean for Texas sample is significantly different from means for Massachusetts, California, and Michigan samples. ^b Mean for Texas sample is significantly different from means for Massachusetts and California samples. ^c Mean for Texas sample is significantly different from means for Massachusetts, California, and Michigan samples. ^d Mean for Texas sample is significantly different from means for Massachusetts and California samples. ^e Mean for California sample is significantly different from mean for Michigan sample. ^f Mean for Massachusetts sample is significantly different from means for Texas, California, and Michigan samples.

Table 3
Descriptive Statistics for Preferences of Female College Students in 1984/1985, by Sample Location

Characteristic	Massachusetts			Texas			California			Michigan			Average		
	M	SD	Rank	M	SD	Rank	M	SD	Rank	M	SD	Rank	M	SD	Rank
Good cook, housekeeper	1.12	0.69	15	1.24*	0.68	16	1.30	0.66	15	1.13	0.61	16	1.20*	0.66	15
Pleasing disposition[a]	2.77	0.52	3	2.69	0.47	4	2.62	0.57	4	2.62	0.51	4	2.68*	0.52	4
Sociability	2.34*	0.62	6	2.31*	0.60	8	2.34*	0.67	8	2.23	0.66	8	2.31*	0.64	8
Similar education background[b]	2.05	0.80	10	1.96*	0.80	12	2.19*	0.80	10	1.97*	0.73	10	2.04*	0.78	10
Refinement, neatness[c]	1.75	0.75	11	1.97	0.72	11	1.86	0.68	12	1.69	0.74	12	1.82	0.72	12
Good financial prospect[a, c]	1.59*	0.90	12	2.14*	0.79	10	2.02*	0.78	11	1.83*	0.74	11	1.98*	0.80	11
Chastity[d]	0.31	0.74	18	0.77*	0.96	18	0.40*	0.76	18	0.34*	0.69	18	0.46*	0.79	18
Dependable character	2.77	0.56	3	2.78*	0.48	3	2.74*	0.51	3	2.79	0.56	3	2.77	0.53	3
Emotional stability, maturity	2.80	0.47	2	2.82*	0.39	2	2.99*	0.09	1	2.82*	0.39	2	2.86*	0.34	2
Desire for home, children[c]	2.21	0.93	8	2.56*	0.71	5	2.40*	0.78	7	2.30	0.85	7	2.37	0.82	7
Favorable social status[c, e]	1.23*	0.88	14	1.65*	0.81	15	1.64*	0.88	14	1.34	0.88	14	1.47	0.86	14
Good looks[f]	1.47*	0.73	13	1.73*	0.68	13	1.68*	0.72	13	1.69*	0.60	12	1.64*	0.68	13
Similar religious background[d]	1.08	1.06	16	1.71	1.04	14	1.06*	1.07	16	1.34	1.11	14	1.30*	1.07	16
Ambition, industriousness[g]	2.29*	0.68	7	2.52*	0.60	7	2.41*	0.61	6	2.52*	0.56	6	2.44*	0.61	6
Similar political background[d]	0.87	0.91	17	1.16*	0.94	17	0.94*	0.92	17	0.86	0.87	17	0.96*	0.91	17
Mutual attraction, love	2.97	0.17	1	2.96	0.20	1	2.99	0.09	1	2.98	0.13	1	2.98*	0.15	1
Good health	2.07	0.71	9	2.21	0.63	9	2.20	0.59	9	2.12	0.59	9	2.15	0.63	9
Education, intelligence	2.60	0.56	5	2.53*	0.57	6	2.62*	0.52	4	2.53*	0.54	5	2.57*	0.55	5

Note: See note to Table 2.

[a]Mean for Massachusetts sample is significantly different from mean for California sample. [b]Mean for Texas sample is significantly different from means for Massachusetts and Michigan samples. [c]Mean for Texas sample is significantly different from means for Massachusetts, California, and Michigan samples. [d]Mean for California sample is significantly different from means for Massachusetts and Michigan samples. [e]Mean for California sample is significantly different from means for Texas, California, and Michigan samples. [f]Mean for Massachusetts sample is significantly different from means for Texas and Michigan samples. [g]Mean for Massachusetts sample is significantly different from means for Texas and Michigan samples. [h]Mean for California sample is significantly different from mean for Michigan sample. [i]Mean for Texas sample is significantly different from means for California and Michigan samples.

identified in Tables 2 and 3 with superscript letters appended to the relevant mate characteristics.

Regional differences. Table 2 shows that men in the Texas sample, more than men in the other samples, valued a potential wife's cooking and housekeeping skills, financial prospects, and chastity. Additionally, men in the Texas sample reported greater preference than did men in at least two other samples for a wife who embodied refinement and neatness, social status, a similar religious background, and ambition and industriousness. Table 3 shows that the differentiation of the Texas sample from the other samples is not specific to the mate preferences reported by men. Women in the Texas sample, more than women in the other samples, valued refinement and neatness, good financial prospects, chastity, desire for home and children, social status, and similar religious and political backgrounds in a potential husband.

Sex differences. We followed the significant multivariate effect for participant sex with independent means t tests for sex differences in the 18 preferences, for each sample separately, and then for the four samples combined. The Bonferroni procedure was used to correct for increased Type I error rate. By the Bonferroni procedure, statistical significance was reduced from .05 to .003 (.05/18), two-tailed. The results are displayed in Tables 2 and 3. Significant sex differences are indicated by an asterisk appended to the relevant preference mean. Three of the 18 characteristics were differently valued by men and women across all four samples. Women, more than men, valued good financial prospects and ambition and industriousness in a potential spouse. Across all four samples, men, more than women, valued good looks in a potential spouse. Across three of four samples, men, more than women, valued chastity in a potential spouse. Also across three of four samples, women, more than men, valued sociability, similar educational background, dependable character, emotional stability and maturity, and education and intelligence in a potential spouse.

The rightmost column of Tables 2 and 3 displays descriptive statistics and ranks for each of the 18 characteristics, collapsed across all four samples. Only two of these characteristics are not differently valued (at $p \leq .003$, two-tailed) by men and women: good health and refinement/ neatness. Women, more than men, valued a pleasing disposition; sociability; similar educational, religious, and political backgrounds; good financial prospects; dependable character; emotional stability and maturity; desire for home and children; social status; ambition and industriousness; mutual love and attraction; and education and intelligence in a potential mate. Men, more than women, valued cooking and housekeeping skills, chastity, and physical attractiveness in a potential mate.

Similarities across regions and sexes. Despite regional and sex differences, there was substantial similarity across regions and between the sexes. We computed Spearman rank-order correlations among the four samples on the 18 preferences, aggregated across participants within a sample, for men and women separately. Additionally, we computed Spearman correlations between the aggregate preferences of men and women for each of the four samples. The cross-sample correlations ranged from .96 to .99 for men and from .97 to .99 for women. The cross-sex correlations ranged from .86 to .91 (the full set of correlations is available from the first author on request). The magnitudes of these correlations suggest great similarity in the relative valuation of the mate characteristics across samples and between sexes.

DISCUSSION

Three conclusions can be drawn from this study. First, regions within the United States appear to differ in the values they place on a marriage partner, perhaps reflecting differences in the impact of various cultural changes in this century. The Texas sample, in particular, appears to differ from the other samples in placing a greater value on chastity, good financial prospects, social status, and a similar religious background. Second, several consistent sex differences were found that transcended sample. Men in all samples placed more importance on good looks, whereas women in all samples placed more importance on good financial prospects and ambition and industriousness. Third, despite a few significant differences between regions and sexes, there was tremendous similarity across regions and sex in the overall ordering of the values. Both sexes in all four samples, for example, rated mutual attraction and love as the most important value in selecting a marriage partner.

STUDY 2: MATE PREFERENCE IN 1996

METHOD

Participants. Three convenience samples of undergraduates participated in this study from three different geographic regions within the

United States (we were unable to collect repeat data from Massachusetts and California): the University of Texas at Austin ($n = 326$); the College of William and Mary in Williamsburg, Virginia ($n = 176$); and the University of Michigan at Ann Arbor ($n = 105$). The total sample consisted of 607 undergraduates, 226 men and 381 women. Table 1 provides all available demographic information for each sample and for the total sample. Participants voluntarily completed a mate preferences survey during an introductory psychology class.

Mate selection survey. Participants completed the same survey used in Study 1.

RESULTS

Tables 4 and 5 show the preference means, standard deviations, and rank orderings for the 18 characteristics for the three samples separately, and for men and women, respectively. A MANOVA on mean values for the 18 mate preferences by participant sex and sample (Texas, Virginia, Michigan) revealed overall ef-

Table 4

Descriptive Statistics for Preferences of Male College Students in 1996, by Sample Location

Characteristic	Texas			Virginia			Michigan			Average		
	M	*SD*	Rank	*M*	*SD*	Rank	*M*	*SD*	Rank	*M*	*SD*	Rank
Good cook, housekeeper[a]	1.51	0.74	13	1.25	0.64	13	1.20	0.71	15	1.40	0.72	14
Pleasing disposition	2.51	0.53	4	2.47*	0.59	4	2.48	0.59	4	2.49*	0.55	4
Sociability	2.24	0.70	7	2.00	0.68	9	2.16	0.55	7	2.16	0.69	7
Similiar education background	1.75*	0.90	12	1.66*	0.78	12	1.96	0.79	10	1.75*	0.86	12
Refinement, neatness	1.82	0.72	11	1.72	0.86	11	1.56	0.77	12	1.76	0.77	11
Good financial prospect	1.51*	0.91	13	1.22*	0.86	14	1.44	0.82	13	1.42*	0.89	13
Chastity	1.29	1.04	16	1.15	0.99	15	0.84	0.85	17	1.20	1.01	16
Dependable character	2.70	0.53	2	2.75	0.47	2	2.68	0.48	3	2.72	0.51	2
Emotional stability, maturity	2.66	0.53	3	2.57*	0.59	3	2.72	0.46	2	2.64*	0.54	3
Desire for home, children	2.13*	0.93	9	2.14	0.95	6	1.88	1.01	11	2.10*	0.94	9
Favorable social status	1.25	0.91	17	1.11	0.97	16	1.12	0.83	16	1.20*	0.92	16
Good looks	2.14*	0.71	8	2.03*	0.61	8	2.24*	0.60	6	2.12*	0.67	8
Similar religious background[a]	1.43	1.15	14	1.02	1.05	17	1.36	1.08	14	1.31	1.13	15
Ambition, industriousness	1.97*	0.77	10	1.91*	0.76	10	2.12	0.67	9	1.97*	0.76	10
Similar political background	0.81	0.86	18	0.74	0.80	18	0.80	0.91	18	0.79	0.84	18
Mutual attraction, love	2.92	0.37	1	2.95	0.21	1	2.92	0.28	1	2.93	0.32	1
Good health	2.30	0.65	6	2.06	0.73	7	2.16	0.55	7	2.22	0.67	6
Education, intelligence	2.42*	0.63	5	2.34	0.57	5	2.44	0.65	5	2.40*	0.61	5

Note: See note to Table 2.

[a]Mean for Texas sample is significantly different from mean for Virginia sample.

fects for both independent variables, $F(1,18) = 12.83$ and $F(2,36) = 2.49$, respectively (both $ps \leq .001$). To identify within-sex, between-sample differences, we conducted a one-way ANOVA on each of the 18 preference means by sample, for men and women separately. Significant ($p < .05$) main effects were followed by all possible post hoc comparisons. To control for increased Type I error rate, a Bonferroni correction for alpha inflation was employed. By the Bonferroni procedure, statistical significance was reduced from .05 to .017 (.05/3), two-tailed. Significant between-sample differences are identified in Tables 4 and 5 with superscript letters appended to the relevant mate characteristics.

Regional differences. Table 4 shows that men in the Texas sample, more than men in the Virginia sample, valued cooking and housekeeping skills and a similar religious background in a potential wife. Table 5 shows that women in the Texas sample, more than women in the Virginia sample, valued cooking and housekeeping skills, pleasing disposition, and good financial prospects in a potential husband. Additionally, women in the Texas sample, more than women in the Michigan sample, valued refinement and neatness and similar religious background in a potential husband. Finally, women in the Michigan sample valued chastity less in a potential husband than did women in the Texas and Virginia samples.

Sex differences. We followed the significant multivariate effect for participant sex with independent means t tests for sex differences in the 18 preferences, for each sample separately and then for the three samples combined. The Bonferroni procedure was used to correct for increased Type I error rate. By the Bonferroni procedure, statistical significance was reduced from .05 to .003 (.05/18), two-tailed. The results are shown in Tables 4 and 5. Significant

---

Table 5
Descriptive Statistics for Preferences of Female College Students in 1996, by Sample Location

Characteristic	Texas			Virginia			Michigan			Average		
	M	*SD*	Rank	*M*	*SD*	Rank	*M*	*SD*	Rank	*M*	*SD*	Rank
Good cook, housekeeper[a]	1.36	0.61	16	1.17	2.73	16	1.18	0.73	15	1.27	0.64	16
Pleasing disposition[a]	2.57	0.56	5	2.73*	0.50	4	2.71	0.48	4	2.64*	0.53	4
Sociability	2.31	0.57	8	2.24	0.59	8	2.34	0.57	8	2.29	0.58	8
Similar education background	2.11*	0.75	11	2.07*	0.71	10	2.18	0.73	9	2.11*	0.73	10
Refinement, neatness[b]	1.86	0.68	12	1.68	0.65	12	1.59	0.76	13	1.75	0.70	12
Good financial prospect[a]	2.15*	0.15	10	1.75*	0.72	11	1.95	0.73	11	1.99*	0.73	11
Chastity[c]	1.23	1.10	17	0.96	1.09	17	0.54	0.81	18	1.01	1.08	17
Dependable character	2.80	0.44	2	2.86	0.34	2	2.76	0.54	2	2.81	0.44	2
Emotional stability, maturity	2.66	0.53	2	2.84*	0.39	3	2.76	0.53	2	2.80*	0.40	3
Desire for home, children	2.48*	0.76	6	2.41	0.83	6	2.37	0.91	7	2.44*	0.81	6
Favorable social status	1.48	0.83	15	1.34	0.81	15	1.42	0.87	14	1.43*	0.83	15
Good looks	1.62*	0.72	13	1.58*	0.61	13	1.72*	0.66	12	1.63*	0.67	13
Similar religious background[b]	1.58	1.06	14	1.43	1.06	14	1.11	1.06	16	1.44	1.07	14
Ambition, industriousness	2.39*	0.66	7	2.35*	0.53	7	2.46	0.66	6	2.39*	0.62	7
Similar political background	0.90	0.89	18	0.95	0.87	18	0.80	0.81	17	0.89	0.87	18
Mutual attraction, love	2.95	0.28	1	3.00	0.00	1	2.95	0.22	1	2.97	0.22	1
Good health	2.25	0.68	9	2.08	0.66	9	2.13	0.56	10	2.18	0.65	9
Education, intelligence	2.61*	0.51	4	2.48	0.57	5	2.62	0.51	5	2.58*	0.53	5

Note: See note to Table 2.
[a]Mean for Texas sample is significantly different from mean for Virginia sample. [b]Mean for Texas sample is significantly different from mean for Michigan sample. [c]Mean for Michigan sample is significantly different from means for Texas and Virginia samples.

sex differences are indicated by an asterisk appended to the relevant preference mean. Men, more than women, valued good looks in a potential spouse across all three samples. For two of the three samples, women, more than men, valued similar educational background, good financial prospects, and ambition and industriousness in a potential spouse.

The rightmost column of Tables 4 and 5 displays descriptive statistics and ranks for each of the 18 characteristics, collapsed across all three samples. Women, more than men, valued a pleasing disposition, similar educational background, good financial prospects, emotional stability and maturity, desire for home and children, social status, ambition and industriousness, and education and intelligence in a potential mate. Men, more than women, valued physical attractiveness in a potential mate.

Similarities across regions and sexes. To gauge overall similarity in the ordering of values, we computed Spearman correlations among the three samples on the 18 preferences, aggregated across participants within a sample, for men and women separately. We also computed Spearman correlations between the aggregate preferences of men and women for each of the three samples. The cross-sample correlations ranged from .94 to .98 for men and from .98 to .99 for women. The cross-sex correlations ranged from .94 to .98 (the full set of correlations is available from the first author on request). As was documented for the 1984/1985 assessment period, the magnitudes of these correlations suggest high levels of similarity in the relative valuation of the 18 mate characteristics across samples and between sexes.

DISCUSSION

Three general conclusions can be drawn from these data. First, as in Study 1, significant regional differences were discovered. In 1996, Texas continued to place a greater value than the other samples on a mate with a similar religious background. In a decade-later replication, Texans also continued to value chastity more than Michiganders. In fact, this regional difference increased slightly during the intervening decade, reflecting an increasing importance that Texans, particularly Texas women, place on chastity in a potential mate. Second, the greater importance that men attach to physical attractiveness continued in this decade. The greater importance that women attach to good financial prospects continued for two of the three samples, but failed to reach significance for the Michigan sample, perhaps reflecting a slight attenuation of the sex difference in this region. Third, despite these regional and sex differences, the samples of both sexes from all three regions showed a strikingly high degree of similarity in the overall valuation attached to these mate characteristics.

GENERATIONAL STABILITY AND CHANGE IN MATE SELECTION CRITERIA

DEMOGRAPHIC INFORMATION FOR SAMPLES FROM 1939, 1956, 1967, AND 1977

The 1939 sample (Hill, 1945) included 346 male and 282 female undergraduates at the University of Wisconsin at Madison. No additional demographic information was provided. The 1956 sample (McGinnis, 1958) included 120 undergraduates (distribution by sex not specified) at the University of Wisconsin at Madison. No additional demographic information was provided. The 1967 sample (Hudson & Henze, 1969) included 337 male and 229 female undergraduates at one of four universities (distributions by university or by sex by university were not provided): Arizona State University at Tempe, University of Nebraska at Omaha, the State University of New York at Stony Brook, and the University of Alberta at Edmonton. Across the 1967 samples, the median age was 21.6 years for men and 20.4 years for women. Seventy-six percent of the men and 82% of the women were single. No additional demographic information was provided. The 1977 sample (Hoyt & Hudson, 1981) included 132 male and 184 female undergraduates at Arizona State University at Tempe. The median age was 21.0 years for men and 20.2 years for women; 87% of the men and 88% of the women were single. No additional demographic information was provided.

Table 6 displays the ranks based on mean ratings for the 18 characteristics, separately by sex and by assessment year. Ranks connected by dashed lines highlight a preference change of at least three ranks from the first to the sixth assessment periods. Underlined ranks highlight preferences for which there is at least a one rank sex difference, in the same direction, across all six assessment periods. Because variances were not provided in earlier reports, statistical tests for generational differences could not be performed. Several clear trends, however, were apparent in these data.

GENERATIONAL SHIFTS IN MATE SELECTION CRITERIA

For both men and women, there appeared to be an overall increase from 1939 to 1996 in the valuation of mutual attraction and love, education and intelligence, sociability, and good looks. In contrast, there appeared to be a general decrease in the valuation of refinement, neatness, and chastity, for both men and women. In addition to the changes that occurred for both sexes, several generational shifts appeared to be unique to sex. For men, there was an overall increase in valuation of similar educational background and good financial prospects and an overall decrease in valuation of good cook and housekeeper. For women, there was an overall decrease in valuation of ambition and industriousness.

Table 6
Rank Ordering of Mate Preferences Across 6 Decades, by Participant Gender

Characteristic	Men						Women					
	1939	1956	1967	1977	1984/1985	1996	1939	1956	1967	1977	1984/1985	1996
Dependable character	1	1	1	3	3	2	2	1	2	3	3	2
Emotional stability, maturity	2	2	3	1	2	3	1	2	1	2	2	3
Pleasing disposition	3	4	4	4	4	4	4	5	4	4	4	4
Mutual attraction, love	4	3	2	2	1	1	5	6	3	1	1	1
Good health	5	6	9	5	6	6	6	9	10	8	9	9
Desire for home, children	6	5	5	11	9	9	7	3	5	10	7	6
Refinement, neatness	7	8	7	10	10	11	8	7	8	12	12	12
Good cook, housekeeper	8	7	6	13	13	14	16	16	16	16	16	16
Ambition, industriousness	9	9	8	8	11	10	3	4	6	6	6	7
Chastity	10	13	15	17	17	16	10	15	15	18	18	17
Education, intelligence	11	11	10	7	5	5	9	14	7	5	5	5
Sociability	12	12	12	6	8	7	11	11	13	7	8	8
Similar religious background	13	14	13	14	12	12	14	10	11	13	15	14
Good looks	14	15	11	9	7	8	17	18	17	15	13	13
Similar education background	15	14	13	12	12	12	12	8	9	9	10	10
Favorable social status	16	16	16	15	14	17	15	13	14	14	14	15
Good financial prospect	17	17	18	16	16	13	13	12	12	11	11	11
Similar political background	18	18	17	18	18	18	18	17	18	17	17	18

Note: Ranks connected by dashed lines highlight a preference change of at least three ranks from the first to the sixth assessment periods. Underlined ranks highlight preferences for which there is at least a one rank gender difference, in the same direction, across all six assessment periods.

GENERATIONAL CONTINUITIES IN MATE SELECTION CRITERIA

Despite the apparent generational shifts, several characteristics appeared to attain high levels of continuity in valuation across the six assessment periods. As shown in Table 6, dependable character, emotional stability and maturity, and pleasing disposition retained high levels of valuation for both sexes across the six assessment periods. Similar political background retained low levels of valuation for both sexes across the six assessment periods.

In addition to these cross-sex generational continuities, six major sex differences recurred in each assessment period. Across all six assessment periods, men placed a higher premium than did women on good health, good cook and housekeeper, and good looks. In contrast, women placed a higher premium than did men on ambition and industriousness, similar educational background, and good financial prospect.

Cross-generational continuity in relative valuation of the 18 characteristics is suggested by Spearman correlations calculated among the 6 decades of mate preferences. The average correlation among the male samples was .92, ranging from .76 to .98; the average correlation among the female samples was .94, ranging from .76 to .99 (the full set of correlations is available from the first author on request). The magnitudes of these correlations suggest substantial continuity in relative valuation of the 18 characteristics, for both men and women, across the 6 decades of assessment.

Notwithstanding the cross-generational sex differences, the average cross-sex correlation was .84, ranging from a low of .75 in 1956 to a high of .92 in 1996. Noteworthy was an apparent increase in similarity between the sexes in relative importance placed on the 18 characteristics. We assessed the statistical significance of the difference between each of the cross-sex correlations, using Fisher's r-to-z transformation. To control for increased Type I error, we reset alpha from .05 to .003 (.05/15) using the Bonferroni correction for alpha inflation.

These analyses revealed that although the 1956 cross-sex correlation ($r = .75$) was not significantly smaller than the 1967 correlation ($r = .77$; $z = -0.47$, $p = .319$, one-tailed), it was significantly smaller than the 1977 ($r = .89$), 1984/ 1985 ($r = .87$), and 1996 correlations ($r = .92$; all $zs > 3.75$; all $ps < .001$, one-tailed). Additionally, the 1984/1985 and 1977 correlations were significantly larger than the 1967 correlation (both $zs > 5.70$; both $ps < .001$, one-tailed). Finally, the 1996 correlation was significantly larger than the 1984/1985 correlation ($z = -5.31$, $p < .001$, one-tailed) and marginally significantly larger than the 1977 correlation ($z = -2.40$, $p = .008$, one-tailed). Overall, the mate preferences of men and women became more similar over the last 5 decades of assessment.

GENERAL DISCUSSION AND CONCLUSIONS

The importance that people attach to specific characteristics in a mate provides one assay of values. In a rare research opportunity, we were able to assess the cultural evolution of these values in samples spanning more than half a century within America (including one Canadian sample in 1967), using six different time periods ranging from 1939 to 1996. By assessing four different regions in the mid-1980s and three different regions in 1996, we were able to evaluate whether different regions within the United States represent different "cultures" or whether they show enough similarity to be treated as a single culture. A few consistent regional differences did emerge at both time periods. The Texas sample, in particular, placed greater value on potential mates who show chastity and a similar religious background. These differences, however, were dwarfed by the overwhelming similarity in the value ordering of the mate characteristics at both time periods. The cross-regional Spearman correlations ranged from .96 to .99 in the mid-1980s, and from .94 to .99 in 1996. These findings suggest that it is reasonable to aggregate the data and consider the different samples to represent the same "culture" for the purpose of evaluating change over time.

This aggregation for the 1984/1985 and 1996 assessments raises an important limitation of the current study—the assumption that the earlier assessments of college samples taken in 1939, 1956, 1967, and 1977 were reasonably representative of the values of college students of those times. Because we cannot go back in time to assess other samples from former decades, we cannot directly test this assumption. The fact that the different samples taken from widely varying geographic locations in the United States show strong similarity provides circumstantial support for the assumption. Nonetheless, the fact that we cannot test the assumption directly represents a limitation, albeit an unavoidable one, that must be considered when evaluating and interpreting the results. With this limitation in mind, we discuss the nature and implications of the most important findings.

CHASTITY

The value placed on chastity in a potential mate shows one of the most striking cultural changes over time. Among the 18 mate characteristics men desired, it emerged as the 10th most important in 1939, 13th in 1956, 15th in 1967, 17th in 1977, 17th in 1984/1985, and 16th in 1996. Analogous decrements for women occurred, moving from 10th in 1939 to 17th in 1996. Clearly, the cultural value attached to virginity has declined over the past 57 years. Although identifying a single causal factor among the multitude of possibilities may be impossible, it is not unreasonable to suppose that the increased dissemination of birth control devices and the concurrent sexual revolution of the 1960s contributed in some measure to this shift.

During the mid-to-late 1980s, awareness of the specter of AIDS increased dramatically. The premium placed on chastity in a mate provides one assay of the degree to which this awareness had an impact on values, at least in the mating domain. The current data show a slight increase in the importance that both sexes attach

to chastity, moving from a mean rating of 0.80 to 1.20 for men and from 0.46 to 1.01 for women in 1984/1985 and 1996, respectively. In the two samples that are directly comparable from these assessments, the Texas sample showed the greatest increase in the importance attached to chastity; the Michigan sample showed an increase as well, but it was slight. Whether this slight trend continues in the new millennium remains a question for future empirical work.

PHYSICAL ATTRACTIVENESS

Another large shift in values pertains to the importance attached to good looks. Both sexes show a steady climb. For men, it jumped from 14th in 1939 to 8th in 1996. For women, it jumped from 17th in 1939 to 13th in 1996. Both are large changes by any standard. Circumstantial evidence supports the notion that this shift in values is reflected in actual behavior. The cosmetics, diet, and cosmetic surgery industries, for example, have reached $53 billion a year, and increasing numbers of men are apparently partaking of these appearance-enhancement efforts (Wolf, 1991). Again, it is impossible to identify with any certainty a single cause from among the bewildering array of possibilities, but it is not unreasonable to speculate that the surge in visual media—television, movies, Internet images, and virtual reality—have contributed to this shift. Future studies could profitably examine these shifts in other cultures as visual media become increasingly prominent in them.

FINANCIAL RESOURCES

A third clear trend is the increasing importance of good financial prospects in a potential marriage planner. Both sexes show the trend, but men more strikingly than women. This variable ranked 17th for men in 1939, increased to 16th by 1977, and showed the largest jump in the past decade, reaching 13th in importance. In absolute terms, men rated this variable 1.02 in 1984/1985 and 1.42 in 1996, a significant mean increment. Women showed a smaller change, ranking good financial prospects 13th in 1939, 12th in 1956, and 11th in 1977, 1984/1985, and 1996. During the past decade, therefore, the sex difference in the importance attached to economic resources in a mate has diminished. Contrary to the expectations of the structural powerlessness hypothesis (Buss & Barnes, 1986), however, the change is not due to a decrement in the importance that women give it. Rather, it is due to the increasing importance that men attach to this characteristic. One may speculate that the increasing personal access that women have to economic resources, and perhaps the greater variance among women in their degree of personal access to resources, has triggered this shift in what men value in a partner.

GOOD COOK AND HOUSEKEEPER

The sexes also have converged to some extent in the importance they attach to mates who are good cooks and housekeepers. As with the change in the value attached to financial resources, this shift is primarily driven by changes among men. Across the decades, men show a curvilinear relationship, ranking it eighth in 1939, seventh in 1956, and sixth in 1967, but then displaying a trend reversal with a ranking of 13th in 1977 and 1984/1985 and 14th in 1996. Women's ratings, in contrast, show no change over time—domestic skills are 16th in importance at each of the six time periods. Thus, trends toward more equitable sharing of housework, with the emergence of occasional "house-dads," appear to have had no impact on women's valuation of domestic skills in a marriage partner. Perhaps the rise in hiring domestic help among career couples has contributed to the decline in the importance men give to domestic skills in a mate.

MUTUAL ATTRACTION AND LOVE

The final dramatic shift in values centers on the importance of mutual attraction and love. Although important across all decades, it was not considered primary in 1939 or 1956, achieving a rank of fourth and third for men in these decades and fifth and sixth for women. From 1967 on, however, mutual attraction and love steadily increase in importance for both sexes, reaching second for men in 1967 and first in the two most recent assessments. For women it reached third in 1967 before it landed at first in 1977, where it remains in the two most recent assessments. This shift suggests that, for samples of college students in North America, marriage may be evolving from a more institutional form to a more companionate form.

Precisely why this shift in values has occurred is unclear. One might be tempted to speculate that the decline of the extended family and delay of childbirth has created an increased importance of marriage as the primary source of social satisfaction. But this speculation does not square with the finding that mutual attraction and love achieve primary value nearly universally. Among 34 of the 37 cultures worldwide for which this factor has been examined, including cultures varying widely on the nature of family and number of children (Buss et al., 1990), both sexes rated it as one of the most important three factors among the 18 factors examined. The notable exceptions are Nigeria (both sexes placing it fourth), the Zulu tribe (men placing it 10th and women placing it 5th), and China (men placing it fourth and women placing it eighth). With increasing globalization, it will be interesting to see whether these few cultures that do not give it primary importance shift in their values.

CONVERGENCE BETWEEN THE SEXES

Perhaps one of the most important findings from this study is the convergence between men and women in their mating values over the past 3 decades. Using Spearman's statistic to calculate overall similarity, the sexes show significantly greater similarity in 1977 and 1984/1985 than in 1967, and the convergence continues, showing more similarity in 1996 than in the previous decade of assessment. This change cannot be attributed solely or even primarily to changes in the values of women. If anything, men appear to have shifted more in their values to approach those of women, attaching greater importance, for example, to a mate's financial prospects and attaching less importance to a mate's domestic skills. The current convergence may reflect a broader trend toward a common standard by which both men and women are evaluated. Precisely why the mate preferences of men and women might be converging is a topic for future work.

CONTINUITIES OVER THE GENERATIONS

Despite the profound changes that have occurred over the generations, considerable continuity remains. First, several characteristics showed nearly identical levels of valuation across all six generations of assessment. Notably, dependable character, emotional stability, and pleasing disposition retained high levels of valuation at all time periods, and similar political background remained unimportant or irrelevant at all time periods.

Second, the overall ordering of the characteristics remained similar, showing Spearman correlations across the generations that ranged from a low of .76 (e.g., between 1939 and 1996 for men) to a high of .99 (between 1984/1985 and 1996 for women). The average cross-generational correlation was .93, suggesting considerable continuity in values.

Third, despite the real convergence between the sexes, several key sex differences remained strong for each of the six time periods. Most notably, men from 1939 to 1996 have placed greater importance than women on mates who are physically attractive, and women have placed greater importance than men on mates with good financial prospects—sex differences that appear to transcend cultures as well as generations (Buss, 1989). The stability of sex differences, in concert with the relative convergence between the sexes in mate preferences over the past half century, suggests the value of an interactionist approach that integrates "evolutionary" factors with "cultural" factors. A hallmark of modern evolutionary science is precisely this integration of evolutionary psychology and cultural psychology (see, for example, Buss, 1999).

CONCLUSIONS

This article perforce has been heavy on empirical data and light on theory. The historical changes responsible for the cultural evolution of values are numerous, interrelated, impossible to duplicate within the laboratory, and inherently nonreplicable. Perhaps the data and speculations offered in this article will spark greater attention to the development of theories that can explain the cultural evolution of values. We have established with reasonable certainty, within the limitations noted above, the conclusion that values have indeed changed in important ways over time within the United States, and these changes must be interpreted within the context of moderately high levels of continuity.

References

Buss, D. M. (1989). Sex differences in human mate preferences: Evolutionary hypotheses tested in 37 cultures. *Behavioral and Brain Sciences, 12,* 1–49.

———. (1994). *The evolution of desire.* New York: Basic Books.

———. (1999). *Evolutionary psychology.* Boston: Allyn & Bacon.

Buss, D. M., et al. [54 co-authors]. (1990). International preferences in selecting mates: A study of 37 cultures. *Journal of Cross-Cultural Psychology, 21,* 5–47.

Buss, D. M., & Barnes, M. (1986). Preferences in human mate selection. *Journal of Personality and Social Psychology, 50,* 559–570.

Hill, R. (1945). Campus values in mate selection. *Journal of Home Economics, 37,* 554-558.

Hoyt, L. L., & Hudson, J. W. (1981). Personal characteristics important in mate preferences among college students. *Social Behavior and Personality, 9,* 93–96.

Hudson, J. W., & Henze, L. E. (1969). Campus values in mate selection: A replication. *Social Forces, 31,* 772–775.

Kasser, T., & Sharma, Y. S. (1999). Reproductive freedom, educational equality, and females' preference for resource-acquisition characteristics in mates. *Psychological Science, 10,* 374–377.

Kenrick, D. T., & Gutierres, S. E. (1980). Contrast effects and judgments of physical attractiveness: When beauty becomes a social problem. *Journal of Personality and Social Psychology, 38,* 131–140.

Kenrick, D. T., Neuberg, S. L., Zierk, K. L., & Krones, J. M. (1994). Evolution and social cognition: Contrast effects as a function of sex, dominance, and physical attractiveness. *Personality and Social Psychology Bulletin, 20,* 210–217.

McGinnis, R. (1958). Campus values in mate selection: A repeat study. *Social Forces, 36,* 368–373.

Wiederman, M. W., & Allgeier, E. R. (1992). Sex differences in mate selection criteria: Sociobiological or socioeconomic explanation? *Ethology & Sociobiology, 13,* 115–124.

Wolf, N. (1991). *The beauty myth.* New York: Morrow.

Chapter Four
Symbolic Interactionism Theory

Keiko and Thanh are leaving the house to attend a cocktail party sponsored by Thanh's company. It's important that he be there, since he's up for a big promotion this year and wants to make sure those in charge know who he is and can connect his face with his name, since his name is so unusual in the United States. Keiko is tired from working all day and getting the children taken care of before they leave the house, so she is dreading the party. Thanh, however, is very excited.

They are greeted at the door by the company vice president and a very loud band. Thanh introduces his wife with pride and accepts champagne for both of them to sip as they mingle in the crowd. He is really in his element, speaking to everyone he passes, introducing his wife, and keeping his hand on the small of her back to make sure she feels comfortable and included. Since she doesn't know anyone there, he wants to make sure she is close so he can introduce her to everyone and make her feel like a part of the group. He is enjoying the music and expensive champagne and can't wait for the dancing to begin. Thanh says to his wife, "Isn't this the best party you've ever been to?! And can you believe who all is here—all the important people, and I've gotten to talk to all of them. I can't imagine a more perfect evening."

As Keiko looks at him, he knows something is wrong. He asks, "Aren't you enjoying yourself?" She doesn't know what to say to him. After all, the place is too loud and too crowded, and people are drinking way too much. She wonders how he can stand knowing that everyone he speaks to is judging both

of them. And why does he have to be so controlling of her? Everywhere they go he is right by her side, as if he does not trust her to go out on her own for fear she will say something that would make him look bad. It is one of the worst nights of her life! How can two people in the same place have such different opinions about what is going on?

So, who was right—was it the best party they had ever been to or a night of being controlled and judged? Was the party incredible or incredibly boring? The answer to those questions, according to symbolic interactionism, is that they are both right. People define situations based on their own personal experiences and sense of self. Thus, two people can be in the exact same situation and have different interpretations of what is going on in that situation. We'll learn more about this as we discuss this multifaceted and exciting theory.

HISTORY

IMPORTANT EARLY CONTRIBUTIONS

Of all the theories discussed in this text, symbolic interactionism has probably had the greatest impact on the study of families. Not only is this theory rich in history, since it has been in use since the early 1900s, but it is still one of the most commonly used theoretical perspectives in the field today. The longevity and popularity of this theory is due in part to its emphasis on a conceptual framework that is not only rich in content but also adaptable to any time period. It is also due to the fact that symbolic interactionism was born out of both qualitative and quantitative research (LaRossa and Reitzes 1993).

Unlike most theories, there is no one person who is most commonly associated with its development. Thus, the historical review of symbolic interactionism will be longer than most of those in this text, since there are many people whose work needs to be reviewed in order to fully understand the basic assumptions of this theory. While who is covered in this section will vary from one writing to the next, this discussion is based on the guidance of LaRossa and Reitzes (1993).

Symbolic interactionism has its earliest roots in the United States in the pragmatic philosophers of the early 1900s, such as William James, John Dewey, Charles Pierce, and Josiah Royce (Vander Zanden 1987). Not only were these scholars themselves influential in the development of the theory, but perhaps more important, they trained their students who in turn became the primary contributors to the assumptions and concepts that make this theory what it is today. The pragmatists did, however, contribute four important ideas that laid the foundation for the development of symbolic interactionism.

The first important contribution of the pragmatists was to view the world as something that was always changing rather than a static structure whose history is predetermined. Second, the pragmatists argued that social structure is not something that is fixed in time but rather is constantly changing and developing. Third, they were perhaps the first to suggest that meaning comes not from objects themselves but from our interactions with objects. For example, the meaning of a table depends on the person who is viewing or using the table at the time. Finally, "they exhibited an ideological commitment to progress and to democratic values" (La Rossa and Reitzes 1993, 136) that could be advanced through science. Thus arose the notion that we could use research to figure out how society, and people, grow and change and how they do so within the confines of a democratic society that is always evolving.

These four ideas came about at a time in history when people were desperate for information about how the changing structure of society was going to affect them. This was the time of the industrial revolution, when people were going from working at home on the farm to working at the factory, which also meant moving from rural areas to urban areas closer to work (Mintz and Kellogg 1988). As you can imagine, all of these changes left people feeling like they had little control over their lives any-

more, which meant they certainly had little control over society. However, the ideas of symbolic interactionism allowed people to feel as if they gained a little more of that control back, since it is based on the idea that people are not victims of some predetermined course of history but instead are able to change how things happen in society through communication and interaction (LaRossa and Reitzes 1993).

Not only did these ideas appeal to society in general, but they were also accepted by scholars because they were grounded in research. Symbolic interactionism provided the means by which to study social interactions in a scientific fashion. It was at this time that people began to study the family just as a scientist would study a specimen or an astronomer would study a constellation (LaRossa and Reitzes 1993).

PRINCIPAL SCHOLARS

As was previously stated, one thing that makes symbolic interactionism unique is that it is a combination of the efforts of many different researchers. Although there are many people who made important contributions to the development of this theory, we will focus on just a few: George Herbert Mead, Charles Horton Cooley, William Isaac Thomas, and Herbert Blumer.

George Herbert Mead. George Herbert Mead, whose primary contributions focused on the self, is probably the most recognized of all those who have influenced symbolic interactionism. He believed that we learn about ourselves through interactions with others that are based on *gestures* (Mead 1934/ 1956). A gesture can be thought of as any action that causes a response or reaction in another person. We can all think of a few finger gestures that are sure to create a response in others, but Mead used the term more broadly to include such things as language and facial expressions as well. We develop a sense of self-consciousness when we can anticipate how other people will respond to our gestures. Because of this, it takes interactions with others to fully develop a sense of self.

How does this process take place? Mead (1934/1956) believed there were two stages people follow to develop a sense of self. In the first, the *play stage,* the child tries to use gestures to practice the behaviors associated with different roles, such as that of mother, father, firefighter, or teacher (Vander Zanden 1987). For example, if you have ever watched preschool children play house, you have probably seen a girl imitate things she has seen her mother do, such as cooking dinner, changing a baby's diaper, or helping another child with homework. Boys, on the other hand, if they are in the dramatic play area at all, are likely to be doing such things as pretending to drive the family to an event or organizing a play activity for the children. During this dramatic play experience, children are able to imagine the attitudes of the mother or learn to take the perspective of another person. During this stage, children usually assume the role of only one person at a time.

In the second stage, however, children begin to take on the perspective of many people at one time and to see how the individual fits within that group (Mead 1934/1956). This is called the *game stage,* and you can use almost any childhood game as a good example. For instance, when you play soccer, you have to think about not only what you are doing on the field, or the purpose of your position, but also about what everyone else on the field is doing as well. Another good example is that of the family. During this stage children can understand what each person's role in the family is, including their own, and how the behavior of one family member affects the interactions of other family members.

The final step in this process is being able to anticipate how one's behaviors affect not only those in our immediate environment but also in society at large. Mead (1934/1956) called this being able to take the role of the *generalized other,* which means understanding social norms and expectations so that one can guess how other people will react to a specific gesture

or interaction. An example of this is the young man who nervously looks around as he purchases a pornographic magazine. Although he is of legal age, he has internalized the social perception that viewing pornography is lewd and engaged in only by sexual deviants. He is apprehensive that someone he knows will come into the store and see him buying this magazine, thus forming a bad opinion about him.

Finally, Mead (1934/1956) believed that the self is not a thing but rather a process based on constant movement between the "I" and the "me." The "I" is the spontaneous acts we engage in, which are unpredictable and unstable. The "me" (the social self), on the other hand, is those learned roles that are determined by interactions with others. In other words, the social self (or "we") is all of our learned experiences, whereas the "I" is our immediate reaction to situations.

Charles Horton Cooley. Many of the researchers who developed symbolic interactionism focused on the self. For example, Charles Horton Cooley is perhaps best known for his idea of the *looking-glass self,* which is based on the premise that individuals think about how they appear to others, make a judgment about what the other person thinks about them, and then incorporate those ideas into their own concept of self (Longmore 1998). For this process to take place, we must interact with others. Cooley (1956) believed that most of this learning took place during face-to-face interactions with others, especially in small groups, which he called primary groups. The best example of a primary group is a family. Thus, it is in our families that we learn about ourselves, since families teach us about social expectations for behavior, things that we are good at, and many other thoughts and behaviors that come together to make up who we are.

William Isaac Thomas. So when did the concepts included in symbolic interactionism first start being used in family studies? Most believe it was when William Isaac Thomas (and Floarian Znaniecki) wrote *The Polish Peasant in Europe and America* (1918–1920).

This book was one of the first to state that the family has a role in the socialization process (LaRossa and Reitzes 1993). It pointed out that families construct their own realities so that one's culture, or social structure, influences both family and individual behavior.

Thomas is also well-known for coining the phrase *definition of the situation,* which is another foundation of symbolic interactionism. According to this idea, you cannot understand human behavior without also understanding the subjective perspectives of the people involved in the situation. For example, parents are often faced with two siblings who carried on a conversation and then came to the parents for a "final ruling." It becomes obvious during the parents' conversations with each of the siblings that although they were both a part of the same conversation, each person had a different interpretation of what was said by the end of the discussion. This is because each sibling's reaction to the conversation was based on his or her individual, subjective experience. Thomas took this idea further in what is called the Thomas theorem, which states that "if people define situations as real, they are real in their consequences" (LaRossa and Reitzes 1993, 140). Thus, each sibling in the conversation above makes comments based on his or her own interpretation, making each person's subjective opinion valued. So if they were to ask their parents "whose point of view is right," according to Thomas the parents' answer would be "they both are because your point of view is based on your interpretation of the conversation, taking into account your own personal experience." This is probably not the answer the disagreeing siblings want to hear!

Herbert Blumer. It should be obvious at this point that there are many people who have influenced the development of symbolic interactionism. In fact, there are many more than can be discussed here, but one thing we haven't covered yet is who was the first person to use the phrase *symbolic interactionism,* and that was Herbert Blumer. He is also credited with developing the three primary premises of symbolic interactionism, which will be discussed momentarily. Therefore, the influence of Herbert Blumer cannot be overlooked in a historical discussion of this theory (1969).

BASIC ASSUMPTIONS

Perhaps the best way to understand symbolic interactionism is to review the seven basic assumptions of this theory as developed by many researchers in this field, although they are based on three overarching themes which were originally developed by Blumer (1969). All of these assumptions spring from the idea that we understand and relate to our environment based on the symbols that we know or those that we learn. The organization of this discussion is based on the writing of LaRossa and Reitzes (1993).

FIRST OVERARCHING THEME

The first overarching theme (Blumer 1969) is that meaning is an important element of human behavior that cannot be overlooked. This is best explained by reviewing the three assumptions that developed from this primary belief.

People will react to something according to the meaning that the thing has for them. In other words, people live in a symbolic environment and will respond to something based on their definition of that symbol. A cigarette, for example, is a symbol of relief from withdrawal for one person and a "death stick" to another. Thus, the first person would pick up a cigarette and light it, wheras the second person would probably destroy it.

We learn about meaning through interactions with others. This assumption is drawn from the work of Allen and Doherty (1998). While different researchers in this area have varying beliefs about the origins of meaning, most would agree that meaning is learned and processed through our social interactions. People make value judgments about which symbols are positive and negative, and react to them based on these values. Where do we learn about these values? Through interactions with others.

As people come into contact with different things and experiences, they interpret what is being learned. In other words, people are both actors and reactors. We are not passive people who simply respond to the world around us; instead, we are active people who choose which parts of the environment to respond to. So if we enter a room in which we are uncomfortable, rather than simply stand there and feel nervous, hoping someone will come talk to us, we can actively seek out someone we know and go talk to them to put ourselves at ease. In this case, we are taking an active part in controlling our environment.

SECOND OVERARCHING THEME

The second overarching theme has to do with our self-concept. Because humans are active social beings who interact with others based on their meaning of the situation, they must have a sense of self for this to take place.

A human infant is asocial. This means that infants are not born with predetermined ideas about who they are but rather develop these as they interact with people along the way. An example of this is the notion of "the looking glass self" (Cooley 1956), which was discussed earlier. A social interactionist, then, would not say that a child has misbehaved because of a mischievous temperament but rather that this child has learned and interpreted this behavior as a result of his or her interactions with the environment.

Once individuals develop a sense of self, this will provide motivation for future behavior. Because humans are reflexive, they will always reflect on what they experience and use this as a guide for future behavior. This process entails not only a sense of self but also a sense of how others view you. For example, people often respond to a situation based not only on their own beliefs and values but also on how they think others will perceive that behavior (whether positively or negatively). This reflexive process takes an understanding of the self, as well as the *generalized other* discussed previously.

THIRD OVERARCHING THEME

The final overarching theme moves from a discussion of the self to a discussion of society. Whereas the previous themes and their underlying assumptions have focused on more individual aspects, this theme is based on the idea that infants are not born into a social vacuum. Instead, the environment of an infant has symbols and values that were assigned at birth. One only has to go into a nursery to see an example of this. If the room is decorated in pinks and is filled with dolls, what do we assume? We presume, of course, that the infant is a girl. Parents have often used the color pink and dolls as symbols of what is feminine, or as an example of the types of things infant girls will come to value.

Individuals are influenced by society. Individuals are influenced not only by their own self-concept, and the values, symbols, and beliefs of their families, but also by the cultural norms and values of the society in which they live. Perhaps the changing nature of fathering behaviors best exemplifies this. Whereas just a generation ago it was unusual for men to show physical affection to their children, it is now common for this to take place in today's families. This is because of the changing societal expectations of fathers, which state that both parents should show their children they love them not only with words but also with actions, such as hugs (Smith 1996).

People learn the rules and values of society through everyday interaction within that culture. What is the best way to learn about life in Japan? Although it is helpful prior to a visit to that country to read about their cultural norms so you do not begin your stay there offending people, the best way to learn about Japanese individuals and families is to spend some time living among them. You can learn many things during these common, daily experiences that can never be taught in a book.

PRIMARY TERMS AND CONCEPTS

So how do the ideas of all those early pioneers and the basic assumptions given above come together in a practical way to allow us to use and make sense of symbolic interactionism? Again, because of the history of this theory it is difficult to summarize it in a succinct way that will encompass all of its diverse parts. Thus, perhaps the best way to proceed is to discuss some of the primary concepts used in this theory and how they relate to the things we have already reviewed. There are numerous terms and concepts associated with this theory, many of which have been covered within the previous discussion. Terms commonly associated with symbolic interaction include, but are not limited to, symbols, interaction, gestures, social norms, rituals, roles, salience, identities, social act, and definition of the situation. Some of these are covered below.

SYMBOLS

The title of this theory combines two terms that are of utmost importance in this theory: symbols and interaction. Symbols are the products of social interaction. This means that we are not free to use symbols in any way we choose. Rather, their meaning is given to us by the way we see others using them. Thus, the meaning of a symbol in one situation may not be the same in a different situation. For example, how often have you seen professional basketball players swat each other on the butt as they come off the court for a time out? Now, what if you saw a man and woman walking down the street and the man reached over and swatted the woman on the butt. Does the action of hitting the person on the butt represent the same thing in each of these situations? Obviously not. We would assume in the basketball example that it is symbolic of encouragement or praise, whereas it might be evidence of intimacy in the example of the couple on the street. How you define the symbol is based on the context of the situation or the current environment, and it is something you learn from interacting with others in this environment.

INTERACTION

As you can tell, it is difficult to talk about the word *symbols* without also talking about *inter-*

action, as the two terms are dependent upon each other. Interaction, therefore, is a social behavior between two or more people during which some type of communication takes place causing each person to react to the situation and, as a result, modify his or her behavior (Burr, Leigh, Day, and Constantine 1979). This communication can be verbal, but it can also be nonverbal.

GESTURES

Gestures, a good example of nonverbal communication, are acts that represent something else (Vander Zanden 1987). We all know some popular, and some not so popular, hand gestures that are used in the United States, such as touching the thumb and forefinger together in a circle to represent that something is OK. These gestures and symbols are meaningless if there is not someone around to interpret and react to them, thus making interaction a necessary part of socialization.

SOCIAL NORMS

If interactions with others teach us what symbols and gestures mean, this also means that interactions teach us appropriate social norms. Social norms can be defined as expectations about how to act in a given situation. Is your behavior with your friends the same when you are with your parents as it is when you are alone together? My guess is your behavior changes in each of those situations, based on what are appropriate interactions for each of those environments. Interactions with each of these groups, our parents and our friends, teach us what behaviors they find acceptable, and we adapt our behavior based on the social norms followed within each situation.

RITUALS

These ideas come together in families in the form of rituals. For example, think about how your family celebrates holidays such as Thanksgiving. Many of us have elaborate rituals, such as who sits where at the table, who is in charge of carving the turkey, and whether or not a prayer is said before the meal and, if so, who says the prayer. Do you eat your big meal in the afternoon or evening? Who does the cooking? The cleaning? What happens after the meal? Each family has its own social norms for how they interact with each other during holidays and which symbols and gestures are an appropriate part of those rituals. Problems can arise when individuals marry and attempt to negotiate which family's rituals will be carried out in the new married couple's household, since people often enter into marriage assuming their family's traditions will be continued. Thus, it would be good to talk about this before marriage takes place so that you can decide which behaviors to adopt.

ROLES

Another thing that can influence our behavior in any social situation is our self-defined role. A role is a set of social norms for a specific situation, or "part." Think about actors in a play, each playing a character or a role. The same is true of each of us in life. What are some roles you play? Maybe you are a son or daughter, brother or sister, roommate, athlete, or even a husband or wife. Are the expectations for each of these roles the same? Not only do the expectations differ across roles, they can also differ across people who have the same role. For example, all of you reading this book right now are probably doing so not because of some burning desire to know more about family theories but because it was assigned to you in one of your courses in your role as a student. Some people think the role of a student is to read assigned chapters prior to class, participate in class discussion, study for exams, and complete assignments on time. Others, however, see their role as a student as enjoying an active social life, perhaps playing a sport, attending class when it is convenient, and completing assignments when they have time. For still others the role of student means attending class and completing assignments when time permits after working a 40-hour week and taking care of a family as well. The bottom line is that each person defines for him- or herself

what is appropriate behavior for each role he or she plays.

SALIENCE

So how do you decide which of your roles is most important, or which one is going to get the most of your time? According to Stryker (1968), we divide our time among each of our roles based on the amount of salience that role has in our lives. The more salient or important a role is to us, the more time we invest in this role. In the previous example the first student described probably sees his or her role as student as the most salient at the moment, meaning they identify most with the role of a student and will perform those tasks associated with that role first. A student might not go home on a long weekend to see his parents, for example, in order to finish a big paper due the following week at school. One possible explanation for this is that he sees his role as student as more important right now, or more salient, than his role as a son.

Although each individual defines for him- or herself the behaviors associated with a role, there are also social norms or expectations for roles. This does not mean, however, that roles are static—we have evidence in many of our family roles that these do indeed change over time (LaRossa and Reitzes 1993). Perhaps the best example of this is the role of mothers and fathers. While traditionally dads were responsible primarily for the financial support of the family while mothers were responsible for the care of the house and children, this is changing in today's society as more women enter the workforce and more men become highly involved fathers. Therefore, roles help us anticipate or predict behavior, but we must never forget that they are also both individual and social constructions.

Because the idea of roles is easy to discern in families, and thought by many scholars to be of utmost importance, an entire theory has emerged based on the idea that families interact based on the assignment of roles. For example, historically males preformed the "instrumental role"—being the financial provider for the family—while females performed the "expressive role"—taking care of the house and children (Parsons and Bales 1955). As you can guess, this notion came under attack by feminist scholars, who asserted that it did not account for the role of power and inequality in gendered or socially constructed relationships (Osmond and Thorne 1993). Thus, while role theory is still used today in many ways to discuss the various roles that individuals play within families, it has also changed from its original form to include more modern notions of families.

IDENTITY

As you can probably guess, those roles that are most salient for us are also those that most likely define our identity. There are several points to take into consideration here. First, this is a mental process in that our mental events determine our behavior. Once we have figured out what something means, we use that definition to determine our future behavior. This determination is made based on its relevance to our identity. Thus, those roles that are most salient to us, or which best identify who we think we are, are given priority in our lives. It is those interactions in which we choose most often to engage and indeed at which we most often attempt to excel (McCall and Simmons 1978).

It is here where we come full circle in our discussion of this theory. Socialization begins with the individual who is born asocial. Humans begin to learn about their environment, and themselves, through interactions with others, including family, friends, and school. These environments are symbolic representations of meaning. In other words, we are born into a culture and thus must learn what the social norms of a culture are through interaction with others in the same culture. Through this process, people learn about themselves and others, and learn not only which roles and behaviors are deemed most socially acceptable but also those that best represent who each of us is as an individual. This helps us decide which roles are most salient to us, or which best form our sense

of identity. This in turn influences our future interactions with others, as we interpret our own behaviors, and those of others, based on these beliefs. Because of this, some people respond to one thing in a situation while others in the same situation respond to something entirely different. Our world is, after all, socially constructed.

COMMON AREAS OF RESEARCH AND APPLICATION

There are many areas of research that have used the concepts and assumptions of symbolic interactionism, beginning with the work of the early founders previously discussed. However, this is a theory that is still widely used today in areas such as transition to parenthood (LaRossa and LaRossa 1981), issues unique to African-American families (Allen and Doherty 1998; Hollingsworth 1999), and studies of the self such as how accurate people are in perceiving how they are viewed by others (Cook and Douglas 1998; March 2000). This theory is also mentioned often in studies concerning family relationships or how families cope with tragedies such as death or living with Alzheimer's disease. Finally, whereas this theory was originally used to explain the changing family role associated with industrialization, it is currently being used to explain how families are dealing with the increasing number of women with young children entering the workforce and how this is affecting family and individual roles, perceptions of self, and social norms.

AFRICAN-AMERICAN FAMILIES

Think about the first overarching theme we discussed, which states that meaning is an important element of human behavior that cannot be overlooked. The research on African-American families is a good example of this theme, as it is based on the fact that although Blacks and Caucasians are raised in the same geographical areas in the United States, their lives are often very different. This is because different ethnic groups often teach different roles and values. For example, whereas household work is often divided based on traditional gender roles in Caucasian families, the same is not usually true in Black families. Specifically, while traditional white families define cooking and cleaning as behaviors associated with the role of wife and/or mother, in African-American families these behaviors are typically performed based on work hours and type of tasks first rather than specified gender roles (McLoyd, Cauce, Takeuchi, and Wilson 2000).

DEVELOPMENT OF SELF

The second overarching theme was more focused on the development of the self. Recent research using Mead's concept of "the looking-glass self" exemplifies current research of this nature. Cook and Douglas (1998) sought to discover how good people, particularly young children and adolescents, are at predicting how other people perceive them. Not surprisingly, they found that whereas children of all ages were good at predicting how their parents felt about them for some things, they were not good at others. It was also found that the age of the children makes a big difference as well, which lends credit to many of the components of this theory, including the role of cognition in assigning meaning to symbols and the attention given to social norms, which is greater during some parts of the life span than during others. In addition, interactions with others change throughout the life span, which would lead one to believe that perhaps adolescents aren't as aware of how their parents perceive them because they are more focused on the appraisals of their friends.

SEXUALITY

The final overarching theme focused on the role of society. An interesting area of research illustrating this topic is the work of Longmore (1998), which focused on the role of symbolic interactionism in the study of sexuality. Longmore quotes an interesting statement made by Kimmel and Fracher (1992, 473): "that we are sexual beings is determined by a biological imperative towards reproduction, but how we are sexual—where, when, how often, with whom, and why—has to do with cultural learning, with meanings transmitted in a cultural setting" (Longmore 1998, 44). Symbolic interactionism has been used to analyze and explain things such as bar behavior, dating behavior, the development of a sexual identity, and more recently such things as cybersex and on-line dating.

METHODOLOGICAL ISSUES

A final strength of symbolic interactionism which has led to continued use is its acceptance of both qualitative and quantitative methodologies. This means that researchers are not limited to one means of data collection, such as giving people a survey to find out how they feel about a certain topic. This theory also supports the use of observations, interviews, and, as you would guess, interactions with others in order to gain a deeper understanding of how people come to define their realities. Thus, its history is rich with people who have used a variety of methods to determine what makes individuals and families interact as they do.

CRITIQUE

Although symbolic interactionism has been used for many decades, it is not without its critics. We will review some of the most common criticisms of this theory below. Keep in mind during this discussion that these comments are often directed toward an individual using symbolic interactionism ideas rather than the theory in general. Stryker (1980) provided a summary of the criticisms of this theory, a few of which will be reviewed here. First is the idea that people find the key concepts confusing, since they are difficult to define and thus difficult to test using research. However, as LaRossa and Reitzes (1993) note, there has been a plethora of work in this area over the last several decades to address this problem. Thus, while perhaps this was true at the time of Stryker's writing, this is no longer as valid today.

A related criticism is that the ideas and concepts of individual scholars in this field have not been combined into one central theory. In other words, wheras most theories have a basic set of assumptions, lists of concepts, and organized guidelines, some believe this does not exist in the same sense for symbolic interactionism. Some authors have attempted to develop these theories, but there is no agreement as there is with other theories covered in this text. Thus, for some scholars this theory does in fact have specific guidelines and assumptions, but for others these are not well-developed enough to meet their needs; it depends on your school of thought. Further, while some scholars see this as a strength, since it allows them to pick and choose among the various concepts relevant to their particular research, many would say this is indeed a flaw with the theory in general. This makes it difficult to describe the theory to others in a logical fashion, as well as to test the central tenets of the theory, since they are so diverse.

Stryker's (1980) third criticism is that symbolic interactionism does not give enough attention to either the importance of emotions or the role of the unconscious. Although few would argue with this statement in a general sense, there are some aspects of this theory which do, in fact, address this issue. Cooley (1956), for example, states that people have feelings about themselves, or emotions, that drive the looking-glass self. Similarly, recently researchers have started to study the role of emotions in many individual and family contexts using the basic assumptions of symbolic interactionism. Thus, while this criticism holds true of many aspects of this theory, it does not for others.

A fourth criticism, offered by researchers such as Goffman (1974), is that symbolic interactionism places too much emphasis on the ability of individuals to create their own realities and doesn't pay enough attention to the fact that we live in a world that we do not create ourselves. LaRossa and Reitzes (1993) provide the best example of this when they state that whereas researchers can spend a lot of time studying how parents feel about being a new parent, and how they are going to divide up the tasks associated with rearing an infant based on

their symbolic environments, the bottom line is that someone still needs to feed and clothe the infant for it to survive. The point to remember from this is that while concepts such as the definition of the situation are valid and important, one cannot neglect an assessment of the physical realities of the environment as well.

A current criticism of this theory is its lack of attention to the role of biology. Although there are some scholars who attempt to address the genetic inheritance factor within this framework, as a general rule symbolic interactionists are more concerned with biology only as it pertains to cognition, which in turn influences social interactions (LaRossa and Reitzes 1993).

Finally, it is best to think of symbolic interactionism as a framework for organizing or influencing research rather than as a completely integrated theory in and of itself. While there are obviously some problems with this approach, symbolic interactionism also has some valid strengths that have contributed to its duration in the field. One example is that the theory is able to grow and change with the times, meaning that it is just as applicable today as it was when it began in the 1920s. Another strength of the theory is the focus on family interactions and the role individuals play in those social acts. In other words, one cannot look at any situation as being static but rather must recognize that each person in that situation is viewing things from his or her own perspective and acting with the hope of influencing the outcome of the interaction. Finally, symbolic interactionism reminds us that we are all social beings, playing roles and learning from each other.

APPLICATION

Now that we have covered symbolic interactionism in its entirety and evaluated its strengths and weaknesses, let's see how well you understand this theory by answering some questions as they pertain to our married couple at the beginning of this chapter, as well as how they pertain to your own lives.

1. Using the concepts and language of symbolic interactionism, explain how the spouses at the beginning of this chapter could have such different opinions about the cocktail party they attended.

2. Think about what roles you play. Make a list of them and the behaviors and responsibilities of each of those roles. Which of those roles is most salient for you? How does this influence your behavior?

3. Describe a situation you have been in recently that was similar to the one given at the beginning of this chapter. What was the specific setting? How did you react to the situation? How did the other people involved respond? How did your identity influence your behavior in this situation?

4. What are the social norms for the college or university you attend? How are these norms similar to or different from those of your family? How did you discover what those social norms were? How did you respond initially? List ways your behavior has changed as a result of these social norms and your interactions with others within the college environment.

5. Write an example of an experience you have had in your life that exemplifies the concepts of the generalized other and "the looking-glass self."

SAMPLE READING

Stryker, S. (1968). Identity salience and role performance: The relevance of symbolic interaction theory for family research. *Journal of Marriage and the Family* 30: 558–564.

This reading addresses some of the issues we have covered in this chapter, such as spending more time on and placing more importance on those roles we see as being more salient.

References

Allen, W. D., and Doherty, W. J. (1998). "Being there." The perception of fatherhood among a group of African-American adolescent fathers. In H. I. McCubbin, E. A. Thompson, A. I. Thompson, and J. A. Futrell (eds.), *Resiliency in African-American Families*. Thousand Oaks, CA: Sage.

Blumer, H. (1969). *Symbolic Interactionism: Perspective and Method*. Englewood Cliffs, NJ: Prentice-Hall.

Burgess, E. W. (1926). The family as a unity of interacting personalities. *The Family* 7: 3–9.

Burr, W., Leigh, G. K., Day, R. D., and Constantine, J. (1979). Symbolic interaction and the family. In W. R. Burr, R. Hill, F. I. Nye, and I. I. Reiss (eds.), *Contemporary Theories About the Family* (vol. 2, pp. 42–111). New York: Free Press.

Cook, W. L., and Douglas, E. M. (1998). The looking-glass self in family context: A social relations analysis. *Journal of Family Psychology* 12 (3): 299–309.

Cooley, C. H. (1956). *Social Organization*. Glencoe, IL: Free Press.

Goffman, E. (1974). *Frame Analysis: An Essay on the Organization of Experience*. New York: Harper and Row.

Hollingsworth, L. D. (1999). Symbolic interactionism, African American families, and the transracial adoption controversy. *Social Work* 44 (5): 443–453.

Kimmel, M. S., and Fracher, J. (1992). Hard issues and soft spots: Counseling men about sexuality. In M. S. Kimmel and M. A. Messner (eds.), *Men's Lives* (p. 473). New York: Macmillan.

LaRossa, R., and LaRossa, M. M. (1981). *Transition to Parenthood: How Infants Change Families*. Beverly Hills, CA: Sage.

LaRossa, R., and Reitzes, D. C. (1993). Symbolic interactionalism and family studies. In P. G. Boss, W. J. Doherty, R. LaRossa, W. R. Schumm, and S. K. Steinmetz (eds.), *Sourcebook of Family Theories and Methods: A Contextual Approach* (pp. 135–163). New York: Plenum Press.

Longmore, M. A. (1998). Symbolic interactionism and the study of sexuality. *The Journal of Sex Research* 35 (1): 44–57.

McCall, G. J., and Simmons, J. L. (1978). *Identities and Interactions: An Examination of Human Associations in Everyday Life* (rev. ed.). New York: Free Press.

McLoyd, V. C., Cauce, A. M., Takeuchi, D., and Wilson, L. (2000). Marital processes and parental socialization in families of color: A decade review of research. *Journal of Marriage and the Family* 62: 1070–1093.

March, K. (2000). Who do I look like? Gaining a sense of self-authenticity through the physical reflections of others. *Symbolic Interactionism* 23 (4): 359–373.

Mead, G. H. (1934/1956). *On Social Psychology: Selected Papers* (Anselem Strauss, ed.). Chicago: University of Chicago Press.

Mintz, S., and Kellogg, S. (1988). *Domestic revolutions: A social history of American family life.* New York: Free Press.

Osmond, M. W., and Thorne, B. (1993). Feminist theories: The social construction of gender in families and society. In P. G. Boss, W. J. Doherty, R. LaRossa, W. R. Schumm, and S. K. Steinmetz (eds.), *Sourcebook of Family Theories and Methods: A Contextual Approach* (pp. 591–623). New York: Plenum Press.

Parsons, T., and Bales, R. (eds.) (1955). *Family, Socialization, and Interaction Process.* Glencoe, IL: Free Press.

Smith, S. R. (1996). A qualitative investigation of how men come to define themselves as fathers. Unpublished doctoral dissertation, University of Georgia, Athens.

Stryker, S. (1968). Identity salience and role performance: The relevance of symbolic interaction theory for family research. *Journal of Marriage and the Family* 30: 558–564.

——. (1980). *Symbolic Interactionism: A Social Structural Version.* Menlo Park, CA: Benjamin/Cummings.

"Symbolic interactionism as defined by Herbert Blumer" (1996). The Society for More Creative Speech. Retrieved May 9, 2001, from the World Wide Web: *http://www.thepoint.com/~usul/text/blumer.html.*

Thomas, W. I., and Znaniecki, F. (1918–1920). *The Polish Peasant in Europe and America* (vol. 5). Boston, MA: Badger.

Vander Zanden, J. W. (1987). *Social Psychology* (4th ed.). New York: Random House. ✦

Identity Salience and Role Performance

The Relevance of Symbolic Interaction Theory for Family Research

Sheldon Stryker

Framing this paper is the question: [W]hat research problem and hypotheses suggested by symbolic interaction theory give promise, if pursued, of significantly advancing the sociology of the family? The problem delineated revolves around the concepts of identity and commitment. After explication of a set of premises and needed refinements in concepts basic to symbolic interaction theory, a number of hypotheses are offered. These purport to account for the position of identities in a salience hierarchy and tie identity salience to role performance. Finally, it is noted that these hypotheses could profitably be studied in the research setting of responses to first pregnancy.

This paper explicates a general research problem and a set of hypotheses to deal with that research problem. Its starting point is a paragraph from the writer's chapter on symbolic interaction as theory and as theoretical framework in the *Handbook of Marriage and the Family*.[1] Set in the context of a discussion of the possibilities for exploiting the symbolic interaction framework in family-related research, that paragraph raised a set of questions around the concept of identity:

The question of self-conception or identity in relation to the family remains virtually virgin in many respects. What accounts for the differentials which obviously exist in the salience of family identities? What are the consequences of . . . differentials in degree of commitment to a family identity for parent-child relations, for husband-wife relations, for the family as a functioning unit? . . . What determines whether or not a family-related identity is invoked in a given situation?[2]

These questions can be supplemented by others which are closely related. What accounts for the varying degrees of ease or difficulty with which persons adopt novel familial identities? Why is it that some experience little difficulty in modifying the salience of a family identity they hold, while for some such modification occurs—if at all—only with considerable stress?

To answer questions of the sort posed requires that one have a theory. The latter implies the specification of the premises and assumptions entering into the theory; the development of the conceptual apparatus in terms of which the theory is stated; and the articulation of a set of hypotheses, deriving from the premises and assumptions, stating expected relationships among the phenomena pointed to by the concepts. It is to these tasks that the writer now turns.

UNDERLYING PREMISES

1. The ultimate objective of students of the sociology of the family is the explanation of variability in family *behavior*. From the standpoint of a sociological theory of the family, this premise asserts, investigations of familial role expectations as dependent variable, or studies which relate familial role expectations as independent variable to the structure of the self as dependent variable, are incomplete. While such concerns are certainly legitimate from the standpoint of numerous theoretical concerns, and while research on such problems as the impact of family on self is pat-

93

ently important, sociological students of the family must require their theories to specify the consequences of familial role expectations or of self for familial role performance.

These assertions should not be misread. It is not necessary, to make them, to assume that any discrete set of variables can account for all the variability in family behavior. Nor is it necessary, having recognized that any discrete set of variables will always leave a residue of unexplained variance, for the sociological student of the family to invoke theoretically extraneous variables—genetic, biological, psychological, economic, etc.—in a search for "complete" explanations of family behavior.

2. The generalized symbolic interactionist model (to use a word that may not be technically appropriate) has it that:

a. Behavior is premised on a "named" or classified world, and "names" or class terms carry meaning consisting of shared behavioral expectations emergent from the process of social interaction.[3] One learns, in interaction with others, both how to classify objects with which he comes into contact and how he is expected to behave towards these objects. The meaning of the classifications one constructs resides in the shared expectations for behavior the classifications invoke;

b. Among these class terms are symbols used to designate the stable, morphological components of social structure usually termed "positions," and it is these positions which carry the shared behavioral expectations conventionally labeled "roles";

c. Actors within this social structure name one another, in the sense that they recognize each other as occupants of positions, and in naming one another invoke expectations with respect to one another's behavior;

d. Actors within this social structure name themselves as well—it is to these reflexively applied positional designations that the concept of self is typically intended to refer—and in so doing they create internalized expectations with respect to their own behavior;

e. Social behavior is not, however, given by these expectations (either reflected or internalized). That behavior is the product of a role-making process,[4] initiated by expectations but developing through a subtle, tentative, probing interchange among actors in given situations that continually reshapes both the form and the content of the interaction.

3. Empirical work which has sought to make use of the model generalized above has suffered from a failure to go beyond Mead's formulation of the self as "that which is an object to itself." It is essential to treat the self as a complex, differentiated unit rather than as an undifferentiated unity.[5]

4. Empirical work has also suffered from the failure to take sufficiently seriously the idea that the self is an organized structure.

NECESSARY REFINEMENTS IN CONCEPTUAL FRAMEWORK

It has been asserted that the self must be seen as complex and differentiated if one is to advance the understanding of familial role performance, i.e., that the self must be conceptualized as constructed from diverse "parts." The parts which can be taken to comprise the self are discrete identities. One can speak meaningfully of familial identities (e.g., father, husband, in-law), political identities (e.g., senator, candidate, ward captain), occupational identities (e.g., doctor, salesman, employee), and so on, all of which are incorporated into the self as that which is an object to itself.

The meaning, and in degree the implications, of the concept of identity are well stated by Gregory Stone, whose writing presages in part the argument of this paper:

> When one has an identity, he is situated—that is, cast in the shape of a social object by the acknowledgement of his participation or membership in social relations. One's identity is established when others *place* him as a social object by assigning him the same words of identity that he appropriates for himself or *announces*. . . .
>
> Such a conception of identity is, indeed, close to Mead's conception of the 'me,' the self as object related to and differentiated from others. . . . Identity is intrinsically associated with all the joinings and departures of social life. To have an identity is to join with some and depart from others, to enter and leave social relations at once.[6]

Identities, in this usage, exist insofar as persons are participants in structured social relationships. They require that positional designations be attributed to and accepted by participants in the relationships.

It has also been asserted that the self must be viewed as an organized structure. The self may be said to be organized in at least two relevant senses. One may postulate that the discrete identities which comprise the self exist in a hierarchy of salience, such that other things equal one can expect behavioral products to the degree that a given identity ranks high in this hierarchy. The concept of identity salience may be defined as the probability, for a given person, of a given identity being invoked in a variety of situations. Alternatively, this concept may be defined as the differential probability among persons of a given identity being invoked in a given situation. With either formulation, a rank order of probabilities defines the hierarchy of salience.

A caveat must be added at this point. The invocation of an identity—i.e., the perception of an identity as relevant to a particular interaction—may be purely situational: a baby crying in the middle of the night does not ordinarily invoke a political identity in a parent. To the degree that situations are structurally isolated, the hierarchy of salience in which identities exist within the self is irrelevant to the prediction of behavior. It may be, however, that saliency interacts with situations to affect the threshold of invocation of an identity: it is not inconceivable that for some a political identity is so salient that it is indeed invoked in the "baby crying in the middle of the night" situation. In fact, it is implicit in the definition of salience previously given that this concept is best operationalized in precisely these terms.

In general, the hierarchy of salience becomes important in the prediction of behavior in the event of what may be called structural overlap, that is, when analytically distinct sets of relationships are mutually contingent at some point in time and so do invoke concurrently different identities. More often than not, perhaps, one faces situations in which more than one of his identities is pertinent: the interaction of one man with another who is both his employee and his brother-in-law can serve as an example. Concurrently invoked, different identities do not necessarily call for incompatible behavior. But sometimes they do, and it is under this circumstance that the hierarchy of salience becomes potentially an important predictor of behavior. Thus, to follow through with the foregoing example, there is presumably a much higher probability that the familial identity will be invoked in a "typical" representative of a strong kinship society such as Italy than in a "typical" representative of American society, and, therefore, there is presumably a much higher probability that conflicting behavioral expectations will be resolved in the direction of meeting kinship-linked expectations in the Italian case.

The self may be said to be an organized structure in a second sense. The self is, by definition, a set of responses of an organism to itself. These responses are differentiated, as well as in the manner noted above, along cognitive—conative—cathectic lines. Although the meaning of any of these may be said to reside in interpersonal behavior, the assumption here is that it will make a difference with respect to behavior whether the organism responds to itself by, in effect, beginning an assertion with the stem "I am," "I want," or "I feel." Presumably, these modalities of response to oneself are not randomly related to one another; it is a reasonable assumption that the "I want" and "I feel" modalities of reflexive response to oneself are, for a given person, linked in a systematic way to the variety of "I ams" of the self. Thus, some identities can be expected to be linked with strong feelings, and some can be expected to be perceived as closely connected with the achievement of wants.[7]

One more concept, namely, that of commitment, needs to be introduced, for it will play a central part in the development of the theory that follows. Commitment, here, is used in the sense Kornhauser[8] used this term in analyzing the retention and loss of membership in political groups; it refers to the relations to others formed as a function of acting on choices, such that changing the pattern of choice requires changing the pattern of relationships to others. To the degree that one's relationships to specific others depend on one's being a particular kind of person, one is committed to being that kind of person. In this sense, commitment is measured by the "costs" of giving up meaningful relations to others should alternative courses of action be pursued.

Three points concerning the concept of commitment need to be noted. First, while the writer will be concerned in what follows to hypothesize relationships among identity salience, the modalities of response to oneself outlined above, and commitment, the latter concept is analytically independent of the former. That is, relations formed with others as a function of choices are not the same thing as the probability that a given identity will be invoked in a situation, nor as cognitive, cathectic, or conative responses to self.[9]

Second, commitments are premised on identities insofar as entering into relationships requires the attribution and acceptance of po-

sitional designations. A man's relationships to his wife, her relatives, her friends, the member[s] of the couples' bridge club, etc., presuppose his identity as husband.

Third, there appear to be two dimensions of commitment: the sheer number of relationships entered by virtue of an identity, or extensivity of commitment; and the depth of the relationships entered by virtue of an identity, or intensivity of commitment. In what follows, commitment will be used to refer to both dimensions indifferently. Proceeding in this manner obviously ignores a number of significant theoretical and empirical problems. Are there systematic individual or group differences in preference for and importance attached to extensive versus intensive relationships? Is there a functional equation relating these two dimensions of commitment? Are these two dimensions functionally equivalent in their impact on identity salience and role performance? Such questions deserve answers which cannot at this time be forthcoming.

A RESEARCH PROBLEM AND A SET OF HYPOTHESES

What has been said to this point can serve as the basis on which to sketch a general research problem that seems to be strategic to advances in knowledge in the sociology of the family.

The empirical problem is set by the kind of commonplace observations that lay behind the abstractly stated questions with which this paper began. One man takes into consideration the probable impact of a new physical and social environment on his family in the process of arriving at a job-relocation decision. Another does not. A Mayor Wagner decides not to pursue another term of office in New York, apparently on the grounds that to do so would impair his relationships with his sons. That some reacted to his announcement with incredulity indicates that, for some, a family identity does not have the salience which would make that rationale a sufficient motivator of behavior rather than a convenient rationalization. For some, a trip to the library with the children takes precedence over a trip to the golf course; for others, the priorities are reversed. For some, parenthood is the occasion for a restructuring of activities which make the home the center of life; for others, change on the occasion of parenthood is minimal. The research problem, obviously, is to account for such variability in behavior as is exhibited in these observations.

A set of hypotheses giving promise of doing this job can be proposed. The most general hypothesis is the familiar one to the effect that the self mediates the relationship between role expectations and role performance. This general hypothesis, apart from being almost an article of faith of symbolic interaction theory, is (a) true and (b) not very powerful. That is, the evidence supports the validity of this proposition, but also leaves much to be desired by way of accounting for the variability of role performance. If the foregoing conceptual analysis is reasonable, this state of affairs is a function of widespread failure to see the self as composed of differentiated identities and to recognize that these differentiated identities exist in a hierarchy of salience. Given this specification of the concept of self, what is required in order to improve the predictive power of self theory are (1) hypotheses which can account for the position of given identities in the salience hierarchy and (2) hypotheses which tie identity salience to role performance.

The previous discussion suggests the following hypotheses with regard to, first, the position of an identity in the salience hierarchy and secondly, the relationship between identity salience and role performance. These are not intended to be exhaustive; undoubtedly other major as well as derivative hypotheses could be formulated. While it may be too much to say that these hypotheses issue deductively from the previously sketched theoretical model, together with the suggested modifications of it, they do in fact relate strongly to these.

Hypothesis 1. The greater the commitment premised on an identity, i.e., the more exten-

sive and/or intensive the network of relationships into which one enters by virtue of a given identity, the higher will be that identity in the salience hierarchy.

1a. The greater the commitment premised on an identity, the more that identity will be invested with a positive cathectic response; and the more a given identity is invested with a positive cathectic response, the higher will be that identity in the salience hierarchy.[10]

1b. The greater the commitment premised on identity, the more that identity will be perceived as instrumental to NwantsN of the person; and the more a given identity is perceived as instrumental to "wants," the higher will be that identity in the salience hierarchy.

Hypothesis 2. The more a given network of commitment is premised on a particular identity as against other identities which may enter into that network of commitment, the higher will be that identity in the salience hierarchy.

Hypothesis 3. The more congruent the role expectations of those to whom one is committed by virtue of a given identity, the higher will be that identity in the salience hierarchy.

Hypothesis 4. The larger the number of persons included in the network of commitment premised on a given identity for whom that identity is high in their own salience hierarchies, the higher will be that identity in the salience hierarchy.

These hypotheses, relating salience to commitment, elaborate a fundamental theme of symbolic interaction theory, namely, that it is out of social relationships that the self emerges. Each develops from the assumption that the investment one has in his network of social relationships reinforces the significance to the person of the identity on which this network is based.[11]

The first hypothesis above is a straightforward consequent of this assumption. Hypotheses 1a and 1b suggest the bases of the linkage between commitment and the position of an identity in the salience hierarchy. The evidence is quite clear that man's behavior is vitally affected by affect and by wants. Theoretical ideas deriving from George Herbert Mead have been properly criticized for their almost total emphasis on the cognitive components of man's experience. These two hypotheses seek to take into account these other ways in which men characteristically respond to themselves, but to do so in a manner retaining the basic insights of Mead.

Cathectic and conative responses can be expected to have a cumulative impact on the position of an identity in the salience hierarchy. That is to say, the combination of a strongly positive cathectic and a highly valued "want" response presumably would be especially potent in fixing an identity at a high salience level. There appears to be no basis at the present time on which to estimate the differential impact on identity salience of the strong cathectic-low want versus the weak cathectic-high want combinations, and it is therefore preferable not to present any hypothesis with respect to this differential impact.

Hypothesis 2 refers to the situation in which multiple identities are involved in a given network of commitment. For example, one may relate to members of a couples' bridge club not only through one's identity as husband but also through one's identity as friend. The hypothesis asserts that the more these relationships require the husband rather than the friend identity, the higher will be the husband identity in the salience hierarchy. The operational test of such a ranking is whether or not the specified relationships are more likely to continue given the disappearance of the former versus the latter identity.

When others to whom an actor relates by virtue of an identity hold role expectations which are congruent, their behaviors vis-à-vis that actor are likely to be consistent. Consistent behaviors are likely to be cumulatively reinforcing to an identity through providing the actor opportunity to respond consistently in terms of that identity.[12] Conversely, when such role expectations are incongruent, the actor's behavior in terms of an identity is likely to be confused. Such confusion is likely to result in a lowering of the identity in the salience hierarchy. While it may be that people can live with

more dissonance than is implied by cognitive dissonance theory, the reasoning incorporated into hypothesis 3 assumes that dissonant expectations from within the same commitment network will motivate a reduced investment in a given identity.

If an identity as husband is important to all other members of the couples' bridge club, rather than being important to only a few others, that identity as husband is likely to be important to a given member. Hypothesis 4 generalizes this example and assumes the operation of the mechanisms suggested above in support of the preceding hypothesis.

The writer turns now to the relationship between identity salience and role performance.

Hypothesis 5. The higher an identity in the salience hierarchy, the higher the probability of role performance consistent with the role expectations attached to that identity.

This hypothesis makes the important assumption that identities are themselves motivators of human action,[13] an assumption built into the assertion that class terms carry meaning consisting of shared behavioral expectations. But, clearly, motivation to perform in keeping with an identity is insufficient to produce that performance: the structure of opportunities is relevant as well. As stated, hypothesis 5 also assumes the equivalence among persons, or for a given person over situations, of opportunity. In this light, the next two hypotheses are perhaps especially interesting. They are interesting, as well, because they translate into researchable terms the assumption of symbolic interaction theory that human beings are actors as well as reactors.[14]

Hypothesis 6. The higher an identity in the salience hierarchy, the higher the probability that a person will perceive a given situation as an opportunity to perform in terms of that identity.

Hypothesis 7. The higher an identity in the salience hierarchy, the higher the probability that a person will seek out opportunities to perform in terms of that identity.

The hypotheses thus far stated are in static form, but each can be converted into a statement relating changes in component parts (e.g., increases in the commitment premised on an identity will result in the movement upward in the salience hierarchy of that identity). They then can be used in the attempt to account for shifts in the position of an identity in the salience hierarchy or to account for shifts in role performance variables. Rather than running through the exercise of altering the form of hypotheses already reviewed, two having specifically to do with identity change can be stated.

Hypothesis 8. External events which cut existing commitments ease the adoption of a novel identity.[15]

Hypothesis 9. The more the perceived consequences of a projected identity change are in the direction of reinforcing valued commitments, the less the resistance to that change. Conversely, the more the perceived consequences of a projected identity change are in the direction of impairing valued commitments, the greater the resistance to that change.

A SPECIFIC RESEARCH SUGGESTION

All of the hypotheses that have been stated have been formulated at a fairly high level of abstraction in order to suggest that they may have explanatory power over a wide variety of family (and other) situations. It may be useful, however, to conclude by suggesting a concrete setting within which these hypotheses could be tested.

A number of years ago, a psychologist remarked to the writer that the major difference between the psychologist and the sociologist conducting experiments was that the sociologist would let things happen naturally while the psychologist was not afraid to personally manipulate variables in strength. The implicit argument was that sound experimental procedure requires that variables be investigated throughout their range of variation. The concrete setting for research to be suggested has to do with the occasion of first pregnancy. This setting was chosen not to argue that sociologists ought to emulate the psychologists' orientation to experimentation, but rather to note that it can provide certain advantages deriving from an experimental research model.

First of all, the evidence is that, for both males and females, reactions to first pregnancies are variable to an extreme. Thus, the central variable of concern in this paper—position of an identity in a hierarchy of salience—is likely in this situation to be found distributed widely over the salience hierarchies of subjects.

Secondly, the situation of first pregnancy is likely to provide maximal variation in other variables incorporated into the hypotheses. For example, it can be expected that there will be sizable proportions of parents-to-be whose commitments involve them with persons whose identity as parent is highly salient, as well as sizable proportions whose commitments do not so involve them (this is a function of the age at which persons typically meet the first pregnancy situation).

Third, this situation not only involves an existent familial identity subject to change—namely, that of husband or wife—but also a new familial identity—namely, that of father or mother.

Fourth, a first pregnancy is obviously a first exposure event. While one certainly can expect differential reaction as a function of differences in anticipatory socialization, it seems a great advantage to be dealing with an event which one is sure is occurring for the first time.

Fifth, the drama of first pregnancy and ultimate initial parenthood takes place in a relatively restricted period of time and makes feasible a longitudinal study whose time bounds are reasonable.

Sixth, relevant populations are relatively easily enumerable and accessible, as well as being sufficiently large.

Seventh, relevant controls exist to implement an experimental design, for example, unmarried persons of comparable age or married couples with comparable length of marriage who are not in the first pregnancy situation.

A final remark: no claim is made that research into the questions raised in this paper, utilizing the framework of symbolic interactionism, will have revolutionary impact on the state of knowledge in the sociology of the family—significant impact, yes; revolutionary impact, no. The field is much too complex for simplistic faiths.

Endnotes

1. Sheldon Stryker, "The Interactional and Situational Approaches," in *Handbook on Marriage and the Family*, ed. by Harold T. Christensen, Chicago: Rand McNally, 1964, pp. 125–170.

2. *Ibid.*, p. 163.

3. This view of class terms, which emphasizes the function of symbols in arousing expectancies, has received support in recent years in the work of psychologists interested in psycholinguistics and in the processes of thinking. See, for example, Rodger W. Brown, *Words and Things*, Glencoe, Illinois: Free Press, 1958; and J. S. Bruner, J. J. Goodnow, and G. A. Austin, *A Study of Thinking*, New York: Wiley, 1956.

4. Ralph H. Turner, "Role-taking: Process versus Conformity," in *Human Behavior and Social Processes*, ed. by Arnold M. Rose, Boston: Houghton Mifflin, 1962, pp. 20–40.

5. This point of view is taken in a recent work, appearing after this paper was initially prepared, which in many respects parallels the development contained herein. See George J. McCall and J. L. Simmons, *Identities and Interaction*, New York: Free Press, 1966.

6. Gregory P. Stone, "Appearance and the Self," in *Human Behavior and Social Processes*, ed. by Arnold M. Rose, Boston: Houghton Mifflin, 1962, pp. 93–94. For a closely related formulation of the concept of identity, see McCall and Simmons, *op. cit.* See also Anselm Strauss, *Mirror and Masks*, Glencoe, Illinois: Free Press, 1959.

7. Just as identity is related to the "me" aspect of Mead's concept of the self, the conative and cathectic modalities of response are related to the "I" aspect. See George Herbert Mead, *Mind, Self and Society*, Chicago: University of Chicago Press, 1934.

8. William Kornhauser, "Social Bases of Political Commitment: A Study of Liberals and Radicals," in *Human Behavior and Social Processes*, ed. by Arnold M. Rose, Boston: Houghton Mifflin, 1962, pp. 321–329. For somewhat different, but nevertheless related, usages of the concept of commitment, see McCall and Simmons, *op. cit.*; Howard Becker, "Notes on the Concept of Commitment," *American Journal of Sociology*, 66 (July, 1960), pp. 32–40.

9. Identities are, of course, cognitive categories in terms of which individuals respond to themselves. But not all cognitive categories are identities. There is, that is, a difference between responding to oneself by saying, "I am a sociologist," and by saying, "I am honest." The former announces an identity; the latter does not.

10. The writer is aware that one may hate his strongest attachments, i.e., that negative affect may be linked to commitments. Empirically, one supposes, this linkage is comparatively rare: the probability of commitments generating positive rather than negative affect is high. Hypothesis 1a assumes this high probability. This hypothesis may be seen as a variant of Homan's hypothesis to the effect that high rates of interaction lead to high rates of liking. See George C. Homans, *The Human Group*, New York: Harcourt, Brace, 1950. For those cases in which commitment generates negative affect, the writer would argue that hypothesis 1a remains as stated. However, the link between salience and role performance, as expressed in hypothesis 5, would have to be altered.

11. Each of these hypotheses, it should be noted, is in effect a double hypothesis insofar as the concept of commitment has the double referent of extensivity and intensivity.

12. Alexander and Simpson explicitly note a convergence among a variety of theories which is implicit throughout this paper, but nowhere more pointed than in connection with this discussion of hypothesis 3. In their words, "Theories of balance, congruity, dissonance, equity, expectation, and justice are based on the same general postulates and are headed in the same direction. . . . [T]here is sufficient similarity of these approaches to justify reference to them all as balance theories. . . . The basic postulate of the balance theories is that there exists a need for the socialized human

being to establish and maintain stable and consistent orientations toward the self, other persons, and the non-person environment.... In an unorderly flux the consequences of action would be indeterminate; it can be assumed that such lack of predictability is psychologically stressful and that the individual will engage in behaviors oriented toward maintaining a state of stability and consistency." C. Norman Alexander, Jr. and Richard L. Simpson, "Balance Theory and Distributive Justice," *Sociological Inquiry*, 34 (Spring, 1964), p. 183.

13.   Nelson N. Foote, "Identification as the Basis for a Theory of Motivation," *American Sociological Review*, 16 (February, 1951), pp. 14–21.

14. For a more detailed statement of this assumption, as well as of other assumptions of the theory, see Sheldon Stryker, *op. cit.*, pp. 134–135.

15. There is supporting evidence for this hypothesis in Sanford M. Dornbusch, "The Military Academy as an Assimilating Institution," *Social Forces*, 33 (May, 1955), pp. 316–321.

Chapter Five
Conflict Theory

Deborah and Jackie live together with their mother and children in Chicago. Deborah, the older sister, works as a licensed practical nurse on the evening shift at a hospital downtown. Her two boys stay with their grandmother when they get home from school. They do not see their father. Jackie, the younger sister, works the day shift at the local bakery and occasionally picks up an extra shift on the weekends. Her daughter goes to the day care center down the street from her house and spends the weekends with her father.

Deborah and Jackie were out shopping. They wanted to buy some new clothes for their children's Christmas but didn't have the money to shop at the fanciest clothing shops in the mall. In fact, they had driven 40 miles out of town to an outlet mall to find some bargain shops. As Jackie drove, she lamented their financial state. "I wish that, for once, I could just go to the mall and tell all those snooty salespeople to wrap up anything I want for the kids and us. I know that the kids feel badly because they don't have the 'coolest' clothes. And I'd love to buy Mom a cashmere sweater. Just think—I could tell them to wrap it up and deliver it! Wouldn't that be great?"

Deborah replied, "Yeah, Sis, it would be, but you know it isn't ever going to happen. We were born poor and we're always going to be poor. All we can hope for is that our children will go to college somehow and maybe get good jobs and not have to always worry about money."

Deborah and Jackie had a fun afternoon shopping together but stayed too late and were driving home too fast. A police officer pulled them over for speeding, and despite their pleas, they received a ticket for $150. On the drive home, Jackie and Deborah began to argue with each other. Jackie lamented, "We went all that way to save money and look what happened! We don't have the money to pay for this! Why does this stuff always happen to us? Now we're going to have to work overtime just to pay for this speeding ticket."

"What do you mean we? You were the one who was driving! How can you be so irresponsible? You should have been watching the speed more carefully!" replied Deborah.

"I wasn't driving that fast. Did you see that Mercedes pass us? He was doing 85 miles per hour and he didn't get pulled over. I bet if we'd been driving a BMW, we wouldn't have been stopped either!" Jackie continued. "You know I can't afford to pay this ticket. How am I supposed to get overtime when they are laying off people? I thought I could count on you to help cover this—after all, you were in the car with me!"

"This is just the kind of thing you always do. You get yourself in over your head and you always expect me to bail you out. I'm tired of it. This was clearly your fault, and this time you are on your own!" Deborah cried.

"You are the worst sister in the world!" Jackie shouted.

By this time, both sisters were emotionally overwrought and drove home the rest of the way in silence.

HISTORY

Conflict theory is rooted in sociology, where it is used to explain differences between classes within society and the competition for scarce resources, including economic wealth, political power, and social status. In some earlier (as well as some current) societies, people were born into their roles in society as defined by their social class (such as slave, serf, working class, or aristocracy), and remained there for life. Some social theorists believed that, if conditions were right, eventually those who were in the lower classes could move into the higher classes, but this would happen only as the result of conflict.

The famous social philosopher Karl Marx (1818–1883) is sometimes referred to as the father of conflict theory. His thinking was profoundly influenced by an earlier German philosopher, Georg Wihelm Friedrich Hegel (1770–1831). Hegel's theory about the evolution of ideas, known as the Hegelian dialectic, postulated that an accepted idea (the thesis) would eventually be challenged by its opposite (the antithesis) until a stable middle ground was reached that combined aspects of both extremes (the synthesis). The synthesis would then become the new thesis, and the whole pendulum process would begin again (Russell 1945/1972).

Whereas Hegel's philosophy focused on the conflict of ideas, Marx focused on much more pragmatic issues—the economic well-being of individuals in society. Marx took Hegel's approach and applied it to a theory of social and economic change. He studied social change throughout history and proposed that such change followed a dialectical form. He maintained that ruling classes in a society (the ones controlling the economic wealth and the political power) were always overthrown by the oppressed classes through conflict, after which they in turn became the ruling classes, which were likewise eventually overthrown by those classes that they had oppressed (Russell 1945/1972; Turner 1998).

Marx envisioned a time when the laborers (the oppressed and exploited proletariat) would unite their forces and overthrow the capitalist landowners and industrialists (the oppressive and exploitative bourgeoisie) and create a world where everyone had equal access to resources. This was the basic idea in his now famous *Communist Manifesto* (1848). But before a communistic society could prevail, there had to be many years of class conflict, in which the focus was on how the distribution of scarce resources played out and on whom ultimately maintained the power in those communities.

Whereas Marx was a major proponent of conflict theory, his focus was primarily on the economic impact of the theory. Later sociologists focused on its interpersonal uses, most notably Max Weber, Georg Simmel, and Lewis Coser. Simmel (translated 1998) added interpersonal dimensions of love, ownership, valuing, and jealousy to the perspective of conflict

in families, noting that we seem to move from one extreme to the other in interpersonal relationships but find a synthesis in our need for loving. Human interaction has, within its structure, components of inequality (Sprey 1999). Coser said that conflict can solidify and unify a group, as well as promote cohesion and adaptability within groups. This is because dealing with conflict brings flexibility to the system's structure and increases its capacity to change (Turner 1998).

Although these sociologists were important in helping us understand the uses of conflict in society at large, one theorist has been most important in helping define the need for understanding conflict in families—Jetse Sprey. Sprey (1969, 1979, 1999) wrote that conflict was a part of every relationship, including those in families. He outlined how conflict may be understood in families by specifying the components of the theory, by helping researchers to generate ways in which to classify conflict in families, and by distinguishing conflict in families as unique from other types of conflict.

BASIC ASSUMPTIONS

Conflict theory focuses on the explanation of orderly as well as disorderly societal processes. In the context of marriage and family studies, it explains "how and why stability and instability occur, and under what conditions harmonious interpersonal bonds are possible" (Sprey 1979, 130). All humans engage in conflict situations, and understanding the management of conflict will lead to an understanding of stability and instability in marriage and family.

The nature of humans is that they are self-oriented. Conflict theorists make certain assumptions about human nature. They assume that the individual is self-oriented or focused on self-interests. They believe that individuals are symbol-producing, which means that they are able to ascribe value to things (such as a corner office, shares of a piece of cake, or praise from parents). This ability sets up the system of scarce resources for which individuals are in competition. Conflict theorists also believe that humans have unlimited potential to hope, which means they have unlimited potential to desire power, prestige, and privilege, thereby setting up relationships with other humans as real or potential competitors (Farrington and Chertok 1993; Sprey 1979).

Societies operate under a perpetual scarcity of resources. Conflict theorists also make certain assumptions about the nature of society. Societies represent organized systems for species survival. They operate under a perpetual scarcity of resources, and this leads to perpetual confrontations. According to conflict theorists, such confrontations keep societies in a state of flux and lead to upheaval, social change, and growth. Like structural functional theorists, conflict theorists recognize that inequality is an inevitable aspect of most relationships; unlike other theorists, conflict theorists try to manage the inequality rather than resolve it.

Group dynamics are different in families than in other groups. When applying conflict theory, one must recognize the differences between groups and families. The demand for resources varies between groups and families, since some crises can drain family resources. For example, an illness in a family can cause a family to stress its resources to the maximum, whereas an illness in a group will generally not. Membership in a group is voluntary, whereas membership in a family is generally involuntary. If membership in a voluntary group becomes too intense or too competitive, a member may choose to leave. However, it is more difficult to leave a family than it is to leave a group. Relationships in a family are by definition more intense because they are closer in proximity and generally have a longer history. Also, dissolution of a family is more threatening than having a group break up. It takes two to form a group but only one to dissolve it. Thus, the person with the least interest has the most power. The ability to dissolve a family group is great power indeed, so families generally tolerate a higher degree of conflict than groups (Sprey 1979).

The power differentials are also different in voluntary groups. Groups often consist of just one sex, so there is more equality of status. Also, group power remains rather static for the life of the group, but power changes over the life cycle of the family. As children age, they gain more power; as adults age, they lose power. These changes keep the family dynamics of power continuously fluid (Farrington and Chertok 1993).

Conflict is a confrontation over control of scarce resources. Conflict is categorized as either internal or external. Internal conflict is conflict originating from inside the social system (be it between individuals, families, or societies). In closely knit groups, members may suppress conflict. Negative emotions may accumulate and intensify, a phenomenon which social psychologists refer to as "gunny-sacking." When the conflict finally boils over, it is intensified. Not only is the conflict a problem, but it is compounded and magnified by the expression of conflict. Thus, one outcome of conflict theory is the study of conflict management.

External conflict is conflict originating from outside the social system. One cannot deal with internal conflict while also using energy to fight external conflict. An example might be the conflict between political parties over tax policies (an internal conflict with respect to the country). But if war is declared on a foreign aggressor, the parties put aside their differences to concentrate on dealing with a war against another country (an external conflict). Likewise, a couple may be going through a difficult time and feeling as though their marriage is "on the rocks." Then they learn that their young child has a life-threatening illness. They bond together for the sake of the child to fight the aggressor—in this case, the disease.

One of the advantages of conflict is that, in the context of discussions, arguments, negotiations, and management, people come to new understandings of one another. This is often the case in families, when couples or parents and their children learn about each other in the course of an argument. Thus, conflict can produce new or different values and revitalize existing norms. For example, in a disagreement with her 14-year-old daughter, a mother might learn that the curfew of 9 p.m. every night was too early to allow her to see even the early movie with her boyfriend. The mother, while still maintaining strict control over her adolescent daughter's dating habits, might be willing to negotiate a 10 p.m. curfew for weekends while maintaining the 9 p.m. deadline for all other nights. The negotiation maintains social structure in that the mother maintains the power, although neither mother nor daughter is truly satisfied with the outcome (the mother probably doesn't want her daughter to date at all and the daughter probably doesn't want a curfew at all), but the social order is maintained. Furthermore, the conflict allows for growth to occur in the relationship between the daughter and mother as they both learn something about power, negotiation, family relationships, growing up, letting go, and communication skills.

Conflict can be classified. There are two major ways of classifying conflict in families—from a macro-social perspective and from a micro-social perspective. Depending on one's educational orientation (more sociological or more developmental), the questions and focus (and related research) are different. Conflict theory is one of the few theories that can be used in both ways, although it does make the theory a bit more complex to fully understand.

As noted above, the conflict perspective allows us to see society as a place that generates and perpetuates inequality, which leads to conflict and change. Unlike structure-functionalists, who see society as basically finding its own equilibrium, conflict theorists see that, as a society, we ascribe meaning and value, and stratify people into unequal roles, with varying levels of power and access to resources (Farrington and Chertok 1993). When we apply the theory to families, we analyze how families are classified based on their access to scarce resources and determine who has the power to

maintain those value structures. For example, conflict theorists analyze the unequal distribution of power and social status based on social class, gender, race, ethnicity, and education.

From the macro-social perspective, conflict theorists look at issues of conflict between classes of people who have privilege or dominance and those who are disadvantaged—the "haves" vs. the "have-nots"—(e.g., men vs. women, rich vs. poor, whites vs. blacks, those with access to health care vs. those without, employed vs. unemployed, heterosexuals vs. gays and lesbians, adults vs. children, married vs. single, married vs. divorced). This is not to imply that any one individual has more or less than another but rather that a group as a whole has more privilege than another group, and those privileges impact the families and their opportunities and choices. Conflict theorists are concerned with how people manage the discrimination and stigma they face, how they negotiate their inequality in the face of unyielding privilege, and how society creates a shared value about what people "deserve" (Seccombe 1999, 2000).

A conflict theorist who studies families from this perspective might, for example, study how adoption placements are made. Consider the various levels of privilege and disadvantage of the following five potential parents for an adoption placement: a White, married, upper-income heterosexual couple; a White, middle-class lesbian couple; a Hispanic, single, upper-class gay man; a single, upper-class Black woman; and a White, previously divorced, lower-class married couple. If you were the adoption caseworker, how would you rank order the placement, if all other factors were equal? What aspects of stratification enter into that decision? Generally, it is not the case that families fit neatly into stereotypical distinctions, and at times, values about certain families are based on myths rooted in class-consciousness.

From a macro-social perspective, conflict theorists help to deconstruct and analyze the ways in which our society ascribes values, and how this leads to inequality in the family. They focus on broad social issues such as economic inequities between men's and women's salaries, differing societal expectations of men's and women's responsibilities for child-rearing, and the acceptance of violence toward women and children. Family conflict theorists make the link between these broad social issues and family dynamics. In this way, feminist family theory and conflict theory share common goals.

From the micro-social perspective, conflict theorists look within the family system at the elements that can bring about conflict. Two major structural distinctions in families are gender and age. These structural differences bring about a distinct asymmetry in member resources and authority (Farrington and Chertok 1993). Regardless of the intent of the family members, society gives them access to resources in different ways. Adults have access to resources that children do not have (for example, money, freedom, and power); males frequently have access to resources that females do not have (for example, physical power, higher salaries, and opportunity). Additionally, children have an involuntary membership in families. In most other societal groups, membership is voluntary or the result of one's behavior. But children join families without any consultation. Thus, despite their perspective on membership, they must stay within the group and be governed by those in authority within the group.

The family life cycle also affects the long-term balance of resources within the family. Resource utilization and contribution may be different at various stages of the life cycle. In the earlier stages of the life cycle, parents have the power while children have little power. But in the later stages of the life cycle, the children typically gain power while the parents often lose power. This power shift may create conflict.

The interplay between the various macro-social influences on intrafamily dynamics can be seen in the example of how power shifts over the life course. In our culture, power tends

to decrease as one approaches old age. People are valued by their ability to contribute financially, and the elderly are thought of as being "past their prime" in this regard. In some other cultures, power tends to increase as one approaches old age. The wisdom and experience acquired over the years is regarded as a valuable resource, and so the elderly are held in high esteem, even if their physical abilities are not what they once were.

Marital conflict is the most dramatic form of conflict in families in many ways. First, whereas it takes two to make a relationship, it takes only one to end it. So, as in exchange theory, the person with the least interest in maintaining the relationship has the most power in the relationship. Secondly, marital conflict can be intense simply because it is dyadic. By definition, in a conflict there are differences, and in a dyad there are no other allies. Third, marital conflict can also be intense because the marital relationship can come to an end. In contrast, other family relationships are for life. Whenever the stakes are high, the level of conflict can easily escalate.

The outcomes in marital conflict can be assessed in two ways. The first method is to determine the patterns of "winning" and "losing"—that is, "keeping score." The idea of keeping score includes calculating the importance of the battles won and lost as well as the numbers of battles won and lost. The second method is to answer the question "What are the consequences for the relationship after conflict?" Conflict in a relationship ends either constructively or destructively. Marital dissolution affects the family as a whole but does not end it. At any given point, families are seen in the midst of their life course, at different points of conflict, growth, and change along the way (Sprey 1999).

Conflict has positive aspects. Conflict theorists believe that, ultimately, conflict is good, which is to say that the aftermath (the result) of conflict is beneficial. They argue that conflict is actually at the root of progress and change. (This is the legacy of Marx.) Conflict brings about the process of assimilation and compromise. It brings solidity and unity within groups and challenges the values and power we ascribe to those in other groups.

We learn as we change and grow in families, and the process of learning to negotiate, communicate, and manage conflict is a positive aspect of development in families. Indeed, in close relationships it is less important that there are conflicts than how the conflicts are handled (Mace and Mace 1980). Facing conflict can bring relationships to new levels of intimacy, relieve tension and resentment, help to identify problems, increase understanding, and bring about a renewed appreciation for the relationship (Farrington and Chertok 1993; Stinnett, Walters, and Stinnett 1991). Macrosocial conflict theorists believe that conflict theory promotes change by identifying the inequities in society and in families and by promoting a reflection and critique of the structures and values that perpetuate oppression.

PRIMARY TERMS AND CONCEPTS

COMPETITION

Sprey (1979) defined conflict as the "state of negative interdependence between the elements of a social system" (p. 134). When one member of the family or group gains, others lose. Groups that exist over time, such as families, have highly honed abilities to function within a system of competitiveness and to recognize their interdependence. They realize that they can take turns winning and losing and make decisions whereby members jointly win or lose, depending on their willingness to negotiate, cooperate, and seek compromise.

CONFLICT

Conflict is the direct confrontation between individuals or groups over scarce resources. It occurs when people use controversial means to obtain their goals or when they have incompatible goals, or some combination of these. Conflict implies a direct confrontation between opponents, whereas competition is more indirect and less personal. Conflict behavior can include physical force and litigation or the use of

other external powers to achieve one's goals. Conflict can end only when both parties reach a mutually recognized agreement (for example, one party gives up, a settlement is negotiated, or a peace treaty is signed). This does not, however, eliminate the underlying competitive basis.

CONFLICT MANAGEMENT

Conflict management involves dealing with the conflict while acknowledging the continued existence of the underlying competitive structure. It requires recognizing that there are (a) at least two competing perspectives, (b) that there are scarce resources, and (c) that each side should have an opportunity for access to those resources. Through negotiation and bargaining, conflict management can help competitors decide whether they wish to participate in a reciprocal sequence of access to resources (win-lose now, but lose-win later), a compromise in which both lose some resources, or a win-win option in which both sides jointly win. Conflict management does not negate the conflict, but seeks ways to keep it from escalating.

CONFLICT RESOLUTION

Conflict resolution refers to both the end state of conflict and the process of a given conflict's ending. Conflict resolution is different from conflict management, in which the conflict is maintained but negotiated into a stable state. In conflict resolution, the parties no longer see the issue as competition for scarce resources; there is no more conflict (on a particular matter), and resolution is the outcome. This may require redefining the situation so that conflict is no longer perceived as present.

Let's consider the difference between conflict management and conflict resolution by examining a rather common conflict in new relationships: money. A young couple begins their relationship with two separate bank accounts. Each pays half of the bills for housing, food, and other shared expenses; they spend the rest of their income on whatever they choose. But conflicts arise as their relationship begins to change and they want to buy a house, invest in expensive furniture, and save for their future. Who should be responsible for giving up their "fun" money for clothes, CDs, or going out? A conflict-managed solution might be for the couple to continue to pay one-half of the bills and for each to put some percentage of their extra funds into shared funds for future expenses (for example, a down payment for a house, furniture, and other items) and continue to maintain control of the rest of their money. A conflict resolution would have occurred if this couple decided to combine their incomes into a joint checking account and then set up saving funds for their long-term goals. All the bills are paid, but now they are jointly focusing on their goals together, rather than seeing themselves as competitors. Because of a shift in their perspectives, money is no longer seen as an individual resource to be hoarded but rather as a resource that has shared value for them as a couple.

Consensus

Consensus refers to a stable state in which society, groups, or families exist, sharing common awareness or knowledge of given issues, values, and norms. Consensus is reached when all parties "see things the same way." Unanimity, reached during decision-making and negotiation, is a special case of consensus that occurs when all parties agree to a given course of action or perception of a situation. Conflict management seeks consensus of the involved parties.

Negotiation and Bargaining

According to Sprey (1979), much conflict behavior is actually focused on negotiation and bargaining rather than fighting per se. These terms refer to the exchange process designed to reach a collective agreement on a disputed issue. Although the exchange may be heated or passionate as individuals and groups explain their positions, the underlying position is that they are trying to maintain access to their share of scarce resources and must, at least for the purposes of this exchange, per-

ceive those "on the other side" as adversaries who seek to take scarce resources away from them. At times negotiation and bargaining can be associated with hostility, but that is not always the case.

Power

Power refers to the ability to control the direction or course of action of others. It may apply to individuals or groups. It is a particularly salient concept in the analysis of families, since structures in families give authority to parents over children, and society has historically and culturally given power to men over women and boys over girls. Power can also be a function of personality and temperament, since some people tend to be more able to be persuasive (or overpowering interpersonally, regardless of age, gender, or status. Conflict theory looks at the degree to which interpersonal uses of power enter into the reciprocal interactions, identifying ways in which power can be used either positively, as a resource (for example, authority or privilege), or negatively (for example, to unduly control others).

Assertion and Aggression

Assertion is acting in a way that affirms one's rights and positions but does not necessarily do so at the expense of others. This is in contrast to aggression, which is a behavioral use of power to get others to behave to suit one's own advantage, even at the expense of others. Whereas assertion is most typically used in verbal statements, aggression can escalate to psychological and physical overpowering of others.

Threats and Promises

Threats are messages, not behaviors, that communicate the delivery of punishment if demands are not met at some point in the future; promises are messages, not behaviors, that communicate the delivery of something positive or rewarding if demands are met at some point in the future. These messages, verbal or otherwise, require shared understandings of symbols and meanings, making them sometimes more meaningful to groups and families who have had similar shared experiences and less meaningful to outsiders who do not see their inherent power. For example, a wife may threaten to ruin her husband's reputation if he leaves her or a husband may threaten to leave his wife poor and destitute if she leaves him. Either of these constitute threats, are coercive, and have a negative impact on the relationship by maintaining power, although no physical aggression is necessary.

COMMONS AREAS OF RESEARCH AND APPLICATION

CONFLICT MANAGEMENT

For those studying conflict theory, it is often difficult to separate the difference between having a conflict with someone from seeing the relationship in the context of conflict. We all know that being in conflict with someone is draining, frustrating, and often disheartening. In intimate relationships, it is difficult to figure out that there are winners or losers—both partners lose when conflict is destructive. Although it seems intuitive that conflicts need to be resolved for relationships to be stable, conflict theorists believe that growth and change are necessary to achieve true stability. Thus, conflict theorists reject the notion that conflict between partners should focus on resolution and instead believe that the focus should be on conflict management (Alberts 1990; Cahn 1990; Sprey 1979). The focus then turns to how couples and families communicate their needs and manage their individual desires as a group.

Power in the marital dyad has been studied extensively. Blood and Wolfe (1960) used the concept of power to understand decision making between husbands and wives. Goode (1964) defined a negative authority as someone who could prevent someone else from doing something and indicated that this hidden power was often found in the husband's role. Cromwell and Olson (1975) defined three types of power in intimate relationships: power bases, power processes, and power outcomes. *Power bases* are what we bring into the relationship, or our personal assets such as knowledge

or skills, that might serve as a reward for the other partner. *Power processes* refer to the techniques we use to gain control in relationships. These might include our abilities to be assertive, persuade, problem-solve, or coerce. *Power outcomes* refer to the final decision that is made. These elements of power have been used to evaluate many components of family dynamics and decision making.

Although other factors, such as money, education, and employment, contribute to the balance of power in social conflict, communication seems to be one of the key factors in interpersonal conflict (Richmond, McCroskey, and Roach 1997). One of the best-known researchers in the past 20 years in the field of couples' communication is John Gottman. Research by Gottman and his associates (1976; 1979; Gottman and Notarius 2000) has demonstrated the differences between the ways distressed and nondistressed couples communicate, illustrating that those who have negative communication patterns also have higher degrees of marital dissatisfaction and conflict. Furthermore, even highly distressed couples who reported high levels of conflict could be taught to manage their conflict in more positive and satisfactory ways, leading to more positive outcomes and higher marital satisfaction. Conflict management, then, is not a static skill but rather one that improves over time (Gottman 1979; Mackey and O'Brien 1998). The Gottman team's research was so precise that they could predict the outcome of a disagreement 96 percent of the time by the amount of criticism and negative emotion apparent at the beginning of the conflict (Gottman and Notarius 2000). Further, they found that the single most important predictor of divorce is that negative emotion escalates in a disagreement (for example, anger is met with contempt).

When coupled with the concept of power, negative communication takes on additional meaning. For example, some people have a higher tolerance for conflict than others and can use that power to escalate a conflict. Those partners would be classified as *demanders*, and their partners are often *avoiders*. Researchers used to see those labels simply, with the demanders having more power in the relationship than the avoiders. But more careful analysis of communication and power clarified several points. First, couples who avoided conflict entirely were less satisfied with their relationships than those who confronted one another (Gottman and Krokoff 1989). Second, avoidance was not always found to be a negative or deficient element in a relationship; it was found to be a beneficial skill used by couples to postpone discussions until they had the time and energy to discuss issues (Alberts 1990). Combining power dimensions with communication also is one of the emerging avenues of research on domestic violence and power discrepancies (Babcock, Waltz, Jacobson, and Gottman 1993).

Gender is also an important variable in the assessment of power in relationships. In fact, conflict theory forms the basis of some aspects of feminist theory, since it underscores the inevitability of conflict between men and women who have unequal access to resources in our society, which is often reflected in the power relationships of intimate relationships. This is discussed in much more detail in the chapter on feminist theory.

Divorce

Obviously not all conflicts can be managed, and divorce is the result when marital conflicts cannot be resolved. Researchers studying divorce have identified various processes that correspond to the divorce experience, including the emotional, economic, and societal divorce (Shehan and Kammeyer 1997). These processes represent resources that impact the couple differentially and will impact the divorce experience for each partner differently. For example, if one partner has more emotional power by having more emotional closeness to the children, then custody arrangements might be of most importance for that member in the divorce proceedings. If the couple has vast economic holdings and no children, then perhaps the economic settlement may be the most important. If the couple lives in a small community, then perhaps the social aspect of the divorce will carry the most weight. In the worst-case scenarios, these resource issues collide as one partner spreads rumors of drug use or child molestation in order to ensure child custody, or another partner declares bankruptcy in order not to have to pay child support to retaliate for the ex-spouse winning child custody. Obviously, in these conflict-habituated relationships, conflict did not lend itself to the positive growth and change that the theorists envisioned but still demonstrated the use of competition, power, and attempts to access scarce resources.

Developmental Changes

Of particular interest to developmental family scholars is how family dynamics change over the life course and how power differentials change as individuals age. For example, parents and adolescents are generally expected to have more conflict than parents and children because adolescents are seeking to gain power as individuals (Smetana and Gaines 1999; Steinberg 1989). Before their children reach adolescence, parents have all the power, but as adolescents age, they have increased power, through increased access to social and financial networks and, particularly for males, increased physical power. Yet, for most families, the conflicts are generally about minor things, such as daily activities (for example, chores, keeping rooms clean, choice of foods and snacks) (Dacey and Kenny 1997). The research on parent-adolescent conflict also reflects, though, that the frequency and magnitude of conflict in parent-adolescent relationships depend on whom one asks. When adolescents were surveyed, they reported that adolescence was not particularly conflicted (Gecas and Seff 1990), but parents reported adolescence as more turbulent (Pasley and Gecas 1984). Despite this difference in perspective, it is important to remember that conflict can serve to teach adolescents how to appropriately manage and negotiate conflict as they age and leave home.

The interplay between developmental issues and macro-level social issues can be seen in families as they struggle to negotiate the myriad of pressures that adolescents face. One level of conflict is found in the internal conflicts within emerging adolescents as they enter formal operational thought. For example, their cognitive ability to consider the real versus the ideal enables them to imagine idealized versions of themselves, their families, and their society. A second level of conflict exists as the adolescent seeks to individuate from the family while still maintaining some connection to the family. A third level of conflict exists as the adolescent seeks to connect with society at large but may not have the resources to do so. A fourth level of conflict exists if the adolescent can, in fact, connect with society but must "leave the family behind" to do so.

ABUSE

Conflict theory has frequently been used in family studies to clarify issues in family violence and abuse. The clear dynamics of conflict and power are a part of abusive relationships, and family scholars have analyzed these relationships to determine how and why abuse occurs, what the predetermining factors are, why people stay in abusive relationships, and what motivates people to leave such abusive relationships.

Typically, when we consider couple violence, we often consider physical strength as the power in the relationship, but conflict theorists broaden our perspective. The 1950s picture of domestic violence was of a strong man telling "his woman" what to do, and forcing her, if necessary, to bend to his will. The twenty-first century picture of domestic violence must take into account dating and courtship violence, cohabiting violence, violence perpetrated on men by women, same-sex relationship violence, and our increasing knowledge of the many forms of abuse (Johnson and Ferraro 2000; Miller and Knudsen 1999). "Wife abuse" is no longer a term sufficient to include the types of abuse found in intimate relationships today. Even such labels as partner abuse, child abuse, and

elder abuse are not sufficient. Within couples we must now distinguish between common couple violence, intimate terrorism, and violent resistance (Johnson and Ferraro 2000). Conflict theorists have helped us to analyze the complexity of the many forms of violence perpetrated in families.

One of the most important predictors of domestic violence is inequity in power (Sagrestano, Heavey, and Christensen 1999). Couples with more egalitarian distributions of power in their relationships are less likely to report violence than those with unequal power (Coleman and Straus 1986). Further, the severity of the abuse toward a female is dependent on the abuser's perception of her power (Claes and Rosenthal 1990). Power differentials can be seen in communication patterns, since verbal coercion can be a form of emotional abuse and a precursor to physical abuse (Babcock, Waltz, Jacobson, and Gottman 1993). Ironically, despite the hope that women would be empowered by educational and occupational achievement, violence against women is greater in couples when the woman's economic, educational, or occupational status is higher than the man's (Claes and Rosenthal 1990; Sagrestano, Heavey, and Christensen 1999).

CRITIQUE

One of the criticisms of conflict theory is that it analyzes families in destructive, negative terms—that is, conflict, power, and competition. Many family theorists prefer to focus on constructive and positive terms—cooperation, equity, and compassion. In other words, it simply does not fit our ideal of what relationships "ought" to be and therefore provides a less positive model for study.

Another criticism is that conflict theory, once it has described relationships in terms of its components of competition, power, and access to resources, does not propose how families can improve. Other theories focus on order and being able to make predictions about families. Conflict theory, by definition, does not engender a static view of families but rather an always-changing perspective. Thus, conflict theory does not lend itself to research or application outcomes that are immediately transferable to skill building. One exception is the work by Gottman, but his focus has been on conflicts at the interpersonal level and not at the social level.

Despite some scholars wishing that families were safe and happy places, conflict theory does, in fact, describe situations where families are not. Conflict theory raises our awareness of situations that families face regarding inequities in health care, in income, in access to education, and in equal opportunity (both legally and subtly). It encourages us to see families in their complex social systems. Additionally, conflict theory takes into account the ever-changing elements brought into families by development, by social events, by social pressures, and by internal and external forces.

APPLICATION

1. How is Deborah and Jackie's socioeconomic status illustrated by the case study? What elements of class conflict are apparent in their situation?

2. How might the elements of class conflict that are expressed by Deborah and Jackie earlier in the day be a part of the interpersonal conflict experienced between the sisters later in the day?

3. Find an example of each basic assumption in the case study.

4. There were examples of both conflict and competition in this case study. Identify some of them and discuss how socioeconomic, educational, gender, or power components combine to make the situations more complex.

5. Discuss your perspective on the conflict between Jackie and Deborah. Was it positive or negative? Was it good or bad for the relationship? How? In what ways?

6. Discuss some of the consequences of the conflict between the sisters on the family as a whole. What if the children were present during the argument? Would that have made a difference? What other ways, aside from observing parents arguing, do children learn how to manage conflicts in their lives?

7. In this family there are three generations living together. What additional issues of power and conflict management does this family face because of the extended family system?

8. In the chapter by Seccombe, is the conflict represented a macro-level or micro-level conflict? Can the level of conflict at one level (either macro or micro) create conflict at the other level for women in these circumstances? Give some examples.

9. Discuss some of the societal restrictions that inhibit full access to resources for women who are on welfare. What are the negative consequences of continued scarcity of resources from a conflict perspective? Are there any positive consequences?

SAMPLE READING

Seccombe, K. (1999). "Why Welfare?" In *So You Think I Drive a Cadillac? Welfare Recipients' Perspectives on the System and Its Reform.* Boston: Allyn and Bacon.

This chapter reveals some of the many reasons why women are on welfare, despite the stigma and negative perceptions of being on welfare. Drawing from interviews of 49 women, Seccombe analyzes their stories, outlining the social stratification and conflict issues in society and exhibiting how scarce resources are distributed in the United States.

References

Alberts, J. K. (1990). The use of humor in managing couples' conflict interactions. In D. D. Cahn (ed.), *Intimates in Conflict* (pp. 105–120). Hillsdale, NJ: Lawrence Erlbaum.

Babcock, J. C., Waltz, J., Jacobson, N. S., and Gottman, J. M. (1993). Power and violence: The relations between communication patterns, power discrepancies, and domestic violence. *Journal of Consulting and Clinical Psychology* 61: 40–50.

Blood, R. O., and Wolfe, D. M. (1960). *Husbands and Wives, the Dynamics of Married Living*. New York: Free Press.

Cahn, D. (1990). *Intimates in Conflict: A Communication Perspective*. Hillsdale, NJ: Lawrence Erlbaum.

Claes, J. A., and Rosenthal, D. M. (1990). Men who batter women: A study in power. *Journal of Family Violence* 5: 215–224.

Coleman, D. H., and Straus, M. A. (1986). Marital power, conflict, and violence in a nationally representative sample of American couples. *Violence and Victims* 1: 141–157.

Cromwell, R. E., and Olson, D. H. (1975). *Power in Families*. New York: Wiley.

Dacey, J., and Kenny, M. (1997). *Adolescent Development* (2nd ed.). Madison, WI: Brown and Benchmark.

Farrington, K., and Chertok, E. (1993). Social conflict theories of the family. In P. G. Boss, W. J. Doherty, R. LaRossa, W. R. Schumm, and S. K. Steinmetz (eds.), *Sourcebook of Family Theories and Methods: A Contextual Approach* (pp. 357–381). New York: Plenum.

Gecas, V., and Seff, M. A. (1990). Families and adolescents: A review of the 1980's. *Journal of Marriage and the Family* 52: 941–958.

Goode, W. (1964). *The Family*. Englewood Cliffs, NJ: Prentice Hall.

Gottman, J. M. (1979). *Marital Interaction: Experimental Investigations*. New York: Academic.

Gottman, J. M., and Krokoff, L. J. (1989). Marital interaction and satisfaction: A longitudinal view. *Journal of Consulting and Clinical Psychology* 57: 47–52.

Gottman, J. M., and Notarius, C. I. (2000). Decade review: Observing marital interaction. *Journal of Marriage and the Family* 62: 927–947.

Gottman, J., Notarius, C., Gonso, J., and Markman, H. (1976). *A Couple's Guide to Communication*. Champaign, IL: Research.

Johnson, M. P., and Ferraro, K. J. (2000). Research on domestic violence in the 1990's: Making distinctions. *Journal of Marriage and the Family* 62: 948–963.

Mace, D., and Mace, V. (1980). Enriching marriages: The foundation of family strength. In N. Stinnett, B. Chesser, J. DeFrain, and P. Knaub (eds.), *Family Strengths: Positive Models for Family Life* (pp. 89–110). Lincoln, NE: University of Nebraska.

Mackey, R. A., and O'Brien, B. A. (1998). Marital conflict management: Gender and ethnic differences. *Social Work* 43: 128–141.

Miller, J. L., and Knudsen, D. D. (1999). Family abuse and violence. In M. Sussman, S. K. Steinmetz, and G. W. Peterson (eds.), *Handbook of Marriage and the Family* (2nd ed., pp. 705–741). New York: Plenum.

Pasley, K., and Gecas, V. (1984). Stresses and satisfactions of the parental role. *Personnel and Guidance Journal* 2: 400–404.

Richmond, V. P., McCroskey, J. C., and Roach, K. D. (1997). Communication and decision-making styles, power base usage, and satisfaction in marital dyads. *Communication Quarterly* 45: 410–426.

Russell, B. (1945/1972). *A History of Western Philosophy*. New York: Simon and Schuster.

Sagrestano, L. M., Heavey, C. L., and Christensen, A. (1999). Perceived power and physical violence in marital conflict. *Journal of Social Issues* 55: 65–79.

Seccombe, K. (1999). *"So you think I drive a Cadillac?" Welfare Recipients' Perspectives on the System and Its Reform*. Boston: Allyn and Bacon.

———. (2000). Families in poverty in the 1990s: Trends, causes, consequences, and lessons learned. *Journal of Marriage and the Family* 62: 1094–1113.

Shehan, C. L., and Kammeyer, K. C. W. (1997). *Marriages and Families: Reflections of a Gendered Society*. Needham Heights, MA: Allyn and Bacon.

Simmel, G. (translated 1998). On the sociology of the family. *Theory, Culture and Sociology* 15: 283–293.

Singh, G. K., Matthews, T. J., Clark, A. C., Yannicos, T., and Smith, B. L. (1995). Annual Summary of births, marriages, divorces, and deaths: United States, 1994. *Monthly Vital Statistics Reports*. Hyattsville, MD: National Center for Health Statistics, 43, 13.

Smetana, J., and Gaines, C. (1999). Adolescent-parent conflict in middle-class African American families. *Child Development* 70: 1447–1463.

Sprey, J. (1969). The family as a system in conflict. *Journal of Marriage and the Family* 31: 699–706.

———. (1979). Conflict theory and the study of marriage and the family. In W. R. Burr, R. Hill, F. I. Nye, and I. L. Reiss (eds.), *Contemporary Theories About the Family: Vol. 2. General Theories/Theoretical Orientations* (pp. 130–159). New York: Free Press.

———. (1999). Family dynamics: An essay on conflict and power. In M. Sussman, S. K. Steinmetz, and G. W. Peterson (eds.), *Handbook of Marriage and the Family* (2nd ed., pp. 667–685). New York: Plenum.

Steinberg, L. (1989). *Adolescence* (2nd ed.). New York: Knopf.

Stinnett, N., Walters, J., and Stinnett, N. (1991). *Relationships in Marriage and the Family.* New York: Macmillan.

Turner, J. H. (1998). *The Structure of Sociological Theory* (6th ed.). Belmont, CA: Wadsworth. ✦

Why Welfare?

Karen Seccombe

Why do women use welfare? Given the stigma that surrounds welfare use, and the negative perception of welfare mothers, why would women choose to receive welfare? Laziness? Lack of motivation? Desperation?

Women on welfare often disassociate themselves from other welfare recipients. They tend to attribute their own welfare use to circumstances that are largely beyond their control. They need welfare, they told me, because "there are no jobs"; "how can I take care of all my kids and work too?"; "I would be fine if he would just pay child support"; "I was raped"; "I was beaten and abused"; "he deserted us, and I'm trying to get my feet on the ground"; "I'm trying to better myself"; "the welfare system penalizes me if I get a job." In the lives of women, these are not small or trivial reasons.

Rhonda, like most women interviewed, believes that she has little in common with other welfare recipients. She says that she knows many other women who receive welfare for their families whom they raise alone: her friends, her neighbors, and her son's father's family. She perceives that they "enjoy" being on welfare and ". . . getting everything handed to them." But what about herself and her son? Why is she on welfare? Her situation is entirely different, she told me. She elaborated on the circumstances that brought her to welfare: Can't find a permanent job; her son's father pays no child support; her son has a chronic medical condition. Exactly how is her situation different? Despite her belief that her circumstances are highly unusual, her story has a familiar ring to it.

Rhonda is a 28-year-old white woman, with a five-year-old son named Bobby, who is in kindergarten. She has been off and on welfare for five years since her son was born. Rhonda remains in contact with Bobby's father who lives out of state; he is a truck driver and visits his son regularly once each month. During that visit he will take Bobby out, buy him clothes, and take him to dinner at McDonalds. He, however, does not pay child support. Rhonda and Bobby's father remain cordial, and she appreciates the monthly visits, clothing, and dinners for her son. She expects little else from Bobby's father, financially or otherwise, and receives little else.

Rhonda and her son's father never married. They were romantically involved, but the relationship ended shortly before Bobby was born. After the birth of her son, she lived with her mother briefly. But it was difficult having two families under one small roof. Rhonda wanted to be on her own, so she applied for welfare.

When I interviewed Rhonda, she and Bobby had recently moved from a trailer to an apartment within a subsidized housing project. They had lived there for six months, and she detested it. Neither she nor her son socialize with neighbors; they were abusive to her son, she told me. She also believes they are criminals, dependent on the system, and have no interest in "bettering themselves."

The apartment in which Rhonda and Bobby live is cramped, dingy, and run down. There is no carpeting, just dark brown linoleum that is peeling in many places. Two chairs, one end table, and a television are about all that fit in her tiny living room. She stays in the projects because, after losing her job, the eleven-dollar monthly rent is all she can afford. A sizable chunk of her $241 welfare check goes for utilities, which cost approximately $140 a month, because her apartment is poorly insulated. Heat and air conditioning (nearly a requirement in Florida's sweltering six-month summers) escapes through the windows and door cracks. After paying for car insurance, which runs $22 a month; for cleaning supplies, laundry soap, and other miscellaneous expenses, Rhonda has little money left over. When her budget permits, she buys clothes for her son who is growing rapidly, often from the Salvation Army or Goodwill.

Rhonda does not see herself as dependent on the welfare system. During the five years she has been off and on welfare, she has held a variety of jobs. She has worked in the housekeeping department of a hospital, as a cashier, at a warehouse where she sorted lids for a printing company, and she recently ran a daycare center out of her home. She took great pride in her daycare center, and claimed it is her ideal job, and one that she would like to try again someday. She enjoys young children. Having children around the house taught her son Bobby responsibility, and her job did not take her away from Bobby for eight or nine hours a day. Like other women who were interviewed, and consistent with the views of women with greater financial means, an ideal job was seen as one that interfered as little as possible with her responsibilities as a single parent. Unfortunately, Rhonda was forced to close her daycare because many of her clients were considerably delinquent in paying their childcare bills. Unable to force them to pay the money they owed her, Rhonda wasn't able to keep up with her own bills. She had to close her daycare.

Rhonda told me that she "hates welfare." Then why is she receiving it? She, like so many others before and after her, told of having a very difficult time finding a permanent job that pays well enough for her to take care of her family. She had an easier time securing employment when she lived in Maryland. She moved to Florida to be near her sister and father, but has had a difficult time finding a full-time permanent job in a university town. Moreover, her job options are limited; Rhonda quit school in the 10th grade, eventually earning her GED after Bobby was born. She says she actively looks for work, but usually can only turn up temporary jobs that expire after a period of several months. Rhonda told me that she desperately wants to work because she sees it as a ticket to a better life for her and Bobby.

Since he's now enrolled in school she will not have to shell out the $200 a month for daycare like she used to do. A job, she believes, holds promise for a better life. She enthusiastically told me about a job lead she had from her sister. A nearby factory may be hiring over twenty new people, and she is hopeful that she will be one of them. She submitted her application last week. She knows that by securing a job, her rent will go up, her welfare check will be eliminated, and her food stamps will likely be significantly reduced. She acknowledges that these are "disadvantages" but she insists that she prefers "to be out working, meeting people, you know. Making it better for me and my son."

But Rhonda is concerned about losing her medical benefits. As a welfare recipient she receives virtually free medical care for herself and Bobby. Finding a job that would provide medical benefits poses a challenge. But given Bobby's condition, medical benefits are of paramount importance. Bobby suffers from lead-paint poisoning. As a baby he ingested paint peeling off a wall in a house they rented. Lead-paint poisoning is a serious and common problem in old, dilapidated structures that the poor often inhabit. An estimated three million poor children may be at risk of impaired physical and mental development related to ingesting lead-based paint flaking off the walls of older homes (Needleman, Schell, Bellinger, Leviton, & Allred, 1990). Low income preschoolers are three times more likely than children living in moderate income families to have lead levels in their bloodstream of at least 10 micrograms of lead per deciliter of blood, a level at which harmful effects have been noted. Lead exposure damages the brain and central nervous system. Consequently, one study reported that second grade children with high levels of lead in their bloodstream were six times more likely to have a reading disability, had significantly lower IQ rates, and lower scores on vocabulary tests. When researchers followed these children over time, they noted that the children were seven times more likely to drop out of high school (Children's Defense Fund, 1994). Bobby continues to suffer serious bouts from the poisoning several years after ingesting it. He endures frequent pain, and during these episodes is lethargic and without an appetite. His flare-ups occur every few months, and physicians closely monitor him. He continues to be in and out of the hospital with regularity.

Despite what Rhonda may think, her situation is fairly typical. She receives no child support from her son's father. She has difficulty finding permanent work with pay sufficient to pull her above the level she would be at if she stayed home and received welfare. Moreover, a job necessitates that she will lose most of her welfare benefits, including Medicaid. Given the health problems in her family, losing medical benefits is a steep price to pay for a minimum wage job. Despite her insistence that she will be off of welfare very shortly, would we be surprised to find that she later returned to the system?

The truth is that Rhonda is on welfare because of structural problems more so than personal shortcomings. She is not particularly lacking in personal drive or initiative. Since having a baby on her own she has earned a GED and has opened her own business—fair accomplishments for someone who is the sole parent to a young child; a child with a serious illness. She describes one of her personal strengths as being "responsible." Rhonda ingeniously sought to combine work and motherhood so that she could excel at both, and neither would suffer. She struggled as a small business owner, as do many small business owners, until she was forced to close her business due to clients who refused to pay their bills. Rhonda is hardworking and is motivated to improve her circumstances in life. In these ways, she is quite typical of many women I met who receive welfare. Despite her thinking to the contrary, she was not the exceptional case.

Women on welfare, including Rhonda, largely point to two general explanations to explain their own use of welfare: They cite the problems inherent in our social structure, and they cite fate. Neither perspective focuses on the individual as much as to external forces largely outside of her control. A structural perspective attributes poverty and welfare use to economic or social imbalances that restrict opportunities for some people. Fatalism assumes that poverty and welfare use can be traced to bad luck, unpredictable quirks of human nature, or simply to chance. These explanations generally are not accorded to other welfare recipients. They are, however, used routinely by recipients to elucidate why they themselves receive aide.

THE INFLUENCE OF SOCIAL STRUCTURE

Women on welfare commonly attributed their reliance on welfare to problems and concerns related to the way our social structure is organized. Their concerns, they told me, primarily revolved around (1) a lack of jobs paying a living wage; (2) lack of good quality and affordable daycare; (3) lack of father involvement and child support enforcement; (4) inadequate transportation systems; (5) broader problems in our social structure, such as racism or sexism; and (6) a welfare system that penalizes women for initiative and eliminates their welfare benefits prematurely.

EMPLOYMENT

Many women talked about the difficulty of finding employment, particularly a job that pays a living wage. Although the unemployment rate in the nation is a low 5.2 percent, many women told me of submitting application after application, to no avail. "You can't make someone hire you," they said.

One woman, Cassandra, told me of her frustration after applying for job after job, with no luck at landing one. Her responsibilities related to taking care of her home and her children are not considered legitimate work experience, even for service sector occupations. She described her frustration after applying for a job as a custodian.

> I even applied for custodial work at the University, and I know I'm qualified to sweep floors. And the lady even told me at

the desk that I'd be competing with people who already have experience in this area. Now, I know I'm qualified to sweep floors. If I'm going to do it at home for free, I might as well get paid to do it.

Sarah, a white 30-year-old divorced mother who, after an extended job search, finally landed a part-time job at a fast food franchise while also attending college in pursuit of an A.A. degree. She commented on her difficulty in finding even minimum wage work. She has many years of experience, including as a manager in the fast food industry. She wondered if her difficulty in finding work was due to the fact that she has been on Workman's Compensation, and therefore was viewed as a high risk by potential employers. But too many others voiced similar complaints for her case to be an isolated incident.

> It is very hard to find a job. Because people are picky and some of these places, you'll only get a job if you know someone. I spent a year looking for a job, and Colonel Sanders was the first place to hire me. I've gone places, because when you are on Workman's Comp you have to fill out a list every month, and how many jobs you've applied in. I've applied for 20 to 100 a month. And this was the first place that even contacted me in a year. It's not that I'm not qualified. I've had 6 years of management.

Moreover, when women do find work, most are employed in service sector jobs, such as the fast food industry, which generally pay minimum wage and offer no fringe benefits. Fast food franchises such as Wendy's, McDonalds, Burger King, Hardees, and several others offer the most recurrent avenues of employment to women on welfare. They generally do not require a high school diploma nor extensive experience. Yet, despite their possibilities, these jobs do not pay enough to support a family or even pull them above the poverty line. At $5.50 an hour, working 40 hours per week yields approximately $900 a month before taxes. Working 52 weeks a year, an employee would earn approximately $11,800 per year. Taxes take a sizable chunk out of these earnings. For even the smallest families who have only one child, living and surviving on minimum wage poses a challenge.

Yet, many women were eager to take on this challenge. They told me that they want to work, and enthusiastically told me about leads or tips that they had heard regarding which businesses were hiring, and at how much pay. Although most women did not shun minimum wage jobs, jobs that paid eight dollars an hour or more were highly sought after. Women felt confident that they could live on the nearly $16,000 a year that such jobs would provide. Several women told me that they heard the postal service might be hiring—the postal service is notorious for paying "good money." Three other women told me about jobs in the nearby jails or prisons which also offer wages substantially higher than minimum wage.

> They are hiring and so I want to submit my application for this corrections job. They pay $5 an hour to start out with the training. Then, when you get past the correctional course, then you go to the prison and you start working. But they don't pay $5 an hour for being a correctional officer. They pay more than that. They pay you about nine or ten dollars an hour! Plus benefits. See, I'm looking for where the money is at!

It is easy to reduce the number of people on welfare; simply make them ineligible for benefits after two or three years, as many states have done. In this sleight of hand, statistics can be pulled out and dangled to the public showing that welfare use, thus poverty itself, has declined. This, however, is incorrect. The true extent of poverty will not decline until the poor are paid higher wages for the work that they do.

CHILDCARE

The question of who will care for children is one of the most pressing and perplexing questions of our time. If we expect poor single mothers to be employed, who then, will care for, socialize, nurture, discipline, play with, teach, and love their children? And, how much will this cost, both financially, and socially?

Concern over the lack of safe and affordable childcare emerged as a common structural reason why women turned to, or remained on welfare. They know that children need more than custodial care in large and crowded day care centers in order to thrive. Yet, for most poor and working class families, childcare is often patched together in a fashion that leaves mothers anxious. Some told me that they did not feel comfortable leaving their children with strangers. They preferred to depend on other family members, but acknowledged that their mothers, sisters, or other female relatives cannot always be counted on. They have their own family responsibilities and obligations, and cannot always provide day care when needed. Living in high density and high crime areas, they worried about the safety of their children. "I'm not going to leave him with someone I don't know until he's old enough to tell me what happened." And they worried about the psychological effects of inadequate care—crowded, dirty, or impersonal conditions—upon their children.

Moreover, mothers worried about the cost of daycare. Unless a program within the welfare office subsidized childcare, costs for childcare within the interview area approximated $300 to $500 a month, depending on the type of care provided. The size of an AFDC grant for a mother and one child in the region is $241 a month, obviously making full-time childcare an impossibility, prompting many women to comment, "I had to quit—the money went to the baby-sitter." Childcare costs vary dramatically across the country, with costs in many communities in Florida being well below averages costs in other communities, yet still beyond the reach of most poor and low income families. A recent study which compared childcare costs in six communities around the nation found that average costs for care of a two-year-old ranged from $3,100 a year in Birmingham Alabama, to almost $8,100 in Boulder Colorado (Clark & Long, 1995). Not surprising, then, a study sponsored by Wellesley

College found that more than 15 percent of low-income parents reported that their 4 to 7-year-old children regularly spent time all by themselves or in the care of a sibling under the age of 12 (Alter, 1998). Their parents cannot afford the costs of childcare.

Moreover, Rhonda, who has a GED, reminded us that jobs that welfare recipients take are often in the service sector, and they are therefore required to work evenings and weekends when childcare might not be available. Her son Bobby is only five years old, far too young to remain at home alone at night while she works.

> My hardest problem is—I can find a job— it's trying to work around my son. On weekends I ain't got nobody on weekends to watch him. Like my sister, she's busy with her own kids. And my dad, he's kind of a senior citizen, you know. And that's the only problem I have. It's like they always want nights and weekends. See I can do days while he's in school, you know. It's hard.

Childcare is not simply an issue for mothers of young children. Mothers with older, school-age children also face considerable dilemmas about how to juggle employment and parental responsibilities. Low-income children are less likely to live in neighborhoods that have Before and After-School programs. In 1993, only 33 percent of schools in low-income neighborhoods had these school programs, compared to over 50 percent of schools in more affluent neighborhoods (U.S. Department of Education, 1994). Yet these programs have been shown to help low-income students perform better academically, and they help improve student conduct and study habits (Posner & Vandell, 1994).

Some mothers interviewed suggested that parenting is more time consuming and labor intensive as children become teenagers. Peer pressure is strong, including pressure to act out and behave in destructible ways. They feared that their children would get into trouble with the law; that they might use, abuse, or sell drugs; that they may get pregnant; or that they may drop out of school. Mothers here, as well as those responding to nationwide studies, clamored for more organized activities for their school-aged children (Center for Research on Women, 1996; Meyers & Kyle, 1996). Moreover, because they are the sole parent to their children, they have no one to share the burden and responsibilities of childcare. They do not have a spouse, and generally they cannot rely upon the father of their children for assistance or relief from their duties.

Women on welfare juggle their employment and parental responsibilities in a variety of ways, but one aspect was very clear: Their children are more important than any specific job. Their jobs were seen as "work;" they were not careers, with the degree of commitment that careers entail. While "work" was considered important psychologically and financially, under no circumstances should it interfere significantly with family responsibilities. Their first and foremost responsibility was perceived as being a "good mother" to their children. So, how do women on welfare reconcile being good mothers with working? Many women did not want to work before their children were in preschool. Some women refused work that entailed weekends. Others preferred to work the night shift so that they could be home in the afternoons to help their children with their homework after school. Others wanted to work in the afternoons so that they could get their children up and off to school. Others insisted that they could only work part-time so that they could be available to their children in the morning and at night. And finally other women pursued or dreamed of work that allowed them to stay at home, such as Rhonda's childcare center, or several other women's stated desire to be cosmetologists working out of their home. The structure of the desired workday or setting may differ significantly, but the underlying theme is that work should be built around their family schedule and important family events, rather than vice versa. This, however, is not easily accomplished.

One woman, Cassie, revealed a strong preference for working the night shift, leaving her children home alone at night despite the fact that they are only twelve, nine, eight, and six years of age. Although some people might abhor the thought of leaving children this age alone at night, she saw it as the best possible alternative because it allowed her to spend her days with them. She further explained that her oldest daughter has experience getting the kids up and ready for school. All her children chip in with chores and are very responsible, she elaborated.

> I'd rather work at night. I could be home with my kids when they get home from school. Yeah, I'd have the whole afternoon to be with them. It's from 12 midnight to eight. And at midnight I'd be gone to work, I'd come home at eight and get me some sleep. And when they come home I'll be fresh and ready to go again. . . . My daughter was getting them up when I worked at XXX food franchise, and she was not but nine. Eight or nine. I had to be at work at six o'clock in the morning, so I would call home and she would be up, and everybody would be up and ready to go to school. I taught her to help me, and that's what she's been doing.

FATHER'S INVOLVEMENT

A third structural problem cited was the lack of involvement on the part of the children's fathers. Fathers' participation in the emotional or financial upbringing of their children was noticeably absent in the vast majority of cases we examined. Absentee fathers represent a growing and alarming national trend. Less than half of fathers who are court ordered to provide child support payments pay the full amount regularly (U.S. Bureau of the Census 1997b, Table 609, p. 389).

The women I interviewed were required to report the name and whereabouts of the fathers of their children, if known, when they signed up for welfare. When the children's fathers did pay child support, the money went to the welfare agency, and mothers were given an additional fifty dollars per month in their check. This fifty dollars is designed to serve as an incentive to provide information on the children's fathers to the welfare agency, just in case women are reluctant to do so. Yet, despite the mandatory ruling that fathers be identified, the apparent eagerness of women to comply with this ruling, and the welfare agency's supposed vigorous search for the fathers, the majority of the women interviewed continued to received no, or very sporadic, child support. Some women resented this. They resented the freedom that their children's fathers have, while they themselves are stigmatized for receiving welfare. A divorced African American mother who received welfare for her two children responded typically to our question as to whether she received child support.

> No, I don't. And with my ex-husband, he was court ordered to pay child support. He works. But I don't get child support from him. They have money—they can go out and buy themselves cars and they can save money in the bank, but they're not supporting their kids. And I don't like it. I don't think the government should have to take care of a man's kids, especially if he can take care of his own kids. I don't understand it. They are so hard on us, but where is my child support? My kids deserve that money.

She and many others acknowledged that mothers on welfare are stigmatized for caring for their children, whereas fathers are rarely stigmatized for their failure to support their children. Pearl summarized the sentiment of many when she expressed that their fathers' resistance to paying child support has cheated her children. She is a 48-year-old African American woman who is divorced. Pearl has born eight children, three of whom still reside in the home and receive welfare. They live in the housing projects, where she has lived for 25 years. Pearl's life has been hard. She only finished school to the 8th grade, quitting so that she could work as a farm laborer and help support her siblings. She's been married twice, divorced because of her husbands' continual infidelity. She has worked on and off for most of her life—hard jobs, such as farm laborer and

housecleaner. Now alone, she dreams about taking her younger children out of the projects to live in the country where she envisions a safer life for them, free from the pressures of drugs and dropping out of school. The likelihood of her dream materializing is extremely slim. She complained of health problems, and has not held a job in many years. The father of her oldest children is in prison, as are her two oldest sons. The father of the youngest children previously contributed to their support, but quit paying child support a few years prior to this interview. He remarried, "he figured he got a new wife and shouldn't have to pay," she told me. Pearl continued:

> All my kids' daddies owe child support. I used to talk to their daddies about that. I said, well, if you would have been willing to help take care of your kids, they would have had a living and wouldn't have had to been on welfare.

Until the dismal trends in child support are altered through stricter enforcement and through changing norms of greater paternal involvement, it will be very difficult for women to fully support their children on their own.

TRANSPORTATION

It also became clear in the interviews that transportation was a major structural barrier to women getting or keeping jobs. Women on welfare cannot afford to buy reliable automobiles. Those few women who owned newer models likely received them as gifts from family members or boyfriends. Often they did not put the car in their name, hiding it from the welfare office even if they were the sole driver, because it would jeopardize their welfare benefits. The personal asset value of an automobile (value minus debt) must be less than $1,500; otherwise it disqualifies one for welfare. This poses a dilemma for a rational person—how can I find and maintain a respectable job, if I am not allowed to have reliable (e.g., more expensive) transportation? Most women who had cars, even those exceeding the maximum asset level, owned older models that were in a constant state of disrepair. Many cars guzzled gas. Car maintenance is expensive. One woman explained that her car, although a necessity in many respects, also assisted in keeping her poor.

"It's either your tires, or extra gas, or a part tearing up on your car. No, I can never really get caught up." Obviously, women on welfare are not driving Cadillacs.

Public transportation, and walking, are the primary alternatives to the private automobile. While public transportation is available in the largest community in the county, women complained that it was expensive (one dollar, plus an additional 25 cents per transfer) and inconvenient. Moreover, public transportation, even with all its logistical problems, was completely unavailable in some of the smaller communities within the county.

Communities built since the 1950's are often spread out, not geared toward pedestrians or public transportation systems, but geared instead toward private automobile ownership. A strong, central, vibrant downtown area for work, shopping, and entertainment are memories of a bygone era in most communities. Instead, numerous "strip malls" are spread throughout the city limits and fringe areas. Sidewalks may not exist, traffic whizzes by at 45 miles per hour, and without a central core, walking, bicycling, or relying on public transportation becomes difficult and inconvenient. While offhand it is easy to say, "you can walk to work," reality may dictate something else. In many communities walking to work can be more than just inconvenient, it can be dangerous or impractical. Walking through high crime neighborhoods or crossing highways, especially at night, poses special dangers. Walking can add an hour or two to childcare bills, and may necessitate being away from one's children for 9, 10, or 11 hours a day instead of the usual eight. Moreover, in inclement weather, such as heavy rains or snow, it is impractical to expect women to walk for miles and still appear freshly groomed and ready for work. Life without a car is difficult in most cities and towns in the United States. Even with the best intentions, it is not surprising that women without cars find it difficult to maintain steady work.

Several women revealed to us elaborate transportation logistics that allowed them to work or go to school, including commutes of an hour to an hour and a half each way. One African American mother, Dee, who is studying to become an accountant, lives five miles from campus and described her transportation ordeal using the city bus:

> I leave here by 6:45 to get to school at 8:00. So that's an hour and 15 minutes. I leave school at 2:00 to get home by 4:00, so that's 2 hours. So that's 3 hours and 15 minutes I spend. I could leave here at 7:30 and be there by 8:00. And then I have 3-hour breaks in between so I could be home relaxing or doing something.

Transportation problems prevent many women from seeking work altogether, and they inhibit other women from staying at their job. Several women told me that they quit otherwise "good" jobs because of inadequate transportation schemes. When they worked at night, after the buses stopped running, they were forced to rely on friends, family, or a taxi service for rides home after work. Friends and family, although well meaning, were sometimes unreliable. Taxis were expensive. Consequently, the risk of job failure increases, often becoming an eventuality. Many might ask, why try?

> I just had a job in September where I worked six days. But I had to quit my job because I had to pay transportation. And transportation was costing me, like $40 a week. Sometimes at night it was difficult because the shift that I was working was three to twelve—three in the afternoon to twelve at night. And a lot of people don't want to get up and come get you. So, I had to quit the job because of the transportation costs that I had to pay.

In this instance, and several others like it, a recipient sought work despite the obstacles, explored alternative transportation with some optimism, and finally quit due to rational personal economics. People who have always had reliable personal automobiles often overlook the magnitude of this issue for many would-be workers. Growing urban sprawl increases the likelihood of distance to the workplace, and therefore reduces the likelihood of regularly getting to a job without a personal automobile.

RACISM AND SEXISM

Racism and sexism are unpleasant realities in our polarized society. The famous tennis star, Arthur Ashe, before he died of AIDS in 1993, disagreed with a reporter who assumed that AIDS must be the heaviest burden he has ever had to bear. "No, it isn't," Ashe told the reporter. "Being black is the greatest burden I've had to bear. Having to live as a minority in America...because of what we as a people have experienced historically in America, and what we as individuals experience each and every day" (Ashe & Rampersad, 1994:139–141). Likewise the social construction of gender permeates all aspects of life, and people continually distinguish between males and females and evaluate them differently.

Racism and sexism generally have three components: (1) negative attitudes toward minority group members and toward women; (2) stereotypical beliefs that reinforce, complement, or justify the prejudice; and (3) discrimination—acts that exclude, distance, or segregate minorities and women (Lott, 1994). They can be blatant or more subtle. Blatant racism and sexism can take the form of not being hired in the first place, being passed over for a job promotion or a pay raise, or being fired prematurely. A few African American women told us directly that racism had hindered their ability to get, or keep, a good paying job. One woman spoke of her neighbor in the housing project who "has a problem with, excuse my language, white people. They did her real bad."

Racism and sexism can also be more subtle, and this form is sometimes referred to as "institutional" racism or sexism. Patterns of inequality may be woven into the fabric of society, so that it becomes institutionalized, or normative. It may be imbedded in our culture or our social policy. It often goes unnoticed. And, when pointed out, sometimes people will fail to grasp its significance. For example, job opportunities for women are limited in ways that men's generally are not, in part due to the ways women are socialized. Women may not seek training in the higher paying skilled trades, for example, because they have been taught that these are "unfeminine" occupations.

Stephanie, a 26-year-old mother who is in the nursing program at the university, explicitly acknowledged that sexism, as well as racism was likely to limit opportunities for social mobility. She is the mother of one young daughter, and is attuned to issues of social inequality. Like many of the women I interviewed, she was married when she had her daughter, and assumed that her marriage would last forever. Instead, after a painful divorce, her husband has never once paid child support or contacted his daughter.

> Why are people on welfare? There have to be at least a thousand reasons why people are on welfare. Like I tell my daughter, life isn't fair. Things happen. And you have to do the best you can. There are lots of socioeconomic groups in this country, races, blacks, Hispanics, women who don't really have the same opportunities that most people consider normal opportunities. I mean, for myself, look who got stuck taking care of the child?

THE WELFARE SYSTEM BREEDS 'DEPENDENCE' ON THE SYSTEM

Finally, a reoccurring theme throughout most narratives was that the welfare system itself is responsible for their reliance on welfare. A few respondents felt that the welfare system can indeed make people get lazy, and lose their motivation to work, as some social conservatives have argued. A 29-year-old African American woman with 3 children who has been on and off the system repeatedly said:

> Sometimes I think people get a little too satisfied with it and stay on it a little longer

than they should. Once you start getting this check [the] way we do, you get a little lazy sometimes.

However, the majority of women who expressed concerns with the welfare system said *it wasn't that it made recipients lazy per se, but rather that the welfare system had built-in disincentives or penalties for work.* Working, especially at minimum wage jobs which usually lack health insurance and other critical benefits, would not achieve their goals of self-sufficiency, and in fact would jeopardize the health and well being of their children because they would lose critically needed benefits. Moreover, as good mothers, they said, they would never want to jeopardize their children's well being. From these interviews, it became clear that without continued assistance with (a) health insurance; (b) childcare; (c) transportation; (d) food stamps; and (e) subsidized housing, working becomes not only prohibitive, but sometimes was seen as downright dangerous. Many women claimed that they want to work, or that they could find a job, or even that they had a job previously, but felt compelled to quit because working, and the automatic reduction in their welfare benefits, actually lowered their standard of living or jeopardized their children's health. They expressed frustration that the welfare system, as currently structured, actually discourages them from working by raising their rent, eliminating Medicaid, and cutting them off of needed social services before they had a chance to establish themselves. Jo, a mother of two young children claimed:

I've had a job before, and I know I can get a job. It's just really hard. It's like, I got a job at Hardee's (fast food franchise) and I had a friend take me back and forth. I was paying her 20 dollars a week for gas. I got off the system. I was honest about it and told them I had a job. They took my assistance away, and they raised my rent 200 dollars. And they said they weren't going to give me any Medicaid for them either, and I didn't have any health insurance. I had a baby at the time, and she was only a year old. She had to go the periodic appointments and stuff,

and I was like, "okay, well I'm going to try to do it." And I had to work there six months to a year to get health insurance. I was really scared, like, what am I going to do? But I'm gonna do it. So I started doing it, and then I started realizing that, you know, that after about 2 months, was under the welfare level. I mean, by making minimum wage I couldn't keep my bills up, and I could never afford to take her to the doctor. It wasn't getting me ahead. I was being penalized for trying to get off the system, and it's happened to all my friends that are on welfare. It's like a trap, and they don't help.

Jo did what our society expects of welfare mothers—she found a job. But with that job, her financial picture became even more bleak. She told me it caused her to be "under the welfare level." Jo's situation was not an isolated case. Therefore, without considerable change, what hope is there for her, and for other mothers trying to get off welfare?

Concern about losing Medicaid was commonly expressed. Medicaid is a program designed to pay the health care costs of the poor. Not all poor are eligible for Medicaid, however. Like other welfare benefits, Medicaid has specific eligibility requirements, some of which are established at the state level. Today, less than 50 percent of the poor are covered by Medicaid, down from 71 percent in 1975 (Lewin, 1991). Each state is required to extend Medicaid to recipients of AFDC, and now TANF, and to recipients of Supplemental Security Income (SSI), which covers the impoverished elderly and the disabled. However, it is up to state discretion whether to cover others who are impoverished, such as the homeless, or the working poor. Medicaid benefits are a primary reason why women stayed on welfare as long as they have. If they leave welfare, they risk joining the ranks of the uninsured. More than 37 million Americans, or 18 percent of the population have no health insurance from any source whatsoever (U.S. Department of Health and Human Services, 1997). Nearly three-quarters of these individuals are employed or are the dependents of an employed adult, usually working at a low wage, part-time, or temporary position. Over ten million of the uninsured are children under age of fifteen. Another 25 to 48 million people are "underinsured"— meaning that their insurance is inadequate to meet the needs of their family because of extraordinarily high deductibles or co-payments, or because certain procedures are not included, or specific family members are not covered.

It is well documented that persons without health insurance or with inadequate insurance use the health care system less frequently than do others, resulting in a variety of negative health outcomes (Cornwell, Berne, Belzberg, Asensio, Velmahos, Murray, & Demetriades, 1996; Seccombe, 1995; U.S. Congress, Office of Technology Assessment, 1992). The uninsured are more likely than both privately and publicly insured individuals to lack a usual source of care; to have fewer episodes of inpatient hospital care and lack preventative services; and to report delays in receiving health care. They typically seek care at hospital emergency rooms, which are increasingly turning people away and transferring the most serious cases to public hospitals (Cornwell, Berne, Belzberg, Asensio, Velmahos, Murray, & Demetriades, 1996). Consequently, without health insurance, adults and children, are more likely to experience unnecessary pain, suffering, disability, and even death. Women on welfare know this. They fear joining the ranks of the uninsured or underinsured if they were to take a job. Stephanie, in school to become a Registered Nurse, echoed this concern with losing Medicaid. Her daughter has several specific health problems:

> We gripe and we gripe about the fact that we are paying all this money for people who don't seem to be doing very much for themselves, but if you looked at the system from an insider's point of view, you would see that there are actually penalties built into the system for a person with initiative, going out to get a job, or doing something to try to better themselves. As soon as you earn a buck, they take it away from you. You are penalized if you have any kind of asset whatsoever. You have to be so damn poor

that it's not even funny. . . . Next summer in nursing school there are no classes. Yet I can't work. And I will tell you why. I would like to work as a nurses aide, and that is something I can do with my training that I have had. But I can't afford to lose my benefits, specifically my medical benefits. Because if I went to work, they would cut me off. Even though I would not be making enough to pay my bills, I would be cut off from Medicaid. And I can't afford that, you know? It's part-time, usually a nurses aide gets $5–6 an hour, which is not that much above minimum wage. And you know, you work 20 or 30 hours a week. No health benefits, no nothing. So I can't work. It's not that I don't want to work. I'd love to work. But I can't.

An African American mother of two, who works part-time as a nurses-aide, but continues to receive a partial welfare benefit, explains how her benefits were reduced when she began to work:

> The thing that gets me, being a single parent, once my income exceeds a certain amount, I'm in a Project, and my rent goes up. It has been close to $300 for this [she laughs and sweeps her arms around the room]. And then I have to end up paying expensive childcare, and the Medicaid stops for me and my children. You know, most jobs the health insurance is so expensive you can't afford it. Then, you pretty much be where you started from. You end up with nothing.

These interviews, which are grounded in the real-world receipt of welfare, suggest that the presumed link between social programs and welfare dependency touted by social conservatives is flawed. Yes, on a cursory glance, the welfare system does appear to "reduce" one's incentive to work, but a more thorough examination from an *insider's perspective* reveals that welfare programs do not encourage laziness or dependency. Both white and African American women talked about desperately wanting to work, but felt that employment reduced their already meager standard of living and often placed their children at risk because it eliminated or reduced their eligibility for critical medical and social services. They repeatedly pleaded that the welfare system be changed so as to not penalize them by cutting them off of critically needed services, at least temporarily, while they "pull themselves up by their bootstraps." Rather than being lazy or dependent on the system, they are making the most rational, intelligent choice they can, given their circumstances.

In summary, these women frequently cited concerns related to the social structure when explaining their welfare use. Problems with finding inexpensive or reliable childcare; a scarcity of jobs, particularly those which pay a livable wage; lack of father involvement with their children, and ineffective child support policies; inadequate public transportation systems; racism and sexism; and a welfare system that prematurely reduces income and benefits, were recognized as factors which inhibited their upward social mobility.

FATALISM

Bad luck, unfortunate circumstances, and soured relationships—these events come under a heading that others have coined "fatalism," which many women alluded to in their responses. They need welfare for personal reasons that are not their fault. They felt that they simply couldn't help it; they turned to welfare as a way out of a desperate, unplanned, and unfortunate situation.

BAD LUCK

For example, many discussed their bad luck at becoming pregnant. Several, who were unmarried teenage girls when they had their first child, told me that they were surprised at becoming pregnant—they didn't know that sexual activity caused pregnancy, or they didn't know that they could get pregnant the first time they had sexual intercourse. They were confused and unknowledgeable about sex. Many disclosed that they had intercourse as a way to please a boyfriend, or because of peer pressure from their girlfriends at school or in their neighborhoods. They rarely used birth control. Either they didn't know it was necessary, or their partner complained about wearing a condom and they acquiesced to his wishes. When they discovered they were pregnant, they were surprised. How did this happen? Abortion was rarely a consideration among the women interviewed. Instead, these young girls accepted that they somehow got "caught," and had their babies.

Terri Lynn, the young mother previously introduced who works at the bowling alley to support herself and her six-year-old son, told me of her surprise at becoming pregnant. She did well in high school, and never suspected that it would "happen" to her.

> Sure, I don't want to be on AFDC, but I don't have a choice. You know, I didn't plan to get pregnant with him, but it just happened. You know? I don't want to be on AFDC. I'm going to get off it as soon as I put him in school.

An African American woman with four children commented on the bad luck that young women have in their encounters with young men. Her attitude indicated that teenage pregnancies are unfortunate, but that not much can be done about it. It's acceptable, or at least unavoidable. Her greater concern is with women who have multiple births out of wedlock, but having one child "just happens":

> I know a first baby is a mistake. You know what I'm saying? It happens. You go out there, you young, you have sex. It's a mistake. I mean, they got birth control methods, but guys are so persuasive about sex these days. Girls don't think about rubbers or birth control. They just think about impressing him, so they have sex. So they get pregnant. If they keep having babies then they should get a job and help support the rest of those kids, but not the first child.

As both women allude to, peer pressure to have sex is powerful, and difficult to avoid. One recent study involving 1,000 girls in Atlanta found that 82 percent said the subject they wanted to learn most about in their sex education class was "How to say no without hurting the other person's feelings" (reported in Besharov, 1993).

National data indicate that over 20 percent of 14-year-olds have had sexual intercourse, and this increases to 30 percent by age 15, 42 percent by age 16, and up to 59 percent by age 17. Approximately half of women aged 15 to 19 have had sexual intercourse regardless of race, income, religion, or residential location. Nearly one-quarter of teenage women never use contraceptives. Others use contraceptives sporadically. The United States' rate of premarital pregnancy, at 97 pregnancies per 1,000 women under the age of 19, is more than double that of most of western European nations and Canada, nearly three times that of Scandinavian nations, and nearly ten times that of Japan. Although nearly half of teen pregnancies in the United States are aborted, our birth rate among teens is among the highest in industrialized nations (Forrest & Singh, 1990; Sonenstein, Pleck, & Ku, 1989).

POOR HEALTH

For other women, health concerns interfered with their ability to look for, or keep a job, and thus they continued to rely on welfare. Nearly one-third of women interviewed complained of health problems, including asthma, depression, high blood pressure, or back pain.

Many other women told us that their children were sickly, or had emotional problems, and consequently they did not feel comfortable leaving their children with baby-sitters.

Poor children are more likely to suffer a wide array of ailments, both chronic and acute, than are more affluent children (Children's Defense Fund, 1994). For example they are more than three times as likely to be iron deficient; 1.5 times more likely to have frequent diarrhea or colitis; two times more likely to suffer from severe asthma; and 1.5 times more likely to suffer from partial or complete blindness or deafness. These are due to a variety of prenatal and postnatal factors. One important culprit is that poor children are more often born with a lower birthweight than are other children, due to the mother's poor nutrition, lack of prenatal care,

stress, youth, insufficient weight gain, or smoking or other drug use. Moreover, poor children are also more likely to die. According to the Children's Defense Fund, "poor children are about three times more likely to die during childhood as their non-poor peers," (Children's Defense Fund, 1994). Thus, the effects of poverty on the health and well being of children, and adults, is not exaggerated. They are significant, long-term, and can cause considerable heartache, consternation and chaos in the lives of families.

Mothers expressed worry that their children would not get the attention, physically and emotionally, that they might need. Jasmine, for example, has a history of working full-time, often at several different jobs in order to make ends meet. She is divorced, and has a ten-year-old daughter who lives with her ex-husband's sister, and a five-year-old daughter and an infant to care for. Doctor's appointments are routine for Jasmine and her two young children, but they are stressful nonetheless. Both of her children have severe cases of asthma. She's been on welfare for four years, because of "the sickness of the children," she told me. She gives them breathing treatments on and off, as needed. For Jasmine, as was the case with many other women we interviewed, being a "good mother" means being there physically to care for her sick or needy children. Women routinely told us that they did not feel comfortable leaving their sick children in day care, with a baby-sitter, or even with family members for extended hours. They see, first and foremost, that their job is to provide the direct care that they believe their child needs. Among the more affluent, these "family values" would be applauded. Returning to more traditional "family values" is a popular theme espoused by Democrats as well as conservative Republicans. However, among poor women who receive welfare, such values are not applauded, they are, instead, suspect.

THE TERMINATION OF RELATIONSHIPS

A primary reason that women turned to welfare was that a relationship which ended, and they could not support their family on their own. When married or living together, a spouse or partner may have provided an important source of income for the family. When a relationship ends, that income is abruptly halted. Some women find that they are unable to secure a job providing wages above the poverty line. Or they may have no experience working, and do not know how to go about finding a job to support the family. The termination of a relationship was a primary reason that women turned to welfare. As a 35-year-old divorced African American woman told me,

> What made me get on was, I guess, my broken marriage. Because when I was married, I wasn't on AFDC. My husband was employed, and I was working.

The United States has the highest rate of divorce of any country in the world. Our divorce rate rose dramatically in the 1960's, and has since then stabilized to approximately 19.8 divorces per 1,000 married women over the age of 15 (Singh, 1995). Divorce is more prevalent among lower socioeconomic classes, despite the economic hardships it creates. One national study of men and women between the ages of 25 and 34 found that people who had only high school diplomas were significantly more likely to divorce than were people who had bachelor's degrees (Glick, 1984). This is due to a variety of reasons, including younger age at marriage; greater likelihood of premarital pregnancy and childbirth; and greater stress, crises, and disruptions in their lives related to economic vulnerability. When people marry young, for example, they are less prepared for marital responsibilities. They are more unhappy about their partners in terms of love, affection, sex, wage earning, companionship, and faithfulness. They also are more likely than their older counterparts to complain that their spouses are moody, jealous, spend money foolishly, or get in trouble with the law (Booth & Edwards, 1985; Teti, Lamb, & Elster, 1987).

African Americans are nearly twice as likely to divorce as are whites (Saluter, 1994). This is due to many factors, including that African Americans are disproportionately poor or have low incomes, and therefore face many poverty-related stresses. Moreover, they are more likely to marry earlier, have a premarital pregnancy, and have a child born out of wedlock. These factors increase their odds of divorce.

Lillian Rubin, in her book, *Families on the Fault Line* (1994), re-interviewed 32 working-class families 20 years after their original interviews, and found that 56 percent of them had divorced sometime during this period. All but one of the men had remarried, and the lone exception was already in a serious relationship after being separated for only a few months. In contrast, Rubin found that divorced women fared differently. They remained single for a longer period of time after a divorce, and over half needed either welfare or food stamps during this financially difficult period. Over one-third of the women had not remarried. For most of these women, life continued to be a series of economic struggles.

Although both men and women go through financial adjustments after divorce, women's income declines more dramatically than does men's.

Most women have little experience being the "primary" breadwinner in relationships. When they are forced to do so, while taking care of the children as well, it can be overwhelming. Many women reported that receiving welfare was perceived as a method of regaining control over their lives. It allowed them the opportunity to take stock of their situation, to regroup, to assess their options, or to attend school or find a job. Some women reported that they were deserted by their partners, and left alone to care for their children. One such case was Dee, an African American woman with three small children under the age of five. Dee served five years in the Army, a career that she enjoyed. But her husband pressured her to quit, saying that her job was too hard on the family. She quit, and became a housewife at her ex-husband's insistence. Then, when she was dependent on him for financial support, he left her without warning.

My husband left us with no food. The rent was due. You know, when he left he just split. It was like he was never there, no clothes, nothing.

Stephanie, the nursing student at the University, spoke about the shock of having to raise her child alone. Since the divorce, her husband has never once paid child support, nor visited or contacted their daughter. She, like all women, thought that their marriage would last forever, and that he would support both her and their child. She made a wrong choice, but she had no way of knowing it was wrong at the time. It was a choice that any woman could make. She never imagined that she would be on welfare.

I gave birth thinking—he begged me to keep the child when I found out I was pregnant—thinking that we would be a couple, that we would always be together, and he would always want her. And now, it's four years later, and I am by myself, and I am doing this by myself. Even the best-laid plans sometimes go down the drain.

Both Dee and Stephanie, and many others that we interviewed, saw welfare as a critical, but temporary form of assistance, which enabled them to take care of their children immediately after a husband or partner disappeared, or when the marriage or relationship ended. Welfare made it possible for them to pursue further training so that they could be the sole support of a family, or it provided some base level of financial support while they reassessed their life options. They did not see themselves as being irresponsible. Instead, the temporary receipt of welfare was viewed more positively. It allowed them to take control of their lives and provide a better home environment for their children until they could provide it themselves.

VIOLENCE

Some detrimental relationships involved violence and abuse. Violence, or its threat, is a part of every woman's reality. No woman is really exempt from this threat. A rape, for example, is reported in the United States every five minutes (U.S. Federal Bureau of Investigation, 1995), and most rapes remain unreported. Two women interviewed told us that they bore children as a result of rapes. They credit welfare with giving them the opportunity to bear and raise their children, rather than forcing them to have abortions or give up the child for adoption.

Although no direct question about violence was asked, many other women volunteered that they were fleeing abusive relationships or had left an abusive relationship in the past. Violence in the home has reached staggering levels. It is a critical social problem affecting the lives of millions, poor or rich. The true rate of domestic violence can perhaps never be known, as it often occurs, "behind closed doors," where a "man's home is his castle." Groundbreaking research by Straus and Gelles, referred to as the national Family Violence Surveys, was conducted in 1975 and 1985 with a national probability sample of 8,145 husbands, wives, and cohabiting couples. They define violence as "an act carried out with the intention, or perceived intention, of causing physical pain to another person," synonymous with the legal definition of assault. The respondents of these surveys were asked about their involvement in violent acts such as: throwing something at the other; pushing; grabbing; shoving; slapping; kicking; biting; hitting with fists; hitting with an object; beatings; burning, scalding, or choking; threatening with a knife or gun; and using a knife or gun. Together, the two surveys found that in 16 percent of the couples, at least one of the partners had engaged in a violent act against the other during the previous year. In other words, these data reveal that, every year in the United States, approximately one out of every six couples have at least one act of violence in their relationship. Moreover, Straus and Gelles found that, over the course of the entire marriage, 28 percent of the relationships, or nearly one out of three couples, contained violence (Straus & Gelles, 1986, 1988). The true rate may be even higher (Straus, 1991).

Other data from the National Crime Survey by the United States Justice Department estimates that over 600,000 cases of violence between intimates occurs each year—murders, rapes, or assaults committed by spouses, ex-spouses, boyfriends, or girlfriends, or former lovers. This represents more than 13 percent of violent crimes committed within these categories each year (U.S. Department of Justice, 1994). As many as three thousand women are killed by their husbands or boyfriends each year.

Although domestic violence occurs in all social classes, the preponderance of data indicate an inverse relationship between social class and likelihood of violence. That is, women who have lower incomes and lower levels of education are more likely to be victimized than are more affluent or well educated women. Some of this difference may be due to social class differences in the likelihood of reporting violence. Nonetheless, a 1996 Justice report, for example, stated that women living in households with annual incomes below $10,000 are four times more likely to be violently attacked than are other women, usually by their intimate partners. When income and educational levels are taken into account, white, African-American, and Hispanic women have equivalent rates of domestic violence being committed against them.

One battered woman who fled violence, Molly, turned to welfare for support after escaping while her husband was asleep. She has three young sons, the oldest of whom was four at the time she fled. They lived in a rural mountainous area, thirty miles from the nearest town. Her husband deliberately kept her isolated from family and friends, and put a block on the telephone. He was abusive to both her and the children:

I left my husband when he was asleep. I stayed in a shelter. I grabbed some clothes for the kids and left. My mom came up and got us. I had no car, no nothing. No furniture. Zero. That was August of '92. So I had to start completely over from scratch. I got a few of my things back, but basically I lost everything that I had.

Molly has been on welfare for three years, continuously, since leaving her husband. During that time she had nearly completed an AA degree at a community college, and intends to transfer to the University to work on her Bachelor's Degree. At the same time, she cares for her three young children, the oldest of whom is now seven years of age. Two of her children have been diagnosed with Attention Deficit Disorder (ADD), a disruptive and challenging learning disability. They had difficulty in school until they were correctly diagnosed, and began to take appropriate medication. Working through these issues by herself, she cannot imagine what her life would be like without the help she received from welfare. She receives no child support, and doubts that her ex-husband will ever pay the tens of thousands of dollars that he currently owes.

The belief that poverty and welfare use are something that is not one's fault and is beyond one's control, something that was forced upon them, was commonly used to explain their own use of welfare. Because of bad luck with relationships, or being raped or victimized in abusive relationships, many women felt that they had no other choice but to turn to welfare to help them out of an unplanned, but potentially desperate situation. Many women implied that turning to welfare was the *responsible* and *rational* thing to do for their children, and for themselves. They indicated that they were not to blame, and in fact, for many, welfare was a source of empowerment. It allowed them to be independent of an abusive spouse, retain custody of their children, or to take care of their family when a husband or lover deserted them. These are laudable goals, ones that our society would support, at least in theory. Who would really suggest that a woman remains in an abusive situation, lose custody of her children simply because of money, or move her family to a homeless shelter? The women interviewed were likely to see welfare as a short-term phenomenon, a temporary helping hand while they planned the next step in their lives. Each woman interviewed, with the exception of two, was confident that she would be off welfare within five years. Women were less optimistic about the lives of other women who receive assistance.

WHY THE INCONSISTENCY BETWEEN EXPLANATIONS OF THEIR OWN AND OTHERS' USE OF WELFARE?

These interviews revealed an important contradiction: Women perceived that their own use of welfare was due to structural factors, or fate, or to the idiosyncrasies of the welfare system itself; but welfare use by other women, in contrast, was often attributed to laziness, personal shortcomings or other inadequacies. This was the case for both the African American and the white women interviewed. They perceived the economic hierarchy in the United States as essentially fair, and that one's placement in the hierarchy tends to reflect work effort and motivation. They generally believed the popular constructions of the "welfare mother," but evaluated their own situation as distinctly different from the norm. They tended to segregate themselves from other recipients, and saw structural constraints as applying uniquely to themselves. "I'm sure people look at me and say the same thing, but I really do have a legitimate excuse;" or "my situation is different because I injured my back," they told me.

Janie, who has been on welfare since being ganged raped and giving birth to her daughter two years ago, denied being on welfare altogether:

> I'm not on welfare. I don't even know exactly what welfare is. I'm just receiving AFDC, and that might be considered welfare, I'm not sure. As it stands, most of them get on it because they don't want to work, they don't want to take care of their kids. I've seen more people on welfare lose their kids because of it, rather than to take care of themselves. Why they do that is beyond me.

Given the strong negative messages about welfare and welfare recipients, perhaps it is not surprising that both white and African American women who receive welfare also subscribe to Individual or Cultural of Poverty blaming perspectives. Critical theorists, such as Foucault (1980), suggest that our social structures produce cultural ideologies of truth and knowledge that are disadvantageous to the less powerful. These cultural ideologies camouflage the self-serving interests of the powerful by making them appear as though they are natural, normal, and serving the interests of everyone. Likewise, Gramsci's (1971) notion of "ideological hegemony" refers to the process by which consensus is obtained between dominant and subordinate groups, such as the rich and the poor. Social arrangements, which are in the best interest of the dominant group, are presented as being in everyone's best interests. Subordinates come to accept these interests as their own, and the contradictions inherent in the interests of the dominant and subordinate groups are ignored. Thus, the ideology becomes "commonsense" and normative, and cohesion is created where there would otherwise be conflict. The ideologies reflect the interests and perspectives of the elite, but the poor, who fail to see the shared political nature of their problems, also internalize them. Instead, poverty and welfare use is relegated to the realm of a personal problem, rather than a social problem (Mills, 1956). Consequently, like others who are more affluent, women on welfare essentially deem that the popular construction of the "welfare mother" is just. They accept the dominant ideology that stigmatizes welfare recipients.

However, it is important to note that these women infused Structural and Fatalistic perspectives in their worldviews as well, constructed out of their own experiences. They suggested, at least in so far as their own experiences were concerned, that their needs for welfare were due to circumstances over which they had little control.

This research is not alone in these findings. A classic study by Briar (1966), using a sample from 92 African American, white, and Mexican American families receiving AFDC, also found that the respondents almost never referred to welfare recipients as "we" but instead used the word "they." The tendency to view oneself as an atypical recipient, disassociating oneself from other recipients was identified as a coping mechanism for dealing with stigma. More recently, interviewing 16 women in focus groups, Davis and Hagen (1996) also found that welfare recipients had the tendency to view themselves as atypical recipients. For example, while they were quick to condemn others for being welfare frauds, they did not see their own actions as fraudulent. Instead, they were merely "beating the system" by working to get extra money to pay for necessary items that their checks could not pay for.

What then, may explain why many women do not see the commonalties of their experience? One explanation may be found in attribution theory, which proposes that people have a tendency to overestimate the degree to which other people's behavior is caused by individual traits or dispositions, and underestimate the degree to which it is caused by structural factors. And, in contrast, although we tend to attribute other people's actions to their own personal traits or dispositions, we are more likely to attribute our own behaviors to the social structure or situational factors over which we have little control (Jones & Nisbett, 1972).

Consistent with attribution theory, our respondents assigned individual traits or dispositions to other women to explain their use of welfare, ones that are well touted in the media and within the larger cultural milieu. Recipients were accused of laziness, of lacking sufficient motivation to improve their condition, of having deficiencies in human capital such as low education or few job skills, of having little desire to "better themselves," and of living in cultural surroundings that encourage welfare use. It appears that welfare recipients, just like the more affluent, overestimate the degree to which individualistic notions of very negative personality traits or dispositions shape welfare use behavior. Yet, when it comes to explaining the causes of their own welfare use behavior,

also consistent with attribution theory, they tend to blame it on structural or situational causes that are beyond their control. They assess little personal blame; it is simply not their fault. "There are no jobs"; "How can I take care of all my kids and work too?"; "I would be fine if he would just pay child support"; "I was raped"; "I was beaten and abused"; "He deserted us, and I'm trying to get my feet on the ground"; "I'm trying to better myself"; "the welfare system penalizes me if I get a job," were frequently voiced. While all of these factors may be justifiable reasons why a woman would turn to welfare, they are reasons that can apply to all women, and indeed, they did apply to the majority of women interviewed. Women assumed they were exceptions to general trends, however these "exceptions" were common and widespread. They were grounded in their experiences as women in a patriarchal society. Few women were nonchalant about welfare. Instead, most were embarrassed, pained, appreciative, or resigned, and applied for welfare as a last resort. As Rhonda bluntly told me,

It's not what I want for me and my son. It's just that there are a lot of disadvantages to it. I just don't want to be on it. I'd rather be out working, meeting people. Making it better for me and my son.

References

Acs, G., & Loprest, P. (1995). The effects of disabilities on exits from AFDC. Paper presented at the 17th Annual Research Conference of the Association for Public Policy Analysis and Management, November 2–4.

Alter, J. (1998). It's 4:00 p.m. Do you know where your children are? *Newsweek,* April 27, 29–33.

Ashe, A., & Rampersad, A. (1994). *Days of grace: A memoir.* New York: Ballantine.

Bernstein, A. (1997). Off welfare—and worse off. *Business Week.* December 22, p. 38.

Booth, A., & Edwards, J. N. (1985). Age at marriage and marital instability. *Journal of Marriage and the Family,* 47, 67–75.

Bourdieu, P. (1977). *Outline of a theory of practice.* New York: Cambridge University Press.

Briar, S. (1966). "Welfare from below: Recipients' views of the public welfare system." *California Law Review,* 54, 370–385.

Burns, J., Ballew, M., Hsiao-Ye Yi, & Mountford, M. (1996). "Child care usage among low-income and AFDC families." October. Washington, DC: Institute for Women's Policy Research.

Center for Research on Women. (1996). *School-age child care project—"I wish the kids didn't watch so much TV": Out-of-school time in three low income communities.* Wellesley, MA: Wellesley College: Center for Research on Women.

Chandler, D. (1998). "Workshop calls for challenge to welfare." *The Gainesville Sun.* Pp. 1B, 3B.

Children's Defense Fund. (1998). *The state of America's children yearbook 1998.* Washington, DC: Children's Defense Fund.

——. (1994). Wasting America's Future. Washington DC: Children's Defense Fund. July.

Clark, A. L., & Long, A. F. (1995). *Child care prices: A profile of six communities—Final report.* Washington, DC: The Urban Institute. p. 54.

Cornwell, E. E., Berne, T. V., Belzberg, J. A., Velmahos, J. M., & Demetriades, D. (1996). Health care crisis from a trauma care perspective. *Journal of the American Medical Association,* 276, 940–947.

Dahrendorf, R. (1959). *Class and class conflict in industrial society.* Stanford: Stanford University.

Davis, L., & Hagen, J. (1996). Stereotypes and stigma: What's changed for welfare mothers. *Affilia,* 11, 319–337.

Della Face, R. L. (1980). The meek shall not inherit the earth: Self-evaluation and the legitimacy of stratification. *American Sociological Review,* 45, 955–971.

Enda, J. (1998). Proposal expands child care. *The Gainesville Sun.* January 8. Pp. 1A, 7A.

Forrest, J. D., & Singh, S. (1990). The sexual and reproductive behavior of American women, 1982–1988. *Family Planning Perspective,* 22, 206–214.

Foucault, M. (1980). In Collin Gordon (Ed.), *Power/Knowledge: Selected Interviews and Other Writings, 1972–1977.* New York: Pantheon.

Glick, P. C. (1984). Marriage, divorce, and living arrangements: Prospective changes. *Journal of Family Issues,* 5, 7–26.

Gramsci, A. (1971). *Selections from the prison notebooks of Antonio Gramsci.* Edited and translated by Quintin Hoare and Geoffrey Nowell Smith. New York: International.

Habermas, J. (1973). *Legitimation crisis.* Boston, MA: Beacon.

Herbert, B. (November 20, 1997). The game is rigged. *The New York Times.* [Online]. Available: *http://www.nytimes.com/1997/11/20/oped*

Jones, E. E., & Nisbett, R. E. (1972). The actor and the observer: Divergent perceptions of the causes of behavior. In Edward E. Jones, David Kanouse, Harold Kelley, Stuart Valins, and Bernard Weiner (Eds.), *Attribution: Perceiving the Causes of Behavior.* New York: General Learning.

Kaplan, A. (1998). *Transportation and welfare reform.* [Online]. Available: *http://www.welfareinfo.org/transita.htm*

Lewin, T. (April 28, 1991). The ailing health care system: A question of access. *The New York Times.* Pp. 1, 28.

Loprest, P., & Acs, G. (1996). *Profile of disability among families on AFDC.* Washington, DC: Urban Institute report to the Henry J. Kaiser Family Foundation.

Lott, B. (1994). *Women's lives: Themes and variations in gender learning* (2nd ed.). Pacific Grove, CA: Brooks/Cole.

Marx, K., & Engels, F. (1959). Manifesto of the communist party. In L. S. Feuer (Ed.), *Marx and Engels: Basic Writings on Politics and Philosophy.* Garden City: Doubleday.

McElroy, S. W., & Moore, K. A. (1997). Trends over time in teenage pregnancy and child-bearing: The critical changes. In R. A. Maynard (Ed.), *Kids Having Kids: Economic Costs and Social Consequences of Teen Pregnancy.* New York: Urban Institute.

Meyers, J., & Kyle, J. E. (1996, March). *Critical needs, critical choices: A survey on children and families in America's cities.* Washington, DC: National League of Cities.

Meyers, M. K., Lukemeyer, A., & Smeeding, T. M. (1996). Work, welfare, and the burden of disability: Caring for special needs children in poor families. Syracuse, NY: Center for Policy Research, Maxwell School of Citizenship and Public Affairs, Syracuse University, Income Security Policy Series, Paper No. 12.

Mills, C. W. (1956). *The power elite.* New York: Oxford University.

Needleman, H. L., Schell, A., Bellinger, D., Leviton, A., & Allred, E. N. (1990). The long-term effects of exposure to low doses of lead in childhood. *New England Journal of Medicine,* 322, 83–88.

Pavett, L., & Duke, A. E. (1995). *Increasing participation in work and work related activities: Lessons from five welfare reform demonstration projects.* Report prepared for the Office of the Assistant Secretary for Planning and Evaluation, U.S. Department of Health and Human Services. Washington, DC: The Urban Institute.

Peterson, R. R. (1996). A re-evaluation of the economic consequences of divorce. *American Sociological Review,* 61, 528–536.

Posner, J., & Vandell, D. L. (1994). Low-income children's after-school care: Are there beneficial effects of after-school programs? *Child Development,* 65, 440–456.

Presser, H. B., & Cox, A. G. (1997). The work schedules of low-educated American women and welfare reform. *Monthly Labor Review,* April, 25–33.

Rubin, L. B. (1994). *Families on the fault line.* New York: Harper Collins.

Saluter, Arlene F. (1989). *Singleness in America.* U.S. Bureau of the Census, Current Population Reports, Special Studies, Series P-23, no. 162. Washington, DC: U.S. Government Printing Office.

Seccombe, Karen. (1995). Health insurance coverage and use of services among low-income elders: Does residence influence the relationship? *The Journal of Rural Health,* 11, 86–97.

Sonenstein, F. L., Pleck, J. H., & Ku, L. C. (1989). Sexual activity, condom use, and AIDS awareness among adolescent males. *Family Planning Perspectives,* 21, 152–158.

Straus, M. A. (1991). Physical violence in American families: Incidence, rates, causes, and trends. In Dean D. Knudsen and JoAnn L. Miller (Eds.), *Abused and Battered: Social and Legal Responses to Family Violence* (pp. 14–36). New York: Aldine de Gruyter.

Straus, M. A., & Gelles, R. (1988). How violent are American families? Estimates from the National Family Violence resurvey and other studies. In Gerald T. Hotaling, David Finkelhor, John T. Kirkpatrick, and Murray A. Straus (Eds.), *Family Abuse and Its Consequences: New Directions in Research* (pp. 14–36). Newbury Park: Sage.

——. (1986). Societal change and change in family violence from 1975 to 1985 as revealed by two national surveys. *Journal of Marriage and the Family,* 48, 465–479.

Teti, D. M., Lamb, M. E., & Elster, A. B. (1987). Long-range socioeconomic and marital consequences of adolescent marriage in three cohorts of adult males. *Journal of Marriage and the Family,* 49, 499–506.

U.S. Bureau of the Census. (1997). *Statistical abstract of the United States* (117th ed.). Washington, DC: U. S. Government Printing Office.

U.S. Congress, Office of Technology Assessment. (1992). *Does health insurance make a difference?—Background Paper.* (OTA-BP-H-99) Washington, DC: U.S. Government Printing Office.

U.S. Department of Education. (1994). *The condition of education: 1993.* Washington, DC: National Center for Education Statistics.

U.S. Department of Justice. (1994). Violence between intimates. *Bureau of Justice statistics selected findings: Domestic violence.* Nov. No. NCJ-149259. Washington, DC: U.S. Department of Justice, Office of Justice Programs.

U.S. Federal Bureau of Investigation. (1995). *Crime in the United States 1994.* Washington, DC: U.S. Government Printing Office.

Weitzman, L. (1985). *The divorce revolution: The unexpected social and economic consequences for women and children in America.* New York: Free Press.

Chapter Six
Family Stress Theory

Marsha and Sean Peabody have been married for five years; this is the second marriage for both. While Sean has a child from his previous marriage (8-year-old Billy) who spends every other week, holidays, and one month during the summer with them, they have wanted to have an "ours" baby for some time. After trying to become pregnant for several years they started infertility treatment—which worked! Marsha, a corporate manager at a large software company, had to leave work six weeks early because of a difficult pregnancy—she's having twins! Sean, a salesman at a television station, spent three weeks running back and forth between work and the hospital. Finally, Alicia and Barry were born, but five weeks prematurely, which led to health complications for both but especially little Barry. Although Alicia was able to come home after just two weeks, Barry was in the hospital for one month. Thus, Marsha and Sean spent a lot of time running back and forth between work, home, and the hospital. This also impacted Billy's visitation schedule, which left him feeling unwanted and angry.

Marsha was not able to return to work because of the health needs of the twins, and the fact that child care for two would consume most of her paycheck. Sean kept his job but was able to take off only one week once the twins were born. Needless to say, life has been stressful for the Peabody family!

The twins are now three months old and are getting stronger by the day. They still wake up every three hours needing to be fed, and each is taking different medications that must be administered at different times. Marsha's parents live nearby and are taking turns spending the night and helping with the feedings. Other friends and family members are coming over during the day to help Marsha take care of the twins. Both parents are still exhausted and constantly worry about the health of the twins. They often turn to prayer when they feel overwhelmed and find that it comforts them. They are also both very optimistic people and take it all in stride. They were so desperate to be parents that the lack of sleep and complete loss of any activity outside of taking care of the twins seems like no big deal in comparison to the joy Alicia and Barry bring them. Now if they could just convince Billy how wonderful it is to be a big half-brother!

HISTORY

Whereas families have experienced stress since time began, the scientific study of how families deal with stress is a relatively recent phenomenon. The depression of the 1930s was the impetus for this research as Angell (1936) and Cavan and Ranck (1938) sought to discover how families were dealing with the loss of household income and the stress associated with unemployment. Angell discovered that a family's reaction to the sudden loss of income during the depression was based on two things: integration and adaptability. Integration means how close a family feels, how economically interdependent they are, and having a sense of family unity, whereas adaptability means how flexible families are in talking about problems and making decisions as a group. Angell found that families who are both integrated and easily able to adapt their family roles to meet the needs of the situation are most capable of dealing with stress such as that caused by job loss during the depression. Similarly, Cavan and Ranck (1938) studied families both before and after the depression and found that those who were organized and cohesive prior to the depression were best able to deal with economic losses, whereas disorganized families faced further breakdown.

Koos (1946) also researched how families deal with economic loss. His research was then built upon by that of Hill (1949), who developed the "roller-coaster profile of adjustment to crisis" (p. 14). According to Hill's model, families go through four stages when faced with a crisis: crisis, disorganization, recovery, and reorganization. The crisis phase is obviously the stress-provoking event that sent the family into crisis. This can be anything from the birth of a new child to the death of a family member. Once the family is faced with a crisis, a period of disorganization follows as family members attempt to cope with the situation. For example, new parents attempt to develop a schedule of feeding and/or waking up with the child at night so that each parent is able to get some sleep. They also must attempt to cope with little sleep, meeting the needs of the infant, and changing how they view each other now that they are parents as well as spouses.

As families figure out how to handle the situation they enter the stage of recovery, which can be either fairly quick or long-term. According to Hill (1949), families will eventually reach a new level of organization; for some it will be the same as the previous level of organization, for others it will be better than it was before; but for still others things become stable but not as good as they were prior to the stressful event. Thus, some new parents eventually find a schedule that fits all of their needs and are able to continue much as they did prior to the birth of their child. Other first-time parents become closer and find that their marital relationship is better because they have bonded over the birth of their child. This may also lead to better communication skills as a result of figuring out how to manage a newborn. Unfortunately, some parents find having an infant in the home overwhelming and never really learn to adjust. In these families lines of communication break down, resentment and jealousy form, and often divorces occur as the couple is not able to return to a satisfactory level of interaction.

The roller-coaster model of adjustment to crisis was the predecessor to Reuben Hill's (1949) ABC-X model of family stress, which is the foundation of family stress theory. His early research on how families attempt to adjust to the crisis caused by separation and reunion during wartime led to the development of a theory that has remained virtually un-

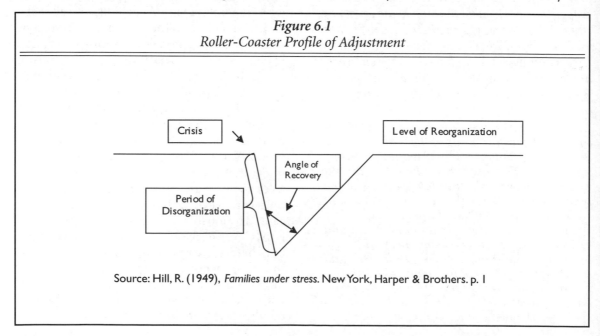

Figure 6.1
Roller-Coaster Profile of Adjustment

Crisis

Level of Reorganization

Angle of Recovery

Period of Disorganization

Source: Hill, R. (1949), *Families under stress.* New York, Harper & Brothers. p. 1

changed over the last five decades. Although other scholars have added to (McCubbin and Patterson 1982), attempted to simplify (Burr and Klein 1994), or built upon (Lazarus and Folkman 1984) this theory, the basics as Hill wrote them have remained primarily unchanged. The rest of this chapter will discuss Hill's ABC-X model.

BASIC ASSUMPTIONS

The basic assumptions of family stress theory revolve around the central components of the model. Thus, this section will focus on the theory itself, and then we will focus more specifically on defining each of those components. As was previously stated, stress theory is based on the ABC-X model, with *A* being the stressor event, *B* the family resources or strengths, and *C* the family's perception of the event, or how they define or attribute meaning to the event. If the event or stressor is such that the family cannot immediately figure out how to solve the problem, this will lead to crisis, the *X* component of the model (Hill 1949). Because of the nature of this theory, the format will be a little different for this chapter.

STRESSOR EVENTS (A)

Now we'll look at each component of the model a little more closely, beginning with the stressor. The first point to remember is that the stressor event itself is neither positive nor negative, since events or situations are neutral prior to our interpretation of them. It is also important to remember that both positive and negative events can cause stress. For example, while it is obvious that events such as loss of a family member are stressful, the birth of a much-wanted child or winning the lottery can also cause stress even though both are events that cause celebration.

Lipman-Bluman (1975) has come up with ten criteria that affect the degree to which a stressor will impact a family, eight of which are commonly used in stress theory and will be addressed here.

1. The first criterion is whether the stressor is internal or external to the family. An example of this would be whether a mother chooses to return to work after the birth of a child versus the mother who loses her job following the birth of her child. In the first case the mother makes the choice to quit her job to take care of her child, so this is a decision made internally. In the second case, however, her boss fires her because she is always late to work and is falling asleep on the job; thus, external circumstances control the decision.

2. Whether a stressor is focused on one member of the family, or all members of the family, can make a difference. For example, is a stressful workplace causing one family member to come home unhappy, which might then disrupt the family, or has a recession caused both spouses to lose their jobs, causing the entire family to deal with a loss of income?

3. Suddenness versus gradual onset revolves around how much time a family has to anticipate the stressors' arrival. Whereas an unexpected illness might cause immediate crisis, pregnancy gives couples time to adjust to the idea of being parents.

4. The severity of a stressor can also make a difference. Are you dealing with the death of a child or the purchase of a new home, for example?

5. How long families have to adjust to a stressor can affect how they cope. Whereas the first day of kindergarten happens only once, learning how to care for a spouse with cancer is a long-term stressor event.

6. Whether the stressor is expected or not can also make a difference. We can expect to have difficult times while our children are adolescents, but we do not expect to be the victim of a road rage crime.

7. The seventh criterion is whether the stressor is natural or artificial/human-

made. For example, are you trying to deal with the damage left behind by Hurricane Hugo or are you dealing with the loss of a job because of increased technological advantages at your canning plant?

8. Finally, the family's perception of whether or not they are able to solve the crisis situation can determine how they react to the stressor. It is much easier to respond to something such as being a member of a blended family than it is to deal with a terrorist attack, over which we feel little control. Thus, when looking at the *A* component of this model, use these eight criteria to determine how to define and describe the stressor event in a determination of how it will affect the family.

RESOURCES (B)

Once a stressor has affected a family, the family must figure out how to deal with the event or situation. One way this is done is by accessing resources, the *B* component of this model. Recall the work of Angell (1936), who described the ideas of family integration and adaptability. The ability to pull together as a family and to be flexible based on the circumstances are both resources. These two resources were further developed into a more complex model by Olson and McCubbin (1982), but the premise remains the same: Family members must learn to balance being cohesive and being individuals while also finding ways to retain their boundaries as a family, unless doing so brings harm to the family. In other words, family members stick together as a cohesive unit when facing a crisis and pull together to help one another, but they also learn when they need to go outside the family and seek help.

McCubbin and Patterson (1985) state that we should think of resources as falling within three categories: individual, family, and community. For example, one way to deal with the loss of a job is to figure out what you can do to solve the problem or find another job. In this case, individual resources would be level of education, job experience, perseverance, and

work ethic. One can also use family resources to deal with unemployment by being supportive and encouraging to one another, making contacts with those you know in the job market, helping your spouse with a résumé, and sharing household responsibilities to allow more time for a job search. Finally, one can also turn to the community for such help as job relocation services, headhunters, having people at church help you make contacts and keep you in their prayers, and having other friends help with some of your current tasks to allow you more time to search for a job. The more resources you have available, the better you are able to cope. Thus, the best response to stress is to use a variety of resources.

According to McKenry and Price (2000), social support is one of the most important resources we can access. This can be provided by families instrumentally (that is, with household chores or writing a résumé), emotionally, and through the building of increased social networks. Being supported also has the added benefit of building one's self-esteem because our feelings of self-worth increase when others are willing to help us—it is seen as a sign of love and support. We can also receive social support from community resources such as increased networking, help with problem-solving skills, and providing assistance in accessing valuable resources.

DEFINITION OF THE SITUATION (C)

Lazarus and Launier (1978) suggest that what individuals think about or how they interpret the stressor is as important as accessing resources when determining how a family will react to a crisis. This is often assessed in research concerning coping with a chronic illness such as cancer. Cognitive appraisal and coping processes are thought of as mediators of individual psychological responses to stressors such as being diagnosed and living with cancer (Folkman 1999; Lazarus and Folkman 1984). Optimism, or the belief that more good things will happen than bad, helps a person to view a stressor as more challenging than threatening, which has been associated with more positive outcomes in breast cancer patients (Carver et al. 1993; Epping-Jordan et al. 1999). The appraisal process in turn influences the thoughts and behaviors used to manage stress—coping. Thus, individuals with cancer who are optimistic about their chances of survival are better able to deal with their diagnosis than those who see it as an insurmountable problem (Soliday and Smith 2001).

The self-fulfilling prophecy, which is "a prediction of behavior which biases people to act as though the prediction were already true" (Papalia and Olds 1996, 487), also influences our perceptions of stressors. Burr (1982) relates this to stress theory by saying that individuals and families who believe that a stressor cannot be solved are dooming themselves to failure. In contrast, those who can cognitively reframe the problem as being something they can handle are better able to manage the stressor. For example, if a student convinces herself she cannot pass an exam, she is likely to study less than she would otherwise, which may lead to her actually failing the exam. In contrast, if she had confidence that she could pass the exam, or her perception was that she was able to pass the exam, she would probably study more, which would most probably lead to success.

An important part of this process is how the stressor is broken down into manageable tasks. For example, rather than looking at the problem in its entirety, such as moving to a new town to take a new job, make a list of things that have to be done in each location. That way you're focusing on only one item at a time rather than being overwhelmed with all that has to be done. Cognitive reappraisal is a part of this process as well; we attempt to decrease the intensity of the emotions surrounding the situation as much as possible. Rather than viewing the move as tearing you away from a place you love, focus on the endless adventures that await you in a new town and a new work environment. This changes the emotional energy from negative to more positive. Finally, family members should encourage each other to maintain their normal lives rather than allow the problem to consume them. In this example that would mean spending time with friends you care about and doing things in your community as a family while still working toward completing the tasks necessary to make the big move.

STRESS AND CRISIS (X)

Whether or not a family will enter a state of crisis is determined by the previously discussed components of the ABC-X model. A crisis is reached when the family is no longer able to maintain its usual balance because of the stressor event. It is important to note that not all stressors will lead to crisis. In addition, just because a family faces a crisis does not mean the family will be broken apart because of it. In fact, families often function better and are more cohesive after a crisis than they were before, as was shown previously, when the roller-coaster model of adjustment to crisis (Hill 1949) was discussed in the example of how differently couples adjust to having a newborn.

PRIMARY TERMS AND CONCEPTS

STRESSORS

Now that we know the basics of the theory, it is important to define a few of the concepts in more detail, which will be done following the ABC-X model. Olson, Lavee, and McCubbin (1988) define stressors as "discrete life events or transitions that have an impact upon the family unit and produce, or have the potential to produce, change in the family system" (p. 19). Notice that this definition uses the word discrete, which implies that stressors are singular. In other words, in this model we deal with one stress-producing event at a time. It is also important to note that stressors are neither positive nor negative by themselves but become one or the other based on how we define the situation. Thus, what is negative for one person might be a positive event for another. Think about a 15-year-old with plans to attend medical school who becomes pregnant versus Marsha and Sean from the beginning of this chapter, who have taken extraordinary measures in an attempt to become pregnant. Both families are faced with the same event, pregnancy, but what is a painful and difficult predicament for the teenager is a cause for celebration for the Peabody family.

NORMATIVE EVENT

Similarly, while stressors can be both positive and negative, they can also be normative or non-normative. A normative event has three primary components: It is something that occurs in all families, you can anticipate its occurrence, and it is short-term rather than chronic (McCubbin and Patterson 1983). Examples of normative stressors would be the birth of a child, learning how to deal with a teenager, buying your first home, and facing retirement. We are better able to deal with those stressors that are normative, since we've had some time to think about how we will handle the situation, or what resources we can access. Non-normative stressors such as losing an infant to sudden infant death syndrome or the separation of family members due to war are not anticipated and, thus, are more likely to lead to a crisis.

RESOURCES

The *B* component of the model—resources—are characteristics, traits, or abilities of individuals, families, or communities, as was previously discussed (McCubbin and Patterson 1985). One resource not already mentioned is that of *coping,* which is what we do in an attempt to deal with a stressor. Coping is really an interaction of our resources and our perceptions as we choose those resources we draw upon based on our perceptions of what will work and what won't. For example, if a student has a big paper due on Monday, and it's now Sunday night and he is sick but hasn't started the paper yet, there is a problem. One way for him to cope with that problem is to simply admit that the paper won't be his best work but that he can still get it done if he locks himself in his room with his reference materials and his computer. In this case he has defined the prob-

lem as solvable and used the resources at his disposal—his work ethic, self-confidence, and perhaps a roommate who will type for him—to write the paper. If, on the other hand, he decides that he just can't get it done and he'll explain it to his professor tomorrow, he might cope by going to bed, which in turn is likely to result in a failing grade on his paper.

Lazarus and Folkman (1984), among others, believe there are three primary ways to define how families cope: using direct actions, intrapsychically, or by controlling the emotions associated with the stressor itself. *Direct actions* mean actually doing something, such as searching the community for resources, writing a new résumé, or seeking counseling to help deal with a problem. *Intrapsychic coping* refers to cognitively reframing the problem so that it does not seem so overwhelming or insurmountable. Finally, while some people *control the emotions* caused by the stressor in positive ways such as talking with a friend or going to a religious service, others use more destructive means, such as turning to alcohol or drugs in an attempt to dull the pain or alleviate the emotions. Regardless of how a family copes, the ultimate goal is to return the family to its previous state of functioning—in other words, trying to solve the problem so things can return to normal.

CRISIS

Here it is important to make a distinction between stress and crisis. Whereas *family stress* is something experienced by families that causes a change in the family or upsets their sense of normalcy, *crisis* is a state or period of disorganization that rocks the foundation of the family. One should also bear in mind that whereas families can experience different degrees of stress, one is either in crisis or not in crisis. When does stress become crisis? When the family can no longer maintain the status quo using their existing resources, or is so overwhelmed as to be incapacitated, they have entered a crisis state (Boss 1988).

ADAPTATION

The level of family adaptation is usually thought to fall somewhere between *bonadaptation,* a positive result to the crisis, and *maladaptation,* an unhealthy or dysfunctional resolution of the crisis. For example, whereas some families deal with the job loss of one spouse by pulling together and pooling resources until a new job is found (bonadaptation), other families fall apart in this situation, begin fighting with each other, and turn to alcohol to cope with the loss (maladaptation).

COMMON AREAS OF RESEARCH AND APPLICATION

In their review of the use of family stress theory during the 1970s, McCubbin et al. (1980) point out that while much research has taken place to provide support of Hill's (1949) original theory, there was also a good deal of research on normative life events such as the transition to parenthood, adjusting to widowhood, relocation and institutionalization, and adapting to retirement. Interestingly, similar research is still taking place using stress theory as a basis for analysis and discussion.

INFORMAL FAMILY CARE

For example, Fredrikson and Scharlach (1999) noted that this theory has been used extensively in the study of informal types of care. Their research focuses on the outcomes of working and caregiving at the same time and the stressor pileup that can result from having multiple, conflicting roles. They suggest that stressors such as caring for disabled family members or finding alternative sick child care can be dealt with using resources such as social support and professional caregivers. It was also found that the greater the intensity of the stressor—job demands, degree of child or parent disability, or accessibility to caregiving resources—the higher the level of stress and greater potential for crisis.

WORK AND FAMILY

Bernas and Major (2000) also studied a variation of this topic as they looked at the stress associated with work and family conflict and resources that can alleviate this stress, or at least prevent it from leading to crisis. They focused on social resources such as friends, family members, and coworkers, as well as personal resources such as hardiness (that is, being committed to each role, having a sense of control over roles, and the ability to positively frame stressors as challenges rather than unsurmountable obstacles). They found that both types of resources positively impact a parent's, particularly a mother's, ability to balance work and family roles.

ADOLESCENT COPING

Another normative stressor currently being researched using stress theory is the work of Plunkett and Henry (1999), who studied how adolescents' level of stress, and the type of coping resources they access to deal with these stressors, affect adolescent family life satisfaction. One thing that led to lower levels of adaptation for adolescents was their perceptions of parental overt conflict (hostility, mocking, insulting, screaming, or threatening). They also found that "adolescents who perceived increased stress due to the pileup of life event stressors reported decreased family life satisfaction" (p. 616). In addition, the use of detrimental coping strategies such as drugs or alcohol to escape stress also resulted in lower family satisfaction, whereas those who used social support to cope with stress had more positive views of family life. Thus, one must recognize the multitude of things that cause stress for adolescents, analyze how they perceive each of these stressors, and encourage the use of positive coping strategies to keep adolescents from entering a crisis state, which may lead to problems.

NON-NORMATIVE STRESSORS

Many non-normative stressors are also being assessed using family stress theory. Although the process of divorce is becoming more normative in its existence, it is still considered a non-normative event, since couples do not enter a marriage expecting to divorce. Wang and Amato (2000) studied how families adjust to divorce based on divorce stressors (loss of income, loss of friends, moving), perceptions (positive versus negative views), and resources (supportive friends and family, education, employment, and income). While their research, in contrast to previous research in this area, found only minimal support for stress theory, they did determine the importance of obtaining a participant's subjective assessment of whether or not the divorce was a positive or negative event. In other words, perhaps one of the most important parts of the model for this topic is the individual's perception of the divorce itself: Having a more positive attitude toward the divorce and available social resources leads to better post-divorce adjustment.

Non-normative Caregiving

Whereas we discussed some of the caregiving literature focused around normative events, there can also be unexpected situations, such as mental or physical illness, that require a caregiver as well. Provencher, Fournier, Perreault, and Vezina (2000) reviewed measures using a family stress theory framework that is available to assess how caregivers of individuals with schizophrenia cope. Primary emphasis was placed on the fact that although much of the literature in this area identifies how caregivers respond to the stress of caring for the behavioral needs of individuals with schizophrenia, there is little study of how caregivers perceive their roles or how they cope with caring for the individual. It seems obvious that each of these components would influence the behaviors of caregivers as discussed in the ABC-X model.

With 10 percent of American grandparents today raising their grandchildren, this is another caregiving situation that is increasing in prevalence (Heywood 1999). Stressors for this population include financial problems, health problems, returning to employment after retirement, and a decreased social life due to re-

turning to child care activities. Because of this, access to resources such as child and medical care, counseling, and social support is important. Since many of these grandparents are putting their "golden years" on hold to become full-time parents once again, it is also important that they make the choice willingly or perceive the event as being positive. The incredible amount of stress experienced by this population has led to a good deal of research using family stress theory (Sands and Goldberg-Glen 2000).

Finally, one more area of non-normative caregiving is taking care of someone with, or living with, a chronic illness. As was previously stated, much of the research in the area of chronic illness uses a stress theory approach to determine how individuals and families cope with the diagnosis of a chronic illness such as cancer. This is especially difficult when the form of cancer is extremely rare, as in the case of carcinoid cancer (Soliday and Smith 2001). Much of the stress for these patients comes from uncertainty about the disease itself, as well as the knowledge that there is currently no cure. It was found that the perception of the diagnosis as either a death sentence or something that can be coped with by living life to the fullest affects patient levels of depression. In addition, coping strategies differed widely from one individual to the next, again supporting the need to address both individual and family reactions to stressors, as well as to make inferences to large populations only with extreme caution (Smith and Soliday 2001).

Thus, if there is one thing we can conclude from this review of current literature based on family stress theory, it is that the theory is as relevant today as it was in its inception in the 1930s. One would predict that as people face more and more stressors in their lives, and society becomes increasingly complex, the use of this theory will remain stable. Perhaps the most common approach will be a combined theoretical orientation as authors discuss issues such as those above using this theory in addition to other theoretical approaches more specific to their topic of study.

CRITIQUE

Despite the fact that this theory has been widely used since its introduction in the 1930s, many have identified problems in the theory. Perhaps the most well-established problem is the fact that this is a linear model trying to explain complex families and situations. In other words, it is often not one single event that causes a family to become stressed to the point of crisis but rather an accumulation of events. To address this problem, McCubbin and Patterson (1982) developed the Double ABC-X model, based on their research on families who had a member either captured or unaccounted for after the war. The model begins with the traditional ABC-X model and treats this as the precipitating event. However, it adds the post-crisis period of adjustment, which takes into consideration the fact that families must respond not just to the initial crisis itself but to the events that precede and follow that event as well. With that in mind, the Double ABC-X model uses the traditional model as its base and then replicates this model with a different interpretation to represent post-crisis adjustment.

THE DOUBLE A FACTOR: STRESS AND CHANGE

There are three components to the double A factor: the initial stressor, changes in the family, and stressors resulting from attempting to cope with the initial stressor. Therefore, if you're attempting to deal with the loss of a job, the initial stressor event, you often have other things that happen at the same time that compound the stress. Perhaps the family has to change roles to accommodate the husband now being at home while the wife is the only parent working. In this case, the father will now take on housework and child care responsibilities, which can be stressful for him as he learns to balance those duties while also searching for employment. It is also possible that the resources you access to help you deal

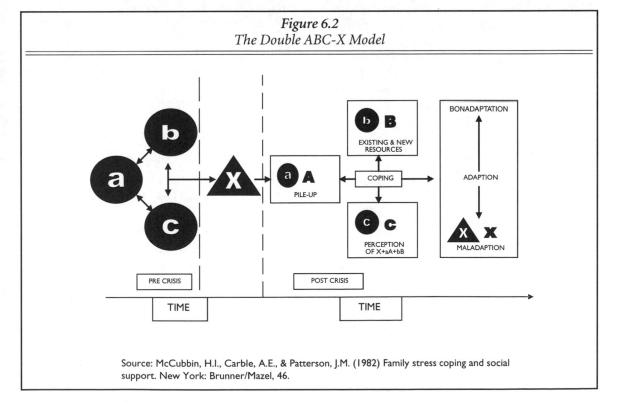

Figure 6.2
The Double ABC-X Model

Source: McCubbin, H.I., Carble, A.E., & Patterson, J.M. (1982) Family stress coping and social support. New York: Brunner/Mazel, 46.

with the loss of a job, such as having an in-law come and help out with the kids since you can no longer afford child care, are in and of themselves a source of stress. Having multiple stressors at one time is called stressor pile-up.

THE DOUBLE B FACTOR: FAMILY RESOURCES

While the initial stressor caused the family to access those resources that were immediately available, often those resources are not enough to keep the family from entering a crisis state. When those resources fail, families must turn to new sources, learn new skills, or strengthen old skills in order to cope. Thus, the double B factor takes into account the fact that sometimes those resources on which we rely cannot help us solve the problem, in which case we must seek out new opportunities.

THE DOUBLE C FACTOR: FAMILY PERCEPTION

The double C factor component is concerned not only with the family's response to or beliefs about the initial stressor but also with how they interpret their previous responses to the crisis situation itself. For example, a family faced with the death of a child will assess how they interpret the death of the child and then how they assess their ability to cope with that loss. How a family perceives its ability to respond to situations such as this can determine how they will continue to cope with the ramifications of this event.

THE DOUBLE X FACTOR: FAMILY CRISIS AND ADAPTATION

In the double X factor the post-crisis adaptation hinges on how the family has adapted to the initial crisis, as well as how it has adapted to the new level of family functioning. In other words, does the situation break the family apart or build the family up? This time, however, we're referring to the entire family system rather than just how the family responded to one event or situation.

MUNDANE EXTREME ENVIRONMENTAL STRESS MODEL

It was thought by Peters and Massey (1983) that family stress theory does not truly represent the experiences of those who experience oppression on a continual basis, such as Black family members do. In fact, these researchers thought that racism and discrimination were so much a part of their daily lives that they were not an additional stressor as implied by Hill's (1949) model but instead were a part of everyday life. Thus, they developed the mundane extreme environmental stress (MEES) model, which adds three components to the original ABC-X model. The first addition is an A factor, which represents constant exposure to racial discrimination, most of which is both chronic and unpredictable. In this case it's not another stressor but simply a piece of the puzzle that must be examined when studying Black family stress. The second addition is the D factor, which is the pervasive environmental stress associated with being of minority status in the United States. This is more anticipated, since it is a part of daily living. Finally, the Y factor is the lens through which crisis situations must be viewed for Black families, since their experiences are different from those of majority status. Thus, this model simply builds upon the traditional family stress theory by adding the need to take racial discrimination into account when studying Black families.

FAMILY ADJUSTMENT AND ADAPTATION RESPONSE (FAAR) MODEL

A final extension of family stress theory, which addresses critics who say that this is only an individual theory focusing on one specific topic, is Patterson's (1988) FAAR model, which basically expands the previous theory to be more inclusive of family systems. In this framework, families attempt to balance the demands they face with their capacity to deal with them, as influenced by the family meaning or definition/interpretation of the situation. When these demands are beyond the family's ability to deal with them, the family experiences crisis. Thus, the model looks at the processes families use in an attempt to restore balance while also including what is added by individual family members, the family unit itself, and the community.

This model has been further tested in the field of family resiliency (Patterson 2002). Resiliency means thriving or succeeding despite adverse circumstances. The focus here is on why some families do well while others are torn apart by stressful or high-risk situations. It is hoped that by determining the process that allows those families to thrive, we can help those families that are unable to balance their demands on their own.

Another common criticism of family stress theory is that it focuses on only one issue: stress. Because of this, the theory will perhaps never be considered a grand theory or a theory that one can apply to any discipline or situation. However, this should not overshadow the primary strength of this theory, which is its applicability to real-life situations. There is a great deal of literature using this theory as a basis for therapy. For example, you can help a couple deal with their lack of communication by having them analyze each component of the ABC-X model in an attempt to keep them from entering crisis, or if they're already in crisis to help them adapt positively. Similarly, this theory is helpful when studying any topic that produces stress that has the potential to lead to crisis for an individual or a family. In addition, this is one of the few theories reviewed that has shown continual development, as is illustrated in this critique. Although it may not have reached the status some would like in order for it to be included in a textbook on family theory, it's a great example of an evolving theory with more and more application to family situations in modern times. Thus, while the scope of the theory is perhaps limited to dealing with stress, it's applicability is far-reaching.

APPLICATION

1. Think about the story of the Peabody family at the beginning of this chapter. How does the ABC-X model apply to their lives? What is the stressor? Resources? Definition of the situation? How are they coping? Would one of the other models covered be more useful here? If so, why?

2. Name three things that are causing you stress right now in your life. How would you use the ABC-X model to analyze each situation and figure out how to keep those stressors from leading to crisis?

3. Look at your list of stressors again. Which of these would be better explained by using the Double ABC-X model? Analyze the situation again using this model.

4. Early family stress research was focused on the depression and the effects of war on families. What are some events in society today that could benefit from research using this theory? Outline the basic components of the model as they apply to current situations.

5. What do you think the ABC-X model is missing? How do current models address these issues? What is still missing and how could it be added?

6. Which finding surprised you the most from the Lipman-Blumen reading? Based on this article, and family stress theory, would you predict the same results if we were to have a World War III?

SAMPLE READING

Lipman-Blumen, J. (1975). A crisis framework applied to macrosociological family changes: Marriage, divorce, and occupational trends associated with World War II. *Journal of Marriage and the Family* 37:4, 889–902.

This article is a unique application of family stress theory as it utilizes the principles of the theory to discover how families (both individually and as a society) coped with a major social crisis—World War II. The stressor affects not only individual families but also the entire country, which makes this analysis especially interesting.

References

Angell, R. C. (1936). *The Family Encounters the Depression.* New York: Charles Scribner.

Bernas, K. H., and Major, D. A. (2000). Contributors to stress resistance: Testing a model of women's work-family conflict. *Psychology of Women Quarterly* 24 (2): 170–178.

Boss, P. (1988). *Family Stress Management.* Thousand Oaks, CA: Sage.

Burr, W. R. (1982). Families under stress. In H. I. McCubbin, A. E. Cauble, and J. M. Patterson (eds.), *Family Stress, Coping, and Social Support* (pp. 5–25). Springfield, IL: Charles C. Thomas.

Burr, W. R., and Klein, S. R. (1994). *Reexamining Family Stress: New Theory and Research.* Thousand Oaks, CA: Sage.

Carver, C. S., Pozo, C., Harris, S. D., Noriega, V., Scheier, M. F., Robinson, D. S., Ketcham, A. S., Moffat, F. L., and Clark, K. C. (1993). How coping mediates the effect of optimism on distress: A study of women with early stage breast cancer. *Journal of Personality and Social Psychology* 64: 375–390.

Cavan, R. S., and Ranck, K. H. (1938). *The Family and the Depression.* Chicago, IL: University of Chicago Press.

Epping-Jordan, J. E., Compas, B. E., Osowiecki, D. M., Oppedisano, G., Gerhardt, C., Primo, K., and Krag, D. N. (1999). Psychological adjustment in breast cancer: Processes of emotional distress. *Health Psychology* 18: 315–326.

Folkman, S. (1999). Thoughts about psychological factors, PNI, and cancer. *Advances in Mind-Body Medicine* 15: 236–259.

Fredrikson, K. I., and Scharlach, A. E. (1999). Employee family care responsibilities. *Family Relations* 48 (2): 189–196.

Heywood, E. M. (1999). Custodial grandparents and their grandchildren. *Family Journal* 7 (4): 367–372.

Hill, R. (1949). *Families Under Stress: Adjustment to the Crisis of War Separation and Reunion.* New York: Harper and Brothers.

Koos, E. L. (1946). *Families in Trouble.* New York: Kings Crown Press.

Lazarus, R. S., and Folkman, S. (1984). *Stress, Appraisal, and Coping.* New York: Springer.

Lazarus, R. S., and Launier, R. (1978). Stress-related transactions between person and environment. In L. A. Pervia and M. Lewis (eds.), *Perspectives in Interactional Psychology* (pp. 360–392). New York: Plenum.

Lipman-Blumen, J. (1975). A crisis framework applied to macrosociological family changes: Marriage, divorce, and occupational trends associated with World War II. *Journal of Marriage and the Family* 3: 889–902.

McCubbin, H. I., Joy, C. B., Cauble, A. E., Comeau, J. K., Patterson, J. M., and Needle, R. H. (1980). Family stress and coping: A decade review. *Journal of Marriage and the Family* 42: 855–871.

McCubbin, H. I., and Patterson, J. M. (1982). Family adaptation to crisis. In H. I. McCubbin, A. E. Cauble, and J. M. Patterson (eds.), *Family Stress, Coping, and Social Support* (pp. 26–47). Springfield, IL: Charles C. Thomas.

———. (1983). Family transitions: Adaptation to stress. In H. I. McCubbin and C. R. Figley (eds.), *Stress and the Family Vol. 1: Coping With Normative Transitions* (pp. 2–25). New York: Brunner/Mazel.

———. (1985). Adolescent stress, coping, and adaptation: A normative family perspective. In G. K. Leigh and G. W. Peterson (eds.), *Adolescents in Families* (pp. 256–276). Cincinnati, OH: Southwestern.

McKenry, P. C., and Price, S. J. (2000). Families coping with problems and change: A conceptual overview. In P. C. McKenry and S. J. Price (eds.), *Families and Change: Coping with Stressful Events and Transitions* (pp. 1–21). Thousand Oaks, CA: Sage.

Olson, D. H., Lavee, Y., and McCubbin, H. I. (1988). Types of families and family response to stress across the family life cycle. In D. M. Klein and J. Aldous (eds.), *Social Stress and Family Development* (pp. 16–43). New York: Guilford Press.

Olson, D. H., and McCubbin, H. I. (1982). Circumplex model of marital and family systems V: Application to family stress and crisis intervention. In H. I. McCubbin, A. E. Cauble, and J. M. Patterson (eds.), *Family Stress, Coping, and Social Support* (pp. 48–72). Springfield, IL: Charles C. Thomas.

Papalia, D. E., and Olds, S. W. (1996). *A Child's World: Infancy Through Adolescence* (7th ed.). New York: McGraw-Hill.

Patterson, J. (1988). Families experiencing stress: The family adjustment and adaptation response model. *Family Systems Medicine* 5 (2): 202–237.

Patterson, J. M. (2002). Integrating family resiliency and family stress theory. *Journal of Marriage and the Family* 64 (2): 349–360.

Peters, M. F., and Massey, G. (1983). Chronic vs. mundane stress in family stress theories: The case of black families in white America. *Marriage and Family Review* 6: 193–218.

Plunkett, S. W., and Henry, C. S. (1999). Adolescent perceptions of interparental conflict, stressors, and coping as predictors of adolescent family life satisfaction. *Sociological Inquiry* 69 (4): 599–620.

Provencher, H. L., Fournier, J. P., Perreault, M., and Vezina, J. (2000). The caregiver's perception of behavioral disturbance in relatives with schizophrenia: A stress-coping approach. *Community Mental Health Journal* 36 (3): 293–306.

Sands, R. G., and Goldberg-Glen, R. S. (2000). Factors associated with stress among grandparents raising their grandchildren. *Family Relations* 49: 97–105.

Smith, S. R., and Soliday, E. (2001). A qualitative investigation of the stressors and coping techniques of patients with carcinoid. Manuscript in preparation.

Soliday, E., and Smith, S. R. (2001). Psychological adjustment in carcinoid cancer patients: Test of a stress and coping mediated model. Manuscript submitted for publication. Washington State University.

Wang, H., and Amato, P. R. (2000). Predictors of divorce and adjustment: Stressors, resources, and definitions. *Journal of Marriage and the Family* 62 (3): 655–668. ✦

A Crisis Framework Applied to Macrosociological Family Changes

Marriage, Divorce, and Occupational Trends Associated With World War II

Jean Lipman-Blumen

A *conceptual framework for analyzing role change (dedifferentiation) as a system response to crisis is presented. A typology of crises is developed to be used [in] conjunction with critical aspects of the social system at the time of crisis to predict both crisis period and postcrisis (reconfiguration) period role changes. The crisis framework is then applied to macro-changes in family structure in response to an archetypal crisis, World War II. Structural changes in the family are indicated by macrostructural data (i.e., marriage and divorce rates, as well as occupational role shifts for women). Although census data are not sufficiently detailed to permit more elaborate analysis, they generally indicate support for the hypotheses derived from the crisis/dedifferentiation perspective.*

Crisis provides a condition that inevitably affects family structure in various ways. Social scientists have studied the impact of crisis on family structure and functioning from several perspectives.

One group of investigators has studied microstructural changes within the family in the face of personal, individual or small group crises. This genre of work includes, among others, studies of death and subsequent bereavement (Lindemann, 1949; Rapoport, 1963), illness (Davis, 1963), poverty (Rainwater, 1959; Komarovsky, 1940, 1962), and natural disaster (Drabek, 1968).

A second group of researchers has focused upon large-scale societal crises and questioned their impact upon a limited group of families or family members within a given research sample. Bettelheim's (1960) study of the intrapsychic and role changes experienced by concentration camp internees and their families in Germany during World War II exemplifies this approach. Hill's (1949) work on families separated and reunited in wartime acts as a bridge between these two research strategies.

Still a third school of investigators has investigated macro-aspects of family structure, reflected in divorce, marriage, and remarriage rates, and related them to macrosocietal factors (Kunzel, 1974; Pinard, 1966). Within this genre are numerous studies of the relationship between divorce and occupational level (Weeks, 1943; Kephart, 1955; Duncan and Duncan, 1969; Goode, 1951). The major macrosocietal condition that has caught the imagination of researchers has been the business cycle (Wilcox, 1893; Thomas, 1927; Gulden, 1939; Ogburn and Thomas, 1922; Goode, 1951; Glick, 1974), while the effects of war on family structure have been noted mostly *en passant* (Davis, 1950; Pinard, 1966; Goode, 1963).

The present paper, which falls within the third group of studies, attempts to investigate macrosocietal indicators of changing family structure in response to a macrosocietal crisis, World War II. More specifically, the objectives of this paper are (1) to develop a conceptual framework for understanding how roles change as a system response to crisis, and (2) to apply this conceptual scheme to macrostructural family changes in response to

World War II, the archetype of a large-scale crisis.

Toward a Conceptual Framework for Crisis

Definition

By crisis, we mean *any situation which the participants of a social system recognize as posing a threat to the status quo, well-being, or survival of the system or any of its parts, whose ordinary coping mechanisms and resources are stressed or inadequate for meeting the threat* (Lipman-Blumen, 1973). Crisis requires maximum rational use of resources, including resources often held in reserve or deliberately repressed. Crisis commonly requires reallocation of both material and nonmaterial resources. Social roles, including familial, occupational, political, generational and sex roles, may be conceived as resources and often prove to be critical in crisis periods.

Crisis is a sufficient, but not a necessary, condition for role change. All genuine crises produce role changes of varying degrees, types, and duration in the social systems in which they occur. The exact nature of the role change to be expected in response to crisis depends upon the relationship between two major factors: (1) the nature of the crisis, and (2) the state of the social system at the time of crisis.

A Typology of Crises

The nature of the crisis is a significant variable influencing the type of role change to be expected. There are numerous dimensions of a crisis, and the description of a crisis according to at least ten dimensions will permit a very clear characterization of any given crisis. The ten most important dimensions of crisis (presented here in "polar opposites" form) may be conceptualized as the following continua:

(1) Internality versus Externality: refers to whether the source of the crisis was internal or external to the social system affected.

(2) Pervasiveness versus Boundedness: refers to the degree to which the crisis affects the entire system or only a limited part.

(3) Precipitate onset versus Gradual onset: marks the degree of suddenness with which the crisis occurred, i.e., without or with warning.

(4) Intensity versus Mildness: involves the degree of severity of the crisis.

(5) Transitoriness versus Chronicity: refers to the degree to which the crisis represents a short- or long-term problem.

(6) Randomness versus Expectability: marks the degree to which the crisis could be expected or predicted.

(7) Natural generation versus Artificial generation: connotes the distinction between crises which arise from natural conditions and those which come about through technological or other human-made effects.

(8) Scarcity versus Surplus: refers to the degree to which the crisis represents a shortage or overabundance of vital commodities—human, material and non-material.

(9) Perceived solvability versus Perceived insolvability: suggests the degree to which those individuals involved in the crisis believe the crisis is open to reversal or some level of resolution.

(10) Substantive content: (This dimension differs from the previous nine in that it subsumes a set of subject areas, each of which may be regarded as a separate continuum graded from low to high.) Using this dimension, the analyst can determine whether the substantive nature of the crisis is primarily in the political, economic, moral, social, religious, health, or sexual domains or any combination thereof.

The State of the Social System

The specific response of a system to crisis is determined, to a large degree, by the relationship between the nature of the crisis (identified by the typology), and the state of the social system at the time the crisis occurs.

The state of the social system involves at least seven crucial aspects:

(1) *the level of system organization* which refers to the degree to which the system is organized into a set of integrated and effectively functioning parts;

(2) *the adaptation coefficient* of the system (or degree of potential flexibility), which refers to the degree to which the system is able to adjust its organized pattern to new situations by creative, meaningful and effective realignment of its parts;

(3) *the available resources* at the time of crisis;

(4) *the previous experience of the system with similar crises,* including the development of coping mechanisms and strategies;

(5) the *effectiveness* of the system in the resolution of *analogous crises* (effectiveness in previous crises may be based upon a combination of the previous four factors);

(6) *the breadth and complexity of the roles prior* to crisis;

(7) *the length of time since* and the *nature of* the most *recent crisis,* including effects of the crisis.

By focusing upon the nature of the crisis (identified by the typology) and its relationship to the state of the social system (measured by the aspects outlined), predictions can be made about different types of role changes that will occur at the height of the crisis, as well as additional role refinements that occur during the reconfiguration period (after the crisis has been resolved). The sharpest role changes occur at the peak of crisis, and roles tend to re-approach the precrisis level following the resolution of crisis.

Except in cases of extremely mild, transitory, gradual, expected and bounded crises that occur in flexible, organized and experienced social systems, roles rarely return completely to their precrisis states. The more severe, prolonged and pervasive the crisis, the greater the permanent residue of role changes. The postcrisis (or reconfiguration) role patterns become solidified or set at a new level of integration, which may remain intact until the next crisis cycle upsets the role configuration. The reconfiguration period of the most recent crisis becomes the precrisis period of the next crisis cycle.

THE STRATIFICATION SYSTEM AND CRISIS

One common concomitant of crisis is the disruption of the stratification system, which serves as a mechanism for ordering priorities of symbols and goals, and is based upon the controlled status of individuals and groups. In times of stability, the stratification system is the major mechanism whereby individuals and groups are rigidly differentiated from one another according to various criteria, such as sex, race, education, occupation, family lineage, and wealth. During periods of stability, the stratification system works to keep individuals and groups with certain characteristics and credentials in certain roles; it simultaneously works to keep others, lacking those qualities, out of these roles.

During stable periods, goals are diffuse, long-range, and difficult to rank. As a result, means often become more important than ends. Goal displacement may occur as means become ends in themselves (Merton, 1957: 199–201). When means are more important than ends or goal attainment, emphasis shifts to *who* is performing a task, rather than *which task* and *how well* the task is being performed. Under these conditions, the stratification system is robust.

By contrast, crisis creates a situation in which goals are quickly and easily identified. Goals usually are immediate or short-range. Survival is such a goal for the immediate present and imminent future. Goals, during crisis periods, are easily rank ordered and commonly focused upon survival or sustenance of the social system and/or individuals within it. The criteria for participation in various roles change, with decidedly less emphasis upon formal characteristics of individuals or groups and more upon whether or not the individual or group can help achieve crucial goals ("deliver the goods"). In this way, the stratification system is seriously impaired, with the result that differentiation between roles begins to break down. Roles are no longer clearly demarcated sets of expectations, tasks, attitudes, rights and responsibilities, separated from one another by distinct entry criteria.

DEDIFFERENTIATION PROCESS

In time of crisis, roles undergo a process of dedifferentiation, whereby the lines of demarcation between roles break down. Dedifferentiation rests upon two basic operations (and combinations thereof): assimilation and overlap.[1] Dedifferentiation has two forms: structural dedifferentiation and occupant dedifferentiation.

In structural dedifferentiation, an element of a role (*i.e.,* usually a task component) ceases to be the exclusive domain of the parent role and may move entirely to another role or may be shared with another role. A simple example involves the task of providing economic support within a family. In traditionally differentiated roles, the breadwinner task belongs solely to the husband's role. In the case of dedifferentiated roles, either the wife takes over this task (assimilation), or both husband and wife share the breadwinning (overlap).

Numerous patterns of structural dedifferentiation occur in which parts of roles may become embedded in other previously existing roles, or may spin off to become totally new and separate roles.[2]

Occupant dedifferentiation occurs when individuals or groups who previously were excluded from a role(s) are permitted, even recruited, into those very roles. In occupant differentiated roles, the criteria for occupancy of two roles are mutually exclusive. All the criteria that indicate which individuals and groups may enter a given role also connote those who are excluded.

As we have been suggesting, roles change in response to crisis. Sometimes new roles emerge in crisis, and some roles emerge only during crisis and then disappear until the next crisis arises (*i.e.,* the comforter and the worrier). Other institutionalized roles are structured around the potential or recurrence of crisis (*i.e.,* fire, police and hospital personnel, as well as military roles). Role dedifferentiation, with the loosening of the stratification system, reduces tension in a system facing crisis. This tension reduction mechanism permits movement in a system in which rigidity would compound the crisis.

In the remainder of this paper, we shall attempt to apply this crisis framework to the macro-changes that were evident in the family and the occupational structure as the result of World War II.

CRISIS FRAMEWORK APPLIED TO MACROSTRUCTURE OF FAMILY DURING WORLD WAR II

TYPE OF CRISIS

World War II, as experienced by American families, was an intense (CD4)[3] crisis arising from external sources (CD1), external not simply to the family, but to the larger American social system. It was a threat to the survival of the United States, dramatically initiated by the Government of Japan (CD7) (artificial generation) in an unexpected (CD3) (precipitate onset) attack on Pearl Harbor in 1941. World War II was perceived immediately by Americans as a pervasive (CD2) crisis, which would have immediate, severe (CD4) and long-range (CD5) implications for the entire American social system, including all families that comprised the nation. The attack was unanticipated (CD6), at least by the general population, and, at the outset, its solvability (CD9) was unclear.

World War II, like most wars, involved scarcity of resources (CD8). At the outset, naval and other military equipment were in dangerously short supply. As the crisis persisted, new shortages of fuel, food, clothing, and personnel developed. But in mobilizing the nation to meet the crisis, surpluses in other areas—such as jobs—occurred. The substantive content (CD 10) of the crisis was primarily political and secondarily economic. There were substantive dimensions of morality, patriotism, and sexuality.

State of the Social System

At the time of the crisis, American families tended to have a role structure (SSD6)[4] that was traditional, differentiated, and simple. Most families consisted of the wife, husband and unmarried child(ren). In 1940, relatively few families had subfamilies (*i.e.*, married children with *their* families, or grandparents) living in the nuclear household. By the end of the war, this situation had drastically changed, with many families "doubling up" (Hill, 1949; Glick, 1974; Current Population Reports, P-20, #10, 1947). The vast majority of these families maintained an adequate level of organization (SSD1), although many had suffered disorganization in the previous decade of the Great Depression (SSD7) (Cavan and Ranck, 1938).

Only Americans in their third decade had recollections of experiences associated with an analogous crisis, World War I (SSD4). As a result, a large proportion of young married and still single people (under age 30) had not had previous analogous experience; therefore, they had not had the opportunity to develop coping mechanisms specific to war conditions.

The available resources (SSD3) varied from family to family, but the median income in 1939 was $1,231 (U.S. Dept. of Commerce, Bureau of the Census, 16th Census of the United States, 1940, Population, Families, Size of Family and Age of Head, Table 8). Many families still were feeling the economic effects of the Depression (SSD7). Few, if any, families had major food, fuel, or clothing reserves stockpiled before December, 1941.

From a role perspective, these families did not have an extensive set of resources (SSD6). There were roles representing two generations and adult roles representing two sexes. The adult roles were the first and primary roles to

undergo dedifferentiation. The dedifferentiation of adult roles within the family, as we shall see, was directly linked to dedifferentiation of roles within the occupational sphere.

In summary, World War II was an intense, pervasive, externally-initiated and artificially generated crisis, characterized by precipitous onset. It was generally unexpected and involved scarcities in many areas. Moreover, it was perceived as a major crisis, whose solvability was not entirely clear, both because of its enormity and because of the uncertainties of political and economic factors which were at the heart of the crisis.

At the time the crisis began, American family structure could be described as highly differentiated and generally traditional. Because of the Depression crisis of the previous decade, most families were not noticeably affluent, and thus had more limited resources than they otherwise might have had.

In addition, only individuals over 30 were likely to have had significant experience with World War I, which would have prepared them for the vast mobilization effort the nation as a whole underwent. Those individuals most likely to be drawn into the Armed Services were largely in precisely that age group which had no prior experience with an analogous crisis.

Predictions

This combined set of factors—a major, large-scale crisis, occurring shortly after a long-term, pervasive crisis of an entirely different nature—would lead to the general prediction that role dedifferentiation would be widespread. Moreover, the reconfiguration (postcrisis) role patterns, while less accentuated than those evident during the height of the crisis, nonetheless would be more advanced than the prewar levels. Further, they would create a greater residue of changes than would be expected for a more limited crisis.

More specifically, we shall propose seven predictions from this model and attempt to test them with available census data.

HYPOTHESIS 1

Hypothesis 1: There would be, at least initially, and probably again in the post-War period, an increase in the number of marriages (individuals dedifferentiating their roles from the condition of single to married individual).

Bureau of the Census figures reveal that

. . . between 1940 and 1943 there were 1,118,000 more marriages than would have been expected under normal peacetime conditions. . . . In these four years, 6,579,000 marriages took place, whereas, on the basis of the average marriage rate for the years 1920 to 1939, only 5,461,000 would have been expected. (U.S. Department of Commerce, Bureau of the Census, *Population,* Series PM-1, No. 3, November 12, 1944, p. 1)

In 1942, the highest marriage rate ever recorded to that time for the United States occurred (13.1 marriages per 1,000 of the population). After 1942, the marriage rate fell off somewhat, but it remained above normal through 1945, and then peaked again during the postwar period (see Table 1).

It is interesting to note that the marriage rate had much the same pattern during World Wars I and II. In each case, the marriage rate increased sharply during the initial and early stages of the war, and then experienced another peak after the crisis.

Some of these marriages, particularly among older couples (ages 25–39), reflect the postponement of marriages during the preceding Depression years. The mobilization for war provided employment, and thus economic stability, for civilian older couples who had en-

Table 1

Number of Marriages and Marriage Rate per 1,000 of the Population 1938 to 1944, and Estimated Normal* Number of Marriages, 1938 to 1944, for the United States

Year	Actual Marriages		Expected Normal Number of Marriages	Excess (+) or Deficiency (–) of Actual From Normal	
	Number**	Per 1,000 of the Population		Number	Percent of normal
1938	1,319,000	10.2	1,332,000	−31,000	−1.0
1939	1,375,000	10.5	1,342,000	+33,000	+2.5
1940	1,565,000	11.9	1,353,000	+212,000	+15.7
1941	1,679,000	12.6	1,362,000	+317,000	+23.3
1942	1,758,000	13.1	1,371,000	+387,000	+28.2
1943	1,577,000	11.8	1,375,000	+202,000	+14.7
1944	1,445,000	10.9	1,378,000	+67,000	+4.9
1945	1,613,000	12.2	1,376,000	+236,000	+17.2
1946	2,291,000	16.4	1,371,000	+920,000	+67.1
1947	1,992,000	13.9	1,364,000	+628,000	+46.0
1948	1,811,000	12.4	1,354,000	+457,000	+33.8
1949	1,585,000	10.7			

*"Normal" marriages based on 1920 to 1939 average annual age-specific marriage rate applied to female population of corresponding ages living in specified year.

**Figures for 1941–1944 are estimated. The figures for these years exclude members of the armed forces abroad. "The inclusion of this group has little effect on the marriage rate in the years under consideration. For 1943, the marriage rate is 11.8 if the armed forces abroad are excluded from the base population, and 11.6 if they are included. For other years the difference is even smaller" (U.S. Department of Commerce, Bureau of the Census, *Population,* Series PM-1, No. 1, July 4, 1944, p. 1.

Sources: U.S. Department of Commerce, Bureau of the Census, *Population* Series PM-1, No. 3, November 13, 1944. p. 2.
U.S. Department of Commerce, Bureau of the Census, *Statistical Abstract of U.S. for 1951,* Table 57.

dured or lived with the threat of unemployment during the Depression years.

Among the younger groups, particularly 18 through 24 years, the increase in marriage rates most probably reflected two distinguishable responses to the crisis. One, there was the emotional impetus to consummate relationships to provide emotional security for men and women, and economic security for some women. Two, there was the realization that dedifferentiation of the single male role to the married male role, in some cases, could lead to deferment from the less desired role of serviceman.

These trends suggest support for Hypothesis 1.

HYPOTHESIS 2

Hypothesis 2: There would be an increase of both younger-than-usual and some older-than-usual individuals entering marriage (*i.e.*, the age criteria for entering the marital role would change during the war, but the age criteria would undergo readjustment—not necessarily to the precrisis level—in the postwar period).

In 1947, the Census Bureau also reported that

> . . . the largest increase in the proportion married has occurred in the age group 20 to 29 years old. In 1947 about 63 per cent of all persons in this age group were married, as compared with only 54 percent in 1940. The number of married persons in their twenties increased by about 20 percent in these seven years, whereas the civilian population as a whole in this age range increased by only about 3 per cent. (U.S. Department of Commerce, Bureau of the Census, *Current Population Reports,* Population Characteristics, Series P-20, No. 10, April 1947, p. 2).

In 1940, the median age at first marriage for *all females ever married* was 21.6. The median age at first marriage for white women *ages 20 to 24 years* was 19.5 and for black women *ages 20 to 24* was 18.8. For all women ever married who were 20 to 24 years old in 1940 (n = 3,115,580), 621,960 were married before they were 18; 1,006,920 were married between 18 and 19; 767,160 were married between 20 and 21, and 274,100 were married between 22 and 24. The

median age at first marriage for all women ever married who were 20 to 24 years old in 1940 was 19.4, compared to a median age of 21.8 in 1939, 21.1 in 1944, and 20.7 in 1949 (U.S. Department of Commerce, Bureau of the Census, *Population,* Special Reports, Series P-45, No. 7, May 28, Table 5; U.S. Department of Commerce, Bureau of the Census, *Current Population Reports,* P-20, No. 239, September 1972, Table D).

Older people also experienced increases in marriage rates. The Census Bureau reports that

> . . . high marriage rates since 1940 have also produced increases in the proportion married among older persons, but these increases have been less striking than those among younger persons. During this period with its high employment level, many thousands of older persons who had passed through the more usual age for marriage during the Depression years of the 1930's married for the first time. (*Current Population Reports,* Series P-20, No. 10, p. 2, 1947)

On the basis of these figures, we submit Hypothesis 2 receives empirical support.

HYPOTHESIS 3

Hypothesis 3: There would be an increase in divorce, particularly following the crisis resolution; and the age groups most involved in divorce would be the younger people most directly affected by the crisis.

The evidence we have of an increase in the marriage rate of younger age groups or the younger age at first marriage during the early war years is a fair predictor of a subsequent increase in the number of divorces among these couples. This is so because of the consistent correlation between young age at first marriage and high divorce rates.

The divorce rate hit an (until then) all-time peak in 1946, with 610,000 divorces and annulments reported in 1946, representing a 25.8 per cent increase from the preceding year. The divorce rate (per 1,000 population) hovered around 1.7 during the Depression years,

Table 2
Marital Status of Males 14 Years Old and Over, by Age, for the U.S.: Civilian Population, April, 1947, and Total Population, April, 1940

Age	Total Ever Married 1940 %	Total Ever Married 1947 %	Divorced 1940 %	Divorced 1947 %
14 to 19 years	1.5	2.4	—*	0.1
14 to 17 years	0.3	0.4	—*	—
18 & 19 years	3.7	7.2	—	0.2
20 to 24 years	27.8	38.0	0.3	1.1
25 to 29 years	64.0	72.0	0.9	1.7
30 to 34 years	79.3	84.2	1.4	1.9
35 to 39 years	84.7	88.5	1.8	2.1
40 to 44 years	87.4	89.9	2.0	2.1
45 to 54 years	88.9	90.9	2.0	2.0
55 to 64 years	89.3	91.0	1.8	1.9
65 to 74 years	89.9	92.3	1.5	1.3
75 years and over	90.9	91.6	0.9	0.8

*Percent not shown where less than 0.1.
Source: U.S. Department of Commerce, Bureau of the Census, *Current Population Reports,* Series P-20, No. 10, Table 1, 1948.

Figure 1
Divorce Rates (Number of Divorces per 1000 Total Population) 1935–1990

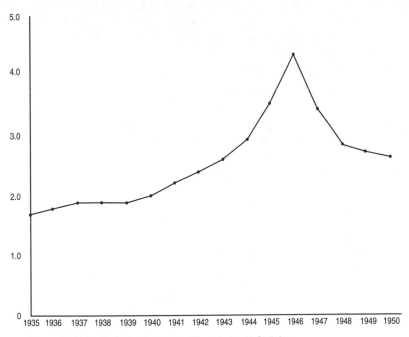

Source: U.S. Public Health Service, National Center for Health Statistics,
"Marriage and Divorce." *Vital Statistics of the U.S.,* 1969

Table 3
Marital Status of Males 18 to 44 by Veteran Status (1947)

	Veteran		Nonveteran
Age	%	Divorced	%
18–24	1.1		0.5
25–34	2.3		1.1
35–44	3.7		1.7
		Wife Absent	
18–24	1.6		1.4
25–34	2.5		2.5
35–44	3.6		2.0

Source: U.S. Department of Commerce, Bureau of the Census, *Current Population Reports,* Series P-20, No. 10, Table II, p. 28.

and increased from 1.9 in 1939, to 2.2 in 1941. Thereafter, the rate rose steadily climbing to 2.4 in 1942, 2.6 in 1943, 2.9 in 1944, 3.5 in 1945 and peaking in 1946 at 4.3. In the postwar years, the divorce rate declined to 3.4 in 1947, and 2.8 in 1948, but never reached the 1939 prewar level of 1.9 (see Figure 1).

Evidence of an increase in divorce among young persons comes from the Census Bureau which reports that

...the increase since 1940 in the proportion of persons divorced (and not remarried) has been particularly large among persons under 25 years old. About 1 out of every 40 persons who had ever been married was divorced (and not remarried) in 1947, as compared with about 1 out of every 48 in 1940. (U.S. Department of Commerce, Bureau of the Census, *Current Population Reports,* Series P-20, No. 10, p. 1)

If we examine the males who were 25 to 29 years old in 1947, we undoubtedly see a large proportion of the men who were marrying between 1940 and 1947. In 1940, these males were 18 to 22. The percentage divorced by 1947 for this group of males who were 18 to 22

Table 4
Labor Force Participation* Rates of Women, by Age, for Selected Years

Age	1940 %	1945 %	1947 %
Total	27.6	37.0	30.0
14–19	20.0	39.9	27.7
14 & 15	2.4	12.2	8.1
16 & 17	13.8	40.8	24.2
18 & 19	42.7	67.3	48.9
20–24	48.0	54.9	44.3
25–34	35.5	40.2	31.2
35–44	29.4	40.7	35.4
45–54	24.5	36.9	32.3
55–64	18.0	27.5	23.5
65+	6.9	9.6	8.1

*Percentage of all women 14 and over in the labor force out of total number of women 14 and over in the population.
Source: U.S. Department of Labor, Women's Bureau, *Women as Workers,* Table 22.

just before the war began was 1.7, almost twice as great as the percentage divorced for those individuals who were 25 to 29 years of age in 1940 (0.9) (see Table 2).

Hypothesis 3a: There would be more divorces among veterans than among nonveterans in the postwar period.

This hypothesis was developed on the basis of several sets of factors. First, many of the males who entered the Armed Services presumably entered hasty wartime marriages for reasons of emotional security, as well as because of the existential climate characterized by the slogan "live today, because tomorrow may never come." Secondly the age at first marriage for many of these servicemen was very young, a factor consistently associated with high subsequent divorce rates.

Third, many of these servicemen were separated for long periods of time from their wives (and children), particularly beginning in 1943 when there was a large contingent of American servicemen overseas. For older servicemen, a proportion of whom may have had less than ideal marriages before the war the separation necessitated by the war resulted in dedifferentiated roles both for husbands and wives. Wives, left at home with children, expanded their roles to include many of the family role tasks formerly exclusively performed by their husbands. Husbands, meanwhile, were experiencing role change in their transformation from family man to serviceman. In addition, many wives, as we shall show below, elaborated their roles to include breadwinning role tasks previously reserved for the husband role. As a result, in the postwar period, many of these families faced reentry crises, which were resolved by further dedifferentiating their roles from a married to divorced status, or simply formalizing through divorce the role changes that already had occurred (Hill, 1949).

Census Bureau statistics reveal that

. . . among male veterans of World War II under 45 years old in 1947, about 56.4 per cent were married and living with their wives. Among nonveterans 18 to 44 years old, about 72.5 per cent were married with wife present. Veterans had a larger percent divorced than did nonveterans. (U.S. Department of Commerce, Bureau of the Census, *Population Characteristics, Current Population Reports.* Series P-20, No. 10, p. 6)

Unfortunately data are unavailable with more refined age categories, which would allow us

	1940		1945		1947		% Change	
	N	% Distr.	N	% Distr.	N	% Distr.	1940–1945	1945–1947
Total	13,840,000	100.0	19,570,000	100.0	16,320,000	100.0	41.4	−16.6
14–19	1,460,000	10.5	2,720,000	13.9	1,820,000	11.2	86.3	−33.1
14 & 15	57,000	0.4	280,000	1.4	170,000	1.0	391.2	−39.3
16 & 17	333,000	2.4	934,000	4.8	530,000	3.2	180.5	−43.3
18 & 19	1,070,000	7.7	1,506,000	7.7	1,120,000	6.9	40.7	−25.6
20–24	2,820,000	20.4	3,270,000	16.7	2,690,000	16.5	16.0	−17.7
25–34	3,820,000	27.6	4,450,000	22.7	3,640,000	22.3	16.5	−18.2
35–44	2,680,000	19.4	4,060,000	20.7	3,580,000	21.9	51.5	−11.8
45–54	1,830,000	13.2	2,969,000	15.2	2,690,000	16.5	62.2	−9.4
55–64	920,000	6.6	1,611,000	8.2	1,460,000	8.9	75.1	−9.4
65+	310,000	2.2	490,000	2.5	440,000	2.7	58.1	−10.2
Median Age	31.9		33.5		35.0			

Table 5
Women in the Labor Force* for Selected Years

*Number by age and percentage of women in the total female labor force.
Source: U.S. Department of Labor, Women's Bureau, *Women as Workers,* Table 21.

to substantiate more definitively the argument presented here.

In addition, the Census Bureau reports that in 1947

> ...about 1 out of every 29 veterans of World War II 18 to 44 years old who had ever married was divorced and not remarried, whereas only about 1 out of 60 ever-married nonveterans in this age range was divorced and not remarried. (U.S. Department of Commerce, Bureau of the Census, *Population Characteristics, Current Population Reports*, Series P-20, No. 10, p. 6)

We might interpret this to mean that those individuals most severely affected by the war were most likely to incur more long-lasting role changes.

Ideally, to demonstrate the validity of this hypothesis, as well as several previous ones, it would be useful to have divorce statistics of veterans and nonveterans categorized by direct information on age of husband and wife at (first) marriage, duration of marriage, length of time veteran was separated from family, overseas duty of veteran, and age at divorce. Unfortunately, the history of American data collection in the area of marriage and divorce statistics has been of a relatively recent and unsystematic nature (Newman, 1949; Cohen, 1941; Bureau of the Census, 1940). The marital status information on veterans represents an even more difficult situation.

HYPOTHESIS 4

Hypothesis 4: There would be an increase of women in the labor force, and the increase in labor force participation would be particularly high among new categories of women (*i.e.,* those who had had low participation rates before the war—such as married women, mothers, older women).

The crisis framework predicts that in times of crisis the criteria for entry into certain roles change drastically, and, thus, new categories of individuals and groups become eligible for roles from which they previously were barred. The stratification system begins to give way, allowing for the reallocation of resources and the utilization of newly perceived or identified resources. The crisis framework also suggests that the dedifferentiation of roles should peak during the crisis period, and then recede, but rarely to the precrisis level.

An overview of the empirical data suggests that, in the United States during World War II, this is essentially what occurred. During this period, blacks (Killingsworth, 1969), women, and other minorities entered the labor force, not only in larger numbers, but in different occupational roles than they had heretofore occupied. Prior to World War II (March, 1940) women represented 25.4 per cent of all workers, and by April, 1945, this figure rose to 36.1 per cent. In the postwar (reconfiguration) period they had dropped to 27.6 per cent—a level below the crisis peak, but above the precrisis point.

Looked at from the perspective of the total female population, we see another reflection of the same phenomenon: in the prewar period (March, 1940) 27.6 per cent of all women 14 years of age and over were in the labor force; however, during the war (April, 1945) the percentage rose to 37, and then dropped to 30 per cent in the postwar period (April, 1947).

Data on variations in labor force participation by age group during the War years are difficult to obtain in detail.[5] However, we know that the median age of women workers was 32 years in 1940, rose to 34 years by 1945, and rose again to 35 by 1947 (U.S. Department of Labor, Women's Bureau, *Handbook on Women Workers,* 1965, p. 12; *Women As Workers: A Statistical Guide,* Table 21).

The participation rate of women in the labor force indicates the ratio of women working or seeking work to the total female population of comparable ages. When we look at the participation rates of women in the labor force by age groups (see Table 4), we see that in 1940, 8.2 per cent of the 14 to 17 year olds, 46.4 per cent of the 18 to 24 year olds, 29.4 per cent of the 35 to 44 year olds, and 24.5 per cent of the 45 to 54 year olds were working. In addition, 18.0 per cent of the 55 to 64 year olds and

6.9 per cent of the 65 years and over group were in the labor force.

By 1945, 26.5 per cent of the 14 to 17 year olds, 61.1 per cent of the 18 to 24 year olds, 40.7 per cent of the 35 to 44 year olds, and 36.9 per cent of the 45 to 54 year old women were in the labor force. Almost 28 per cent of women 55 to 64 years and 10 per cent of the 65 years and over group were working.

By 1947, virtually every age group experienced a drop from the wartime peak; but the only group which returned to the precrisis baseline (in fact dropped below it) was the group of women in prime childbearing age groups. High levels of older and younger women in the postwar labor force reflected a permanent postcrisis residue. The age criteria for women workers had changed in response to the war, and these changes had clear and lasting effects.

Turning now to the restricted population of all women who work outside the home, we note that in 1940 women 14 to 17 years old made up 2.8 per cent of the total number of women workers. Women 18 to 24 years old represented 28.1 per cent of the female labor force, women 25 to 34 represented 27.6 per cent, women 35 to 44 were 19.4 per cent, and women 45 to 54 made up 13.2 per cent of the working women. By 1945, the figures had shifted in the following way: there were increases in all but the early childbearing categories (see Table 5).

When we examine marital status of women workers, we note a large influx of married workers and mothers in the labor force. Their numbers increased during the peak war years, and dropped back somewhat following the war, but never returned to the prewar levels. Since that time, the rate of labor force participation of married women has continued to grow at a faster rate than that of single women. Clearly some of the increase in married women workers during the war period can be attributed to the increased marriage rates. Interestingly enough, the rate of increase in working among married women was even greater in the group with husbands present

than in those with husbands absent (due to military duty, employment elsewhere, voluntary separation, etc.). This suggests that the increase was attributable to changing criteria, based on a changing value system; that is, a married woman did not need to have a husband absent in order to justify entering the labor force.

The figures for mothers in the labor force convey a similar picture. Working mothers were relatively scarce before World War II. In 1940, the Women's Bureau reported 8.6 per cent of all mothers with children under 18 years of age worked outside the home (U.S. Department of Labor, Women's Bureau, *Handbook on Women Workers*, 1965, p. 38). During the war, this group expanded so that by early 1946 18.2 per cent of mothers with children under 18 years were working. If we compare working mothers to all women in the labor force, we see that they increasingly made up a larger portion of working women. Put another way, their participation rate increased

Table 6
Labor-Force Participation Rates of Mothers and of All Women, Selected Years, 1940–1964*

Year	Mothers[1] %	All women[2] %
1964	34.5	37.4
1960	30.4	36.7
1958	29.5	36.0
1956	27.5	35.9
1954	25.6	33.7
1952	23.8	33.9
1950	21.6	33.1
1948	20.2	31.9
1946	18.2	31.2
1940	8.6	28.2

*Women 14 years of age and over.
[1]Data are for March of each year except 1946, 1948, 1952, and 1954, when they are for April.
[2]Annual averages.

Source: U.S. Department of Labor, Women's Bureau, *1965 Handbook on Women Workers*, Table 18, p. 38.

Table 7
Employed Women Workers in Selected Occupational Groups, April 1940, 1945, 1947[1]

	1940[2]		1945		1947	
	N[3]	%	N	%	N	%
Craftsmen, foremen, and kindred workers	110	0.9	300	1.5	160	1.0
Operatives and kindred workers	2,190	18.4	4,610	23.9	3,420	21.7
Professional and semi-professional workers	1,570	13.3	1,510	7.8	1,540	9.7
Domestic workers	2,100	17.6	1,670	8.6	1,690	10.7
Service workers	1,350	11.3	1,980	10.3	1,770	11.2

[1]Estimates of employment by occupation for April, 1940, and April, 1945, were adjusted to be consistent with revised Census totals of agricultural and nonagricultural employment. Estimates subsequent to 1940 are subject to sampling variation which may be large in cases where the quantities shown are relatively small.

[2]Approximately 400,000 employed workers whose occupations were not reported were apportioned according to the distribution of those whose occupations were reported.

[3]Numbers in thousands.

Sources: U.S. Department of Commerce, Bureau of the Census and U.S. Department of Labor, Bureau of Labor Statistics.

faster than working women in general, particularly during the war years (see Table 6).

The Women's Bureau informs us that "since 1946, the percentage of working mothers with children under 18 has steadily increased at a rate of about one per cent a year" (U.S. Department of Labor, Women's Bureau, *Handbook on Women Workers*, 1965, p. 38). The fact that, after an initial drop-off from the peak war years, women's participation rates continued to climb is probably at least partly related to their initial experience during the war years. Severe, prolonged and pervasive crises provide opportunities for learning new roles, and for recognizing the advantages of having new categories of role occupants in certain previously forbidden roles.

Both the role occupants and the gatekeepers develop new perspectives as the result of crisis. Crises of such enormous proportions force the participants of social systems to reorder their priorities, partly on the basis of their crisis experience. The fact that no evidence could be mustered to demonstrate unequivocally that children were harmed by their mothers' wartime working outside the home served to encourage those women who had worked during

the war to remain in the labor market. It also encouraged others who had not worked outside the home to enter the work force in postwar years. Reordering of priorities comes about in connection with changes in values and norms. Value and norm changes, reflected here in shifts in the wife and mother roles, occur most abruptly and surely in the face of crisis demands. As a result, new groups are recruited into previously forbidden roles. Clearly, Hypothesis 4, which predicts increases of women, particularly new groups of women, in the labor force is substantially upheld.

HYPOTHESIS 5

Hypothesis 5: There would be an increase of women in occupational roles which women ordinarily did not enter (women would be dedifferentiating their traditional occupational roles to include nontraditional occupations) and these increases would peak during the crisis period and start to level off after the war, but not return to precrisis levels.

World War II saw not merely a gross influx of women into the marketplace, but clear changes in the internal distribution of women (as well as men) among various job classifications. These internal changes reflected occupant dedifferentiation of certain occupational categories. This can be seen most clearly in the categories of "craftsmen, foremen and kindred workers" and "operatives and kindred workers."[6] (See Table 7.)

As the crisis model predicts, there is an increase in these nontraditional roles for women during the crisis and a recession after the crisis (*i.e.*, in the reconfiguration period), but not to the precrisis low. Thus, in 1940, 0.9 per cent of women workers were craftsmen, foremen and kindred workers; by 1945, their ranks had swelled to 1.5 percent and then dropped to 1.0 per cent by 1947. Similarly, among women working in 1940, 18.4 per cent were operatives and kindred workers. In 1945, 23.9 per cent were in this category, but by 1947 they had leveled off to 21.7 per cent (again, above the precrisis point). Concomitantly, the ranks of professionals, semiprofessionals and domestic workers experienced a departure of women workers during the war years and a resurgence (but not to the precrisis baseline) after the war. (Figures for service workers, another traditional female category, showed a similar trend.)

Thus, we conclude that Hypotheses 4 and 5 are upheld. Women did increase their numbers in the labor market, and new categories of women—married women, older women, mothers—entered the labor force. Women workers, further, dedifferentiated the previously traditional (and narrow) range of occupational roles they held in stable periods to include nontraditional occupational roles during the crisis. The role dedifferentiation peaks that occurred during the crisis became reconfigured following the war and stabilized at a new level—below the crisis peak, but above the precrisis low.

Despite the predictions of labor market analysts and other social scientists that there would be a great exodus of women from the labor market following the war, many women stayed and consolidated, at a somewhat lower level, some of the gains that the crisis period had permitted. The postwar distribution patterns of women in the labor market, and their later increases, reflect the severity and pervasiveness of the crisis. As the crisis model predicts, long-term, intense, pervasive crises are more likely to leave a greater dedifferentiation residue that establishes a new baseline for future change.

SUMMARY

A conceptual framework for analyzing role change (dedifferentiation) as a system response to crisis has been presented. A typology of crises has been developed to be used in conjunction with critical aspects of the social system at the time of crisis to predict both crisis period and postcrisis (reconfiguration) period role changes.

The crisis framework was then applied to macro-changes in family structure in response to an archetypal crisis, World War II. Structural changes in the family were indicated by macrostructural data (*i.e.*, marriage and divorce rates, as well as occupational role shifts for women). Although census data are not sufficiently detailed to permit more elaborate analysis, they generally indicate support for the hypotheses derived from the crisis/dedifferentiation perspective.

References

Bettelheim, Bruno. 1960. *The Informed Heart.* Glencoe, Ill.: Free Press.

Cavan, Ruth and Katherine Ranck. 1938. *The Family and the Depression.* Chicago, Ill.: University of Chicago Press.

Cohen, Bernard. 1941. "Centralized collection of marriage and divorce records and their uses." *American Journal of Public Health* 31 (August): 824.

Davis, Fred. 1963. *Passage Through Crisis: Polio Victims and Their Families.* Indianapolis: Bobbs-Merrill.

Davis, Kingsley. 1950. "Statistical perspective on marriage and divorce." *Annals of the American Academy of Political and Social Science* 272 (November): 9–21.

Drabek, Thomas E. and Keith S. Boggs. 1968. "Families in disaster: reactions and relatives." *Journal of Marriage and the Family* 30 (August): 451–453.

Duncan, Beverly and Otis Dudley Duncan. 1969. "Family stability and occupational success." *Social Problems* 16 (Winter): 273–285.

Glick, Paul C. 1974. "A demographer looks at American families." Burgess Award Address presented at annual meeting of National Council on Family Relations in St. Louis, Missouri, October 25, 1974. Published in *Journal of Marriage and the Family* 37 (Feb., 1975): 15–26.

Goode, William J. 1951. "Economic factors and marital stability." *American Sociological Review* 16 (December): 802–812.

——. 1963. *World Revolution and Family Patterns.* New York: Free Press.

Gulden, Tess. 1939. "Divorce and business cycles." *American Sociological Review* 4 (2): 217–223.

Hill, Reuben. 1949. *Families Under Stress.* New York: Harper and Brothers.

Kephart, William M. 1955. "Occupational level and marital disruption." *American Sociological Review* 20 (August): 456–465.

Killingsworth, Charles. 1969. "Jobs and income for Negroes." Pp. 194–273 in Irwin Katz and Patricia Gurin (eds.), *Race and the Social Sciences.* New York: Basic Books.

Komarovsky, Mirra. 1962. *Blue Collar Marriage.* New York: Vintage.

——. 1940. *The Unemployed Man and His Family.* New York: Dryden.

Kunzel, Renate. 1974. "The connection between the family cycle and divorce rates: an analysis based on European data." *Journal of Marriage and the Family* 36 (May): 379–388.

Lindemann, Eric. 1949. "Symptomatology and management of acute grief." *American Journal of Psychiatry* 101: 141–148.

Lipman-Blumen, Jean. 1973. "Role de-differentiation as a system response to crisis: occupational and political roles of women." *Sociological Inquiry* 43 (2): 105–129.

Merton, Robert K. 1957. *Social Theory and Social Structure.* Glencoe, Ill.: The Free Press.

Newman, Samuel C. 1949. "Needs and future prospects for integrating marriage and divorce data with other vital statistics." *American Journal of Public Health* 39 (September): 1141–1144.

Ogburn, William F. and Dorothy S. Thomas. 1922. "The influence of the business cycle on certain social conditions." *American Statistical Association Journal* 18 (September): 324–340.

Pinard, Maurice. 1966. "Marriage and divorce decisions and the larger social system: a case study in social change." *Social Forces* 44 (March): 341–355.

Rainwater, Lee, R. P. Coleman, and G. Handel. 1959. *Workingman's Wife.* New York: McFadden Bartell.

Rapoport, Rhona. 1963. "Normal crises, family structure and mental health." *Family Process* 2 (1): 68–80.

Social Science Research Council. 1948. *Labor Force in the United States.* New York.

Thomas, Dorothy Swaine. 1927. "Social aspects of the business cycle." *Demographic Monographs* 1. New York: Gordon and Breach Science Publishers.

U.S. Department of Commerce, Bureau of the Census. 1940. "Size of family and age of head." 16th Census of the U.S. Population and Families. Washington, D.C.: U.S. Government Printing Office.

——. 1940. "Tentative plans for the collection of marriage and divorce statistics." *Vital Statistics—Special Reports* 9 (May 9, 1940): 491–495. Washington, D.C.: U.S. Government Printing Office.

——. 1940–1955 Annual Report on the Labor Force. Washington, D.C.: U.S. Government Printing Office.

——. 1944. "Marriages in the United States: 1914–1943." Population. Series PM-1, No. 1 (July 4, 1944). Washington, D.C.: U.S. Government Printing Office.

——. 1946–1952. *The Labor Force.* Special Surveys. MRLF-No. 36 for 1946–1952. Washington, D.C.: U.S. Government Printing Office.

——. 1948. "Characteristics of single, married, widowed, and divorced persons in 1947." Current Population Reports, Population Characteristics. Series P-20, No.10. Washington, D.C.: U.S. Government Printing Office.

——. 1951. Statistical Abstract of U.S. for 1951. Washington, D.C.: U.S. Government Printing Office.

U.S. Department of Labor, Women's Bureau. 1965. 1965 Handbook on Women Workers. *Women's Bureau, Bulletin* 290. Washington, D.C.: U.S. Government Printing Office.

——. n.d. Women as Workers. D-65. Washington, D.C.: U.S. Government Printing Office.

U.S. Public Health Service: National Center for Health Statistics. 1969. "Marriage and divorce." *Vital Statistics of the U.S.* 3. Rockville, Maryland.

U.S. Public Health Service: National Office of Vital Statistics. 1949. "The development and status of vital statistics on marriage and divorce." Released November 22, 1949.

Weeks, H. Ashley. 1943. "Differential divorce rates by occupation." *Social Forces* 21 (March): 334–337.

Wilcox, Walter F. 1893. "A study of vital statistics." *Political Science Quarterly* 8 (1).

Endnotes

1. "Assimilation" is defined as taking over and incorporating into the first of two roles a role element which previously was part of another role, and which the second (counter-) role relinquishes. "Overlap" refers to the process by which a role element which previously was an exclusive part of one role is now a nonexclusive component of two or more roles (Lipman-Blumen, 1973: 107).

2. These patterns include role reversal, role submergence, role obsolescence, institutional substitution, role emergence, role compartmentalization, as well as unilateral and reciprocal patterns of assimilation and overlap. For an extended description of these patterns, see Lipman-Blumen, 1973.

3. "CD" stands for "crisis dimension" described in the section on "A Typology of Crisis."

4. "SSD" stands for "social system dimension" described in the section on "The State of the Social System."

5. According to the Women's Bureau (1965 *Handbook on Women Workers*, p. 17), "data are not available for computing labor force participation rates for all women 18 to 64 years of age prior to 1947, or for non-white women prior to 1954."

6. Although we are focusing on changes in women's roles, men's roles also changed during World War II. Comparable occupational shifts for male workers were recorded during this period.

Chapter Seven

Family Systems Theory

Fred and Cassie have been married for three years. For the most part, they do not have any serious disagreements, or at least any that they can really put their finger on. But sometimes Fred says or does something that offends Cassie. He then feels somewhat guilty for what he has done, but he does not feel that it is totally his fault, and doesn't like the superior attitude she sometimes has when he does apologize. Therefore, he acts defensively instead, giving the impression that he is now responding to a revengeful reaction on her part, even though she has not (at least yet) given one. Cassie can't understand why Fred was mean to her and is angry but doesn't want to show it, so she acts indifferently. Fred notices the indifference and wonders if it is feigned or deliberate. He is afraid to apologize because it would be embarrassing and even more hurtful if the apology were rejected or taken advantage of. Besides, it wasn't like she hadn't done something to him earlier that precipitated his offense. Meanwhile, Cassie wants to hear an apology but isn't sure that it will be enough. She would like restitution but isn't sure that she can demand it. So neither one apologizes or forgives and the relationship spirals downhill. They eventually stop talking to each other without really understanding why and are urged by their friends to seek marriage counseling.

This continuous circular interaction, where each is responding to his or her perception of the other, is at the heart of family systems theory and illustrates its complexity.

HISTORY

It is generally believed that family systems theory emerged primarily in the 1960s. However, the basic concepts that would eventually lead to a coherent theory were being discussed a long time before that. For example, in 1926, Ernest Burgess made a presentation to the American Sociological Association that became a landmark publication. He referred to the family as "a unity of interacting personalities." He explained that this means that the family is much more than its formal or legal definition; instead, it is a living, growing superpersonality that has as its essence the interaction of its members.

Burgess went on to describe two basic family types: the highly integrated and the unintegrated family. The first is characterized by rituals, discipline, and interdependence and the second by a lack of those features. He discussed the importance of the roles played by each family member, how problems result when they conflict, and how one member can be identified as the "family problem."

These insights are all elaborated on in chapter two of Waller's (1938) classic textbook on the family. This chapter, titled "The Family as an Arena of Interacting Personalities," begins by discussing how the family is basically a closed system of social interaction. It also discusses how the family is the greatest source of influence on a child, but that the child's personality also affects the parents. And perhaps most important, Waller explores the idea that family experiences are repetitive and are based on patterns of interaction.

In the same time period, biologist Ludwig von Bertalanffy (1969) was beginning to develop the basic ideas of general systems theory. However, for the most part, systems theory as it relates to families remained hidden as a part of structural functionalism until after World War II. At that point, family therapists (Bateson, Jackson, Haley, and Weakland 1956) began to seek explanations for the patterns of family interaction that seemed to be at the heart of the dysfunctions they were dealing with. Because of this application, this is also referred to as family process theory (Broderick 1993). In general, family systems theory has its greatest utility in communication and clinical applications. Despite this separate use and identity, some sociologists (Winton 1995) still see it as part of structural functionalist theory.

Bronfenbrenner (1989), most well known for his ecological theory of human development, uses systems concepts in his theory. He focuses on the role of different environments, such as home, school, and the community, and how they interact with an active child. We see that not only are children being influenced by parents, the school, and the neighborhood, but that the child impacts those environments and helps to shape them as well.

There are four basic systems that make up our ecological environment. The first is the *microsystem.* This represents the immediate environment of the child, such as the family and school or day care center, church, peers, and so forth. The environment itself interacts with the age, health, sex, and other aspects of the individual. Because of this a child's behavior will vary, based on the microsystem or the environment. The second level is the *mesosystem,* which recognizes that those various components of the child's environment are not independent. Instead, they interact with each other and with the components of the next systems as well. Thus, a child may learn something at school that will make the home environment better.

The *exosystem* is those institutions that are beyond the child's immediate environment but impact upon his or her development in less direct ways. Examples include friends, neighbors, and extended kin, the parent's place of work, social service agencies, and the media. So if a parent has a bad day at work, even though the child never entered that place or environment, he may be affected by the short temper of the parent once the parent gets home. Beyond that is the *macrosystem,* which includes the customs, attitudes, values, and laws of the culture in which the child lives. Each of our lives is af-fected on a daily basis by laws such as speed limits, over which we have no control.

All of these systems must be understood and taken into account if one is to have a full understanding of a child's development. In addition, it should be within the context of a *chronosystem.* This refers to changes in the environment across time (Gardiner and Kosmitzki 2002).

BASIC ASSUMPTIONS

The whole is greater than the sum of the parts. A family is much more than a collection of individuals who live together and are related to each other. It is also a natural social system, with its own rules, roles, communication patterns, and power structure. A basic dictum is that "the whole is greater than the sum of the parts." It is unique from, and more long lasting than, most other systems. One enters a family through birth, adoption, or marriage and remains a member until death. In actuality, a family member may continue to have psychological influence over another even after he or she has passed on. The family in which you are a child is called your *family of origin.* You remain a member of this group even after you grow up and move away because your experiences in that system continue to affect your personality. The family you create when you marry or live together as married is referred to as your *family of procreation.*

The locus of pathology is not within the person but is a system dysfunction. Systems theory requires a *paradigm shift* in the way we think about the world. Most social science theories have taken what we call an intrapsychic viewpoint. Here the individual is the unit of study, and problems are presumed to be "in the head" of that person. However, with systems theory, the *locus of pathology,* or the location of the problem, is not within the person. Rather than saying that an individual has a disease, we say that the system of which he/she is a part is *dysfunctional.* That is, problems are seen as being a function of a struggle between persons. Think of a family as being represented by a circle for each member, with lines connecting them. The lines represent the communication patterns—the ways they speak to and act toward each other—between the members. Systems theorists believe that the problems are in the lines rather than in the circles. This applies to normative or functional behaviors as well, of course, even though clinical applications tend to focus on difficulties. Another way of thinking about it is to compare a system to a child's mobile hanging over a crib. A number of interesting objects are connected by strings or wires. Whenever one is hit, it causes the others to move. Similarly, if you remove one of the objects, the entire system becomes unbalanced.

This interpersonal rather than intrapsychic perspective considers all behavior to be a part of ongoing, interactive, and recurring events, with no real beginning or end points. Therefore, a person who manifests some symptomatic behavior is seen as representing a dysfunctional system. Some are disturbed by this, taking it to mean that individuals are not responsible for their behavior and that they can therefore blame their problems on their family or society. Actually, according to systems theory, time is not wasted on blaming, since the beginning points of a conflict typically cannot be found. We are then free to focus on how to resolve the problem rather than being distracted by trying to find someone to punish for it. It is recognized that individuals are ultimately responsible for their own behavior but that no behavior can be understood in isolation. One's behaviors, emotions, and interactions make sense only within the context of their social world or the environment in which they occur.

As an example, let us say that there is a teen with an eating disorder, which may have resulted in part from having an overcontrolling mother. So is the teen's behavior the mother's fault? Before we answer, let us further assume we find that the mother became controlling in part because of living with an abusive father, who himself grew up under similarly abusive

conditions, which is where he learned that pattern of interaction. Pretty soon we are back in time to where the family ancestors who may have started the behavioral patterns to begin with are all deceased. So, rather than attempt to trace the behavior to its roots in order to place blame, a family therapist can focus on looking for ways to break the present chains of interaction that are maintaining the symptoms.

This paradigm, which is more than a therapeutic approach but actually a new way of conceptualizing human problems and understanding behavior, requires its own *epistemology*. This term refers to the way that knowledge is gained and how conclusions are made. The relationship outlook shifts the attention from content to process, or from the behavior itself to how it is maintained.

Circular causality guides behavior. With *linear causality* the focus is on content. If you believe that one event causes the next in straight-line stimulus response fashion, the observer will be distracted by what a couple is arguing about and how it got started. In contrast, *circular causality* is the idea that with human social interaction there are a number of forces moving in many directions simultaneously. It is all about process. That is, it doesn't matter if the couple is fighting about money or child rearing—it is the repetitive pattern of interaction that is of interest. The focus is on *how* they interact, regardless of the topic, and what can be done to change that pattern into a more functional one (that is, one that leads to happiness rather than unhappiness).

Take as an example a young recently married couple. Desiring to be autonomous, they resent and avoid their parents and in-laws for calling and visiting too often and giving unwanted advice. From their viewpoint, they are running away from the parents because the parents are running after them. However, the parents see it differently—they would not have to call and counsel so often if the adult children would just see them occasionally. Each sees themselves as reacting to the other and believes that the other one "started it." Are the children avoiding because the parents are intrusive, or are the parents intrusive because the children are avoiding? We think linearly, but the behaviors are circular.

Therefore, the entire family is the "patient," rather than a particular individual member. Often one person may manifest more symptoms, or is believed by the others to be the major cause of family problems and is therefore sent for counseling. We call this individual the "identified patient." The key to understanding a family is to refrain from paying attention to the individual members. Instead, it is their behavioral exchanges, what are referred to as the family *rules,* that are of primary importance.

Rules are discovered in retrospect. The repetitive patterns of interaction are identified, and these are the rules that a family lives by. Positive change is made in a family by helping them to change their dysfunctional rules. A few rules are clear and overt—that is, you can ask family members what the rules are and they can consciously identify them and agree on them. They might include a curfew for the teenagers and not talking back to Mom or Dad. Next are the rules that they do not identify as such, but if an outside observer were to point them out, the family would agree. A common one is the unspoken rule about where everyone sits at the dinner table or that Dad gets to control the TV remote. The most powerful rules are the ones that are covert and unstated. They might include such possibilities as the fact that mom can get mad but dad may not; brother can get away with poor school performance but not sister; or that in an argument, one person blusters while the other ignores it.

Rules result from the redundancy principle. Couples begin to create the rules of their relationship as soon as they meet. You cannot have an infinite reservoir of possible behavioral responses for every situation, so a few are selected and used over and over. This is the *redundancy principle,* which results in family rules. Some rules are dysfunctional (such as mom has an asthma attack whenever dad tries to go to work), but once established, they tend to remain. This is because humans have an automatic tendency to maintain a balance or equi-

librium in their lives; this is called *homeostasis.* Fearing the unknown, we generally oppose change, even change that would be good for us. So when a couple asks a therapist for help, they will also sabotage any attempts to change them.

So how do these ideas work in therapy? An example will further explain the basic ideas. A couple comes for counseling due to a problem with domestic battery. The husband is defensive and blames his wife for forcing him to be mean to her because she won't do as she is told. She responds apologetically that if she were just a better housewife, the marriage would be OK. Putting the specific content or presenting behavioral problem aside for the moment, the therapist determines the following repetitive sequence of events: (1) the husband has strict expectations about what his wife should be or when she should have things ready for him; (2) he has been drinking; (3) she fails to meet an expectation, such as arriving late from work when he has been waiting to pick her up; (4) he becomes angry and berates her; (5) she withdraws—becomes quiet and makes no eye contact in the hope that it will blow over; (6) this makes him more upset, so he escalates his abusive behavior to force a reaction from her; and (7) she finally responds, either with an apology or anger. Either way, this ends the sequence and all is well until it starts again.

Think of these behaviors as circular. They represent some of their family rules that are repeated over and over again. The therapist would choose to intervene at the point where it appears the couple would be most likely to be able to make changes. It could be with the husband's attitudes or drinking behavior, or it could be with the wife's tendency to withdraw before responding. Regardless, it is the process that must be dealt with, not just the physical abuse.

Feedback loops guide behavior. When a family member begins to move outside the accepted limits of family behavior, the others will engage in *feedback loops* to get that member back in line. *Negative feedback* is when others punish you for breaking family rules in order to correct you and get you to return to the proper way of acting. This could be when a teen sasses a parent and gets "the look" or is grounded. The same would occur when breaking a dysfunctional rule, so "negative" does not refer to good or bad but is in the context of breaking a rule, whatever it may be.

Positive feedback is a rewarding response for the deviation. In this case the person is encouraged to break out of the homeostatic balance. Therapists will often give positive feedback for attempts to replace dysfunctional rules with functional ones. Also, family members receive positive feedback for behaviors that stay within the rules, whether they are functional or not. Thus, the focus of systems theory is on the quality of communication among family members.

Pathological communication causes relationship problems. Emotional illnesses have generally been considered to be "in the head" of the patient, although we now understand the important role of genetics in these disturbances. Early family therapists, however, discovered some important family connections. For example, a young person would be hospitalized for schizophrenia and receive behavioral and psychoanalytic therapy. As a reward for getting better, his family would be allowed to visit him, but then he would relapse. They initially thought that it had to do with having interactions once again with a cold, rejecting mother and coined the term *schizophrenogenic mother* to describe this situation. This, in combination with a passive, ineffectual father, was believed to result in sons particularly who could become confused and feel inadequate, and thus become schizophrenic.

As the communication theorists refined their work, it became clear that the primary source of dysfunctions such as schizophrenia was communication patterns rather than these gender and parental behavior issues. *Pathological communication* is the term that refers to the various kinds of unclear and confusing ways of relating, which can cause problems in a relationship. One is mystification, in which the speaker denies the reality of a situation by per-

haps saying that nothing is wrong when there clearly is. Another is the indirect communication of beating around the bush instead of coming out and clearly stating one's desires. Volumes have been written about these and other difficulties in communication.

One of the most prominent concepts in systems work is the *double bind*. It is a special form of contradictory communication. Whenever someone speaks, he or she sends two messages: the verbal and the nonverbal. In other words, there is what you say and how you say it. When someone says "I love you" in the proper tone of voice and in an appropriate circumstance, then he or she "affirms" the communication. That is, the two parts of it are congruent, and you believe someone loves you because of the words and the way in which they are said. This is functional because a person sends the message he or she intended to send and it is received appropriately. However, levels of messages sometimes contradict each other, leaving the recipient to decide what the truth is and how to respond. This is particularly difficult for children, who can be stressed into dysfunctional behaviors as a result. It also predictably leads to conflict in adult relationships.

When the two contradicting messages are commands, then it is a double bind. That is, the individual is told to do two things but cannot do one without disobeying the other. Either way, he or she will be punished—the classic "damned if you do, damned if you don't" situation. The person feels compelled to respond, and the family rules are such that one may not comment on the contradiction or leave the situation. It is like the classic joke where the child is given two shirts for his birthday and puts one on. His mother then responds: "What's the matter, you didn't like the other one?" No matter which shirt he does or does not put on, he is in trouble.

Let's return to the case described in Goldenberg and Goldenberg (2000), a schizophrenic son who is visited by his mother. Happy to see her, he goes up and gives her a hug. In response she stiffens, so he withdraws, to which she responds by asking why he doesn't love her anymore. He can hug her and be rejected or not hug her and be rejected. If he points out what she is doing, she will deny it. Instead, he can choose the "schizophrenic way" and withdraw from reality so as not to be responsible for making any decisions. In other words, "crazy" behavior is the logical way to respond to a system with dysfunctional rules. Therefore, we see that the identified patient is often the person in the family who is the healthiest, in the sense of not wanting to endure dysfunctional rules. Even though it is well known now that most serious emotional disturbances have a genetic base, just like any other illness, it is also true that such disorders are most evident in the families with the highest levels of communication deviance. That is, pathological communication patterns are stressful and make things worse, whereas healthy rules result in a calmer family life and therefore fewer symptoms in its members.

All family members take on roles. The fact that we all tend to play out certain roles is part of the redundancy principle. In addition to being a parent, child, student, or athlete, there are common psychological roles that family members take on. Refusing to play one's role can upset the family equilibrium and result in negative feedback. Research on alcoholic families has revealed certain roles that are found to some degree in most families.

Here is the breakdown that we see over and over again in dysfunctional families (Winton 1995). The parent with the chemical dependency (in this example, the father) plays the role of the *dependent* person. His job is to bring grief to the family while blaming others for his abuses. For example, if you did what he asked then he wouldn't have to drink. He denies his problems and manipulates others in order to perpetuate them. His wife is the *enabler* (also referred to as the *co-dependent*), who helps him to avoid the consequences of his behavior. She may call in sick to work for him or encourage the children to stay away from him when he "gets like that." Perhaps there were alcoholics in her family of origin, and her husband was drawn to her because of her traits of covering for others. She often has psychosomatic symptoms due to her repressed feelings of anger and guilt.

The firstborn child is often the *hero*. He or she is the ideal student and caretaker who seems to have it all together. This is a stressful role but one that is difficult to give up because it has many rewards. The second child is the *delinquent.* This is the scapegoated child, who does poorly in school or manifests other acting-out behaviors. It is a negative approach to getting Dad to change, since the hope is that by turning attention to the child it will alleviate the need of the father to drink. The next child is the *invisible child,* who just keeps a low profile in the hope that it will help lessen family tensions. This child, who basically stays out of the way and thus never deals with emotions, is the most likely to suffer from an emotional illness. The last child is the *clown,* who attempts to use humor in dealing with the family problems.

For any one person to change, the entire system must be changed. Instead of focusing on why the father became an alcoholic and how bad that is, a therapist would help some of the others, particularly the enabling spouse, to give up their supportive roles. If the delinquent can straighten up, for instance, then the family can shift attention from that distraction to the real problem—the drinking.

All this occurs at more subtle levels in families with less serious problems. For example, a young woman might marry into an extended family at whose reunions she is expected to babysit all the children while the other adults socialize. No one knows how this happened, or would even admit to it being the case, but trouble ensues if she refuses to play her role. Another might be selected as the family rebel, or star, and be the focus of the same family reunion.

Family types are based on the rigidity of family boundaries. Some researchers (Kantor and Lehr 1975) have identified three basic family types, based on the rigidity of family boundaries and rules. *Open families* are basically democratic, and the rights of individuals are protected and interactions with outsiders are permitted. There is also consensus and flexibility, and family members are bound together by love and respect. This is often called *mutuality,* and healthy children and patterns of interaction are common in these families.

The second type is the *random family.* Here there are almost no boundaries. The members are seen as *disengaged;* that is, they have very little to do with each other. Children often see this level of freedom as a sign of a lack of love and concern from their parents, and social problems are common. In fact, as adolescents they often yearn for the rules imposed on their peers by their parents, since they see the rules as an indication of love, care, and concern. The final type is the *closed family.* In this one, family members are *enmeshed* or overly involved in each others' lives. Individual identities are not allowed, and family boundaries close off much of the outside world. Emotional illnesses can result from this family configuration, since individuals cannot think or function on their own behalf.

As an exaggerated example, assume someone sneezes. In an open family others will respond with "bless you" and maybe offer a tissue. In the random family, no one will notice if you are too weak to get out of bed from the flu that brought it on. In the closed family, you are being rushed off to the doctor and interrogated about everything you have done lately.

Systems clinicians such as Virginia Satir see a loop between one's self-esteem and their ability to communicate. Dysfunctional communication patterns between family members results in low self-esteem, and people tend to defend themselves from threats to their esteem by using defensive and therefore dysfunctional communication styles. Therefore, one leads to the other in a downward spiral. Satir goes back to the family of origin causes and helps the clients to *reframe* (that is, consider less negative motivations for the behaviors of others) their childhood experiences into more positive and generally truthful memories and then teaches congruent and value-building communication styles that raise self-esteem. As self-esteem

rises, so does a person's ability to communicate in a functional manner (Satir 1964).

PRIMARY TERMS AND CONCEPTS

Broderick and Smith (1979) provide us with explanations for the key concepts of systems theory. An updated version is found in White and Klein (2002). For our discussion, the following terms are most relevant to systems theory.

SYSTEM

A system is essentially any set of objects (like the parts of an engine or the members of a family) that relate to each other in a way that creates a new superentity. It is a boundary-maintained unit composed of interrelated and interdependent parts. The family is a social system (Winton 1995).

BOUNDARIES

The limits of the system are its boundaries. A family maintains its boundaries by filtering out any external elements that seem hostile to the goals and policies of the family while at the same time incorporating those that are seen as beneficial. This is similar to the role of the placenta during pregnancy. In addition to the boundaries for the overall household kin group, there can be boundaries between family subgroups, such as the parents and the children. It then becomes possible to classify families on a continuum from open to closed, depending on how permeable or flexible the boundaries are.

ELEMENTS

The various individual members of the system are called *elements*. The terms "units" and "objects" have also been used to describe the people who live in a family system. Since family membership can vary over time, the focus is usually on the roles that family members play. There are various ways in which this can be conceptualized, such as instrumental, expressive, leader, follower, parent, child, sibling, lover, or rebel.

Family Rules

Family rules are the repetitive behavioral patterns, often referred to as the *redundancy principle,* that families engage in. Each family has unspoken guidelines for how it deals with input and change, which govern the behaviors of its members. If they do not have family rules in place, which allow them to respond appropriately to new situations, they may either adjust or simply break down. The typical response is to fall back on an already existing rule, even when it is insufficient to solve the problem.

Feedback

Feedback refers to the response a family member makes to the behavior of another person. It may be *positive* in that it encourages more of the stimulus or input from the other or *negative* in that it discourages change. There are continuous "feedback loops" as each member speaks to, and impacts upon, the behaviors of the others.

Equilibrium

There is a tendency for a system to seek a balance in the variety of its behaviors and its rules. This natural inclination to maintain the status quo and therefore avoid change is usually referred to as *homeostasis,* which means the system has equilibrium.

Clincal Concepts

There are additional concepts that must be understood when applying the theory, particularly in therapy. These are important for understanding how family members affect the emotional lives of each other (Goldenberg and Goldenberg 2000).

Linear Causality

The typical psychological and "commonsense" view that one event causes the next in unidirectional stimulus-response fashion is linear causality. Thus, a specific behavior causes a specific response.

Circular Causality

In contrast, the worldview of systems theorists indicates that many forces are impacting on each other simultaneously. There is a continuous series of circular feedback loops in which everyone influences everyone else and the family without any clear beginning or ending points. Because of this you cannot identify a specific beginning cause or event.

Identified Patient

The identified patient is the member of the family believed to be the one who is "sick" or is causing the problems. In actuality, that individual is simply the symptom bearer in a dysfunctional family, or the one who carries much of the family burden.

Double Bind

A kind of pathological communication in which a person is given two commands that contradict each other is called a double bind. If you obey one request, then you are in trouble for disobeying the other. This confusion leads to emotional or mental distress.

Disengagement

When family members are insufficiently involved in each other's lives due to rigid boundaries, they are considered to be disengaged. This is a characteristic of what is called a *random* family.

Enmeshment

In contrast to disengagement, when boundaries are blurred and family members are overinvolved in each other's lives, they are considered to be enmeshed. This is the characteristic of a *closed family,* and it often results in psychosomatic symptoms due to the lack of personal autonomy.

Mutuality

Mutuality is found in open families in which all are accepted and loved, even with differences of opinion. The opposite is *pseudomutuality,* in which a family gives the surface impression that it is open and understanding when in fact it is not.

COMMON AREAS OF RESEARCH AND APPLICATION

The two areas of greatest research productivity and application of systems theory concepts are family communication and family therapy. These actually overlap a great deal, since therapy often focuses on the communication patterns in families. For this reason, this section of this chapter will not be broken down into specific topical areas. Whitchurch and Dickson (1999) provide an excellent summary of what we presently know about family communication from a systems perspective. David Olson (1995) has developed what is probably the most well-known use of science with therapy in his circumplex model. This approach expands upon Kantor and Lehr's (1975) three family types by categorizing families as to their adaptability and cohesion. Therapists use the information to help families move to a balance between the two traits, which is characteristic of normal families.

Broderick and Pulliam-Krager (1979) do an excellent job of linking the three basic family types to childhood outcomes. They begin by reviewing the various aspects of pathological communication, which they term *paradoxical pressure*. This is then connected to open, closed, and random families. Using a flowchart model, they show how boundary maintenance can result in varying childhood problems. We begin by asking if paradoxical pressure exists in a family—that is, are there double binds or any other type of crazy-making communication patterns? The assumption is that few families can totally escape communication problems, but for the few who do, the result is a child who is an "unchallenged normal." Lacking such pressures, the child will grow up in the normal range but have no motivation to understand those who do have psychological problems. They make good accountants but not great therapists, for instance.

If the answer to the question about dysfunctional communication is "yes," then we move to the next choice point and ask if the family "screened out the deviant perspective." That is,

do the parents protect their children from antisocial elements such as gangs, adult media, drug use, and so forth. If the answer to that question is no, then we see that this is a random disengaged family. The likely childhood outcome is delinquency; the children are not emotionally ill, but they rebel against both a family and society that does not seem to care about them.

However, if the answer had been yes, meaning that the deviant perspective is screened out, then we go to the next choice point and ask if the family "screened out the normative perspective." (See Figure 7.1). In other words, are children also kept from prosocial aspects of society such as school, church, and good friends? If the answer is no, then we have an open family. Here the boundaries keep out the bad elements but, recognizing that they are not perfect, let in good ones. This way the children can compare and gain an understanding of their own families' craziness and avoid it in their own lives. We call these individuals "achieved normals."

If the answer to the last question is yes, then we have a closed, enmeshed family. Here the rigid boundaries keep out all outside forces, either pro- or antinormative. So all the children have is their own family craziness. Without a metaperspective (the ability to compare their worldview with that of others), the outcome for these children is some form of neurotic or psychotic behavior. Therefore, one of the great insights of systems theory is that enmeshment leads to emotional problems. The other families provide an escape from their pathological communication, but in a closed family, developing a symptom is just about the only way to deal with double binds.

Haley (1959) explains that families with an emotionally ill member continuously engage in contradictory and double-binding communication. They not only disqualify whatever anyone else says but also disqualify their own communications as well. This dysfunctional protection, which keeps them from ever being held responsible for their behaviors, is based on the need for love and the fear that if you let

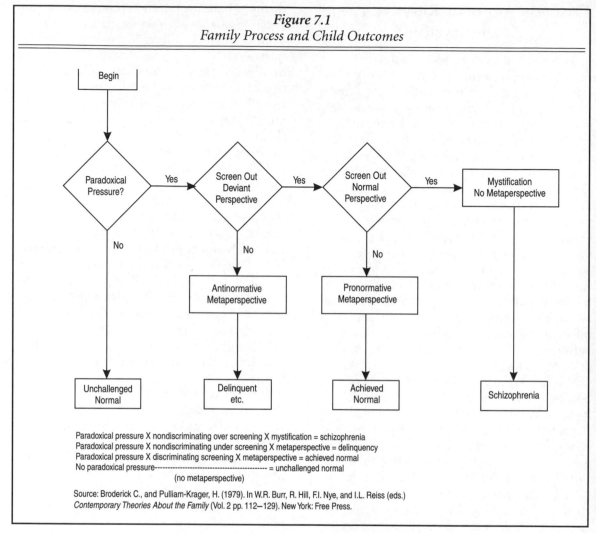

Figure 7.1
Family Process and Child Outcomes

Paradoxical pressure X nondiscriminating over screening X mystification = schizophrenia
Paradoxical pressure X nondiscriminating under screening X metaperspective = delinquency
Paradoxical pressure X discriminating screening X metaperspective = achieved normal
No paradoxical pressure-- = unchallenged normal
                                            (no metaperspective)

Source: Broderick C., and Pulliam-Krager, H. (1979). In W.R. Burr, R. Hill, F.I. Nye, and I.L. Reiss (eds.)
Contemporary Theories About the Family (Vol. 2 pp. 112–129). New York: Free Press.

people act freely, they may choose not to love you. This exaggerated concern comes from family-of-origin difficulties.

The greatest concern about family rules turns out not to be what the particular rules are but rather who makes the rules. Everyone wants life to go his or her own way, so ultimately marriage relations become a struggle for power. Emotional fights are about who should make the rules rather than what they should be. People usually do not recognize this consciously and thus cannot understand why their spouse will not agree to some simple request. This is complicated by the different levels of messages that we communicate.

For instance, a wife wants her husband to pick up his own dirty clothes, indicating that they should have an equal relationship. But if he does so, then he is doing what she says, and the relationship is not equal after all. This may cause him to erupt in indignation without understanding why, and she will be dismayed that he will not do this one little thing. In another example, a wife may want her husband to be the leader in the family and make the big decisions but it is impossible for that to happen if she tells him to do so because then he would just be doing her bidding.

Human communication in all settings is incredibly complex. This becomes especially true in emotional settings like the family. Systems theory may be the approach that can best deal with the levels of complexity and intimacy that are so central to human interaction.

CRITIQUE

There are some legitimate criticisms of systems theory. White and Klein (2002) summarize the three principal concerns that are reviewed here. The first is the belief that systems theory is more of a model or flowchart for conceptualizing, but it does not qualify as a true theory. The major concepts seem to be too vague for true testing and do not predict in the sense of deducing from propositions. This is a valid criticism if you are coming from the dominant epistemology of science, which is the hypothetical-deductive model of empirical testing. However, systems advocates counter that the worldview most appropriate for this theory is the *constructivist* position, in which different models may be useful for different purposes.

The second criticism is that systems theory is too global and abstract, and therefore is virtually meaningless. In other words, it is too "general" to pick up important distinctions that would make it worthwhile. The defense here is that the world is very diverse and that systems can make connections between the natural and social world that discipline-specific theories are not capable of doing.

Finally, some critics claim that the family process theorists in particular make the mistake of reifying the idea of system. That is, instead of remembering that it is just a model for understanding, they slip into considering the system to be reality. They confuse the "model" with the "thing." The response from systems apologists is that all theories have their naive claims and that systems theory is no more prone to reification than any other theory.

One finds validity in these criticisms due to the relative lack of useful mathematical models and predictive propositions that have emerged over the years from this approach. It may be that the kinds of interactions attended to by systems theory are simply too complex for the traditional scientific method to deal with in an understandable fashion. As a result, the theory has been most useful in the areas of family communication and family therapy. Broderick and Smith (1979) list the following as the most productive types of issues for examination by systems theorists:

1. *Sequential patterns of interaction.* Other disciplines, such as economics, have benefited for many years by utilizing such concepts as feedback loops, escalation, and dampening in the context of temporal patterns of everyday life. Systems theory can use the same conceptual tools to understand family interactions.

2. *Communication and control.* Traditional family literature tends to see communication as a variable that ranges in amount and satisfaction, but little else. The family process therapists have accumulated considerable evidence that controlling behavior is the most important aspect of communication.

3. *Goal orientation.* The dynamics of system goal achievement and its relationship to control and family rules appears to be a topic unique to systems theory literature.

4. *Boundary maintenance.* The importance of maintaining systems boundaries is more important to systems theory than it is to any other. There is considerable evidence now that whether a family boundary is relatively open or closed is crucial to its effectiveness.

5. *Complex relationships.* Finally, most other theoretical approaches utilize causal models that are linear, avoid too many interaction effects, and tend to average outputs into mean results. Systems theory recognizes that life is nonlinear, with multiple causal paths and outcomes. Therefore, its models emphasize branching, rather than averaging.

APPLICATION

One of the best ways to understand systems concepts is to apply them to your own family life. The following are some good exercises adapted from Goldenberg and Goldenberg (2000).

1. List the roles that you currently play in their order of importance. How many are family (vs. career or other) roles? Which of all the roles is the most integral to your sense of self?

2. What homeostatic or corrective feedback do you engage in when dealing with conflict with a loved one? How do they respond to it?

3. List some behaviors of friends or family members that irritate you. Now try to reframe the motivations into more positive possibilities. Does this change your feelings toward the person?

4. Most communications between people have a "command" aspect as well as the content of the message. For instance, asking where the salt is at dinner implies a command to go get it. List some common comments in your family that have implicit commands in them.

5. In reference to the situation given at the beginning of this chapter, list examples of circular causality from your own family. What are some examples of endless arguments in which each person blames the other for "starting it"?

SAMPLE READING

Jackson, D. (1965). Family rules: Marital quid pro quo. *Archives of General Psychiatry* 12: 589–594.

This chapter ends with a classic article in which Jackson explains that marriage is much more that a gender-based relationship, and that interactive behavior can be best explained by the concept of "family rules." As you read his exam-ples, see if you can think of the key rules that govern your family.

References

Bateson, G., Jackson, D., Haley, J., and Weakland, J. (1956). Toward a theory of schizophrenia. *Behavioral Science* 1: 251–264.

Bertalanffy, L. (1969). *General Systems Theory: Essays in its Foundation and Development*. New York: Braziller.

Broderick, C. (1993). *Understanding Family Process*. Newbury Park, CA: Sage.

Broderick, C., and Pulliam-Krager, H. (1979). Family process and child outcomes. In W. R. Burr, R. Hill, F. I. Nye, and I. L. Reiss (eds.), *Contemporary Theories About the Family* (vol. 2, pp. 604–614). New York: Free Press.

Broderick, C., and Smith, J. (1979). The general systems approach to the family. In W. R. Burr, R. Hill, F. I. Nye, and I. L. Reiss (eds.), *Contemporary Theories About the Family* (Vol. 1, pp. 112–129). New York: Free Press.

Bronfenbrenner, U. (1989). Ecological systems theory. In R. Vasta (ed.), *Six Theories of Child Development* (vol. 6, pp. 187–250). Greenwich, CT: JAI Press.

Burgess, E. (1926). The family as a unity of interacting personalities. *The Family*, 3–9.

Gardiner, H., and Kosmitzki, C. (2002). *Lives Across Cultures: Cross-Cultural Human Development*. Boston: Allyn and Bacon.

Goldenberg, I., and Goldenberg, H. (2000). *Family Therapy: An Overview*. Belmont, CA: Brooks/Cole.

Haley, J. (1959). The family of the schizophrenic: A model system. *Journal of Nervous and Mental Disease* 123: 357–374.

Jackson, D. (1965). Family rules: Marital quid pro quo. *Archives of General Psychiatry* 12: 589–594.

Kantor, D., and Lehr, W. (1975). *Inside the Family*. San Francisco, CA: Jossey-Bass.

Olson, D. (1995). Family systems: Understanding your roots. In R. Day, K. Gilbert, B. Settles, and W. Burr (eds.), *Research and Theory in Family Science* (pp. 131–153). Pacific Grove, CA: Brooks/Cole.

Satir, V. (1964). *Conjoint Family Therapy*. Palo Alto, CA: Science and Behavior Books.

Waller, W. (1938). *The Family: A Dynamic Interpretation* (revised by R. Hill, 1951). New York: Holt, Rinehart and Winston.

Whitchurch, G., and Dickson, F. (1999). Family communication. In M. Sussman, S. Steinmetz, and G. Peterson (eds.), *Handbook of Marriage and the Family* (2nd ed., pp. 687–704). New York: Plenum.

White, J., and Klein, D. (2002). *Family Theories* (2nd ed.). Thousand Oaks, CA: Sage.

Winton, C. (1995). *Frameworks for Studying Families.* Guilford, CT: Duskin Publishing Group. ✦

Family Rules

Marital Quid Pro Quo

Don D. Jackson

Because they are so obviously and invariably composed of only one man and one woman each, marriages in our society are usually described in terms of sexual differences, which are of course considered innate or at least fixed characteristics of the individuals involved. All manner of behaviors quite removed from primary sexual differences can be brought into the framework of male-female differences, which framework then becomes an explanatory model of marriage. This view pervades our popular mythology of sexual stereotypes, it influences marriage manuals and similar advisory accouterments, and it certainly guides our scientific study of the marital relationship, no matter how inconsistent or unspecific this theory proves to be. The rich variety of forms which anthropologists have shown us "masculinity" and "femininity" take in marriage across the world should indicate something is amiss with the assumption that absolute, specific sexual differences in marriage are a heuristic value. The function of such differences in organizing a special relationship is seldom considered; it may be that a shared belief in any difference at all would serve the same purpose. It is proposed here that the individual differences which are so evident in marital relationships may just as reasonably be a result of the nature of that relationship as of the nature of the individuals who compose the relationship.

Heterosexuality is not the only unique feature of marriage; there is another characteristic which, strangely enough, often goes unnoticed, but may be the most important aspect of marriage: it is the only well-known, *long-term collaborative relationship*. Thus there are several nonsexual aspects which must be considered in any analysis of marriage and marriage problems.

1. It is a *voluntary* relationship, even though undertaken in a culture which views marriage as almost compulsory.

2. It is a *permanent* relationship; that is, it is supposed to be a lifetime contract. ("till death do us part.")

3. Marriage in the western world is an *exclusive* relationship, in which the parties are supposed to be virtually sufficient each unto the other, with a marked exclusion of third parties and outside relationships.

4. It is a broadly *goal-oriented* relationship with many vital mutual tasks to be carried out on a long-term basis and marked by time-bound eras—each with its special problems.

To describe these premises of marriage is not to imply that they are necessarily realized nor that the parties enter into marriage with such concepts in mind. These are shared beliefs about the nature of marriage as an institutionalized relationship, and the assets and liabilities of marriage as a legal arrangement stem, in large part, from the workability of these norms.

Unused as we are to thinking in terms of different kinds of relationships (rather than different kinds of individuals), still we can see that there are probably no other dyadic relationships which, *regardless of the sex of the partners,* can be similarly characterized. For instance, the assumption (not to say the reality) of permanency excludes most other volitional relationships which are not troubled by the curious paradox of "having to want to stay together." The *homosexual "marriage"* comes to mind immediately as a possible example of a relationship in which primary sexual differences are absent but the relationship problems as outlined above are more or less relevant. We might question whether being against the social grain—two against the world—has something to do with the durability of some such relationships. Yet, even in homosexual "marriages" there is the evolution of sex-role differences. Homosexuals may choose for their relatively permanent partners their opposites in terms of "masculinity" and "femininity," (and they often used a sex-role language for their relationship even when parent-child or sibling terms would seem more appropriate). While it can always be asserted that sex-role identification preceded the relationship (i.e., one partner is "really" female), this cannot be proven; so, just as in heterosexual marriage, the differentiation of the individuals along sex lines can be seen as primary *or* as a means of working out the problems posed by the rules of the marital relationship, that is, as effect, not cause.

Other instances in which the same relationship problems seem to be posed are fairly easily distinguished. In the *roommate* arrangement, for instance, volition, relative permanence, and mutual tasks do frequently apply; but there is no expectation that the two will not engage in highly important, independent, third-party relationships. In fact, it would be unusual for each roommate *not* to maintain independence or external coalitions with regard to financial, sexual, intellectual, and even companionship needs. Lacking a premise of virtual self-sufficiency of the dyad, the roommate arrangement also avoids many of the problems which arise in marriage. *Business relationships* are oriented to an explicit and specific central goal, as opposed to marriage which cannot be said to have any single goal. In fact, for marriages we have to make up goals such as "the rearing of children" or "companionship" even when such functions can successfully be carried on without legal or secular blessings. Business relationships are also necessarily diluted by a wide variety of intrinsic factors, not the least of which are the time-defined working day and, again, the vital role of third parties such as customers, staff, even the stock market. There must be enduring, nonhomosexual relationships between, perhaps, unmarried possibly related women; here one thinks of the maiden aunts or old maid school teachers of our American mythology, and one begins to wonder how such relationships are worked out. Unfortunately for our research interests, these relationships seldom come to the attention of professionals. So it seems we are unable by means of counterexample to prove immediately whether marriage is the way it is because a man and a woman are involved, or because it is a unique kind of a relationship for any two people at all. *Thus, it is possible that one could outline marriage as a totally nonsexual affair, nearly excluding all sexual differences, or at least minimizing the casual role usually assigned such differences.*

The sex-role view of marriage is so widely accepted that the position just taken seems nearly impudent. It nevertheless seems important to reconsider some of our beliefs about marriage since our present knowledge of individual theory is quite exhaustive when contrasted with the paucity of systematic knowledge of relationship per se. In our traditional conceptual framework, the individual is held by the boundaries of his skin, and whatever transpires between two such captives—that which is neither clearly "I" nor clearly "thou"—is a mystery for which we have no language or understanding. Our thoughts, research efforts, and even what Benjamin Whorf called "our view of the cosmos" are limited or facilitated by the language which we use. Therefore, we must first have a language which enables, even forces, us to think interactionally. The necessity for a language with which to study interaction may lead to the abandonment of terms which belong to the study of the individual in favor of terms which focus on the relationship. The concept of "family rules"[1] represents one such tool. The observation of family interaction makes obvious certain *redundancies,* typical and repetitive patterns of interaction which characterize the family as a supraindividual entity. One of the simplest such rules is proposed in this paper: the marital quid pro quo, an alternative to the theory of individual differences in marriage.

To suggest that the individual, sex-aligned differences which we witness in marriages may not be due to individual sexual differences, or indeed have anything to do with biological sexual requirements, is not to say these differences do not exist. To the contrary, just such differences can be the basis of working out a relationship. The stresses and success of marriage still need not be attributed to sexual or even individual personality differences, but could conceivably be expected to be true of any hypothetical relationship which is also voluntary, permanent, exclusive, and task-oriented. The actual differences between marriage partners are probably not nearly so important as the difficulty in collaborating; furthermore, any two people in these conditions have to work out rules based on differences or similarities. Sexual differences are readily available, but if there were no real differences to help define the relationship, differences would probably be made up. In this light, our present language of marriage imposes many encumbering myths about maleness and femaleness. For it seems that differences are inevitable in a relationship, especially in an ongoing, goal-oriented relationship such as marriage. Imagine two perfectly identical persons—not real-life identical twins who have long since become distinguishable to themselves and others—but a carbon-copy pair who are in fact the same person in two bodies. If such a pair were to live together, it is obvious they would have to evolved differences which did not before exist. The first time they approached a door that must be entered in single file, the die would be cast. Who is to go first? On what basis is this decision to be made? After it is made and effected, can things ever be the same again? If they fight, someone must win. If one precedes and the other forebears, it cannot then be said they are identical, since one would be aggressive, thoughtless, or "the one who takes the initiative," while the other would be passive, patient, or sluggish. In short, a relationship problem which has nothing to do with individual differences—for there were none in our hypothetical pair—has been solved by evolving differences which may be considered shorthand expressions of the definition of the relationship which was achieved. Later, these differences are available to handle other, similar circumstances wherein identical simultaneous actions are neither possible nor desirable. There is an old European tale of a detective posing as a lodger in a boarding house where a number of mysterious suicides have occurred. He notices across the courtyard from his window an old woman who is weaving. As he becomes entranced by her elaborate movements he begins to mimic them. Then with slow horror it becomes apparent to him that it is she who is following *his* movements, not he who is following hers. As the cause and effect become inextricably tangled, he throws himself out the window at the spinner.

When we consider the work to be done by marital partners—money-making, housekeeping, social life, love-making and parenting—the tasks which must be attempted and to greater or lesser degree accomplished, then we are overwhelmed by the impossibility of sameness and efficiency of differences. In the marital relationship, at least, two individuals are faced with the challenge of collaboration on a wide variety of tasks over an indefinite, but presumably long, period of time. In most of these areas—sexual, financial, occupational—no simple or nonpersonal division of labor is obvious. Cultural stereotypes are of some help, but even these appear to be fluid in middle-class America.

From research done on the parents of white, middle-class families observed at the Mental Research Institute, it seems that the way couples handle this crucial relationship problem is by a marital quid pro quo. When two people get together, they immediately exchange clues as to how they are defining the nature of the relationship; this set of behavioral tactics is modified by the other person by the manner in which he responds. The definition which is agreed to (and if the marriage is to work some sort of agreement must be reached), this definition of who each is in relation to the other can best be expressed as a quid pro quo. Quid pro quo (literally "something for something") is an expression of the legal nature of a bargain or contract, in which each party must receive something for what he gives and which, consequently, defines the rights and duties of the parties in the bargain. Marriage, too, can be likened to a bargain which defines the different rights and duties of the spouses, each of which can be said to do X if and because the other does Y. Quid pro quo, then is a descriptive metaphor for a relationship based on differences, and expression of the redundancies which one observes in marital interaction. One of the most common quid pro quo's observed in white, middle-class, suburban families is the following arrangement: the husband is, broadly, an instrumental type who deals with matters logically and intellectually, and is considered the practical, realistic one; his wife is the more sensitive, affective or "feeling" sort of person who understands people better than things. This sort of quid pro quo is extremely utilitarian for the sort of life such a couple is likely to lead, since the exchange implies a fairly clear division of labor which defines the contribution made by each. Carried to the extreme, this quid pro quo could result in rigidity and misunderstanding, though it is probably not as prone to pathology as some other relationship agreements. That this arrangement has little to do with fixed "sex roles" as we ordinarily think of them has been confirmed by Robert Leik[2] who recently measured this mode of differentiation in actual families as well as "mock family" stranger groups (i.e., stranger groups with the same sex and age composition as the real families tested). He found that:

The traditional male role (instrumental, non-emotional behavior) as well as the traditional female role (emotional, non-task behavior) appear when interaction takes place among strangers. *These emphases tend to disappear when subjects interact with their own families* (italics mine).

And he concluded that:

In general, *the relevance of instrumentality and emotionality is quite different for family interaction than for interaction among strangers.* This major finding poses new problems for the theoretical integration of family research with that based on ad hoc experimental groups. Such integration is possible only through recognition of the fact that the context of the interaction with strangers places a meaning on particular acts which is different from the meaning of those acts within the family group (italics mine).

Thus, though this quid pro quo is a common and culturally convenient arrangement, it is not intrinsic to sex roles in marriage. Quite the opposite—the ongoing family relationship apparently custom-tailors the marital bargain to its own particular situation.

Another type of quid pro quo is a "time-bound" relationship, that is, one in which the marital agreement is seriate. If A says to B, let us do X, spouse B assents because they have established a time-bound relationship in which the next move would be B's. The husband may suggest to his wife that they go to a movie; she says yes, and then she has the right to say, we can have a beer afterwards. Similarly, the wife may take certain rights which the husband will grant because he knows he will have a turn in the near future. This time-binding is finite, and while it may not always be a matter of minutes (as it is in sexual intercourse) or of days, it is probably not months or years. Flexibility in time-binding is probably another word for "trust" in a relationship, and this may be the most workable of quid pro quo's.*

The phenomenon of time in relationships—especially marriage—needs study. Relationships that are not rigidly time-bound have great flexibility, while some of the crises of various periods of family life may relate to time. That is, the unspoken promise never kept may, with the passing of time, become more obviously unlikely to be kept, e.g., that the husband will spend more time with the family as soon as his business gets on its feet becomes less believable as time goes by and the children grow up; at some point the "promise is broken" simply by the passage of time.†

There is then a peculiar relationship which can be observed in both marital and exploitative political situations, when the quid pro quo is not in fact time-bound but is treated as if it is. If A says to B, let us do X, B says yes because A indicates that eventually B will get his reward. B's day is allegedly coming, and though it never does, A keeps acting as if it is going to and B keeps acting as if he accepts this. These are often pathological relationships which in marriage are frequently characterized by depression and even suicide. The vicious cycle aspect of this relationship is apparent—the more B lets himself be conned, the more he has coming eventually and the less free he is to try another game, since he has so much already invested.

If the gist of these examples has been clear, it should not be necessary to point out that the quid pro quo is not overt, conscious, or the tangible result of real bargaining. Rather, this formulation is the patter imposed by the observer on the significant redundancies of marital interaction, and should always be understood metaphorically, with the tacit preface, "It seems as if. . . ." The specifics of marital bargaining are not of interest to us. It is at the level of exchange of definitions of the relationship (and, therefore, of self-definition within the relationship) that we can usefully analyze in terms of quid pro quo. If we were to focus only on the content level of marital interaction, we might miss the probability that the so-called masochist does not like or need to suffer—he gets something out of the relationship by using the one down position as a tactic.

Note, for instance, the following example:‡

H: I wish you would fix yourself up. Take $50 and get a permanent, a facial—the works!

W: I'm sorry, dear, but I don't think we ought to spend the money on me.

H: *!!æ*! I want to spend it on you!

W: I know, dear, but there's all the bills and things. . . .

Here the apparently one-down behavior of the wife is actually quite controlling. If we look beyond the particular $50 about which they are disputing, we can see the relationship they have worked out: the husband is allowed to complain about the wife and act in charge, but the wife indicates she does not intend to follow his orders, that in fact his orders are stupid and, since she sets no time conditions, we do not know if she will ever get a permanent or not. This is one clue to the quid pro quo. Rather than executing a piece of action, this couple is going through a repetitive exchange which defines and redefines the nature of their relationship. Thus on another occasion:‡

H: Hey, I can't find any white shirts!

W: I'm sorry, dear, they're not ironed yet.

H: Send them to the laundry! I don't care what it costs!

W: We spend so much on groceries and liquor, I felt I should try to save a few pennies here and there.

H: Listen for *!!æ*!, I need shirts!

W: Yes, dear, we'll see about it.

Note that just as the wife does not specify *when,* nor whether she is really saying yes or no, the husband does not insist on clear, definite information. It would be misleading to ascribe motivation to this couple. To say he likes to bluster or she likes to frustrate him is senseless and yet irrefutable. What is important is their interactional system: once having established such a pattern of interaction, they are victims of blindness and reinforcement.§ Further, their roles are defined not by "male aggressiveness" and "female passivity," but by the simple fact that wives are supposed to be pretty and to take charge of the laundry and husbands are affected by whether or not wives fulfill these expectations.

This is so obvious, yet we as researchers are victims of the sex-role propaganda, too. Most psychiatrists would probably doubt that a family in which the husband runs the house and the wife brings home the money could rear apparently healthy children. Yet in two such examples brought to our attention this appears to be the case. To understand why these couples function well, we would do much better to analyze their present relationship and seek to identify their particular quid pro quo than to seek the answer in their individual backgrounds and calculate the probabilities that such individuals would meet and marry.

It is becoming more accepted among clinicians that there are no marital relationships which are unbalanced or impoverished for *one* spouse. Observation of the interaction reveals the "bargain" struck between alcoholic and spouse, between wife-beater and wife. The quid pro quo reasoning, then, is still tautological and, within its own sphere of proof, just as irrefutable as notions of human instincts and sex roles. If one believes that marriage is a relationship bargain and is the judge of the terms of this bargain in any particular case, then he can prove his own hypothesis. Again it is important to restate that the concept of family rules in general and of the quid pro quo in particular is only a descriptive metaphor imposed by the observer on the redundancies he observes in interaction. This is not only *true* in the many important areas of the social sciences where the researcher must be both judge and jury, but it is also highly desirable as long as we avoid the pitfalls of reification and acknowledge the fictitious nature of all our constructs. This is a necessary first step if we are to devise a language which will elucidate and convey the process, not the property. Our goal is to do verbal justice to the phenomena in which we are avowedly interested. In our early attempts at interpersonal research, we are constantly limited by the only terminology we have—an ill-fitting bequest from theories of the individual. The notions of family rules and the marital quid pro quo are levers to force us away from the characteristics of individuals onto the nature of their interaction, and are at least somewhat more appropriate to describe the phenomena we will observe in interaction.

It is possible that the formulation of "rules" such as the quid pro quo has enormous predictive potential. If we are reasonably accurate in our formulation of a metaphor for a couple's relationship, we can forecast the likelihood of success or failure and even the fate of children in the family system. For instance:

The "Big Daddy-Baby Doll" arrangement is not likely to be a workable quid pro quo. While Baby Doll may be able to continue her half of the bargain for some time, the material offerings with which Big Daddy must be constantly forthcoming are, after all, finite in number. There are only so many countries to tour and so many jewels which can be bought and worn. No matter what his wealth, her situation will probably eventually endanger the quid pro quo so that the marriage must terminate or find a new level of operation.

Other arrangements may survive the early period of marriage but cannot be expected to accommodate children. For instance:

A couple had a quid pro quo of total independence; each pursued his own career and was succeeding. They scorned the usual financial and housekeeping arrangements, basing all decisions on the maximization of the independence of both. Though one might wonder how it happened in an atmosphere of total independence, the wife became pregnant; her career and way of life were drastically limited. The marriage foundered because the original quid pro quo could not possibly be made to include maternity and motherhood. A new relationship had to be established.

Some parental relationships can survive the onslaught of a little stranger, but cannot accommodate his emotional health:

The family maxim seemed to be "People who live in glass houses shouldn't throw stones." Husband and wife scrupulously avoided even the mildest and—to us—vital criticism of each other, and in turn was not criticized by the spouse. This ban on information, however, provides a poor teaching context for children and is not likely to encourage healthy, spontaneous curiosity. The marriage lasts, but the brighter-than-average son was referred to therapy for marked academic underachievement.

These examples are, of course, retrospective. But our success in postdiction of psychopathology in children from the blind analysis of examples of marital interaction in terms of the quid pro quo leads us to hope that, with refinement, prediction and prophylaxis of pathological systems are possible.

Summary

A theory of marriage is proposed which is based on the relationship rather than the individuals. Specifically, the quid pro quo formulation holds that the similarities and differences between spouses compress the metaphorical "bargain" on which the marital relationship is based. The advantages of this scheme are that (1) we have a language which aids our observation of truly interactional phenomena, and (2) there is the promise of improved predictive power when the "rules" of the relationship are grasped.

National Institutes of Mental Health Grant No. 04916.

Janet Beavin assisted in writing this paper.

References

1. Jackson, D. D.: Study of Family, *Family Process* 4: 1–20 (March) 1964.

2. Leik, R. K.: Instrumentality and Emotionality in Family Interaction, *Sociometry* 26: 131–145, 1963.

Endnotes

* Trust is obviously a key concept in marital and even national relationships. It is a belief that the other will do for you what you just did for him, and since you do not know when this will occur, trust appears not to be time-bound. But these are probably intervening signals which declare A's intent to repay B even though no specific date is ever set. I hope not to have my life insurance cashed, but that ad of the great Rock of Gibraltar constantly refurbishes my trust.

† So-called menopausal depression is often related by clinicians to the onset of woman's inability to have children. My own observations led me to seriously question this. Among other considerations is the fact that the wish for a child may help deny an unsatisfactory marriage.

‡ These are not transcribed examples but were reported in couple therapy.

§ B. F. Skinner has stated that aperiodic negative reinforcement is the most potent conditioner. Because couples are apart a good deal and engage in a variety of contingencies some of their negative interactions take on an aperiodic aspect. This may make it difficult for A to label B in black and white and yet enhance B's vulnerability.

Reprinted from: Don D. Jackson, "Family Rules: Marital Quid Pro Quo." In *Archives of General Psychiatry*, 12, pp. 589–594, 1965. ✦

Chapter Eight
Feminist Family Theory

Bob and Alice Stephens were having dinner at a nice restaurant to celebrate their tenth wedding anniversary. Bob said to Alice, "Isn't this relaxing? A dinner alone without the kids. We should treat ourselves to this more often." Alice smiled politely but was unconvinced that it was such a treat. It's true that Bob suggested that they go out to dinner, but Alice had made the reservations. In fact, Alice had picked up Bob's suit from the cleaners on her way home from work. She had arranged for the babysitter, made dinner for the kids before she left, washed the basketball uniform that Bobby Junior needed for tomorrow's gym class, and helped little Alicia study for her spelling test before she drove downtown to Bob's engineering office, where he changed into his suit for dinner. She felt too tired and anxious to relax.

Alice had been feeling a great deal of stress lately. She enjoyed her job as a lawyer but was worried about making partner in her firm. Two men who had joined the firm after her had already achieved partner status. When she asked the senior partners about it, they explained that she was "off-track" because of the maternity leave she had taken to have her children. They also indicated that her work with the Legal Aid fund was notable but did not bring in the kind of money to the firm that was expected of a partner. Alice worked with single mothers whose ex-husbands had failed to pay child support. But now she had to find ways to bring in clients who could afford to pay more money. And as much as she loved her husband, children, and her work, what Alice really wished for was an evening at home, soaking in a nice hot bath, and some peace and quiet to read a book.

HISTORY

Feminist family theory, not surprisingly, has its roots in the feminist movement. Feminism can be defined as the search for rights, opportunities, and identities women believe they deserve (Thomas 2000). Feminism in the United States might be said to have begun with the Seneca Falls Convention in 1848. Women—most notably Elizabeth Cady Stanton and Susan B. Anthony—fought for the right to vote; a battle that was not won until ratification of the Nineteenth Amendment to the U.S. Constitution in 1920.

The modern feminist movement, or the second wave of feminism, began in the 1960s, concurrent with the civil rights movement, the anti–Vietnam War protests, and the general cultural challenge to the established institutional authorities and the "status quo." Leaders in this movement, like Betty Friedan, Gloria Steinem, and the National Organization for Women (NOW), worked toward resolution of issues such as equal pay and job training for women, reproductive choice, maternity leave, subsidized child care, and an end to sex discrimination (Okin 1997).

The feminist movement of the 1960s and 1970s was characterized by several branches, each with a slightly different emphasis. *Liberal feminists*, like Friedan, saw the subjugation of women, particularly in terms of their career paths. They stressed the importance of challenging laws and customs that restricted women's ability to achieve significant roles in society. *Marxist feminists* focused on the exploitation of women in their reproductive roles and in household labor, which maintained women as "second-class" citizens. *Radical feminists* emphasized male dominance as the problem with society, specifically male power and authority as oppressive to women. Radical feminists proposed that individuals should not be limited by masculine or feminine traits but should strive toward androgyny (a combination of both masculine and feminine traits). Families, as the source for patriarchy (male dominance) and oppression of women, could not be reformed into something positive and should therefore be avoided. *Socialist feminists* focused on women's liberation from the combined aspects of class oppression and patriarchy, particularly as found in families (Okin 1997; Osmond and Thorne 1993). Most feminists in the United States have most closely aligned themselves with the liberal branch of feminism (Shehan and Kammeyer 1997).

Within every field of study, knowledge is advanced by pioneers who propose cutting-edge ideas. Often we see that several extreme philosophies are presented, and after a time, a middle ground is reached that incorporates elements of each but is not as extreme as any individual original branch. This is also the case in feminism. By the 1980s the distinctions between the feminist branches melted away. Feminists focused on issues related to women's second-class status in society and in families, reproductive rights, discrimination faced in the workplace, and how a gendered society affects the socialization of women (Okin 1997).

In the 1960s, one of the dominant theories of the family was structural-functionalism. Structural-functionalists proposed that roles in families should be divided in a "natural" way, generally based on sex. They proposed that families functioned best when men did the instrumental tasks of earning money and caring for basic needs, and women provided the expressive tasks of caretaking of the family members (Baca Zinn 2000). In 1972, sociologist Jessie Bernard wrote *The Future of Marriage*, in which she contrasted male and female perspectives on marriage. Bernard found that there were two marriages—his and hers—and that his was better than hers. This finding was in direct opposition to the ideas presented in structural-functional theory. Based on the work of Bernard and others, feminist family theorists began to consider status in families, analyzing how males may dominate family power, both intentionally and unintentionally. When this happened, males benefited but females did not, thus leading to two types of marriages. Feminist family theorists recognized that male

power and dominance were the result of socialization and challenged the concept that male power was natural and inevitable. They examined how the family was influenced by social institutions and politics and how it was affected by the wider system of societal norms.

Feminist understanding was furthered in the 1980s by the groundbreaking work of Carol Gilligan, who analyzed the psychological and internal development of women's sense of self as different from that of men's. In her book *In a Different Voice*, Gilligan (1982) explored how women defined their identity and understood reality through relationships, particularly intimate relationships. Their experiences must be taken into account in the analysis of their development, particularly as they internalized their sense of self and their moral code. She further clarified that, for women, nonviolence and caring for others dominated their views of justice and equality.

In the 1990s, feminist scholars sought to combine both the societal perspective and the individual perspective of oppression, paving the way for a third wave of feminism. This perspective focused on the multiple forms of oppression that might be experienced on an individual basis as a result of societal oppression. A "matrix of domination" (Collins 1998, 2000) could include oppression because of gender, class, race, ethnicity, sexual orientation, religion, or physical ability. For example, although all women experience relatively less status than men, white women experience relatively more status than women of color, middle-class women have more status than poor women, and heterosexual women have more status than lesbians or bisexual women. Multiracial feminism (MRF) is one example of feminism that developed from this third wave of feminism. MRF focuses on the intersection of gender, race, and ethnicity and challenging the assumptions that gender is the only issue that matters. It encourages us to understand "social location" as a more complex social phenomenon (Lorber 1998).

BASIC ASSUMPTIONS

Whereas there have been many different forms of feminism, feminist family theorists generally base their work on the following basic assumptions (Baca Zinn 2000; Osmond and Thorne 1993; Sollie and Leslie 1994):

Women's experiences are central to our understanding of families. Feminist family theorists begin with the question "What is the perspective of women?" Other theories have investigated the structures, the roles, and the resources people bring to their relationships. Feminist family scholars focus on women's perspectives and feelings, how women have been left out of the social and historical dialogue, and how women's issues have been ignored. Gender becomes the organizing concept. For example, the concept of "work" used to mean only paid work, which used to mean only men's work. Adding women's experience to the conceptualization of the term expanded it to include the unpaid labor that women did for families and communities as well.

According to Katherine Ferguson (as cited in Osmond and Thorne 1993), "Feminist theory is not simply about women, although it is that; it is about the world, but from the usually ignored and devalued vantage point of women's experiences" (p. 592–593). Osmond and Thorne go on to add, "By making women's experiences visible, feminist scholarship reveals gaps and distortions in knowledge that claims to be inclusive but in fact is based on the experiences of Euro-American, class-privileged, heterosexual men. Starting with the life experiences of women, in all their diversity, opens new epistemologies or ways of knowing the world" (p. 593). Feminist family theorists "analyze gender as a central principle of social organization and as something that all people do in their daily activities in every institution" (Osmond and Thorne 1993, 593). Two related concepts are that people exaggerate differences between men and women and that they use "these distinctions to legitimize and perpetuate power relations between men and women" (Osmond and Thorne 1993, 593).

Feminist family theory also addresses the development of women across the lifespan. Because women have been oppressed, their development has been hindered. The theory investigates how their development might be different if society did not constrain them (Thomas 2000) and asks questions about the experience from a gendered perspective (Gilligan 1982).

Gender is a socially constructed concept. When we talk about gender, we talk about something different from sex. Sex refers to biological assignment; gender refers to "the social meanings of masculinity and femininity that are produced through social processes and interactions that produce 'men' and 'women'" (Rutter and Schwartz 2000, 61).

Feminist family theorists make the point that gender roles are defined by society, not by biology. In the past, fathers went to work; mothers stayed home. Doctors were men; nurses were women. Business executives were men; secretaries were women. Boys were football players; girls were cheerleaders. These were socially constructed roles. In today's society, gender roles are changing, but there is still resistance. Women are members of the U.S. military, but they are not allowed in combat. Women are allowed on aircraft carriers but are not allowed on submarines. Contrast that with the Israeli army, in which women are drafted and fight alongside the men.

Language is an important element in socially constructed gender roles. In French, for example, all nouns have a male or female gender, usually indicated by the article (*le pere*—father, but *la mere*—mother). While English is not so obvious, words still have gender connotations. Usage becomes so natural that the implications of the word are not necessarily recognized. For example, using the term *mankind* instead of *humanity* implicitly excludes women.

A subtler example is using the word *spinster* to refer to an unmarried, childless female. What word do we use to refer to an unmarried, childless male? There is no comparable word. We might use the word *bachelor,* but it doesn't have the negative connotation that the word *spinster* has. We define spinsters in terms of what they are not—not wives, not mothers (Allen 1994). Feminists attend to this kind of language use to ensure that women are not excluded from the social conversation.

Putting behaviors and labels together is termed *categorization*. Behaviors and roles are labeled and categorized according to gender. At a very early age, boys and girls learn what boys do, what girls do, what men do, and what women do. Behaviors by parents or others reinforce these categorizations. For instance, if a father were to see his 3-year-old son dancing in a tutu, he might yell at the child care provider, "Don't ever let my son wear that again! I want my son to grow up to be a real man!" The son's exploration in the fantasy play area of the child care center had no social meaning until the father ascribed a strict gendered meaning to it.

Stratification is an outcome of categorization. Once tasks for men and women and boys and girls have been divided, people begin attributing value (even unintentionally) to those tasks. The value attributed to male tasks has generally been greater than the value attributed to female tasks. People who are more highly valued have more power in the society. Feminists refer to those with power as *privileged*. People with less value have less power (are less privileged) and can be oppressed. In gender analysis, stratification is most commonly found when women's behaviors and roles are given less value than men's. For example, "women's work" like housework and child care is unpaid, whereas men's work is given greater value and pay in society. Feminists seek to illuminate the status differences so that women can become empowered.

One way to do this is to bring attention to the ways language influences, and perhaps perpetuates, stratification. For example, a man believes himself to be an equal partner and proudly proclaims that he "helps around the house," as if this were an unusual behavior and therefore notable. This implies that the woman is still in charge of the housework because the man is just "helping out." The old gender roles are still there. Privilege is also evident in race, ethnicity, sexuality, nationality, age, physical ability, and religion (Collins 1998). Recognizing the multiple levels on which privilege is located, and the language that distinguishes status, is a complicated task. Many of the hierarchies we learn are learned in our families (Collins 1998; Walker 1993), and challenging those beliefs can be important but difficult.

Social and historical contexts are important. To understand women and families, we must understand the contexts in which they live. As they define women's roles in families, feminist family theorists look for meaning in both the sociological and the historical contexts. The analytical focus is not just on the individual and interpersonal relationships but also on the larger social forces that influence those relationships (Ferree 1990). Indeed, feminist family theorists contend that one must study the larger contexts to understand the position of women in the family. For example, the idealized concept of the nuclear family is still the norm in family research, despite obvious demographic changes. The historical norm no longer applies to the new forms of family (which we will investigate below). But if a researcher does not take into account the larger social changes that are occurring, the nuclear family might remain the norm by which to measure, and this could lead to incorrect conclusions.

There are many examples of how society may negatively impact women—politically, economically, religiously, socially—and those ultimately impact the family. Some examples are women being paid less for doing the same job; women's standards of living dropping more significantly after divorce than men's; insurance paying for Viagra but not for birth-control pills (even when they are prescribed for noncontraceptive medical reasons); and the fact that in most states the maximum age limit for adoption is higher for men than women. Many women face additional discrimination in terms of race, class, age, sexual orientation, and religion, which adds burdens to their families.

Investigating the influences of religion on culture, families, and women's experiences provides a good example of taking the sociocultural context into account. In the early Judeo-Christian world, women were considered property and were exchanged from father to husband along with a dowry of land, money, and livestock. Although this practice is not acceptable in the United States, remnants of the subjugation of women are still evident in some religious perspectives. For example, predominant in the discussion of women's roles in certain Christian families is the question of whether the man is the head of the home (as Christ heads the Church). The issue of power, as influenced by religious conventions and beliefs, needs to be considered in this important social context and in how it affects women and girls within families.

Trying to understand the multiple levels of influence on women's experiences is the starting point for feminist family scholars. Analyzing these contexts is the basis for understanding how society constructed particular views of what women and men should be. Feminist family scholars refer to the act of analysis as social deconstruction. The reflection on and discussion of that analysis forms the basis of the social discourse of gender roles.

There are many forms of families. Feminist family theorists broaden our view of families. The traditional view of the nuclear family is an inadequate description of families in today's society. Economic forces, divorce, and other social factors have changed the nature of the family in the United States. Today, families include long-term cohabiting couples, single parents and their children, multiethnic families, multigenerational families, same-sex families, stepfamilies, remarried couples, and fictive kin.

Research data indicate that the most successful family relationships are based on loving friendship, models of equality, intimacy, caring, and cooperation. These qualities are applicable to more than simply the traditional nuclear family (Allen and Baber 1992). Limiting families to the traditional nuclear definition restricts women's roles to a subordinate position and discounts the experiences of women in diverse family forms.

Emphasis is placed on social change. One goal of feminist family theory is an activist orientation—that is, challenging the status quo. Feminists seek to empower the disenfranchised or those with less power (Sollie and Leslie 1994). They advocate looking at diverse family forms, challenging sexism, and challenging aspects of our society that act against women and children, including homophobia and male violence, so that we can bring the acceptance of difference and diversity to human interactions. *Feminist praxis* refers to the feminists' struggle to put their beliefs into action.

Not only do feminist family theorists seek to uncover gender biases, they also work to change existing gender relations in society, in the economy, in education, and in families (Allen and Baber 1992; MacDermid and Jurich 1992; Osmond and Thorne 1993). They seek to bring public attention to what had previously been considered private issues, particularly with respect to families. Their slogan is "the personal is political." In other words, what happens personally to women has political and social impact. Given that much of a woman's experience is located within the family, one might also say that "the family is political" as well. You can see the dynamics of power both in society and in families, but power in families (whether of men over women or parents over children) has often been seen as "natural" and therefore less likely to be challenged. Although few in today's society would dispute the fact that family members should not wield their power to the extremes of child or wife abuse, feminist family scholars have continued to uncover less obvious forms of power differentials, such as differing amounts of influence in decision-making, division of labor in the household, and differences in anticipated costs when leaving a relationship (Okin 1997).

One example of the personal made political revolves around the issue of sexual *agency*. Sexual agency refers to the degree of control one has over one's own sexuality and reproductive activity, clearly a personal and a private issue. Early feminists pointed out how power over one's reproductive capacity led to power in one's life, both personally and economically (Baber 1994; Sollie and Leslie 1994; Thompson 1992). Prior to the advent of reliable birth control, women (married or not) who wanted an active sexual life had to be prepared for pregnancy. Until the Pregnancy Discrimination Act of 1975 was passed, women could be fired from their jobs simply because they were pregnant. Years after the federal mandate was passed, young married women were still discriminated against in hiring, because employers feared that they would get pregnant and leave their jobs. Jobs, therefore, were more likely to be given to young men or single women. As birth control became more reliable and the women's movement opened the workplace, women who were pregnant and women who were mothers had increased access to economic opportunities and therefore more power.

However, in the United States women who are pregnant or have children still suffer economically and socially. Pregnant women are not fired, but the law does not require that they be paid for their time off to have the child. When they return to work, they often must pay for child care, thereby reducing their resources. Contrast this with several European countries that actually provide one year paid maternity leave to women after childbirth and subsidize child care so that all children receive the same quality of care when the mothers return to work.

A subtler example of the personal made political may be seen in how women reflect on their roles. Many women believe that they need to stay at home with their children if they can. For economic reasons, most are unable to do that, and they often report feeling guilty about it. These women, and perhaps their families and society in general, interpret their inability to care for their children and work at the same time as a personal failure (Mahoney 1996). This guilt, generally not expressed by men, is an indication of how subtle and pervasive the social inequality is in our society.

There is no objective, unbiased observation of humans. Our observation is influenced by social realities. This is implied by "the personal is political" slogan that we talked about above. Something that is personal is by definition subjective and not objective.

Feminist family scholars have challenged the traditional approach to scientific understanding. Even the questions that we ask are influenced by how we are trained to be scientists (Thompson 1992). Traditional science teaches objectivity and observer-free bias, with an emphasis on neutral "fact." Feminist family scholars challenge this perspective by saying that there is no neutral observation of humans. If our social realities are constructed based on a gendered perspective, then our perspective on reality, and therefore the facts as we know them, are socially constructed. So the real focus for feminists is not about obtaining objective facts but rather about understanding how people's social reality is constructed by understanding their experience (Sollie and Leslie 1994).

Feminist family scholars believe that families should not be treated as a unitary whole. If they are, the lesser voices in the family are oppressed. For example, if an abuser is asked "How is your family life?" he might respond "Fine." His abused spouse probably views the state of the family differently. The question should not be "How is your family life?" but rather "What is your experience of this relationship?" Feminist family scholars seek to uncover the voices in families that have been oppressed or neglected by traditional social science. In order to uncover these voices, feminist researchers are more likely to use case studies, qualitative analyses, and ethnographic studies in addition to traditional survey data.

PRIMARY TERMS AND CONCEPTS

SEX

Sex refers to one's biological assignment as genetically defined at birth—that is, male or female.

GENDER

Gender refers to the social meanings and behaviors ascribed to one's sex, particularly with regard to roles and behaviors expected of someone because of one's sex. Gendered behaviors are learned as a result of socialization and are therefore the result of one's culture, not genetic predisposition. For example, we often give preschool boys trucks and preschool girls dolls to play with because that is what society, not genetics, deems acceptable.

CATEGORIZATION

Categorization is the process of applying labels to behaviors and roles according to one's sex. Certain behaviors, roles, words, and symbols are considered "male" (for example, aggression, playing with trucks, "strong," the color blue), whereas others are considered "female" (for example, being nice, ballet, "soft," the color pink).

STRATIFICATION

Stratification refers to the application of value to different categories. Assigning social value to categories ranks those categories in the social context. For example, is it better to be nice or aggressive? In the first grade of elementary schools, it is probably better to be nice, and girls may be treated more positively than boys by their teachers and their peers in that social context. But in the social context of a Fortune 500 company, it is probably more highly valued to be aggressive than nice, so a woman who has been socialized only to be nice and never encouraged to learn any aggressive skills probably won't ever be hired as a chief executive officer, no matter how well educated she may be.

PRIVILEGE

Privilege refers to the social status given to one with more power and value in society. The concept of privilege urges feminists to ask not only who has power but who does not and to ensure that those who have been previously marginalized and oppressed by those who have had power and privilege are now included in the matrix of voices represented.

SOCIAL DECONSTRUCTION

The first step in the analysis of how views of reality are constructed by social interactions, particularly in light of how gendered meanings are developed, is social deconstruction. It involves the consideration of how society has categorized and assigned values to behaviors and roles according to sex.

SOCIAL DISCOURSE

The next step in the analysis, social discourse, brings the analysis of social deconstruction into the "conversation" of gender expectations and behaviors. Social discourse raises awareness of the analysis into the work of social scientists through examining the ways in which we invite people to participate in the dialogue of deconstruction, ensuring that those who do not have privilege are included in the conversations. It challenges us to question how we focus our questions, and how we analyze the data.

PRAXIS

The step after analysis, in which beliefs and values are put into action, is praxis. For feminist family scholars, this includes advocacy for women, inclusiveness in language and behavior, and reflecting on one's own behavior with intention.

COMMON AREAS OF RESEARCH AND APPLICATION

DIVISION OF LABOR

One of the major areas of feminist research is division of labor within the family. Labor divisions are often constructed according to gender, including both paid and unpaid labor in our society. The stereotypic family has been the traditional, idealized, nuclear family, in which the father is the breadwinner and the mother stays home to care for the house and children. Although the nuclear family is no longer representative of most families in the United States today, we often still see people reacting to women's labor outside the home as "intrusive" because of our societal expecta-

---

Figure 8.1
Analysis of Social Interaction From a Feminist Perspective

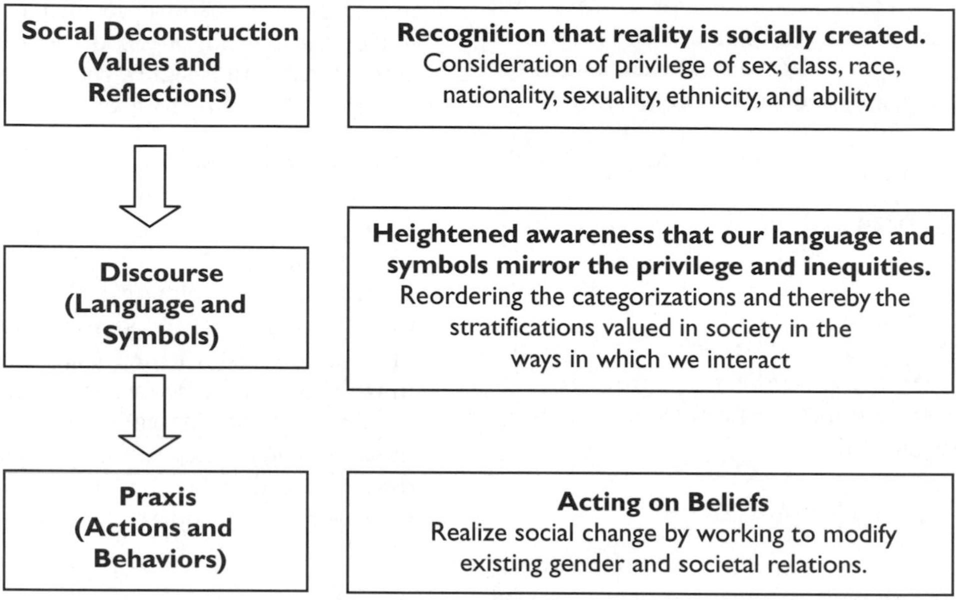

Social Deconstruction (Values and Reflections)	**Recognition that reality is socially created.** Consideration of privilege of sex, class, race, nationality, sexuality, ethnicity, and ability

⬇

Discourse (Language and Symbols)	**Heightened awareness that our language and symbols mirror the privilege and inequities.** Reordering the categorizations and thereby the stratifications valued in society in the ways in which we interact

⬇

Praxis (Actions and Behaviors)	**Acting on Beliefs** Realize social change by working to modify existing gender and societal relations.

---

tions that the woman's first responsibility is the home. Further, unpaid work in our society is not considered "real work." The work that is done at home—maintaining the home, paying the bills, raising the children, tutoring the children, ferrying the children back and forth to their activities, nursing, getting up in the middle of the night, cooking, and cleaning—are not considered valuable work in our society because these jobs do not produce an income.

Even as women enter the workforce in increasingly higher-status, higher-income professional roles, they are still expected to be "wives" in spite of the outside work. Many high-level corporate jobs are structured according to the assumption that a worker has a partner for support, thereby creating what is essentially a two-person career. One partner, typically the male, is expected to work long hours, as if he does not need to worry about the needs of the children and the rest of the family, because those needs will be met by the wife. The outcomes of this arrangement oppress

both men and women and are perpetuated by social norms that feminist family scholars challenge. Furthermore, analyses of dual-earner couples show that women continue to do the majority of household tasks and child care in addition to their full-time jobs.

In her analysis of this "second shift," Hochschild (1989) found that women not only did the work but also often believed that it was their responsibility. Feminist family theorists analyze this division of labor from an equity perspective and also deconstruct the reality of why a woman would believe those jobs are her responsibility.

FAMILY VIOLENCE

A second application of feminist family study is family violence. According to feminist family scholars, in our attempt to maintain privacy in the family, we have failed in our social obligations to identify injustices in the family (Wood 1998). Families are not always the "havens of love, goodwill, and affection" that we would like to believe exist, and families are not safe places for many women and children.

While some homes are places that foster support for many of us, many other homes are places where "abuse, violence, exploitation, cruelty and persisting inequities fester for far too many citizens in our country" (Wood 1998, 129). By drawing attention to such abuse in families, feminist family scholars have identified facts about families that others have not noticed. For example, a violent act against a woman is perpetrated every 12 to 18 seconds in the United States, and four women die each day because of family violence (Wood 1998). In some studies of dating violence, as many as 50 percent of college men admitted that they had sexually coerced a woman against her wishes, and one-third admitted that they would commit rape if they could be certain no one would find out (Wood 1998).

Feminist family theorists studying violence in families have expanded the definitions of violence to include isolation, threats, and forced economic dependence (Thompson and Walker 1995). They have also reflected on the ways in which societal behaviors affect those already oppressed. For example, feminist family scholars have called attention to the fact that police officers sometimes refuse to interfere in domestic disputes or advise victims not to prosecute batterers. They have noted that our music has encouraged women to "stand by your man," our cosmetic counters and lingerie departments have encouraged women to fulfill social prescriptions for femininity, and our junior high schools have stood by a tradition of relegating girls to supporting roles as cheerleaders while boys learn aggression on the sports field.

Although it is part of feminist family scholarship to identify the problems of oppression and inequities in our society, it is also imperative that feminist family scholarship generates alternatives and seeks ways to empower the oppressed and disenfranchised. Feminist family scholars identify issues and also seek ways to advocate on behalf of women and their families through education and support.

CRITIQUE

Feminist family theory can be used to analyze certain aspects of family relations. It includes a wide range of "family types" within its definition of a "family unit." Other theories are narrower in their scope. Feminist family theory sheds light on other issues that are neglected or ignored by other theories, such as the male-oriented perspective of what was previously considered "objective" research. It attempts to lend more equal weight to women's issues in family interactions and to downplay the traditional gender roles of some other theories.

Feminist family theory is not without its critics, though. Feminism has been criticized as being oppressive to men by focusing only on issues that affect women. Feminist family scholars refute this by saying that issues that are important to women in families are important to men as well.

Feminist family theory has been criticized for working outside the parameters and paradigms of the traditional, scientific base of knowledge. Critics say that although science is not totally value-free, we should strive to present the information in the best and clearest way without becoming involved in the data. Feminist family scholars respond that because it is impossible to be truly objective, the most truthful thing is to admit our subjectivity and work hard to reflect on our role as researchers rather than deny its influence in the research process.

Feminist family theorists have also been criticized for their activist position. Social scientists, maintaining an objective stance, have frequently preferred being describers of events rather than facilitators of change. Feminist scholars argue that it is impossible to fully embrace and understand the oppression of the disenfranchised without being ethically bound to do something to alter that reality. Issues of inequity in relationships, such as division of labor in families, economic stability and support, and ways in which society devalues women's work and limits opportunities, should be addressed by those with power and privilege.

Feminist family theorists have also been criticized for working against traditional nuclear families. But the reality is that the traditional nuclear family is no longer the dominant norm. Feminist scholars argue that the inequality within families may actually lend itself to the dissolution of the traditional nuclear family as power differentials enter into the conversations, economy, and distribution of labor in American families.

Finally, some have challenged feminist family theory because, they claim, it pays too much attention to the oppression of one group—women—to the exclusion of other forms of oppression (for example, by race, ethnicity, age, disability, religion, and so forth). The "matrix of oppression" found in the third wave of feminism is an attempt to expand the boundaries of awareness of oppression experienced by members of our society.

APPLICATION

Alice and Bob Stephens seem to have a good marriage, a stable family, and two good jobs. In many ways, they are part of a privileged class. But it is clear that, at least on this night, there are two marriages—his and hers. Bob relies on Alice to take care of the "little things" that keep their family life going smoothly, yet Alice is troubled and feeling overwhelmed by keeping up with all those little things.

1. Compare Alice's experiences and Bob's experiences. What are some of the privileges they have? What are some of the inequities? Identify ways in which those inequities are intentional. Are there some inequities that are not intentional? If so, why do they exist?

2. In what ways are their perspectives on their marriage different?

3. How are Alice's and Bob's lives impacted by social norms and expectations?

4. What social and/or historical contexts should be taken into account when attempting to understand the Stephens' family?

5. Based on what you have learned studying feminist family theory, what recommendations for change might you suggest if Alice and Bob came in for counseling?

6. If Bob and Alice were to divorce, how might the consequences of that divorce be different for each of them? What role would privilege play?

7. If you wanted to study marriages like the Stephens', how might you design your research so that both Bob and Alice had equal voice in the study? What differences do you think you would find between the men and the women?

8. Using the process of deconstruction, discourse, and praxis outlined in Figure 8.1, find examples of each stage of the analysis of social interaction from the interviews in the reading by Blaisure and Allen. Illustrate how the couples' reflection on their ideology and practice build marital equality. What do you think about the concept of "vigilance" as described in this article?

SAMPLE READING

Blaisure, K. R., and Allen, K. R. (1995). Feminists and the ideology and practice of marital equality. *Journal of Marriage and the Family* 57: 5–19.

Using qualitative data, this study considers how couples view marital equity from both ideological and practical perspectives. In their own words, it includes both male and female perspectives about the ways in which they struggle to make their ideals match their behaviors in real life.

References

Allen, K. R. (1994). Feminist reflections on lifelong single women. In L. D. Sollie and L. A. Leslie (eds.), *Gender, Families, and Close Rela-*

tionships: *Feminist Research Journeys* (pp. 97–119). Thousand Oaks, CA: Sage.

——. (2000). A conscious and inclusive family studies. *Journal of Marriage and the Family* 62: 4–17.

Allen, K. R., and Baber, K. M. (1992). Starting a revolution in family life education: A feminist vision. *Family Relations* 41: 378–384.

Allen, K. R., and Fransworth, E. B. (1993). Reflexivity in teaching about feminism. *Family Relations* 42: 351–356.

Baber, K. M. (1994). Studying women's sexualities: Feminist transformations. In L. D. Sollie and L. A. Leslie (eds.), *Gender, Families, and Close Relationships: Feminist Research Journeys* (pp. 50–73). Thousand Oaks, CA: Sage.

Baca Zinn, M. (2000). Feminism and family studies for a new century. *Annals, AAPSS* 571: 42–56.

Bernard, J. (1972). *The Future of Marriage.* New York: World.

Collins, P. H. (1998). It's all in the family: Intersections of gender, race and nation. *Hypatia* 13: 62–82.

——. (2000). *Black Feminist Thought: Knowledge, Consciousness, and the Politics of Empowerment* (2nd ed.). New York: Routledge.

Ferree, M. M. (1990). Beyond separate spheres: Feminism and family research. *Journal of Marriage and the Family* 52: 866–884.

Gilligan, C. (1982). *In a Different Voice: Psychological Theory and Women's Development.* Cambridge, MA: Harvard University Press.

Hochschild, A. R. (1989). *The Second Shift: Working Parents and the Revolution at Home.* New York: Viking/Penguin.

Lorber, J. (1998). *Gender Inequality: Feminist Theories and Politics.* Los Angeles: Roxbury.

MacDermid, S. M., and Jurich, J. A. (1992). Feminist teaching: Effective education. *Family Relations* 41: 31–39.

Mahoney, A. R. (1996). Children, families, and feminism: Perspectives on teaching. *Early Childhood Education Journal* 23: 191–196.

Okin, S. M. (1997). Families and feminist theory: Some past and present issues. In H. L. Nelson (ed.), *Feminism and Families* (pp. 13–26). New York: Routledge.

Osmond, M. W., and Thorne, B. (1993). Feminist theories: The social construction of gender in families and society. In P. G. Boss, W. J. Doherty, R. LaRossa, W. R. Schumm, and S. K. Steinmetz (eds.), *Sourcebook of Family Theories and Methods* (pp. 591–626). New York: Plenum.

Rutter, V., and Schwartz, P. (2000). Gender, marriage, and diverse possibilities for cross-sex and same-sex pairs. In D. H. Demo, K. R. Allen, and M. A. Fine (eds.), *Handbook of Family Diversity* (pp. 59–81). New York: Oxford.

Shehan, C. L., and Kammeyer, K. C. W. (1997). *Marriages and Families: Reflections of a Gendered Society.* Needham Heights, MA: Allyn and Bacon.

Sollie, L. D., and Leslie, L. A. (1994). *Gender, Families, and Close Relationships: Feminist Research Journeys.* Thousand Oaks, CA: Sage.

Thomas, R. M. (2000). *Recent Theories of Human Development.* Thousand Oaks, CA: Sage.

Thompson, L. (1992). Feminist methodology for family studies. *Journal of Marriage and the Family* 54: 3–18.

Thompson, L., and Walker, A. J. (1995). The place of feminism in family studies. *Journal of Marriage and the Family* 57: 847–865.

Walker, A. J. (1993). Teaching about race, gender and class diversity in the United States families. *Family Relations* 42: 342–350.

Wood, J. T. (1998). Ethics, justice, and the "private sphere." *Women's Studies in Communication* 21: 127–149. ✦

Feminists and the Ideology and Practice of Marital Equality

Karen R. Blaisure
Katherine R. Allen

The literature on marital equality documents the incongruency between the ideology and practice of marital equality. Twenty married female and male feminists were interviewed and asked to describe the influence of feminism on their marriages. This study confirms a distinction between the ideology and practice of equality within heterosexual marriage. However, it also reveals the possibility of upgrading marriage for women and the establishment of marital equality. Couples reported the practice of vigilance, defined as an attending to and a monitoring of equality, within and outside of their relationship. This vigilance of equality appeared as five processes: (a) critique of gender injustices, (b) public acts of equality, (c) support of wives' activities, (d) reflective assessment, and (e) emotional involvement.

In her 1972 book, *The Future of Marriage*, and again in the second edition (1982), Bernard concluded that the future viability of marriage will depend upon "upgrading" marriage for women. After reviewing the literature on marriage, she declared that two marriages exist, his and hers, and that marriage is more attractive and healthier for the former than for the latter. Bernard (1982) was optimistic that couples were struggling to improve marriage to make it beneficial for both spouses, although achieving an equal division of employment and family work was "still more talked about than practiced" (p. 300). According to more recent research, equality between marital partners continues to reflect incongruency between ideology and practice. Individual couples may experience more congruency between talk and action, but for the majority of married couples, the discrepancy remains.

Traditional marital and family life, described as "patriarchal but father-absent" (Luepnitz, 1988, p. 111), is a tenacious script that some couples are attempting to rewrite with much effort and disappointment. Past research has found that when women in traditional marriages assume a feminist identity, they and their relational expectations change a great deal but their husbands have little interest in changing their beliefs and behaviors (Acker, Barry, & Esseveld, 1981).

Hochschild (1989) noted the incongruency between ideology and practice in marriage when she considered "the second shift" (i.e., housework, parental responsibilities, and domestic management). While 18% of the men studied shared the work of the second shift equally with their wives, the majority did not. However, even though research such as Hochschild's reports a continued incongruency for the majority of couples, it also indicates that, for some couples, congruency between the ideology and the practice of marital equality is possible (Gilbert, 1993; Jump & Haas, 1987). Among the men who subscribed to an egalitarian ideology, 70% shared equally, while only 22% of the men subscribing to a traditional ideology and 3% of men subscribing to a transitional ideology shared equally. Certainly an ideology of marital equality increases the possibility of sharing family work, although it is not a guarantee.

FEMINISM AND MARRIAGE

Feminism highlights first and foremost the oppressive character of structural inequality based on gender (Osmond & Thorne, 1993).

Recent theorizing on gender has examined "the process of the social construction of maleness and femaleness as oppositional categories with unequal social value" (Ferree, 1990, p. 868). Distinctions based on gender require the ignoring and even suppression of similarities by "the constant and contentious process of engendering behavior as separate and unequal" (Ferree, 1990, p. 869). Gender becomes, along with race, sexual orientation, class, and age, an organizing category of peoples' lives.

Feminist analyses have provided an excellent critique of relationships as gendered constructions. Over the past two decades, feminists have demonstrated the problematic nature of marital and family life for women (Glenn, 1987). Women are the marital partners responsible for a family's emotional intimacy, for adapting their sexual desires to their husbands', for monitoring the relationship and resolving conflict from a subordinate position, and for being as independent as possible without threatening their husbands' status (Fishman, 1983; Thompson & Walker, 1989). Feminism has provided a critique of traditional gender-structured marriage, resulting in an awareness of its overwhelming cost to women in financial, emotional, and physical dimensions. The problematic nature of marriage for women has been linked to its centrality in patriarchy, the devaluation of women's work, and the hierarchy of gender (Ferree, 1990; Glenn, 1987).

Previously published research indicates a higher involvement of men in family life when married to women with equal or higher education, income, and status (Jump & Haas, 1987; Perry-Jenkins & Crouter, 1990). When the wife's career, as well as the husband's, organizes family life, the chances of marital equality are increased (Atkinson & Boles, 1984; Haas, 1980).

The question of who should remain at home with children typically is resolved along gender lines. Couples can consider themselves equal because they jointly participated in the decision making about child care, which is a process that obscures the inequality of the outcome. Yet the result is predictable for most couples and places women at a greater disadvantage (Haavind, 1984; Hochschild, 1989).

To expose only the oppressiveness of traditional family life for women, however, conceals the supportive aspects of families for women, such as providing resources and self-esteem for minority and working class women (Ferree, 1990) and mutual nurturing between wives and husbands (Thompson, 1993). Family relationships can be empowering for women as well (Baber & Allen, 1992), by providing interpersonal skills in emotional caregiving and self-disclosure.

Using the concept of distributive justice, Thompson (1991) sought to explain why women fail to consider the imbalanced division of family work as unfair. By examining "women's sense of fairness," the imbalance and its excuse become evident. Rather than counting time and tasks, Thompson argued that women want care from their husbands in the form of doing disliked tasks, covering for the women at home so they can have personal time, and responding to requests for help. In addition, by making within-gender comparisons, women consider themselves to be better off than other women with husbands who do less. Finally, justifications for unequal distribution of family work, such as attributing family work to women's personal needs, function to obscure women's entitlement to relational equality.

This present study asks what happens to the practice of marriage when wives and husbands agree on the goal of equality. Specifically, how do feminist women and men practice marriage? Is there a sharing of the second shift? Does a feminist ideology of marital equality result in a marital "upgrade" for women? For feminist couples, does the ideology of marital equality translate into the practice of marital equality?

This research reports on couples in heterosexual marriages who clearly stated their belief in marital equality and used those beliefs to assist them in attempting, and in some cases reaching, a practice of marital equality. This study confirms the difficulty and documents the possibility of congruency between the ideology and the practice of marriage.

METHODOLOGY

A qualitative research design is particularly relevant to the study of marriage because it invites participants to describe and explain their lives in their own words and to assess for themselves to what extent they experience marriage as beneficial and detrimental (Ehrensaft, 1990; Fishman, 1983; Thompson, 1992). Feminists in heterosexual marriages were interviewed because of their stated beliefs of equality and their goal of reconstructing marriage for the wellbeing of women and men. Couples married 5 or more years were included in order for them to reflect on time together past the "honeymoon" phase. We sought couples who could be considered "expert informants" (Acker et al., 1981) on the blending of feminism and marriage. Interviewing self-identified feminist couples yielded empirical data from these informants (Dressel & Clark, 1990) and reflected strategic, or purposive, sampling (Haas, 1980; Kaufman, 1985). While a small number of participants were eventually included in this study, this sampling procedure was driven by theoretical criteria, resulting in a specific group of couples (Fishman, 1983; Gilgun, 1992; Strauss & Corbin, 1990) who could address the topic.

DATA COLLECTION

Theoretical sampling was used to locate couples who met the study's parameters. Over the course of 8 months, intensive efforts were made to find couples in heterosexual marriages who were self-identified feminists prior to marriage and currently and who had been married for at least 5 years. Volunteers were recruited through advertisements and snowball sampling (Rubin, 1983; Taylor & Bogdan, 1984). Advertisements were placed in regional weekly and monthly newsletters of the National Organization for Women (NOW) and in local newspapers. Announcements were made monthly at a regional NOW meeting, and two professors at a local university announced the

study to graduate classes during the fall semester of 1991.

Telephone or face-to-face pilot interviews were done with one or both partners of 23 couples who volunteered for the study. Volunteers were asked questions concerning feminism, length of marriage, and willingness to participate in joint and individual interviews. Thirteen couples were ineligible to participate in the study for the following reasons: One of the partners did not self-identify as a feminist either before or during marriage, one of the partners did not want to participate, couples were married fewer than 5 years, or couples were not legally married. Ten of the initial 23 couples met the requirements for participation and provided, on average, 6 hours of interview time per couple, or 4 hours of interview time per person. A joint interview was completed with each couple to obtain an initial description of their daily lives and a history of their marriage, as well as to provide an opportunity to observe the couple interacting. During subsequent individual interviews, participants were asked to clarify information presented in the joint interview, to talk more about the influence of their feminist beliefs on their marriage, and to note satisfactions and dissatisfaction with their marriage. Interviewing occurred in two sessions, one joint and one individual, for each participant, and took place in the participant's home or office. The two interviews per person provided opportunity for the participants and interviewer to establish rapport, allowed participants to reveal themselves over time, and offered them a chance between interviews to think about the research topic.

Although Rubin (1983) argued for interviewing partners of a couple separately to encourage freedom of conversation, this research design allowed for joint and individual interviews, providing the opportunity for the interviewer to observe partners interacting as well as for the spouses to talk in confidence. Furthermore, joint interviews allowed couples to elaborate on and clarify relational events and thus offer a shared or disparate view of their experiences (Daly, 1992).

ANALYSIS OF DATA

Data analysis was a synthesis of various procedures for managing qualitative data. The analysis was guided by the study's use of a feminist framework, the research questions, participants' experiences of their combination of feminism and marriage, and the authors' individual and collaborative understanding and life experiences. Interviews were transcribed into Hyperqual, a Macintosh computer program for qualitative data analysis (Padilla, 1991).

The data analysis process was informed by the dual purposes of offering a critical interpretation and making use of reflexivity, the process of reflecting upon and examining the research process (Fonow & Cook, 1991). The first author audiotaped observations, data analysis hunches, and feelings towards the couples following each interview. These memos and ongoing reflexive conversations among the authors and several colleagues, both female and male, assisted in keeping a critical perspective toward the self-reported data.

Participants engaged in the construction of this analysis through reading and commenting on what had been written about them (Acker, Barry, & Esseveld, 1983; Thompson, 1992). They were sent a preliminary draft of the results and were invited to respond by telephone or letter with their reactions to the interpretation of their lives. Comments included disagreeing with a presentation of why one woman spent more time parenting than on her career and updating information about decisions couples had made since their interviews. In addition, one man stated that he thought the critique of marriage was overly severe. Participants' comments and corrections were considered during the data analysis.

Coding procedures outlined by Taylor and Bogdan (1984), along with an adaptation by Strauss and Corbin (1990), were followed. A list of each participant's responses to questions and topics was made for comparison. Data analysis continued through the use of three levels of generality: what was characteristic about each individual marriage, what were group differences among the marriages studied, and what was common across all of the marriages studied (Runyan, 1984). An analysis to determine the congruency between ideology and practice of equality proceeded by comparing couples who described sharing family work with those who did not.

DESCRIPTION OF PARTICIPANTS

The selection criteria, including the requirement of self-identification as a feminist and the means of recruitment via newspaper and NOW advertising, resulted in a homogeneous group. The 20 participants interviewed for this study were White and well educated. The median and mode age was 36. All but two women had degrees equivalent or higher than their husbands. Nine couples had children, and three couples had children from previous marriages. The median length of marriage was 10 years. Participants claimed the label of feminist currently, and both members of the couple considered themselves feminists before marriage. The oldest couple considered themselves feminists prior to marriage but did not remember hearing the term feminist until after they had married. Once they had become acquainted with the term, perhaps as early as within a year of their wedding, they began using it.

The participants understood feminism to be the belief in equality, a promotion of women and their strengths, and a political movement dedicated to changing society for the betterment of women and men.

> ELIZABETH: Feminism is basically highly conscious of autonomy and a person's potential for self-development. Feminism remains at its heart seeing the wholeness and the value of the female and wanting women to have these political, social, economic, religious [rights].

Often men discussed their beliefs in a liberal feminist sense—that is, that women are men's equals—a perspective that has been criticized as having an androcentric bias (Tong, 1989). Yet the men also expressed dismay over what passes as masculine and as a result felt isolated from most other men. Three men specifically stated that they felt more comfortable around women than around men, who typically talked in ways that reinforced the idea of women as inferior.

The women began marriage with structural advantages (i.e., age, income, education, and status) not typically found in traditional marriages. Husbands were no more than 3 years older than their wives, except for Carl who was 10 years older than Elizabeth. Elizabeth came to the marriage with a doctoral degree, the same occupation as her husband, and 4 years of work experience. Four women were older than their husbands; three of these women had been married previously. Five women had more education or higher professional degrees than their husbands when marrying. The sample represented a variety of high-status professions.

All of the women described the ability to financially care for themselves and their children and the willingness to divorce, if necessary (see Okin, 1989). Three women currently earned more than their husbands, while another two women earned income equivalent to their husbands'. Half of the women earned less than their husbands; however, their financial contributions were respected. Jennifer's salary was reinvested in her business which was solely in her name. Sarah's income was steady and provided the family with health care insurance, whereas her husband's income from self-employment, although greater in amount, was erratic. Her economic support was crucial for the family's financial well-being. Even though Ruth's husband earned more than she when his housing and other employment allowances were counted, Ruth's part-time salary equaled her husband's full-time salary. Ruth had more control over her work hours than her husband, whose job required him to be continually on call. Although Miriam and her husband shared the same occupation, she historically received smaller salaries due, in their estimation, to sex discrimination. They considered themselves co-providers even though her current professional salary was nearly $8,000 less than her husband's.

Finally, Mary, the only woman who was not employed at the time of this study, had removed herself from the job market to increase the time spent with her children, to escape a poor work environment, and to attend to a chronic illness. She worked a few hours per week at her parents' business and at a small home-based business she and her husband were beginning. She felt financially secure even without a job because, as she quickly stated, should she ever divorce, she could fire her husband from his present job because he worked for her parents' business, and she was on the board of directors. This ability to influence her husband's financial well-being, along with the financial stability provided by a family business, gave her power typically gained by women through employment.

All couples with children were pleased with the degree of the fathers' involvement, although few couples accomplished shared parenting, and some women wanted their husbands to take on more parenting responsibilities. All but two women, Rose and Miriam, had the primary care of their children as babies. In these two couples, both parents considered themselves to be primary parents with equal responsibilities. The couples with stepchildren followed the model that the biological parent would be the primary parent. In one case the children were adults at the time of the parents' marriage to one another. For the other two remarried couples with minor children, the stepfathers were reported to be more emotionally involved with the children than the biological fathers. Both women in these couples reported feeling highly satisfied and comfortable with the level of their current husbands' involvement in assuming many parenting responsibilities. When compared with their own fathers and male friends, all of the men with children cared for them to a great extent while wives pursued their careers,

Table 1
Participant Demographics

Name	Age	Years Married	Education	Work	Number of Children and Their Ages
Barb	30	5	B.A.	government	no children
Dan	33	5	M.A.	government	
Ruth	39	8	M.A.	health care	5-year-old son
Paul	35	8	M.A.	religion	
Sarah	33	10	B.A.	government	5-year-old son and
Shawn	36	10	B.A.	small business	18-month-old daughter
Rachel	43	13	2 M.A.s	mental health	10-year-old son and
Tony	44	13	M.A.	consultant	7-year-old daughter
Deborah	52	13	Ph.D.	education	21- and 23-year-old daughters
Milton	39	13	M.A.	government	from her previous marriage
Mary	36	15	B.A.	arts	8-year-old twin sons
John	36	15	A.A.	small business	
Jennifer[a]	48	7	B.A.	small business	17- and 22-year-old daughters
Calvin[a]	43	7	Ph.D.	education	from her previous marriage
Rose[a]	44	10	Ph.D.	education	8-year-old daughter
Patrick[a]	35	10	Ph.D.	education	
Miriam[a]	33	12	M.A.	research	9-month-old son
Larry[a]	35	12	M.A.	publishing	
Elizabeth[a]	67	22	Ph.D.	both retired	each had 2 adult children at
Carl[a]	77	22	Ph.D.	both education	time of their marriage

[a]Couples who reported a sharing of domestic responsibilities. Whereas all couples described participating in three processes of vigilance (critique of gender injustices, public acts of equality, and support of women's activities), the four couples noted here also participated in two additional processes: reflective assessment of relationship contributions and emotional involvement.

education, and personal interests. These fathers were involved in their children's lives through interacting with them one-on-one for large blocks of time (evenings, 8-hour days, a whole week). Fathers and stepfathers in this study reported feeling very close to their children.

RESULTS

This study confirms a distinction between ideology and practice of equality within heterosexual marriage of feminists. The practice of marital equality in terms of outcome—that is, sharing the second shift (Hochschild, 1989)—does not automatically flow from a stated feminist ideology of equality. However, couples in this study demonstrated some of the ways in which the gap between the ideology and practice of marital equality can be narrowed and possibly closed.

This analysis revealed that all couples participated in at least three processes of vigilance that reinforced the creation of their marriages as supportive locations for feminist thought and practice. However, couples differed in the extent to which they participated in two additional processes of vigilance that further promoted the practice of equality. These five processes are described below following a discussion on how feminist beliefs blend with marriage.

UPGRADING MARRIAGE THROUGH VIGILANCE

Couples reported practicing vigilance, defined as an attending to and a monitoring of equality, within and outside of their relationship. This vigilance began prior to their marriage, and for some, prior to meeting their partner. Women reported feeling empowered to choose their spouses wisely. Feminism offered criteria for the women to use when determining the extent to which they felt comfortable in a relationship.

BARB: I don't want to get involved in a relationship if I have to worry about what I say or I have to go really gently to put feelers out to see how they feel about things.

ELIZABETH: Feminism gives me the strength to demand: Either I get the treatment I think is adequate partnering or I leave. Feminism is a very important part of my life.

Feminism provided women with a screening criterion to assess men as potential partners willing to attend to issues surrounding equality. Wives and husbands clearly stated the importance of having similar world views in choosing to marry one another. Miriam and Larry's discussion of their similarities was typical of all of the participants.

MIRIAM: Feminism is a view that we share. If we didn't share this view, we probably wouldn't have gotten married. So, it was important that we share it in order to be a happy couple. Feminism probably informs our decisions that we make and steers us as a couple in certain directions and away from other choices.

LARRY: In order to get married to someone I had to make sure that almost all our beliefs were completely congruent.

Ruth addressed the importance of entering marriage after acquiring an education, work experience, and self-knowledge, a process she termed "coming into my own."

RUTH: If you look at the traditional understanding of marriage where the man owns a woman, everything is in a man's name, the children take the father's name, that's oppressive. But if you can think of marriage as the commitment of two equals, you see what I am saying about waiting until I was 30 to get married, and how awful it would have been if I had gotten married in my twenties. I met Paul at a point when I had finally come into my own, when I had found a career and a lifestyle that I felt comfortable with. I felt sufficient in and of myself. I decided that even though I wanted to one day get married and have children that I might not do that and that would be okay because I enjoyed what I did.

Participants' experience of feminism was nested in a larger liberal world view. Rachel and Tony considered themselves to be outside of the mainstream, thus their relationship provided a feeling of acceptance for each of them.

RACHEL: I really value his political, social, and religious views because I meet so few people whose views are anywhere near mine.

Foremost, due to their shared ideology, all participants considered themselves to be moving toward something better than what traditional marriage offered. Their dissatisfaction with traditional marriage resulted from observing marriages of friends and family, being aware of its costs to women, and experiencing such marriages with prior spouses. Feminism was identified by these women and men as a crucial component in making their relationships satisfying. They felt benefited by their marriages and believed them to be superior to traditional marriage. Women and men said that others had commented on how strong and supportive the couples' marriages appeared, although they questioned the couples' preferences for having different names, separate recreational interests, or friends of the other sex.

Moving toward something better translated into women being able to have their own identities while in marriage, and men being able to have connection with family members. Women talked about feminism helping them to have a sense of self in marriage.

> JENNIFER: Being married is not oppressive to me. But part of that is, I'm not Mrs. E. I'm not his possession. And I see having his name as being his possession. He's not Mr. N. He's not my possession.

Men described feeling close to their children and to their partners. In explaining why he wanted to marry Jennifer and the benefits of blending marriage and feminism:

> CALVIN: I feel a real emotional attachment and wanted to spend the rest of my life with her. . . . I don't see a contradiction in feminism and marriage. From my experience in being married to Jennifer, I think we have actually been able to both support each other. Feminism is not the reason we got married, but I certainly think that it helps promote support of each other. . . . I don't think I could have handled marriage any other way.

Couples reported the importance of five processes that collectively described a vigilance to the attending to or monitoring of their experiences of equality. All couples described engaging in three vigilant processes: critique of gender injustices, public acts of equality, and support of wives' activities. Of the 10 couples in this study, four couples considered themselves to share the work of the home equally and described satisfactory engagement in an additional two processes, reflective assessment and emotional involvement. The other six couples perceived imbalances in doing the work of the home and reported difficulties with these last two processes.

PROCESSES OF VIGILANCE COMMON TO ALL COUPLES

Critique of gender injustices. Feminism was a lens through which partners together critiqued sexism, gender stereotypes, and "cultural baggage" or gender expectations of their partners. Couples reported an ongoing dialogue based on their critique of messages they heard throughout the day, such as commercials that pigeonholed men as incompetent in the home and women as willing to give up their careers for marriage, male friends who expressed an inability to wash clothes, or men who denigrated their wives at parties. Calvin explained some of the topics he and Jennifer discussed in daily conversations.

> CALVIN: Men are putting this image out of women, virtually anorexic and must have certain characteristics, marvelous skin and tremendous shape, and it's absolutely unfair and very sexist. It is very bothersome to see that. The other thing that we comment on, we see so much of in the papers these days, in the news, is the abuse that goes on in the home situation, mostly of women.

The following example of sexism is typical of incidents related by all couples.

> DAN: They actually asked me, when I made my appointment with the doctor, if I minded that she was female.

> BARB: But I never get asked if I mind if the doctor is male.

> DAN: I'm in there for ulcer treatment. "What is she going to do to me? Do I have to come in and do something strange?" I thought it was a very strange question to ask me.

> BARB: That's when you become aware of it. That's when it becomes very evident to you. That's double standards.

All couples reported spending relationship time addressing the sexism or sexual harassment experienced by the women in educational, social, or work settings.

DAN: I was mad because I felt that Barb wasn't valued for what she was. She worked just as hard as anyone else, and she wasn't appreciated. It made me more supportive of her.

MILTON: There's a real awareness for me that women feel they don't have the authority in a classroom because they are women, which just blows me away. It helps me to understand sometimes Deborah's insecurities about teaching.

Women described feminism as offering a language to help them clarify their experiences of injustice, and thus make sense of their world and define themselves. Naming their experiences of discrimination, sexual harassment, and salary disparities enabled them to make choices to protect themselves, for instance, to demand higher wages or seek a better work environment.

DEBORAH: Feminism gives me a larger context for understanding my private sphere as dependent on a larger society.

Men's participation in identifying gender injustices and introducing them into topics of conversation was common throughout the couples. Women especially noted this activity on the part of their husbands.

DEBORAH: Milton is more likely to run across something [gender injustice] and tell me than the other way around. Probably I am several degrees more radical on a variety of topics including feminism living with Milton.

Men stated that feminism allowed them to better understand the experiences of others, and they expressed their attempts to empathize with women and validate their wives' experiences of gender injustice.

PATRICK: If I were a woman, I would have a much different outlook on life, absolutely. I think I would be a lot more cynical. I think I would be a lot more wary.

DAN: Where Barb works, it's got all sorts of discrimination problems. That affects us in

the sense that on a daily basis Barb has to come home and unload her frustration because her work environment is extremely frustrating.

Women described feelings of confirmation of themselves and their relationship when they determined that the relationship was a place where they could voice their own thoughts. Barb brought attention to this vital part of her marriage by comparing it with a previous relationship with a man who did not respect her views.

BARB: I would not jump out with some of my opinions on things because they were not his opinions, and I didn't feel like getting into an argument. So I was dating different people. Dan was one of them. I wanted to date him because I realized the more we talked, the more I didn't have to worry if it was going to create a problem by bringing up a topic or not.

Public acts of equality. All couples were vigilant in their public demonstration of their concern for the wife's status in the marriage. Different last names and financial decisions were the most common expressions of the importance of the wives' equal status, although other public acts were common, such as John's defense of Mary's right to have lunch with male friends or Larry using flex-time in order to leave work in the middle of the afternoon to care for his son while his wife worked. The financial ability of these women to care for themselves and their minor children demonstrated equality not only to others, but also to themselves.

Eight couples had different last names, a conscious effort to symbolize that their marriage was not based on traditional assumptions of male pre-eminence.

JENNIFER: My husband certainly didn't get anybody with his name. When I got divorced I dropped my ex-husband's name, and I dropped my father's name and I went back to my first and second names. My second name was my mother's father's name. The younger of the two girls now has that same last name. My older daughter kept her father's name. So we have three names in the family.

This act symbolizes the public dimension of a relationship decision.

> PAUL: We can witness to what we believe by living it. We don't make a big deal about it but it does make a statement to folks.

All couples were aware of the symbolic and concrete implications of common financial decisions. They put the wife's name first on the tax return or on a car registration. Some consciously decided to put half of the credit in the wife's name, while others had separate accounts even if they had a joint account for household bills. All couples described careful attention to ensuring that paperwork reflected their goals of equality. One public act that men were quite aware of doing was delaying decisions in order to consult with their partners, despite a tendency to make decisions on their own, especially when others expected them to assume this male privilege.

> LARRY: Well, the world we're in still expects to see the male making all the decisions about what the family is going to do. So people ranging from a car salesman to everything else expect me to make any decision that is confronting what we should do. They talk to me, and I don't like that. I don't want them to talk to me, I want them to talk to both of us.

Husbands' support of wives' activities. Support of women's employment and feminist activities were important in these marriages. All the women said their husbands had directly supported their career or vocation. For example, Carl assisted Elizabeth in completing her book. Deborah's career was considered primary, and her employment prospects had determined the location of their residence. John arranged his work schedule to accommodate Mary's artistic vocation, which required many hours away from the family. During busy seasons, Calvin, the recognized cook of the family, brought dinner to his wife's business for them

to share and then stayed to help her with the work load. In addition, he serviced the business computers, which required many hours of his free time.

Men described their support of their wives' feminist activities as "behind the scenes." For example, Shawn provided child care while Sarah went to marches. Carl supported Elizabeth's multiyear effort to change discriminatory pay practices at her workplace by opening up their home as a meeting place for research and strategy sessions. Other husbands such as Tony and Dan verbally supported their wives' participation in feminist organizations in front of family, friends, and coworkers.

TWO ADDITIONAL PROCESSES OF VIGILANCE

While the three processes of vigilance described above were reported by all of the couples, only four couples reported the use of all five processes. Two additional processes of vigilance, reflective assessment and emotional involvement, were used by four couples who also reported equal sharing of parenting, household, and domestic management tasks. The other six couples, who reported little or one-sided monitoring of equality in their relationship and/or difficulty in emotional involvement, also had an imbalance in the division of tasks. These six couples employed explanations of difference due either to gender or to personality (Hare-Mustin, 1991; Hochschild, 1989) to account for an unfair division of parenting and household tasks.

Reflective assessment. Reflective assessment indicates an ongoing monitoring of one's contributions to the relationship and family life. Among the four couples who described the equal sharing of parenting, household, and domestic responsibilities, both partners described a vigilance in assessing their marital contributions. When both partners participated in an ongoing reflective assessment, this process provided a way to identify and correct imbalances.

> PATRICK: I think it is really possible to have equality or a nonoppressive marriage

but it is not something that sort of happens and you say "Zap, now we got it" and you go on. You have to constantly communicate and sometimes it swings a little bit more toward the other. It is this fluid thing, it is just not static. You just don't say, "Well, we are feminists now so therefore our marriage is equal, and I won't physically hurt or verbally abuse you and so therefore we have equality in our marriage." I think without constant communication the notion of equality probably can't exist. You have to ensure that equality maintains itself. I am convinced that having a sense of equality about the marriage, that the notion that both of you have equal say about what's going in decisions, makes for a better marriage and a better life.

Rose described her reactions to having a partner who attended to the relationship and who was vigilant in monitoring his contributions.

ROSE: I think about Patrick as another responsible partner, an equal person in carrying out this relationship. As I look back on the other marriage, I saw myself as an adult taking care of that relationship. For the first several years, I was continually surprised at what it was like to live with another adult who was also responsible for the work of the home. Because we both do a lot of the same things, we have an appreciation of each other. He's getting lots of good stuff out of this relationship; I think he puts a lot into our relationship.

Through assessments of their financial contributions to the relationship, Jennifer and Calvin created an understanding that "growing a business" is equivalent to bringing a stable salary into the family.

JENNIFER: Several times over the last several years I don't feel like I'm bringing in enough and there are times when I'm anticipating that he would be thinking, "Well, maybe she ought to quit that and go get a decent paying job." And I've said that. That's not his reaction to it at all. He reminds me that I'm growing a business, that it's not the same as getting a salary from someone else because everything in here I own. He's not more important or valuable because he makes more money than I do.

When this reflective assessment was balanced, couples described little struggle between themselves. This process was experienced as an outgrowth of their beliefs.

MIRIAM: Your questions always raise the presumption that there's a conscious effort that we have to work at meshing feminism and marriage, and I don't think we ever have. Since we were feminists before we got married, it's just who we are, and it didn't need to be worked on. If he came out with a wildly unfeminist statement I'd look at him and say, "Who are you? You're not the guy I married." You mold your marriage; we're equal partners and "I'm not going to take any shit from you just because I'm a woman and you're the man."

Although Miriam denied a conscious effort at this process, her last sentence demonstrates the attitude of vigilance that infused their description of their marriage and interactions.

The importance of reflective assessment of the practice of equality was highlighted by the reports of the other six couples in which one partner did more reflective assessment than the other. These couples also reported more disparity in carrying out responsibilities of the home. Couples used justifications based on gender and personality differences to explain the imbalances. Men justified the arrangement by stating, "she has a higher standard," "she's more fussy," or "she's the more organized person." The two couples in which the husbands (Dan and Milton) did more of the domestic tasks explained this arrangement by citing the husbands' shorter work hours as a logical reason for this difference and by referring to one wife's recent illness and prolonged recuperation (Milton).

When reflective assessment was one-sided, wives were the ones who monitored their own and their partners' contributions to the relationship. While imbalances were identified, they were not corrected, leading to feelings of resentment and frustration.

RACHEL: I was disappointed, I felt ripped off. He didn't do 50% of the housework. He maintains that a lot of this stuff is totally unimportant to him, that he doesn't care if the bills are paid. It seems to me that it's a cop-out for him to just say, "Well, I don't care about these things so you do them all if you want them done." I think he certainly benefits a lot. I don't think our degree of commitment to those menial tasks is consistent with the degree to which they are important.

Sarah described two examples of how she is attempting to balance the work load, given she has the responsibility for all of the "planning" activities around the home.

SARAH: I am not afraid of a conflict. I tell him, "You do the expenses from now on, I am not going to do it." I run the household, the planning and the managing. It is more intensified when you have children. . . . A lot of it was me [telling him he needed to take on more responsibility]. "You are going to cook two nights a week, and not only that, you are going to know what we are going to have for dinner, and you are going to do the grocery shopping for it." You see what it gets down to? So, he calls at 4:30 and says, "What do you want for dinner?" putting it back on me. [I say] "I don't know. You decide. Good-bye. Figure it out for yourself."

Regarding discrepancies in parenting responsibilities, four couples with biological children who did not share parenting provided the following justifications: Work demands interfered with the husband's time at home, the special bond between mother and infant became apparent through the early months of an infant's life and so propelled the parents to interact with the infant to different degrees, and/or the mother knew more about emotionally caring for children and thus could provide children with better parenting. The two couples (Mary and John, Ruth and Paul) who used these explanations the most described the most unequal parenting arrangements. Two other couples (Rachel and Tony, Sarah and Shawn) relied on these explanations to a lesser extent. They described conflict when the wives advocated for more participation from their husbands in parenting and in assuming domestic responsibilities.

When these four women compared their husbands as fathers with other men, they voiced strong appreciation for the closeness and involvement their husbands had with the children. Yet when comparing themselves with their husbands as parents, these four women voiced disappointment (Mary and Ruth) and anger (Rachel and Sarah). They wanted their husbands to take on more of the responsibility, management, and awareness that is required for raising children (LaRossa, 1988). On balance, it is important to note that a typical week at Ruth and Paul's house would show him caring for their son on his day off while Ruth worked, visiting him at school, meeting the school bus at noon, and taking their son to day care on the days that both he and Ruth worked. Likewise, the other fathers demonstrated similar or higher degrees of involvement with their children.

Emotional involvement. Couples described the importance of communicating emotions verbally and not withdrawing from conflict. Every couple mentioned the importance of feeling close to the other partner, whether they experienced the presence or absence of this feeling. Those four couples who shared the work of the home equitably, however, described being able to meet each other's emotional needs. In their individual interviews both Miriam and Larry related feeling a special fit between them.

LARRY: I don't know if I could love someone the way that I love Miriam. I think marriage is the second best thing that ever happened to me, our son being the first right now. It's not even the second best. It's not like a hierarchy, this is the first and second. It's just two equal, good things.

MIRIAM: He's my soul mate, and I know I would never find anybody as perfect for me as he is. Other friends are for spice, for variety, for flavor, for a fuller emotional range. I get everything I need from him, but having other people is important, too. And I love him, no matter what. I knew he was the right guy for me.

Again in separate interviews, Rose and Patrick, who also expressed all five vigilant processes, conveyed a sense of wonder at their closeness.

ROSE: I love my husband very much, and I am very happy to be married to him. I feel very grateful to have these two people that I live with and I love so much.

PATRICK: It never struck me that marriage would be an expanding notion. I am a much broader, well-versed person who can see a lot more different perspectives now that I am married and have a child. I know more about people and life and probably myself than I would if I had not gotten married. One of the most satisfying things to me is there is this person that's right there in the house who is my friend who I can say, "What do you think about this?" and get an answer that I really truly want to hear because I need some information, I need to have some sense of where am I on this thing.

Miriam explained how communication is related to the experience of equality.

MIRIAM: You always let the other one know what you're thinking and what you're doing. The way to keep the other person powerless is to deny them sufficient finances, sufficient knowledge. So if you're always open and you're always sharing, then you're not denying the other per- son what they need to establish their power, too.

The ability to use communication to build intimacy was not automatic for these four couples. In the past, Calvin, Larry, and Carl had been confronted on the results of their communication and had worked at changing their interactional styles.

CALVIN: I had to learn that I unintentionally send messages with my body language. When we have a quote "discussion" or argument or whatever, I tend to stand and pace

and they [his wife and their daughters] tend to sit. That is a physical position where you're coming on as being superior. I didn't realize that, but I have tried to remind myself to be the first to sit down in such a situation.

Every couple talked about the importance of communication, including those six couples who described some difficulties. Emotionally shutting down was described as either a lack of communication skills or a power play.

DAN: One thing I can say for us, we talk.

BARB: We value the ability to talk to each other. We really don't seem to have a communication problem. If I'm pissed off at him, I'll tell him. If he's pissed off at me, he will usually tell me. Except he's worse at that, he keeps a lot of things inside. But, we definitely value that part of our relationship.

In Barb's reflections on their communication, she noted Dan's tendency to withhold intense feelings about a difficult issue involving his extended family. She attributed this keeping "things inside" to a lack of skills versus a power play; therefore, she did not feel emotionally vulnerable as some wives did, as noted below. However, Barb also voiced frustration over the greater amount of work she did in regard to this issue. Dan's holding back communication on this particular situation translated into Barb doing more work. This couple's experience highlights the varying degrees of emotional withdrawal in marriage, the variation in interpretation of such withdrawal, and the connection between withholding communication and the perception of workload.

Using communication to establish superiority, withholding talk to control a situation, or exploding in anger were contrary to the establishment of emotional closeness.

DEBORAH: If there are any problems, he shuts down or he wants to ignore them as long as possible. I want to get them resolved as quickly as possible. I am more comfortable talking out personal problems, and he is more, "Let's pull down the curtain, let's stop, let's do nothing." It is like I don't exist. It can be simply pulling up the newspaper, it can be just looking blank or giving me the feedback that he has heard, but what I have said isn't worth listening to.

As a result of this communication pattern, Deborah stated feeling emotionally unsafe at times, so she sought emotional understanding from friends.

Mary said that while her husband, John, was not empathic and open with his feelings, she felt close to him. In contrast to Deborah and Milton, Mary did not experience John's lack of empathy as a control issue, but rather an inability to communicate in a particular way.

> MARY: He also is not very up front about his feelings. Just because you are a feminist doesn't mean you are open with your feelings. You can still be very closed and very inward. He keeps everything inside. I wish I knew what his feelings were. So we'll go through this, "Well, how are you feeling?" and I try to drag things out of him at times when I know he should be depressed and he should be upset.

Yet, although Mary and John both felt very close to one another, like Deborah, Mary sought friendships to provide her with the empathy she wished she had in her marriage.

DISCUSSION

This study confirms that the ideology of marital equality does not translate automatically into an outcome of marital equality. While this incongruency between ideology and practice is commonplace among couples in which the man holds to a traditional ideology, men who have egalitarian ideologies are more likely to share equally in the work of the second shift (Hochschild, 1989). This present study on feminist couples, who could be considered the most ideologically committed to marital equality, also reveals their difficulty in carrying out beliefs of equality, in that six of the 10 couples had difficulty in participating in

two of the five processes of vigilance—reflective assessment and emotional involvement.

Yet this study does reveal the likelihood that a feminist ideology upgrades marriage for women. Wives and husbands who claim a feminist identity strive to enact their beliefs of equality through practices of vigilance, sometimes resulting in a mutual sharing of the second shift work. The second shift was shared by partners who, in addition to providing a safe and supportive location for women's feminist voices, were vigilant in the monitoring of their own contributions and had the interpersonal skills necessary to establish emotional closeness (Baber & Allen, 1992; Vannoy-Hiller & Philliber, 1989).

The men in this study spoke of their feminist beliefs and the benefits accompanying a marriage based on these beliefs and they sought, albeit in varying degrees, to put equality into practice. Upgrading marriage for women is possible; getting the "stalled revolution" into motion again is possible. However, both require the participation of men who are committed to a process of marital vigilance and to a guiding ideology of equality. While their numbers may be few, studies are beginning to note their presence. Recognition of them and their commitment to the creation of an "interdependent union of equals" (Schwartz, 1994, p. 2) is necessary in the ongoing study of heterosexual marriage.

PROCESSES THAT UPGRADE MARRIAGE

All 10 couples practiced the first three vigilant processes that functioned to support women and upgrade their marriages. The processes of critiquing gender injustices, publicly demonstrating marital equality, and supporting wives' career and vocational goals provided a context in which women's identities were validated. Marriages were not experienced as oppressive to women; rather they enabled women to pursue personal, relational, and professional goals.

First, husbands' feminist attitudes and behaviors served a necessary function in upgrading their wives' marriages. Stating frustration and anger at the status quo is not without its negative consequences for women in their personal and professional relationships (Lewis, 1990). However, at home, these women could express their mixed feelings of anger, hope, and fear about sexism and have their feelings validated by their husbands. They felt free to voice their feelings and their understandings of the world to a partner who agreed with and respected them. Husbands' participation in feminism validated the women's understanding of the world. Men's initiation and participation in a critique of gender injustices demonstrated their feminist commitment, reinforcing women's understanding of the marriage as a safe place for them to talk about their experiences and their feelings of anger. In previous research, Acker et al. (1981) found that feminist women who are married to nonfeminist men do not experience the same validation and support for feminist interpretations of the world, and thus often restrict their feminist voices within their marriages. This first vigilant process, the critique of gender injustice, provided emotional space for women to receive validation and support.

Second, couples' public acts of equality, such as different last names, stated to others their intentions of equality, thereby reinforcing their decision to do marriage differently. The women in this study were financially able and willing to leave their marriages, if necessary. Okin (1989) argued that women's ability to exit relationships, largely a factor of finances, is translated into more influence in relationships.

Third, support for women's careers, education, and vocational goals was commonplace as men adjusted their schedules and jobs to offer concrete demonstrations of their support. Such support provided these women with benefits they saw occurring in only a few other marriages.

Processes That Promote the Practice of Equality

The ideology and practice of marital equality were congruent for those four couples who participated in two additional vigilant processes: reflective assessment of personal contributions to their marriage and meeting each other's emotional needs. Six couples who reported difficulty with these two processes also reported inequality in the work of the second shift. This study suggests that reflective assessment and emotional involvement are connected to the outcome of marital equality, supporting Vannoy's (1991) conclusion that, with less powerful social forces maintaining marriage, interpersonal skills and individual ability for emotional intimacy are required of couples.

First, reflective assessment requires the attainment of personal development to make commitments and to participate in mutual emotional support (Baber & Allen, 1992). When individuals in couples reflected on their own contributions and made necessary alterations—that is, when they went against gender prescriptions—they reported less conflict than couples who relied on the wife to monitor relational contributions, and they reported equality in sharing the second shift.

Second, emotional involvement corresponded to reports of equal sharing of the second shift and functioned to validate personal identity. Women's identities, as well as men's, were supported when their partners reacted according to expectations and in ways that were congruent with women's own reactions (Vannoy, 1991). Because of a shared feminist ideology with their husbands, these women's identities were supported, and they experienced marriage as an accepting and fortifying relationship. For some men, feminism revealed the barriers to emotional involvement and motivated them to develop closeness with their partners and children. However, when emotional vulnerability was one-sided, marital equality was inhibited. Erickson (1993) found that husbands' "emotion work" had a positive effect on women's sense of well-being. The present study elaborates this connection by suggesting that meeting partners' emotional needs is vital to the practice of marital equality. The variation in emotional withdrawal and its coexistence with unequal division of domestic work and the differing interpretations of emotional withdrawal require further investigation.

Women's feminist beliefs contributed to their recognition of whether the division of responsibilities was fair or unfair (Thompson, 1991). The couples who experienced disparity in parenting and domestic responsibilities attributed them to personality differences, women's needs, or as indications of the special quality of motherhood. Such explanations function as justifications for inequalities (Hare-Mustin, 1991; Hochschild, 1989).

Fathers' participation as involved parents was evident, but, for four of the six couples who did not practice complete vigilance, it was not quite egalitarian. Yet, these fathers were not traditional; they did not replicate a patriarchal but father-absent family (Luepnitz, 1988; Stacey, 1990). Rather, they enjoyed feelings of closeness to their children and partners and attributed this nontraditional involvement with their family to their feminist beliefs.

Conclusion

A feminist perspective allowed an inquiry into the marital experiences of women and men while assuming the possibility of martial equality and women's well-being as a criterion (Baber & Allen, 1992; Hawkesworth, 1989). These feminist couples considered marriage as part of the relational landscape worth revitalizing. Rather than rejecting marriage as an enduring and unalterable relationship form, these couples' appropriation of marriage for feminist goals resulted in upgrading this relationship form for women. We found that a feminist ideology upgrades marriage for women by promoting a vigilance to equality enacted through five processes: critique of gender injustices, public acts of equality, support of wives' activities, reflective assessment, and emotional involvement. Ideology matched practice when both partners participated equally in the last two processes—reflective assessment and emotional involvement.

This research raises questions to consider when determining equality in a relationship and when exploring what makes marriage equitable for women and men. Do both partners critique gender injustices? Does a woman's feminist voice have a home in her marriage? Does she have the freedom to participate in feminist conversations with her husband? In what symbolic and public ways does the couple demonstrate their goal of marital equality? Is the woman's educational and financial well-being supported and advanced? Can the woman leave the marriage and continue to care for herself and children? Do both partners reflect upon their contributions to the marriage and correct imbalances? Are domestic tasks and childrearing shared? Do both partners do the emotion work of the relationship? Do they have the individual skills necessary to establish and maintain emotional involvement?

We are limited in our predictions of what forms heterosexual relationships will take when women's work receives equitable recompense and value in society, when men and women are equally dedicated to parenting and caring for the young, the old, and the sick, when women and men in equal numbers are in positions of authority in government, education, religion, and health care, and when women do not experience pervasive violence in their lives. Currently, negative consequences, such as emotional isolation or divorce, are real for women who seek equality diligently and do not recoil from expecting reciprocal caring from men. This study suggests that feminist women need not forego relationships with men but can expect them to assume feminist beliefs and to strive with women to enact them.

Note

This research was partially funded by the following grants: the Fahs-Beck Fund for Research and Experimentation, administered by the New York Community Trust; the Graduate Research Development Project Grant, from the Graduate Student Assembly of Virginia Polytechnic Institute and State University; and the Outstanding Proposal from a Feminist

Perspective Award, from the Feminism and Family Studies Section of the National Council on Family Relations. Preparation of this paper was partially funded by the New Faculty Research Grant, Western Michigan University. The authors gratefully acknowledge the valuable comments and suggestions of Alexis Walker, Stephen Marks, Barbara Risman, and two anonymous reviewers.

References

Acker, J., Barry, K., & Esseveld, J. (1981). Feminism, female friends, and the reconstruction of intimacy. In H. Z. Lopata & D. Maines (Eds.), *Research in the interweave of social roles: Friendship* (Vol. 2, pp. 75–108). Greenwich, CT: JAI Press.

———. (1983). Objectivity and truth: Problems in doing feminist research. *Women's Studies International Forum, 6*, 423–435.

Atkinson, M. P., & Boles, J. (1984). WASP (Wives as Senior Partners). *Journal of Marriage and the Family, 46*, 861–870.

Baber, K. M., & Allen, K. R. (1992). *Women & families: Feminist reconstructions*. New York: Guilford Press.

Bernard, J. (1982). *The future of marriage*. New Haven, CT: Yale University Press. (Original work published 1972)

Daly, K. (1992). Parenthood as problematic: Insider interviews with couples seeking to adopt. In J. F. Gilgun, K. Daly, & G. Handel (Eds.), *Qualitative methods in family research* (pp. 103–125). Newbury Park, CA: Sage Publications.

Dressel, P. L., & Clark, A. (1990). A critical look at family care. *Journal of Marriage and the Family, 52*, 769–782.

Ehrensaft, D. (1990). *Parenting together*. Urbana: University of Illinois Press.

Erickson, R. J. (1993). Reconceptualizing family work: The effect of emotion work on perceptions of marital quality. *Journal of Marriage and the Family, 55*, 888–900.

Ferree, M. M. (1990). Beyond separate spheres: Feminism and family research. *Journal of Marriage and the Family, 52*, 866–884.

Fishman, P. M. (1983). Interaction: The work women do. In B. Thorne, C. Kramarae, & N. Henley (Eds.), *Language, gender and society* (pp. 89–101). Rowley, MA: Newbury House.

Fonow, M. M., & Cook, J. A. (1991). Back to the future: A look at the second wave of feminist epistemology and methodology. In M. M. Fonow & J. A. Cook (Eds.), *Beyond methodology* (pp. 1–15). Bloomington: Indiana University Press.

Gilbert, L. A. (1993). *Two careers/one family*. Newbury Park, CA: Sage.

Gilgun, J. F. (1992). Definitions, methodologies, and methods in qualitative family research. In J. F. Gilgun, K. Daly, & G. Handel (Eds.), *Qualitative methods in family research* (pp. 22–39). Newbury Park, CA: Sage.

Glenn, E. N. (1987). Gender and the family. In B. B. Hess & M. M. Ferree (Eds.), *Analyzing gender* (pp. 348–380). Newbury Park, CA: Sage.

Haavind, H. (1984). Love and power in marriage. In H. Holter (Ed.), *Patriarchy in a welfare state* (pp. 136–167). Oslo: Universitetsforlaget.

Haas, L. (1980). Role-sharing couples: A study of egalitarian marriages. *Family Relations, 29*, 289–296.

Hare-Mustin, R. T. (1991). Sex, lies, and headaches: The problem is power. In T. J. Goodrich (Ed.), *Women and power* (pp. 63–85). New York: W. W. Norton.

Hawkesworth, M. E. (1989). Knowers, knowing, known: Feminist theory and claims of truth. *Signs, 14*, 533–557.

Hochschild, A. (1989). *The second shift*. New York: Viking.

Jump, T. L., & Haas, L. (1987). Fathers in transition: Dual-career fathers participating in child care. In M. S. Kimmel (Ed.), *Changing men* (pp. 98–114). Newbury Park, CA: Sage.

Kaufman, D. R. (1985). Women who return to Orthodox Judaism: A feminist analysis. *Journal of Marriage and the Family, 47*, 543–551.

LaRossa, R. (1988). Fatherhood and social change. *Family Relations, 37*, 451–457.

Lewis, M. (1990). Interrupting patriarchy: Politics, resistance, and transformation in the feminist classroom. *Harvard Educational Review, 60*, 467–488.

Luepnitz, D. A. (1988). *The family interpreted*. New York: Basic Books.

Okin, S. M. (1989). *Justice, gender, and the family*. New York: Basic Books.

Osmond, M. W., & Thorne, B. (1993). Feminist theories. In P. G. Boss, W. J. Doherty, R. LaRossa, W. R. Schumm, & S. K. Steinmetz (Eds.), *Sourcebook of family theories and methods* (pp. 591–623). New York: Plenum Press.

Padilla, R. V. (1991). HyperQual (Version 4.0) [Computer software]. Chandler, AZ: Author.

Perry-Jenkins, M., & Crouter, A. C. (1990). Men's provider role attitudes: Implications for household work and marital satisfaction. *Journal of Family Issues, 11,* 136–156.

Rubin, L. B. (1983). *Intimate strangers: Men and women together.* New York: Harper & Row.

Runyan, W. M. (1984). *Life histories and psychobiography.* New York: Oxford University Press.

Schwartz, P. (1994). *Peer marriage.* New York: Free Press.

Stacey, J. (1990). *Brave new families.* New York: Basic.

Strauss, A., & Corbin, J. (1990). *Basics of qualitative research.* Newbury Park, CA: Sage.

Taylor, S. J., & Bogdan, R. (1984). *Introduction to qualitative research methods* (2nd ed.). New York: John Wiley & Sons.

Thompson, L. (1991). Family work: Women's sense of fairness. *Journal of Family Issues, 12,* 181–196.

———. (1992). Feminist methodology for family studies. *Journal of Marriage and the Family, 54,* 3–18.

———. (1993). Conceptualizing gender: The case of marital care. *Journal of Marriage and the Family, 55,* 557–569.

Thompson, L., & Walker, A. J. (1989). Gender in families: Women and men in marriage, work, and parenthood. *Journal of Marriage and the Family, 51,* 845–871.

Tong, R. (1989). *Feminist thought.* Boulder, CO: Westview Press.

Vannoy, D. (1991). Social differentiation, contemporary marriage, and human development. *Journal of Family Issues, 12,* 251–267.

Vannoy-Hiller, D., & Philliber, W. W. (1989). *Equal partners.* Newbury Park, CA: Sage.

Chapter Nine
Biosocial Theory

Ross and Roberta, both single parents in their early thirties, live across the hall from each other, and their children attend the same school. One day they were sitting with some other single parents as they watched their children play a soccer match when they started talking about how difficult it is to find a person to marry in today's society. After all, here are four adults who are attractive, funny, intelligent, and could date all they wanted if they had the time. The problem seems to be that none of them can find long-term relationships that are satisfying and can lead to eventual remarriage and having more children. Roberta stated that the problem was that men are raised differently than women, and that they just don't understand what women want and need in a relationship.

Ross, being a scientist, said that mate selection as it currently exists is the result of thousands of years of evolution and the natural selection of traits that will allow the strongest of each species, in this case humans, to survive. Thus, for men to attempt to survive it is better to have multiple mates to increase their chances of reproducing. For women, however, since they have to invest more time and energy in reproductive activities simply because they are the ones that give birth, it is imperative for them to choose their mates wisely on the basis of who will provide the most resources. From this Ross concluded that women have a greater need to select a good mate and marry than do men, which is why women are desperate to marry and men are desperate to avoid commitment and simply attempt to reproduce with multiple women. And men certainly don't want to use their time and resources on other men's children!

Lisa replied, "OK, I don't understand everything you just said, but I do know that if men would simply wake up and smell the java, they would realize what a great person I am and fall madly in love with me. I mean, really, what's not to love about me? Or any of us, for that matter? And how could they not love my child once they spent some time with him? The real problem is we just don't understand each other." So, who's right? Are the women correct in assuming that society has created the differences between genders that lead to problems in mate selection, or is Ross correct in to assuming that the problems that exist today are related to a genetic predisposition to certain personality characteristics that is born from years of evolutionary selection and change? These questions and more will be addressed in this chapter.

HISTORY

The history of biosocial theory is difficult to discuss with any certainty because there are so many variations. Variations that combine the ideas and beliefs of people from many disciplines are typical of a theory in its formative years, but they are also what make this theory both unique and exciting. Because there are many theories that are similar to biosocial theory—such as evolutionary psychology (Cosmides, Toby, and Barkow 1992), ethology and sociobiology (Thomas 1996), and psychobiology (Cloninger, Svrakic, and Przybeck 1993)—what you read here may not be the same as the treatment of this material in another text.

Whereas biosocial theory is in its beginning stages, it is based on ideas that have been around for some time. One of the earliest publications concerning evolution was *The Origin of Species* by Charles Darwin (1859). In this book Darwin suggests that there is a struggle for survival among species, with nature "selecting" those individuals who are best adapted to the environment. This process occurs over generations, and as individuals are changing to fit the environment, the environment is also changing. Until the last several decades, Darwin's ideas were left basically untapped by social scientists in their understanding of human social behavior. In fact, there was a bias against his principles, with many in this area believing that biology and society were such opposites they would never have a place in the same discussion.

Because of this opposition, much of the early work in this area was done in the medical arena as biologists sought to discover biological causes of individual behaviors, as well as by ethologists who studied animal or human behavior from an evolutionary perspective. Perhaps the first to move the discussion of selection from biological predetermination to possible influences of the environment was W. D. Hamilton (1964a,b). Hamilton believed in the concept of inclusive fitness, which means not only that individuals change and adapt over time in order to survive but also that fitness includes those individuals who surround or are related to the individual. In other words, since we inherit our genetic material, it is in our best interest to support those we are related to, since this promises the survival of our own genes as well. This would help to explain such things as parental investment in children. This idea led other social scientists to consider the genetic nature of human relationships as they exist within a social environment.

Perhaps the most influential writing in this area was by Edward Osborne Wilson, who in 1975 published *Sociobiology*. In this writing he posited that evolution was evident in people across time, and that genes influence individual behaviors, which have evolved in order to ensure survival. While many in the field did not agree with his ideas, the book did generate a great deal of discussion and research concerning the role of genetics in human behavior. Similarly, Hans J. Eysenck (1967; Eysenck and Eysenck 1985) sought to explain the role of genetic predisposition in introversion/extraversion and stability/neuroticism and used this biological basis to explain how individuals interacted differently based on the social situation. These principles have been expanded upon in recent decades to explain human be-

havior in many areas, including mate selection, parenting, child development, behavioral and mental disorders, and the mind-body connection in the treatment of medical diseases. It is important to remember that this brief historical review is far from comprehensive but simply seeks to point out that the ideas of Darwin have been expanded upon and used to understand modern behavior, although there is still disagreement in the social sciences as to which is more powerful—nature or nurture.

BASIC ASSUMPTIONS

Because the assumptions of the theory depend on which version or writing you are discussing, it is important to note that these 12 assumptions are being taken verbatim from a chapter on biosocial perspective written by Troost and Filsinger (1993).

"Humans have an evolutionary origin." This is based once again on the ideas of Darwin and the principle of natural selection. As Mayr (1991) states, "change comes about through the abundant production of genetic variation in every generation. The relatively few individuals who survive, owing to a particularly well-adapted combination of inheritable characteristics, gives rise to the next generation" (p. 37).

"The family has played an important role in human evolution." Because survival of the individual is dependent on survival of the family, the existence of families across time has helped individual family members adapt and thus survive. An example of this is that people everywhere across cultures live in families of some sort, raise children, and attempt to make a living or a means to survive. These similarities are seen as a result of our specific evolutionary history (Fox 1989).

"The evolutionary origin of humans has an influence upon families today." Human behavior today is based upon the genetic and social adaptation of individuals and families since time began. Thus, reactions to current social issues such as parental investment in

children and gendered behavior all have their basis in evolution.

"Proximate biology has an influence on the family, and the family has an influence on proximate biology and the health of its members." *Proximate*, as will be discussed below, refers to interaction between genetic predisposition and social interactions. This simply means that individuals are predisposed to some diseases or medical conditions, which influences how they interact within the family. Maybe they are frequently tired and thus are not as active in family activities. In turn, the behaviors of family members influence the health of other family members (for example, smoking, increased stress, physical abuse, or violence).

"Biosocial influences are both biological and social in character." One cannot discuss the social influences on behavior without also addressing the biological components as well.

"The biosocial domain is concerned with three factors: the biological, biosocial, and social." Although most social scientists do not as of yet have accurate ways to measure each of these factors, the best model is one that would take each of them into consideration. Problems come when you try to disentangle one from the other.

"Human biological and biosocial variables do not determine human conduct but pose limitations and constraints as well as possibilities and opportunities for families." It is important to distinguish between biology driving human behavior and influencing human behavior. The premise of this theory is that genetics sets the stage for certain behaviors but does not necessarily determine how or even if they will be exhibited.

"A biosocial approach takes an intermediate position between those who emphasize the similarity between humans and other animals (Wilson 1975) and those who emphasize the differences (Charon 1989, Mead 1964)." While most who utilize this theory would agree that humans have evolved throughout time, most would also support the notion that we are also a unique species with our own culture and in-

teractions. The reality lies somewhere in the middle.

"Adaptation is assumed to have taken place over a vast period of time. The hundreds to thousands of generations to reach Hardy-Weinberg equilibrium in adaptive evolutionary biology (Birdsell 1981) are vastly different than, for example, human ecology. . . . Conjectures about biological adaptation in the span of one generation or over the course of the twentieth century or the computer age are dubious assertions." The Hardy-Weinberg law is the idea that if a system is at equilibrium, or in balance, the genetic distribution of alternative forms of a gene are also stable. In other words, genetic transitions do not take place until that system is no longer stable. At that point, genes may mutate or change so that some become more dominant than others. This is the basic principle of natural selection. Some mutation takes place to allow for greater fitness or to ensure adaptation that is necessary for survival. Because this process takes a great deal of time, it would be absurd to think we could study this change across just one or two generations; to understand behavior today you must also understand the behavior of our ancestors.

"Adaptations in physiology or conduct vary by environment." Whereas we are born with our genetic structure (our *genotype*), the way that we express those genetic tendencies (*phenotype*) will vary across different environments and situations. Further, the interaction between our genotype and our phenotype necessitates a great deal of diversity across individuals, families, and cultures. This means that two different individuals with the same genetic composition, but entirely different environments, would probably exhibit entirely different behaviors.

"Extant features of human biology can be used to reveal aspects of our adaptation in the past (see Troost 1988a; Turke 1988)." Obviously we cannot go back in time and examine how people in other eras lived their lives on a day-to-day basis, although we do have a good deal of archaeological evidence that provides us with some clues as to what their lives must

have been like. Despite this inability to witness their experiences for ourselves, this theory posits that we can trace current features to their historical roots for at least a glimpse into why those biological features were adaptive at one point in time.

"Proximate, distal and ultimate levels of interpretation can be approached separately; ideally they will be integrated." Definitions of proximate, distal, and ultimate levels will be given in the next section. At this point it is important to note that while you can focus on one piece of the equation at a time, the most fruitful explanations will come from an analysis of all three levels at the same time, since it is difficult to determine where one begins and the next one ends.

PRIMARY TERMS AND CONCEPTS

Since this theory is called *biosocial*, the most logical place to start when discussing primary terms and concepts is with the theory title itself. As mentioned previously, biosocial describes the relationship between the biological and the social. Each component is seen as acting on its own behalf while also working together to produce human experience. The family is a perfect example of a biosocial entity, since its members share some genetic structure, as well as a social environment, with the purpose of advancing its individual members and unified entity (Lovejoy 1981).

ADAPTATION

Based on these ideas, the family has come about because of adaptation. According to the principle of *ultimate causation*, the family has helped to reproduce the species because it provides the support or framework in which adaptation takes place. *Adaptation* is the ability to change or increase the level of fitness in order to increase the chances of survival through greater numbers of offspring.

FITNESS

Fitness refers to the ability to fit within the environment. Generally, one would consider the fitness of an individual. However, Hamilton

(1964a,b) argued that we should also include the fitness of that individual's relatives as being important, which he referred to as *inclusive fitness*. For example, based on the idea of *reciprocal altruism,* individuals work together to better meet the needs of each person. An example of this is parenting, since it is in the best interests of both the mother and the father to work together to bear children and raise them until the children are old enough to have their own offspring. This process ensures survival of the genetic and social structures of all parties involved. Therefore, the ultimate cause of families today is a history of adaptation that has led to the successful reproduction of fit children, which is best done within some sort of family unit. Simply, you cannot analyze families today without recognizing this evolutionary past.

PROXIMATE CAUSES

On the other end of the continuum are proximate causes. Proximate causes, literally meaning nearby or in close proximity, are the day-to-day interactions that take place during regular family life. This includes the interplay of biological and social forces such as learning, language, and culture. If ultimate causes represent the past, and proximate causes represent the present, then *distal* or *intermediate causes* represent how the two interrelate. It should be noted, however, that not all who subcribe to this theory add this distal component. Rather, many assume that behaviors exhibited today are by necessity an interaction between some feature from the past that has been adapted and the current biological and social conditions. As noted above, perhaps it would be most productive to approach studies or topics with the assumption that all three levels should be analyzed and/or considered.

NATURAL SELECTION

It is through natural selection that these terms and concepts come together. Natural selection explains our evolutionary past, since it is through adaptation that those genes most able to ensure survival will be passed along to the next generation. This is known as *survival of the fittest*. In addition, it is through this evolutionary process that modern individuals behave as they do. An individual's genetic material must still interact with the environment. For example, although at conception the genetic material that is transferred controls the development of things such as the central nervous system, muscles, and other body functions and organs that influence behavior, how these genes develop also depends on the environment, such as proper vitamins, minerals, and nutrients; lack of exposure to harmful toxins, gases, or drugs; and a harm-free environment. Thus, one cannot state that the biological is more important than the social, or vice versa, since both must work together to ensure that survival and adaptation take place.

As has been stated numerous times, biosocial theory has many forms and similar areas of research. Whereas this chapter covers terms most commonly seen across readings concerning a biosocial perspective, it is by no means an exhaustive listing of terms often associated with a biosocial approach. However, it is a comprehensive listing of those terms which seem most necessary in order to have a working knowledge of this theory.

COMMON AREAS OF RESEARCH AND APPLICATION

Although it may seem from our discussion thus far that the research in this field will pertain mostly to evolution or perhaps family formation, the reality is that there is a great deal of research done in the last few decades using a biosocial approach to explain topics at both the individual and family level. For example, temperament and personality development have been studied, as well as a variety of gender issues such as the genetic basis of gender differences, theories of incest and rape, and mate selection and sexual interest. We will review some of these areas and then discuss other ways this theory is currently being applied, particularly in the medical and family therapy fields.

TEMPERAMENT

Richter, Eiseman, and Richter (2000) have used a biosocial theory to determine the influence of genetic and environmental factors on personality development, especially temperament. Temperament, our automatic response to stimuli, is thought to be genetically predetermined. However, the environment in which one is raised, or the stimuli to which one has to react, influences how that temperament is displayed. Thomas and Chess (1980) support this idea through cross-cultural research on temperament. For example, they suggest that children will attempt to match their temperament to the standards of the culture in which they reside. Thus, while they may have a genetic predisposition toward certain behaviors, they will not engage in those behaviors because they are not seen as socially acceptable.

Udry (1994) did similar work on temperament, but in this case was studying adolescent problem behaviors. Whereas traditionally researchers assessed delinquency and other adolescent problem behaviors by studying the current environment, such as family and social situations, Udry suggests you must also consider biologically based individual differences such as temperament. In fact, he states that "you can make good predictions of who will use marijuana at age 14 by personality and environmental factors measured in the same children at age 4" (p. 104). This is because children with different temperaments choose different environments that match those genetic predispositions.

The work previously mentioned by Eysenck is another example of using a biosocial perspective at the individual level. His earlier work (Eysenck 1967) was focused on developing a typology of personality that details the various traits and habits of different components of the personality. At this time he identified two primary personality types: introversion/extraversion and stability/neuroticism. He later added the dimension of impulse control/psychoticism (Eysenck 1982). His first step was to identify these dimensions, then to develop a test to measure them, and finally to develop a theory to explain why people have different levels of each of these traits. He did this by using brain research that showed how different people's brains reacted differently to the same stimuli. For example, whereas extraverts have brains that respond more slowly and weakly to stimuli, introverts have brains that react more quickly and strongly. Because of this, extraverts seek environments that provide a good deal of stimulation, whereas introverts seek to avoid chaotic environments (Ryckman 2000). Thus, the genetic predisposition of the personality trait introversion/extraversion is displayed differently depending on the social environment.

Eysenck (1997) continues to develop these ideas and to utilize a biosocial approach. His current research assumes that biosocial influences are a given upon which additional empirical research should build. He supports the movement within psychology of the acceptance of the mind-body connection as a standard from which to develop more scientifically based research. Although this idea has not been accepted by everyone within the field, it has spurred further research into the notion of basing future research on biosocial ideals (Brody 1997).

GENDER

Another area of research that commonly utilizes a biosocial approach is that of the development of gendered behavior and sexual interest. Whereas there are many avenues explored in this general area, we'll discuss a few studies concerning the construction of gender, sexual interest, and the rape and incest theories. For example, Udry (2000) has used a biosocial model to explain how hormones, both present at birth and produced throughout adulthood, combine with the social expectations of each gender to form gendered behavior. By this he means that whereas males and females are genetically driven at birth, the effects of these hormones can be either strengthened or weakened based on the environment and the social beliefs about what's masculine and feminine. While you've probably all heard about this with regard to the importance of hormones during adolescence, and can probably remember what it felt like to experience those peaks and valleys of hormone surges, Udry takes this one step further by suggesting that the environment also influences how these hormones effect us.

Specifically, in one study he measured hormone levels of females during early adolescence and then again when they were between the ages of 27 and 30. He also asked them questions about the types of behaviors their parents encouraged with regard to masculinity and femininity. What he found was that "if a daughter has natural tendencies to be feminine, encouragement will enhance femininity; but if she has below average femininity in childhood, encouraging her to be more feminine will have no effect" (Udry 2000, 451). Thus, although hormones obviously drive some of our behavior, it is also important to consider the social environment when trying to discover why some people are more feminine or masculine than others.

SEXUALITY

Baldwin and Baldwin (1997) also conducted research on gender, but they focused on sexual interest. It is similar to the work of Udry (1994) in that it suggests that using an either/or approach to study gender is inappropriate: Both nature and nurture are important. Baldwin and Baldwin believe that whereas females are more interested in the romantic or love-based notion of sexuality, males are more concerned with the physical pleasure or enjoyment of sexual activities. Biologically it is in the best interest of the male to enjoy sexual activity and to share this with multiple partners in order to increase his chances of producing offspring. However, many believe that sexual interest is controlled by the social or cultural norms that exist. In contrast, Baldwin and Baldwin found that both biological drives and social norms work in concert to produce a diverse range of interests in sexual activity.

Taking this idea of sexual interest in another direction, there has also been a good deal of research which seeks to explain rape and incest from a biosocial perspective. For example, Hendrix and Schneider (1999) state that because it would be to the detriment of families to inbreed, we have a biological predisposition toward sexual inhibition, starting during early childhood, that makes mating with family members unattractive. This will help determine survival of the fittest. In addition, most societies also have cultural taboos against incest, which reinforces this genetic inhibition. They believe that for some cultures the biological drive is stronger, whereas for others the incest taboo is more important. These two pieces together explain why most cultures do not support incest; it will weaken their genetic traits while also going against cultural standards.

Similarly, Ellis (1991) has used both biological and social reasons to explain rape. He believes that the desire to rape is driven by both sex drive and a desire to control and possess, neither of which are learned. In addition, men are genetically predisposed to a stronger sex drive because of natural selection or the need to procreate with multiple partners. Although the drive for sex is inborn, the means for meeting this need is learned through social experience. Finally, there are hormonal explanations for why some people are more prone to committing rape than others. These hormones not only increase the sex drive as well as the need to possess and control but also decreases the person's concern for the suffering of others. Thus, through this combination of biological and social experiences men are more likely to rape than women, and the urge is greater in some men than in others. It is hoped that this discovery will lead to the ability to reduce the risks of rape by manipulating the hormonal and social influences on men predisposed toward rape.

These are just a few of the many areas of research that have benefited from acknowledging both the biological and social influences on behavior. Several fields of study, such as family medicine and family therapy, also take a biosocial approach. There are many reasons this would be helpful in family medicine, in-cluding the importance of genetic risk factors for some diseases (such as alcoholism and some types of cancer), the importance of family involvement in individual compliance with medical treatment, and the effects of stress on both the individual and the family. As has been found with parents who have chronic kidney disease, the illness of one family member also affects the entire family, since that parent is no longer able to maintain his or her pre-disease family roles (Smith and Soliday 2001). In this case, limitations caused by the biological disease affect the social interactions of all those involved. Thus, it is easy to see that medical professionals could benefit from recognizing the mind-body connection for a wide variety of reasons.

As Campbell (1993) suggests, family therapists or other professionals who deal with the family could also benefit from a biosocial approach. When patients come to a therapist with a presenting problem, such as depression, it is important to recognize that this has both a biological component that can be treated with medication and a social component that can be addressed with therapy. This allows for more comprehensive treatment of the problem.

CRITIQUE

The fact that there are many critics of biosocial theory perhaps also means that there are many things one would suggest are limitations of a biosocial theory. However, the following items are based on the assumption that you support the notion of the importance of both biology and environment in human behavior. That said, one valid critique of biosocial theory is that there is disagreement over the basic tenets of the theory and which principles are most important. As was mentioned in the basic assumptions section, where you get your information will determine what items are mentioned as being of primary importance. While this is perhaps not a huge stumbling block, it does make it more difficult than using structural functionalism—for example, everyone agrees as to what that means. The relative newness of this theory is one reason for this disagreement, so we would suggest this will change over time.

Another problem with this theory is that while it makes intuitive sense that both nature and nurture are important, it is very difficult to disentangle the two in research designs. In fact, in some cases it may even be unethical to attempt to determine genetic influences due to the intrusive and perhaps even experimental nature of that research. Thus, we are constrained by the measures that are currently available. Not only that, imagine having to tell individuals who thought they were doing a study on personality that now you need them to give some blood and urinate in a cup. In research of this nature it may be more difficult to find and retain participants.

As you probably could guess from reading this chapter, the theory cannot explain everything. Some research, and some human behavior for that matter, contradicts what we would genetically predict. An example of this is the fact that families today are moving toward having fewer children rather than more children, to the extent of not having enough children to replace themselves. How does this fit with the evolutionary need to carry on your genetic material? Although there is a great deal of speculation, we don't exactly know.

Finally, there is a tendency to confuse a genetic predisposition with a value judgment—that is, it is easy to say that because there is a genetic tendency toward a certain trait, then a certain behavior should follow. An example of that is the genetic and hormonal differences between males and females. While we have said that women have more to be concerned with when it comes to mate selection than do men, because they are physically responsible for bringing a child into this world, it doesn't mean that women should automatically be responsible for the care of that child for the rest of its life. While our cultural beliefs may suggest that's true, that is not entirely biologically based, as some have suggested.

Similarly, while research from this theoretical perspective suggests rape is biologically driven, this does not mean that individuals should not be held accountable for such behavior. Remember, one of our assumptions stated that human biological or biosocial drives do not determine human behavior. In other words, even though an individual may have the genetic predisposition toward rape, this does not mean that he or she must act on that drive. Further, we have strict social norms and laws that guard against this behavior, thus indicating that individuals will benefit by not engaging in such acts. Instead, we should use this information when we treat offenders or engage in prevention efforts. Recognizing the biological or social drives that possibly guide such behavior can provide another avenue of exploration as we strive to decrease its incidence.

Thus, while most social scientists would support the use of a biosocial perspective when researching and explaining human behavior, there is still much work to be done in the development of this theory. This does seem, however, to be the wave of the future.

APPLICATION

1. Refer to the scenario with the group of single parents at the beginning of this chapter. According to biosocial theory, who is right—Ross or the other women?

2. It's exam week and a friend comes to you saying she's not sure she's going to make it through the next exam because she doesn't feel well. She needs to maintain a 3.5 GPA to keep her scholarship and has been studying very hard. You ask her what hurts and she replies, "I don't know, everything!" How would you use a biosocial approach to help her?

3. Think about the role of hormones in your life. What have you learned or been told about how they influence you physically? What about emotionally? Socially? How can you use a biosocial perspective to un-

derstand how hormones influence your behavior, as well as how your environment can effect your hormones?

4. List ways that you are like one of your parents or a sibling. Now go through your list and write ways that each of these could be genetic or socially constructed. How can the interaction of genetics and your family environment be responsible for these similarities?

5. Think about the story at the beginning of the chapter again. How does biosocial theory explain why adults are willing to raise nonbiological children?

6. Which of the research areas from your sample reading do you find most interesting and why? Which application do you find most unbelievable and why?

Sample Reading

Booth, A., Carver, K., and Granger, D. A. (2000). "Biosocial perspectives on the family." *Journal of Marriage and the Family* 62 (4): 1018–1034.

This decade review article provides a topical summary of areas of research that have benefited from the principles of a biosocial perspective. How much has been done in such a short period of time will probably amaze you.

References

Baldwin, J. D., and Baldwin, J. I. (1997). Gender differences in sexual interest. *Archives of Sexual Behavior* 26 (2): 181–210.

Brody, N. (1997). Dispositional paradigms: Comment on Eysenck (1997) and the biosocial science of individual differences. *Journal of Personality and Social Psychology* 73: 1242–1245.

Campbell, T. L. (1993). Applying a biosocial perspective on the family. In P. G. Boss, W. J. Doherty, R. LaRossa, W. R. Schumm, and S. K. Steinmetz (eds.), *Sourcebook of Family Theories and Methods: A Contextual Approach* (pp. 711–713). New York: Plenum.

Cloninger, C. R., Svrakic, D. M., and Przybeck, T. R. (1993). A psychobiological model of temperament and character. *Archives of General Psychiatry* 50: 975–990.

Cosmides, L., Toby, J., and Barkow, J. H. (1992). Introduction: Evolutionary psychology and conceptual integration. In J. H. Barkow, L. Cosmides, and J. Toby (eds.), *The Adapted Mind: Evolutionary Psychology and the Generation of Culture* (pp. 3–136). New York: Oxford University Press.

Ellis, L. (1991). A synthesized (biosocial) theory of rape. *Journal of Consulting and Clinical Psychology* 59 (5): 631–642.

Eysenck, H. J. (1967). *The Biological Basis of Personality.* Springfield, IL: Thomas.

——. (1982). *Personality, Genetics, and Behavior: Selected Papers.* New York: Praeger.

——. (1997). Personality and experimental psychology: The unification of psychology and the possibility of a paradigm. *Journal of Personality and Social Psychology* 73: 1224–1237.

Eysenck, H. J., and Eysenck, M. W. (1985). *Personality and Individual Differences: A Natural Science Approach.* New York: Plenum.

Fox, R. (1989). *The Search for Society: Quest for a Biosocial Science and Morality.* New Brunswick, NJ: Rutgers University Press.

Hamilton, W. D. (1964a). The genetical evolution of social behavior. I. *Journal of Theoretical Biology* 7: 1–16.

——. (1964b). The genetical evolution of social behavior. II. *Journal of Theoretical Biology* 7: 17–52.

Hendrix, L., and Schneider, M. A. (1999). Assumptions on sex and society in the biosocial theory of incest. *Cross-Cultural Research* 33 (2): 193–218.

Lovejoy, C. O. (1981). The origin of man. *Science* 211: 341–450.

Mayr, E. (1991). *One Long Argument: Charles Darwin and the Genesis of Modern Evolutionary Thought.* Cambridge, MA: Harvard University Press.

Richter, J., Eiseman, M., and Richter, G. (2000). Temperament, character and perceived parental rearing in healthy adults: Two related concepts? *Psychopathology* 33 (1): 36–44.

Ryckman, R. M. (2000). Eysenck's biological typology. In *Theories of Personality* (7th ed., pp. 349–390). Belmont, CA: Wadsworth.

Smith, S. R., and Soliday, E. (2001). The effects of parental chronic kidney disease on the family. *Family Relations* 50 (2): 171–177.

Thomas, A., and Chess, S. (1980). *The dynamics of psychological development*. New York: Brunner/Mazel.

Thomas, R. M. (1996). Ethology and sociobiology. In *Comparing Theories of Child Development* (4th ed., pp. 394–412). Pacific Grove, CA: Brooks/Cole.

Troost, K. M., and Filsinger, E. (1993). Emerging biosocial perspectives on the family. In P. G. Boss, W. J. Doherty, R. LaRossa, W. R. Schumm, and S. K. Steinmetz (eds.), *Sourcebook of Family Theories and Methods: A Contextual Approach* (pp. 677–710). New York: Plenum.

Udry, J. R. (1994). Integrating biological and sociological models of adolescent problem behaviors. In R. D. Ketterlinus and M. E. Lamb (eds.), *Adolescent Problem Behaviors: Issues and Research* (pp. 93–107). Hillsdale, NJ: Lawrence Erlbaum.

——. (2000). Biological limits of gender construction. *American Sociological Review* 65 (3): 443–457.

Wilson, E. O. (1975). *Sociobiology: The New Synthesis*. Cambridge, MA: Belknap. ✦

Biosocial Perspectives on the Family

Alan Booth
Karen Carver
Douglas A. Granger

New theoretical models conceptualize families as systems affected by, and effecting change in, reciprocal influences among social, behavioral, and biological processes. Technological breakthroughs make noninvasive assessment of many biological processes available to family researchers. These theoretical and measurement advances have resulted in significant increases in research on family processes and relationships that integrate knowledge from the fields of behavioral endocrinology, behavior genetics, and, to a lesser degree, evolutionary psychology. This review covers a broad spectrum, including the topics of parenthood, early child development, adolescent and middle child development, parent-child relations, courtship and mate selection, and the quality and stability of marital and intimate relations. Our intention is to introduce, by example, the relevance of the biosocial approach, encourage family researchers to consider the application of these ideas to their interests, and increase the participation of family researchers in the next generation of studies.

This is the first appearance of a decade-in-review article devoted to biosocial perspectives on the family. There are several decades of research examining the links between biology and individual development (e.g., perception, memory, maturation), but it is only recently that research has focused on families. Although the information is still fragmented, we now have enough to devote an article to biosocial research as it pertains to families. By biosocial we mean concepts linking psychosocial factors to physiology, genetics, and evolution. This article is a prelude to an explosion of biosocial research related to families anticipated over the next decade. We offer a hint of things to come and hope to perhaps encourage readers to start their own biosocial research project.

Early social scientists, such as William James (1842–1910), assumed that physiological processes were critical components of the behavioral and social phenomena they were studying. Until recently, however, the influence of those assumptions on scientific thinking was limited by significant gaps in knowledge. The nature of many physiological processes was largely unknown, and the technology necessary to operationalize physiological variables was in its infancy. Given these limitations, it is not surprising that research on human development and the family largely focused on the interface between the social environment and individual behavior. Many of those who did study physiological processes looked for simplistic models in which reductionist principles could be applied to reveal "the biological determinants" of behavior. The application of this focus led to clearly drawn boundaries between the social and biological sciences, the exceptions being studies of individual prenatal, infant, and adolescent development.

In the last 2 decades, significant effort has been focused on reversing this trend. Technical and conceptual advances have begun to break down disciplinary walls. Specifically, advances that enable noninvasive and inexpensive measurement of many physiological processes have given behavioral and social researchers new opportunities to integrate biological measures into their programs (Granger, Schwartz, Booth, & Arentz, 1999). In parallel, a series of paradigm shifts have occurred in scientific thinking about the relative contributions of both nature and nurture to behavioral phenomena (McClearn, 1993) and individual development (Gottlieb, 1992).

Dynamic models have replaced the simple reductionist ones of the past. They can best be described as systems models positing that individuals and families are best understood as the product of reciprocal influences among environmental (primarily social), behavioral, and biological processes (e.g., Cairns, Gariepy, & Hood, 1990; Gottlieb, 1991, 1992). In these models, biological functions set the stage for behavioral adaptation to environmental challenge. At the same time, environmental challenges may induce behavioral change that in turn affects fast-acting (e.g., hormone secretion) and slower-responding (gene expression) biological processes. Biological activities that facilitate a particular behavioral response, and behavioral activities that set the stage for changes in biological processes, may be stimulated or attenuated by environmental challenges (immediately or at some earlier stage in the individual's life). Evidence suggests that these interacting factors are capable of affecting differences in developmental trajectories, even for individuals with the same genetic constitution (e.g., identical twins).

Hereafter we focus on topics addressed by family scholars for which methodologically sound biosocial research has advanced knowledge on the topic and for which further research has the potential to yield new information. We focus primarily on behavioral endocrinology and behavioral genetics but briefly cover studies from evolutionary psychology and behavioral pharmacology. Following a primer on each biological topic, this article is organized around the family themes of parenthood, early child development and parent-child relations, adolescents and parent-child relations, courtship and mate selection, and marital and intimate relations. We conclude with notes on next steps in biosocial research and on how family scholars can become involved.

PRIMER ON BIOLOGICAL CONNECTIONS

BEHAVIORAL ENDOCRINOLOGY

The endocrine system produces several hundred hormones and releases them in response to signals from the brain, either nerve signals or other bloodborne chemical messengers. Hormones are chemical messengers that regulate, integrate, and control bodily functions by turning gene expression (influences) on or off. Hormones mediate both short-term processes, such as immediate responses to stress (e.g., fight or flight), and longer-term processes, such as growth, development, and reproduction. Researchers are interested in basal as well as reactive levels of hormones. Behavioral endocrinology is in the forefront of the integration of biological measures into studies of children and families because recent research has shown that hormones may play an integral role in furthering our understanding of individual differences in developmental trajectories, family relationships, and factors that mediate these processes. One of the reasons behavioral endocrinology is at the forefront is that technical advances have made possible the assessment of many important hormones in saliva (Kirschbaum, Read, & Hellhammer, 1992). For introductory reading on the operation of the endocrine system and its role in regulating many aspects of human biology and behavior, we recommend Nelson (1999). The following hormones are discussed in this review.

Testosterone is one of several androgens produced by the endocrine system. Men produce levels several times higher than do women. In women, the primary sources are the ovaries and the adrenal glands, whereas in men the sources are the testes and the adrenal glands. The hormone is implicated in the development of secondary sexual characteristics, reproduction, dominant behavior (which is sometimes antisocial and aggressive), and interest in activities that are traditionally masculine. It also plays an important role in men's competitive activities that involve gaining, maintaining, and losing social status (Mazur & Booth, 1998).

Dehydroepiandrosterone (DHEA) is a hormone produced by the adrenal glands that has a wide range of effects and is a precursor of other hormones. Preliminary studies indicate a possible association with health risk behavior (i.e., alcohol use and smoking), cognitive abilities, and emotionality. There are dramatic developmental differences in DHEA; levels are very low until about age 6 (adrenarche), and then it increases through age 15. In prepubertal children and in females, peripheral conversion of DHEA is the major pathway for testosterone production and may be an early marker for physiological development (McClintock & Herdt, 1996).

Oxytocin affects a variety of cognitive, grooming, affiliative, sexual, maternal, and reproductive behaviors. It is known to be important in parturition and lactation and may be implicated in maternal-infant interactions (Turner, Altemus, Enos, Cooper, & McGuinness, 1999).

Estradiol is the primary female reproductive hormone. It is implicated in the onset of puberty, menstruation, sexual and reproductive capacity, pregnancy, and menopause. It is associated with maternal behavior and may be important to general social affiliative behavior as well (Fleming, Ruble, Krieger, & Wong, 1997).

Cortisol is an endocrine product that enables individuals to adapt to the vicissitudes of life and to environmental changes. Men and women produce the same amount of cortisol. Cortisol regulates metabolism, the fight-flight response, immune activity, sensory acuity, and aspects of learning and memory. Cortisol is particularly interesting because its levels are affected by a variety of environmental processes (the amount of social, physical, and immune stimuli; Stansbury & Gunnar, 1994).

BEHAVIORAL GENETICS

Behavioral genetics is the study of the relative contribution of genes and the environment to individual differences in behavior. The amount of genetic influence may be derived from the correlation of a behavioral measurement within pairs of siblings with known differences in genetic relatedness. For example, the correlation of antisocial behavior within pairs of identical (monozygotic) twins, who share 100% of their genes, is compared with the correlation within pairs of fraternal (dizygotic) twins, who share 50% of their genes. In one study (Reiss, 1995), the correlation for identical twins was .81, whereas for fraternal twins it was .62. To estimate the genetic influence, the difference between the two correlations is multiplied by 2 ($2 \times .19 = .38$). In this example, 38% of the variance in antisocial behavior may be attributed to genetic influences. Studies typically employ multiple sibling pairs (full siblings, half siblings, adopted siblings, siblings from blended families), multiple measures of the same phenomena (child estimates, parent estimates, teacher estimates), and structural equation modeling to determine the fit between genetic relatedness and measures of behavior (Neale & Cardon, 1992; Plomin, 1994).

Environmental contributions are parceled out to those shared by siblings (e.g., home, parents, family wealth, parents' education) and those not shared and which make siblings from the same family different from one another (e.g., parental treatment, sibling gender and age, peers, teachers). The distinction between shared and nonshared environment is important because the influence of the latter is stronger and increases throughout the life course. The portion of variance that is shared can be obtained by subtracting the heritability estimate from the identical twin correlation. In the above example, 43% of the variation would be from shared factors ($.81 - .38$). The remaining variance (19%) would be the effect of the influence of the nonshared environment. A powerful method of estimating genetic influence involves estimating differences in behavior among identical twins who have been reared together versus those who have been reared apart. With a few exceptions, results across methods are similar (Rowe, 1994).

Knowledge about the ways genes influence behavior is limited. Complex sets of genes are instrumental in influencing such things as intelligence and antisocial behavior. Nonetheless, it is unlikely that genes are specifically coded for IQ or criminal behavior. Rather, genes affect such things as memory or speed of processing in the case of intelligence, and impulse control and sensation seeking in the case of antisocial behavior. Some genetic influence is passive, derived from the fact that parents and children share genes. Smart kids live in parent-designed, intellectually challenging environments. Some genetic influence is reactive, stemming from the way parents and others respond to genetically influenced behavior. Antisocial behavior may cause parents to be less affectionate. Finally, some genetic influence is active, that is, genetically influenced behaviors cause children to seek and create environments that in turn affect their behavior. The risk-taking child may seek like-minded individuals as friends.

Two lines of research are of interest to family researchers: one focuses on genetic contributions to measures of family environments (stemming from reactive and active processes); and the other focuses on the way in which environmental factors moderate the expression of genetically influenced behavior. In the former, variance in such independent variables as the home environment, parenting styles, offspring's television viewing, and characteristics of peer groups are subject to genetic influences—especially as the child matures and exercises more control over his or her environment (Scarr & McCartney, 1983). Research on the factors that moderate by amplifying and reducing genetic influences include historical and cohort variables, as well as parenting practices. For example, authoritative parenting may reduce genetic influences, whereas laissez faire practices may increase them.

There are two reasons for introducing genetics into family studies. The first is to correctly identify the source of change in variables such as cognitive development and antisocial behavior to avoid attributing genetic influences to environmental ones and vice versa. The clinical and programmatic significance of this knowledge is that intervention strategies can be targeted to those aspects of the environment that can be altered. The second reason to consider genetic variables is to develop better fitting models to explain dependent variables. Those interested in expanding their understanding of behavioral genetics should read articles by Reiss (1995) and Plomin (1995).

Evolutionary Psychology

Evolutionary psychology focuses on (a) behavior that has enhanced genetic replication in past generations and (b) the way in which contemporary behavior effects reproductive success. In humans, women tend to invest more in offspring than do men and tend to be more selective in their choice of mates—mostly on the basis of men's willingness and ability to make a parental contribution. Men tend to invest less in parenting and may increase their chances of passing on their genetic material by being more promiscuous and concerned about the fidelity of their mates. One example of such behavior is the finding that when compared with biological offspring, stepchildren elect to leave or are "pushed out" of their home earlier (White & Booth, 1985). This may be attributable to the stepparent's lack of desire to invest in children who do not have his or her genetic material.

Theory and research on evolutionary psychology interests family scholars because there is evidence that it affects virtually every aspect of family life. Mate selection and offspring-parent relations, as well as topics such as the quality and stability of stepfamilies, family violence, incest, and the impact of the support capability of the environment, are all considered under the rubric of evolutionary psychology. For introductory reading, we suggest Buss and Schmitt (1993), Daly and Wilson (1983), and Davis and Daly (1997).

Behavioral Psychopharmacology and the Family

Progress made in describing the biological processes involved in regulating behavior has led to breakthroughs in the design and availability of drugs that stimulate or attenuate those processes. Examples include hormone-replacement therapies (i.e., testosterone, estradiol) to resolve midlife changes in negative moods, attitudes, and behavior; Viagra to address impotence and sexual dysfunction; Prozac for affective disorder; and Ritalin for disruptive behavior disorders of childhood. With the exception of Ritalin (Barkley, 1989), little is known about the effect of these agents on family relationships. Although space limitations prevent us from dealing with this topic, family researchers should be on alert for novel opportunities to test and develop theoretical models by studying the impact of the behavioral, cognitive, and attitudinal changes induced by these medications within the broader social ecology of the family.

One of the challenges facing biosocial research is that investigators in each of the fields involved (behavioral endocrinology, behavioral genetics, evolutionary psychology, behavioral psychopharmacology) tend not to be concerned about the other. Their practitioners rarely cite one another. Moreover, they seldom draw on the other fields to help explain the imponderables in their own work. The biosocial sciences can benefit from heeding Wilson's (1998) call for greater unification of the social and biological sciences.

Parenthood

Biosocial research has focused on numerous aspects of becoming a parent. Evolutionary psychology is implicated in establishing a mating relationship. Hormones are examined with respect to the decision to have children, as well as decisions about the timing of sexual intercourse and parenting behavior following birth.

Establishing a Stable Sexual Relationship

To ensure survival, a period of several years of intense parental care is required. By the time they are age 3 or 4 children stand a good chance of reaching adulthood, and the need for intense care wanes. Humans ensure the needed care by establishing monogamous relationships, whereas most other primates do so through other forms of social organization. Compared with men, women are much more discriminating because future investment in offspring will be higher. Women select mates partly based on the resources they control and partly on the resources they can bring to bear on the support of the mother and her offspring (Daly & Wilson, 1983).

Cashdan (1995) added another dimension to reproductive strategies by taking into account women's dominance, status, and access to resources, some of which are associated with the hormone testosterone. Cashdan's research indicated that women with higher testosterone-associated dominance are less in need of a partner and are less selective in the sense they have more sexual partners and are less likely to agree with the statement, "I would not want to have sex with a man unless I am convinced that he is serious about a long-term commitment." On the other hand, women with low testosterone levels who expect or need partner involvement will be more selective and engage in behavior that is more likely to attract a man, such as minimizing assertiveness and sexual activity to assure the man that her offspring are his.

The Decision to Have Children

The decision to have a child is not well understood socially or biologically. Testosterone may be implicated. In a study explaining a wide range of gendered behavior in 250 women aged 27–30, Udry, Morris, and Kovenock (1995) found high testosterone related to a wide range of nontraditional behaviors related to the family, including not marrying, assigning a lower priority to marrying, having fewer children, and enjoying childcare activities less. It would appear that women's decisions to have a child may be related, in part, to basal levels of testosterone.

Not yet examined is whether female engagement in more competitive, aggressive, independent, or solitary activities, or activities with unrelated men, further increases testosterone.

If so, it suggests a feedback mechanism that may help explain participation in parenting. Furthermore, the role of estradiol and other hormones related to reproduction remain to be explored as factors influencing decisions to have children. Whether testosterone or some other hormone influences men's decisions to have children is unknown.

Research supports a moderate heritable component for fertility expectations and desires. Rodgers and Doughty (in press) used the National Longitudinal Study of Youth to investigate ideal, desired, and expected family size. Findings suggest that both fertility expectations and completed fertility have a heritable component, although expectations have a higher level of genetic influence than do outcomes.

Timing of Sexual Intercourse

The role of biological processes in the timing of sexual intercourse is central to parenting. Females of all nonhuman mammals exhibit hormonally related signs of receptivity (visual, pheromonal, behavioral, and combinations of these) at the time of ovulation. The research on humans has been less consistent, mostly because of the difficulty in collecting enough data throughout the menstrual cycle. The only study showing that all the links are present (Van Goozen, Weigant, Endert, Helmond, & Van de Poll, 1997) focused on sexually active, normally, and regularly menstruating women who were not on the pill. Blood samples were obtained every other day, as were measures of sexual activity and mood. Testosterone and estradiol were highest at the ovulatory phase, as were female-initiated sexual activity and interest in sexual activity. It appears that hormones and sexual activity are greatest when women were most likely to conceive. Still, much has to be learned about signals linking the hormones and sexual behavior. Potentially contributing to the functioning of this intricate pattern of linkages between hormones and behavior is interest in having children, early experience with infants or young children, or harsh environ-

ments that threaten infant viability. These topics warrant research.

Parenting Behavior Following Birth

Parenting behavior shortly after birth is linked to biological factors. During pregnancy, many hormones are elevated to levels much higher than at any other time in life. Within weeks of birth mothers' hormone levels decline to normal levels. In cases where postpartum decline in estradiol is gradual, mothers report a greater feeling of attachment to their infants (Fleming, Ruble, Krieger, & Wong, 1997). This may be because estradiol triggers the production of oxytocin (Uvnas-Moberg, 1997), which appears to be implicated in mother's preoccupation with their infant children (Lechman & Mayes, 1998) and in their calm feelings while breast-feeding (Altemus, Deuster, Galliven, Carter, & Gold, 1995). Apparently, breastfeeding itself is a factor in the amount and quality of mother-child interaction. A comparison study indicated that mothers exposed to sucking during skin-to-skin contact shortly after birth talked to their babies more and spent more time with them than did mothers just experiencing skin-to-skin contact (Widstrom et al., 1990). Thus, the links among oxytocin, breast-feeding, and maternal care appear to be important in parent-child relations. Another study implicates the hormone prolactin, as well as oxytocin. Comparisons of women 4 days postpartum and a control group indicated these hormones were associated with lower levels of muscular tension, anxiety, and aggression (Uvnas-Moberg, Widstrom, Nissen, & Bjorvell, 1990). In men, a drop in basal testosterone immediately following the birth of a child has been noted (Storey, Walsh, Quinton, & Wynne-Edwards, in press). This may increase feelings of nurturing on the part of the father. Whether these biological factors continue to play a role as the child develops is not known.

Progress has been made in identifying important biosocial relationships in many phases of becoming a parent. Evolutionary factors that contribute to producing viable offspring have been identified in mate selection. Genetic influences have a role in fertility preferences. Hormones may be important in establishing unions that increase the chances of offspring survival, creating interest in having children, setting the timing of sexual intercourse, and shaping the quality of infant care. The research to date is largely descriptive, however, and little is known about direction of effects or pathways of influence.

EARLY CHILD DEVELOPMENT AND PARENT-CHILD RELATIONS

Hormonal and genetic factors are implicated in the development of gendered behavior and other aspects of cogitative development. They also are linked to the development of the parent-infant bond.

GENDERED BEHAVIOR

Prenatal testosterone production (and perhaps other androgens) during the second trimester of pregnancy affects gendered behavior in adult female offspring in their late 20s (Udry et al., 1995). Gendered behavior refers to one in which males and females differ. More than 20 different measures were used to examine gendered behavior, including such things as marriage, number of births, domestic division of labor, feminine appearance, vocational interests, employment in male-dominated occupations, and personality measures. In this bipolar concept of gender, the higher the score, the more feminine the individual. Using this same data, Udry (2000) found that the greater the mother's testosterone, the smaller the effect of daughter's testosterone on adult-gendered behavior. Moreover, the greater the prenatal (mother's) testosterone, the less sensitive the female child was (during the teen years) to the mother's socialization efforts with respect to feminine behavior. This is probably because the early androgen exposure permanently organizes the brain. Female adolescents with low exposure to prenatal androgen were much more responsive to parental socialization efforts.

The development of gender differences in young children is clear and predictable, with boys preferring aggressive rough and tumble play and traditionally masculine toys and girls preferring more sedentary activities and gender-specific toys. Androgens appear to be implicated in defining the behavior. Most of the research linking hormones and play comes from studies of children with hormone-related disorders (e.g., females with congenital adrenal hyperplasia are exposed to very high levels of androgens from their adrenal glands, and males with idiopathic hypogonadotropic hypogonadalism generate very low levels of androgens). These studies are valuable because they represent essentially natural experiments that randomly assign an affected child and a control sibling to experimental and control conditions. Nonetheless, they may not represent how these processes occur in the population at large (see Collaer and Hines, 1995, for detailed review of the research).

COGNITIVE DEVELOPMENT

A study of genetic influences on the home environment and on its relationship with cognitive development in 1- and 2-year-old children reveals substantial influences (Braungart, Fulker, & Plomin, 1992). The study compares adopted sibling pairs with a matched sample of sibling pairs living with biological parents. The home environment was measured by the Home Observation for Measure of Environment (HOME) scale, which estimates the intellectual resources (e.g., books and other stimulating resources along with material responsiveness and stimulation) available in the home. Cognitive development was measured by the Mental Development Index (MDI). More than one third of the variance in the HOME scores was accounted for by genetic influences, and approximately half the HOME-MDI relationship was mediated by genetic influences. Thus, offspring genetics plays an important role in the family intellectual environment, even in infancy.

PARENT-CHILD ATTACHMENT

Research suggests that infant and early childhood experiences alter short- and long-term patterns of cortisol production. Maternal separation, for example, affects the threshold for cortisol production as well as the size of the cortisol increase (Gunnar, Mangelsdorf, Larsen, & Herstgaard, 1998). Young children with histories of child abuse tend to have atypical cortisol profiles throughout the day (Hart, Gunnar, & Cicchetti, 1995). Even cultural differences in care-giving and child-rearing practices (such as maternal emphasis on emotional expression, consistency in daily schedules, and degree of stimulation) are linked to cortisol profiles in infants (Super, Harkness, & Granger, preliminary data). Studies of institutionalized Romanian orphans indicate that severe social and tactile deprivation in early childhood may result in disruption of the circadian pattern of cortisol production (Carlson & Earls, 1997).

In middle childhood, traumatic events within the family are significant sources of cortisol activation for children. Children from families with high levels of conflict, punishment, serious quarreling, and fighting tend to have the highest cortisol levels (Flynn & England, 1995). Cortisol production increases in response to changes in family composition, such as men migrating in and out of the household for seasonal work opportunities, as well as for children living with a stepfather or distant relatives (Flynn & England, 1995).

The patterns of cortisol production noted above (e.g., basal level, response threshold, size of increase, and daily pattern) have the potential for affecting numerous aspects of child development. Children's cortisol increase resulting from parent-child conflict is associated with high levels of offspring social difficulties, withdrawal, anxiety, and a low sense of control-related beliefs (Granger, Weisz, & Kauneckis, [1996]). In addition, cortisol increases are associated with internalizing behavior problems, symptoms of anxiety disorders, and negative patterns of control-related beliefs (Granger, Weisz, McCracken, Ikeda, & Douglas, 1996). Children's low basal cortisol also is associated with maternal dysfunction and psychopathology and parenting stress, and interrelationships between mother and child cortisol levels (Granger et al., 1998). Taken together, these studies suggest that the individual differences in children's cortisol response to features of the family environment contribute to children's behavioral adjustment and development.

No doubt part of the relationship between cortisol response and family relationships has genetic origins. For example, genetic influences have been observed for several measures of parenting behavior that would affect mother-child attachment. They include parental warmth (Braungart, 1994), affection, punitive parenting (Plomin, Reiss, Hetherington, & Howe, 1994), expressiveness (Plomin, McClearn, Pedersen, Nesselroade, & Bergeman, 1988), and inconsistency (Braungart, 1994). Most of these findings are from twin studies.

Evolutionary psychology also suggests how parental interest in reproductive success influences parent-child attachment in infants. There is evidence that parents are reluctant to invest in newborns if the offspring is of poor quality and unlikely to survive or there is little food or few other resources such that infant care would threaten the reproducing pair or older children. Fathers are reluctant to support newborns if they have doubts about the paternity of the child. Stepparents who have no genetic investment in the child are more inclined to abuse their children than are biological parents (Daly & Wilson, 1988).

Both hormones and genetic influences on measures of the family environment are implicated in the cognitive development of infants. Cortisol has a major role responding to and defining the parent-child bond, as well as offspring internalizing and externalizing behavior. An intergenerational component appears to be in evidence. Behavioral genetic research indicates that offspring genes influence numerous aspects of the family environment. Evolutionary psychology helps us understand aspects of the dark side of parent-child bonds.

Given the range of biological influences, integrated studies are needed to understand how early development is linked to the three biological models.

LATER CHILD DEVELOPMENT AND PARENT CHILD RELATIONS

Adolescent dominance, aggression, and sexual behavior, along with antisocial behavior and depression, appear to have biological links. Special attention is given to gender differences in the link between testosterone and behavior. In addition to children's genetic effects on the environment, we also consider the way environment moderates genetic influences.

SEXUAL DEVELOPMENT

Although puberty is evident around age 12 for girls and age 14 for boys—a time when gonadal development is clearly apparent—the organization of the process is established prenatally. Recent research suggests the early stages of puberty begin at age 6, when the adrenal cortex begins to mature and secrete low levels of the hormone DHEA. The metabolism of DHEA leads to the production of both testosterone and estradiol (McClintock & Herdt, 1996). By age 10, DHEA production is significant and corresponds with children's first sexual attraction, sexual fantasy, and sexual activity. DHEA is a much-overlooked marker with a wide range of behavioral, cognitive, and neural effects. As a precursor to potent hormones such as estradiol and testosterone, its effects may be much larger than current research suggests.

DOMINANCE AND AGGRESSION

The period of adolescence is marked by physiological changes, in addition to a withdrawal (sometimes estrangement) from the family of origin, increased involvement with peers, and an increase in dominance and aggression for both boys and girls. Much of the testosterone and estradiol production goes toward organizing physiological development but some is manifested in behavior. One study of boys in childhood and early adolescence (ages 6 to 13) suggests that taking body mass as well as testosterone into account differentially predicts dominance and aggression (Tremblay et al., 1998). Increasing testosterone and body mass predict dominance, but only body mass predicts physical aggression. Thus, the relation between testosterone and physical aggression in this age group (and perhaps others) may be moderated by body mass. Boys with greater body mass may elicit aggression or find it easier to deal with individuals by being aggressive. Further research is needed to determine whether the relationship holds true for girls.

There remains the question of whether it is hormones or some other variable that produces changes in dominance (and possibly aggression). Evidence that hormones produce the change may be found in a randomized, double-blind, placebo-controlled crossover study of 35 boys and 14 girls who were in treatment for pubertal delay. Administrations of hormones to males and females were followed by an increase in physically aggressive behaviors and impulses but not verbal aggression (Finkelstein et al., 1997). It is noteworthy, however, that there is substantially less information regarding the link between testosterone and dominance in female subjects.

SEXUAL BEHAVIOR

Testosterone change in boys is also associated with changes in sexual behavior. A longitudinal study of 82 boys 12–13 years of age assessed over three years linked normal changes in testosterone with changes in sexual behavior. Monthly changes in saliva testosterone and weekly reports of sexual activity revealed that increases in testosterone were associated with coital initiation, frequency of coitus, and the rising incidence of other sexual behavior (Halpern, Udry, & Suchindran, 1998). Noteworthy is another study of this same sample that found serum testosterone collected semiannually and cumulative reports of sexual behavior over a 3-year period were unrelated. The more frequent collection of testosterone in saliva (which represents an estimate of the biologically active hormone in blood that is available to affect behavior) and improved measure of sexual activity detected changes not revealed in the earlier study. This suggests that longitudinal studies of behavior should make frequent assessments and measure free testosterone so that specific changes can be linked to alterations in behavior close to the time at which they occur.

A behavioral genetics study indicated a moderating effect of environmental factors on the heritability of the age of onset of sexual intercourse. Dunne et al. (1997) showed that genetic factors explained more of the variance in age at first sexual intercourse for a younger cohort (born 1952–1965) of twins than for an older cohort (born 1922–1952). Effects were interpreted to mean that parents of younger twins exercised less social control over offspring behavior.

SEX DIFFERENCES

It is clear that there are marked gender differences in the link between testosterone and risky or nonconforming behavior. Although androgens result in increased interest in such behavior, Udry (1988) demonstrated that social controls (father presence and participation in sports) reduced the relationship between testosterone and sexual activity among adolescent girls, whereas these same controls had little impact on the testosterone-sexual behavior link among boys. The differential impact of social controls on boys and girls suggests that although there are similarities in the hormone-behavior link (e.g., interest in sex and masculine behavior), there are important differences that require exploration.

Nowhere is this more evident than in studies of competition among male subjects. Testosterone is shown to rise in anticipation of competition. Following competition, testosterone remains high or climbs further in winners but drops in losers (Booth, Johnson, & Granger, 1999), a finding that has been replicated numerous times. Nonetheless, testosterone does not have the same role in female competitors. There is no anticipatory rise in female competitors, nor does winning and losing affect testosterone production (Mazur, Susman, & Edelbrock, 1997). In a pilot study (Booth & Dabbs, 1996), it appears that cortisol was implicated in the preparation for and outcome of competitive events. Although untested, DHEA also may have a role in female competition because it is a precursor of testosterone.

The relevance of competition studies to families is that family members confer and take away status from one another. For example, the preferential treatment of one child over another is a way of giving status to one and taking it away from another. Children who receive more favorable treatment may experience an increase in testosterone, which is then expressed in more dominating behavior toward the less favored sibling. Giving and withholding support from spouse in family problem solving is another way status is gained and lost that, in turn, could affect hormone production and may then affect the quality of subsequent family interaction. Given the paucity of research on competing women, it is uncertain how and which hormones may be involved in the conferring and taking away of status from female family members.

PARENTAL RELATIONS, ADOLESCENT DEPRESSION, AND ANTISOCIAL BEHAVIOR

Genetically influenced characteristics of children also affect aspects of adolescent family environment. Significant genetic influences were found for children's and parents' ratings of positive factors (such as warmth, support, empathy, and mutual involvement in enjoyable activities), as well as for negative factors (such as frequency and intensity of disputes and feelings of anger). No influence was observed for control as assessed by monitoring offspring activities (Plomin et al., 1994; Rowe, 1981, 1983). Significant nonshared influences also were noted.

In an analysis of the impact of parents' negativity (anger, coercion, and conflict) on adolescent depression (as assessed by three scales) and antisocial behavior (measured from the Behavioral Problems Index antisocial scale), significant nonshared environment, as well as genetic contributions, were observed for the independent variable and the dependent variables (Pike, McGuire, Hetherington, Reiss, & Plomin, 1996). The nonshared environment contribution was modest in comparison with the genetic influence, accounting for nearly two thirds of the contribution. Moreover, the genetic influence accounts for most of the relation between parents' negativity and adolescent adjustment.

Genetic studies also reveal that environmental factors moderate the genetic influence on adolescent depression and antisocial behavior. Among adopted twins without a biological risk of antisocial behavior (as measured by having a biological parent without an antisocial personality disorder), the correlation between the family environment and becoming antisocial was trivial among those growing up in an adverse family environment. In contrast, among twins with a biological risk, there was a strong correlation between an adverse family environment and antisocial behavior (Cadoret, Yates, Troughtoh, Woodworth, & Stewart, 1995). In other words, children without genetic risk for antisocial behavior do not manifest such behavior, even in adverse environments, whereas children with a genetic predisposition are much more likely to display antisocial behavior in adverse environments than in more positive environments. A similar finding was observed among twins with and without a biological risk of depression. In this case, the interaction was between being at risk for depression and experiencing stressful life events (Kendler et al., 1995).

TRANSITION TO ADULTHOOD

Studies have illustrated the implications of hormone production in youth for problems in adulthood. Numerous adolescents engage in antisocial or deviant behavior. For a few, it extends into adulthood; for others, it is limited to adolescence (Moffitt, 1993). One study revealed that adolescent boys who had been expelled or suspended from school, ran away from home, fought, stole, or were arrested were far more likely to commit a crime as an adult if they had high levels of testosterone than if their testosterone production was average or below (Booth & Osgood, 1993). Social factors such as marriage and full-time employment tended to dampen the impact of testosterone on adult male antisocial behavior. Another study using the same sample of men demonstrated that high testosterone is related to low occupational status and periods of unemployment (Dabbs, 1992). Testosterone-related low occupational success was attributable in part to testosterone-related antisocial behavior during adolescence that got the young men into trouble at school.

Still another study suggests that father's testosterone may be linked to parent-child relationships. Julian, McKenry, and McKelvey (1990) found that fathers with low testosterone had a better quality relationship with offspring 12-18 years of age than did high-testosterone men. Thus, part of the research agenda facing us is to address the issue of why testosterone is related to antisocial behavior in some individuals but not in others. What personal experiences and environmental factors explain the differential impact of the hormone?

One of the few areas of study that combines behavioral endocrinology, genetics, and evolutionary psychology stems from an investigation by Belsky, Steinberg, and Draper (1991), which proposes that early family relationships that are harsh, rejecting, and opportunistic (versus sensitive, supportive, and rewarding) result in an earlier onset of puberty that leads to a precocious and promiscuous reproductive strategy. Although early studies produced mixed results, recent longitudinal studies have clarified the causal paths. There is a genetic influence in that mother's early marriage and childbearing accounts for part of the early onset of daughter's puberty (Ellis & Garber, in press). This study reveals that the mother's low quality romantic relationship with the biological father, stepfather, or boyfriend has an independent effect on the early onset of puberty, as does the presence of a stepfather or boyfriend. The authors suggest that the effect of the presence of an unrelated man may be similar to that observed in studies of other mammals in which pheromones produced by the unrelated adult male accelerate female pubertal maturation (Sanders & Reinisch, 1990). A second longitudinal study suggests that positive care giving from the biological father plays a unique and pivotal role in delaying pubertal development (Ellis, Dodge, Pettit, & Bates, in press). Mother's care giving was found to be redundant of paternal involvement. Further research is needed to clarify the mechanisms involved and to more precisely estimate genetic influences on pubertal maturation.

Hormones have a particularly strong influence on adolescent development. They are related to social dominance and reproductive behavior but seem to have different effects on boys and girls. Testosterone appears to influence behavior that is eventually expressed in adult antisocial behavior and poor socioeconomic achievement. Environmental factors are found to be important moderators of genetic influences on adjustment. Studies combining biosocial models add to our understanding of the onset of female puberty and subsequent promiscuous behavior.

COURTSHIP AND MATE SELECTION

Among the most fascinating—but also puzzling—recent findings are those that suggest an association between a basic feature of the immune system and the process of selecting a mate. Immunologists long ago identified basic features of our cells that enable the immune system to recognize self versus other and subsequently eliminate potentially damaging molecules it determines as other. The basic feature of this part of the immune system is proteins found on cell surfaces called human leukocyte antigens (HLA) or the major histocompatibility complex (MHC). Put simply, the MHC defines for each person a unique "immunological fingerprint." Recent findings suggest that interpersonal cues signal information about individual differences in MHC. Humans can detect individual differences in odors

(sweat) associated with MHC, which influence decisions regarding mate selection and perceived attractiveness (Wedekind, Seebeck, Bettens, & Paepke, 1995). In other words, mate selection might be influenced by olfactory or other cues that signal immunological differences. The greater the immunological differences, the greater the chances of producing a viable infant. Inbreeding avoidance may be the most important function of MHC-associated mating preferences (Potts, Manning, & Wakeland, 1994). Studies of mice suggest that MHC preferences come about through imprinting (Yamazaki et al., 1988). Infants learn how their own MHC type smells, and evolutionary forces have evolved a preference for dissimilar types.

It is of interest that scores of studies find behavioral and social similarity important to understanding mate selection. Winch, Ktsanes, and Ktsanes's (1954) theory of complementary needs never received much support (e.g., Udry, 1964). The MHC studies draw family scholars back to exploring complementarity, albeit in a different form, as an explanatory variable.

This preference for immunological differences would certainly help to explain mate selection studies of Kibbutz marriages and Chinese arranged marriages. Shepher (1971) studied mate selection in Israel Kibbutz where from the time of birth, children were raised in child-care facilities. Parents saw them a few hours a day, but most of the time they were with the care providers and other children. Shepher observed that, upon reaching adulthood, individuals never married someone from the same facility. Wolf (1995) studied arranged marriages in China that took place in the early part of this century. Marriages were often arranged when children were very young. In some communities, the female child would go to live in the male's home where she was treated as one of the children. In other communities, the female remained with the birth parents until mature, whereupon she moved to the male's family. Compared with those who did not reside together until maturity, the couples who lived together as children had unsuccessful marriages. Many were never consummated, and few had children. Men were consistently unfaithful and had children with mistresses. For MHC preferences to be the explanatory mechanism in these studies, we would need evidence of imprinting (akin to the mouse studies) to explain the rejection of kibbutz-mates and sons of foster families.

Family researchers should find this work of interest not only because of its relation to mate preferences and incest avoidance, but also because of its relation to birth outcomes. For example, HLA similarity has been associated with repeated spontaneous abortions (Thomas, Harger, Wagener, Rabin, & Gill, 1985), and lower birth weight (Ober et al., 1987).

Students of contraceptive use also will find the HLA studies of interest. Estradiol reduces women's ability to discriminate immunological differences among potential mates. High estradiol may be found among pregnant women and women on "the pill." A modern contraceptive method may be resulting in poor mate selection from the standpoint of producing children who are less likely to survive. The inability of these women to detect appropriate mates may affect the stability of courtship relationships. Cohabiting pill users have significantly higher rates of union dissolution (controlling for a wide assortment of suspected covariates) than other nonhormonal-based contraceptors (Carver, 1998).

Developments in another line of research bear watching because of their relevance to mate selection. Faces judged to have above average symmetry are regarded as more attractive. Facial symmetry may be associated with greater immunological competence and increased gene variation, which means that mating with such individuals would increase the chances of infant survival (Gangestad & Buss, 1993; Gangestad & Thornhill, 1998; Grammar & Thornhill, 1994; Mitton, 1993; Thornhill & Gangestad, 1993). Preference for masculine facial features has been observed to vary during the phase of the menstrual cycle. When con-

ception is most likely, women prefer less masculine faces than during the rest of the menstrual cycle (Penton-Voak et al., 1999). The masculine faces may signal immunological competence, whereas the less masculine faces may indicate paternal interest and investment in offspring. Gangestad and Simpson (in press) integrate these findings into a theory that suggests women vary their reproductive strategy according to the harshness of the environment. When the environment is difficult, women place more weight on indications of genetic fitness than they do when the environment is less demanding. How these findings, if borne out by subsequent studies, would play out in mate selection or extra-pair sexual relationships is deserving of study.

The integration of measures of basic features of the immune system into mate selection and courtship research serves to increase understanding of incest avoidance, contraceptive use, and unstable courtship relations as they relate to the evolutionary need to produce viable offspring.

RELATIONSHIP QUALITY AND STABILITY

Testosterone's links to marrying and divorcing are considered first, followed by reports of research on the relationship between marital quality and testosterone. Genetic influences on divorce are considered, as is the association between marital conflict and immunity.

MARITAL STATUS

In the preceding section, several biological mechanisms were suggested that may define marital relationship quality and stability. Insight is obtained from evidence that testosterone levels in men drop after they marry. In a 10-year longitudinal study of Air Force officers who underwent four physical exams over that period of time, Mazur and Michalek (1998) were able to compare changes in testosterone with changes in marital status. Unmarried men's testosterone levels were high, but following marriage, they decreased. One scenario is that single men are mostly in the company of other men, and everyday competition (some of which may be over women) keeps testosterone levels elevated (e.g., Booth, Shelley, Mazur, Tharp, & Kittok, 1989). Once married, exposure to other men declined, and the need to compete for women disappeared. Another scenario is that the marriage itself lowered testosterone—similar to what was observed after the birth of an infant. Wives expect men to behave in supportive and nurturing ways, and lowering testosterone may be crucial to successfully enacting the caring spousal and parent roles. Alternatively, biological messages (e.g., pheromones) having to do with sex or reproduction may cause testosterone to decrease.

Relationship Quality

Even though marriage is accompanied by a drop in testosterone, hormones may still be related to marital quality. An analysis of men from a representative sample of 4,462 former military servicemen between the ages of 33 and 42 showed that men with higher testosterone production were less likely to marry in the first place; once married, they were more likely to divorce (Booth & Dabbs, 1993). The likelihood of never marrying was 50% higher for men whose testosterone levels were one standard deviation above the mean compared with those whose testosterone levels were one standard deviation below the mean. Similarly, men at the higher level were 43% more likely to divorce than were those at the lower level. Once married, men with higher testosterone levels were 31% more likely to leave home because of a troubled relationship with their wife, 38% more likely to have extra-marital sex, and 13% more likely to report hitting or throwing things at their spouse. In addition, high-testosterone men were more likely to report low-quality marital interaction, a finding supported by Julian and McKenry (1989). These findings were net of other social variables such as low socioeconomic status or deviant behavior in other arenas. It is important to note, however, that substantial numbers of men with high testosterone had excellent marriages. The mecha-

nism that explains this differential marital success is unknown. There is also the caveat that cross-sectional studies do not clarify whether conflictual marriages raise testosterone.

On the other hand, marriage does play a protective role with respect to the link between testosterone and antisocial behavior and depression. Men with high testosterone levels are at risk of committing a crime and being depressed. Marriage, along with steady employment, reduces the likelihood of both (Booth, Johnson, & Granger, 1999; Booth & Osgood, 1993). Because these studies are based on cross-sectional data, it is not possible to estimate the causal ordering of the variables. The work of Mazur and Michalek (1998) and Gubernick, Worthman, and Stallings (1991) has suggested that marriage may reduce the likelihood that high-testosterone men commit crimes and get depressed. The nature of the mechanism is unclear, however.

We know little about hormones and women's marriages. Having low levels of testosterone may be important to relationship quality, or quality may be associated with hormones associated with reproduction, such as estradiol or oxytocin. Equally important is dyadic research on marital partners to see how hormone-behavior links in one individual are related to hormone-behavior links in the spouse.

Genetics and Divorce

Given that divorce rates are so consistent from society to society (Goode, 1993), it is not surprising that a number of studies have shown genes to influence divorce. Estimates of the heritability of divorce have ranged from .26 (Turkheimer, Lovett, Robinette, & Gottesman, 1992) to .53 (Jockin, McGue, & Lykken, 1996; McGue & Lykken, 1992). Jockin et al. (1996) hypothesized that personality traits play a key role. They demonstrated that between 30% and 42% of the heritability of divorce risk comes from genetic factors affecting personality. This finding is supported by a study of the association between parent and offspring divorce indicating that behavior problems mediate a significant share of the link (Amato, 1996). Analysis is needed that combines methods used by family researchers (survival analysis) with behavior genetics methods to explain the genetic mediation of divorce (e.g., Meyer, Eaves, Heath, & Martin, 1991).

The consequences of divorce for children may also have genetic origins. In a large-scale study of divorce, Block, Block, and Gjerde (1986) and Cherlin and colleagues (1991) both demonstrated that boys' elevated risk for behavior problems observed after divorce disappeared when behavior problems many years before divorce were controlled. Although Cherlin, Chase-Lansdale, and McRae (1998) demonstrated in a later study that the gap between children from divorced and non-divorced families widened as children moved into young adulthood, there remains a significant amount of unexplained variance. It is possible that the behavior problems of the boys before and after divorce are related because of underlying enduring personality characteristics and not because a high-conflict marital relationship generates the problems. This is an example of a finding that could be greatly informed by including a genetic component in the study.

MARITAL CONFLICT, IMMUNITY, AND HEALTH

Data from large epidemiological studies suggest that poor personal relationships are a major risk factor for morbidity and mortality (House, Landis, & Umberson, 1988). The search for mechanisms has revealed substantial evidence regarding the role of immune function. Kiecolt-Glaser, Glaser, Cacioppo, and Malarkey (1998) demonstrated that abrasive marital interactions have important endocrine and immunological correlates. In general, marital separation or divorce, higher marital conflict, and lower marital satisfaction are associated with lower immune function. Such stress-related immunological changes may be a pathway through which close personal relationships influence health (e.g., infectious diseases, cancer, wound healing).

Testosterone is related to poor union quality and stability, as are genetic influences. In contrast, evidence that environmental factors influence hormone levels involves the finding that testosterone declines when men marry. Marital conflict and instability may compromise the immune system, which in turn affects health.

FUTURE DIRECTIONS

RECENT RESEARCH ADVANCES

The biosocial research community is now poised to construct and test multivariate and latent models of the interacting effects of genetic, endocrine, environmental, historical, and behavioral factors that will increase our understanding of family relationships and processes, as well as developmental outcomes (Susman, 1998). Researchers have cleared several major hurdles that now make such advances possible. First, we have reliable and valid noninvasive methods to obtain measurements of biological systems with direct relevance to biosocial research. Second, gene mapping is progressing at a rapid rate, which will advance our ability to disentangle genetic and environmental influences. Third, large public use data sets are now, or soon will be, available that contain biological markers, as well as representative samples of household pairs (twins, siblings, and unrelated adolescents residing in the same household) needed to more accurately estimate genetic variance. The National Longitudinal Study of Adolescent Health (Bearman, Jones, & Udry, 1997), rich in biological, behavior, social, and contextual data, is the premiere study in this category.

INCREASED INVOLVEMENT IN BIOSOCIAL RESEARCH BY SOCIAL AND BEHAVIORAL SCIENTISTS

Contemporary social and behavioral scientists have expressed renewed interest in how the factors they study influence and are influenced by physiological and genetic processes.

A content analysis of articles in three journals that publish family research revealed a substantial growth in the number of articles per issue involving biological variables. Issues from 1990 to mid-1998 were compared to issues from 1980 to 1989. For Journal of Marriage and the Family, the number per issue increased by 47% (.76 to 1.12), for Social Forces, 121% (.28 to .62), and for Journal of Personality and Social Psychology, 18% (1.10 to 1.30).

DEVELOPMENT OF INFRASTRUCTURE SUPPORT

The National Institutes of Health have established new priorities that designate "studies on the interactions between biological and behavioral processes" as being of "high program relevance." The National Science Foundation's Division of Social, Behavioral, and Economic Research has as one of its goals to advance fundamental knowledge about "biological factors related to human behavior." In short, there is now a national agenda to facilitate the integration of biosocial perspectives into research on child and adult well-being and development within the context of the family.

HOW TO GET INVOLVED

This does not mean that family scholars must become biologists to take an active role in this line of research. Rather, we envision family researchers and trainees learning enough biology to become part of an interdisciplinary scientific team. This team approach contrasts with the notion of training one investigator who "knows all" about several fields of knowledge. The latter scenario seems problematic because ultimately depth of knowledge in any one field may be sacrificed to breadth of knowledge. We expect future family researchers to have specialized skills in traditional disciplines but also to have the practical and theoretical biological training needed to speak the common language and facilitate collaboration between investigators who represent different disciplinary perspectives. Family researchers may obtain that knowledge by reading references cited here, attending the meetings of scholarly groups such as the International Society for Psychoneuroendocrinology, Society for Behavioral Medicine, Behavior Genetics Association, and International Workshop on Methodology of Twin and Family Studies.

Note

We are indebted to Paul Amato, Jay Belsky, Ann C. Crouter, Daniel Lichter, J. Richard Udry, Susan Welch, and Lynn White for very helpful comments on earlier versions of this manuscript. This research is supported in part by the Pennsylvania State University Population Research Institute, with core support from the National Institute of Child Health and Human Development, grant 1-HD28263.

References

Altemus, M., Deuster, P., Galliven, E., Carter, C., & Gold, P. (1995). Suppression of hypothalamic-pituitary-adrenal axis responses to stress in lactating women. *Journal of Clinical Endocrinology Metabolism, 80,* 2954–2959.

Amato, P. (1996). Explaining the intergenerational transmission of divorce. *Journal of Marriage and the Family, 58,* 628–640.

Baker, L. A., & Daniels, D. (1990). Nonshared environmental influences and personality differences in adult twins. *Journal of Personality and Social Psychology, 58,* 103–110.

Barkley, R. (1989). Hyperactive girls and boys: Stimulant drug effects on mother-child interactions. *Journal of Child Psychology and Psychiatry, 30,* 336–341.

Bearman, P. S., Jones, J., & Udry, J. R. (1997). *The National Longitudinal Study of Adolescent Health: Research design.* Available at: *http://www.cpc.unc.edu/projects/addhealth/design.html*

Belsky, J., Steinberg, L., & Draper, P. (1991). Childhood experience, interpersonal development, and reproductive strategy: An evolutionary theory of socialization. *Child Development, 62,* 642–670.

Block, J., Block, J., & Gjerde, P. (1986). The personality of children prior to divorce: A prospective study. *Child Development, 57,* 827–840.

Booth, A., & Dabbs, J. (1993). Testosterone and men's marriages. *Social Forces, 72,* 463–477.

———. (1996). *Cortisol, testosterone, and competition among women.* Unpublished manuscript.

Booth, A., Johnson, D., & Granger, D. (1999). Testosterone and men's depression: The role of social behavior. *Journal of Health and Social Behavior, 40,* 130–140.

Booth, A., & Osgood, D. (1993). The influence of testosterone on deviance in adulthood. *Criminology, 31,* 93–117.

Booth, A., Shelley, G., Mazur, A., Tharp, G., & Kittok, R. (1989). Testosterone, and winning and losing in human competition. *Hormones and Behavior, 23,* 556–571.

Braungart, J., Fulker, D., & Plomin, R. (1992). Genetic mediation of the home environment during infancy: A sibling adoption study of the HOME. *Developmental Psychology, 28,* 1048–1055.

Braungart, J. M. (1994). Genetic influences on "environmental" measures. In J. C. DeFries, R. Plomin, & D. W. Fulker (Eds.), *Nature and nurture during middle childhood* (pp. 233–248). Oxford, U. K.: Blackwell.

Buss, D. M., & Schmitt, D. P. (1993). Sexual strategies theory: An evolutionary perspective on human mating. *Psychological Review, 100,* 204–232.

Cadoret, R., Yates, W., Troughtoh, E., Woodworth, G., & Stewart, M. (1995). Genetic-environmental interaction in the genesis of aggressive and conduct disorders. *Archives of General Psychiatry, 52,* 916–924.

Cairns, R., Gariepy, J., & Hood, K. (1990). Development, microevolution, and social behavior. *Psychological Review, 97,* 49–65.

Carlson, M., & Earls, E. (1997). Psychological and neuroendocrinological sequelae of early social deprivation in institutionalized children in Romania. In C. Carter, I. Lederhendler, & B. Kirkpatrick (Eds.), *The integrative neurobiology of affiliation* (pp. 419–428). New York: New York Academy of Sciences.

Carver, K. (1998). *The effect of hormonal contraceptive use on the risk of union dissolution in the United States.* Unpublished manuscript.

Cashdan, E. (1995). Hormones, sex, and status in women. *Hormones and Behavior, 29,* 354–366.

Cherlin, A., Chase-Lansdale, P., & McRae, C. (1998). Effects of parental divorce on mental health throughout the life course. *American Sociological Review, 63,* 239–249.

Cherlin, A., Furstenberg, F. F., Chase-Lansdale, P. L., Kiernan, K., Morrison, D. R., & Teitler, J. (1991). Longitudinal studies of effects of divorce on children in Great Britain and the United States. *Science, 252,* 1386–1389.

Collaer, M., & Hines, M. (1995). Human behavioral sex differences: A role for gonadal hormones during early development? *Psychological Bulletin, 118,* 55–107.

Dabbs, J. (1992). Testosterone and occupational achievement. *Social Forces, 70,* 813–824.

Daly, M., & Wilson, M. (1983). *Sex, evolution, and behavior.* Boston: Willard Grant Press.

———. (1988). Evolutionary social psychology and family homicide. *Science, 242,* 519–524.

Davis, J., & Daly, M. (1997). Evolutionary theory and the human family. *The Quarterly Review of Biology, 72,* 407–435.

Dunne, M. P., Martin, N. G., Statham, D. J., Slutske, W. S., Dinwiddie, S. H., Bucholz, K. K., Madden, P. A., & Heath, A. C. (1997). Genetic and environmental contributions to variance in age at first sexual intercourse. *Psychological Science, 8,* 211–216.

Ellis, B., Dodge, K., Pettit, G., & Bates, J. (in press). Quality of early family relationships and individual differences in the timing of pubertal maturation in girls: A longitudinal test of an evolutionary model. *Journal of Personality and Social Psychology.*

Ellis, B., & Garber, J. (in press). Psychosocial antecedents of variation in girls' pubertal timing: Marital depression, stepfather presence, and marital and family stress. *Child Development.*

Finkelstein, J., Susman, E., Chinchilli, V., Kunselman, S., D'arcangelo, R., Schwab, J., Demers, L., Liben, L., Lookingbill, G., & Kulin, H. (1997). Estrogen or testosterone increases self-reported aggressive behaviors in hypogonadal adolescents. *Journal of Clinical Endocrinology and Metabolism, 82,* 2433–2438.

Fleming, A., Ruble, D., Krieger, H., & Wong, E. (1997). Hormonal and experiential correlates of maternal responsiveness during pregnancy and the puerperium in human mothers. *Hormones and Behavior, 31,* 145–158.

Flynn, M., & England, B. (1995). Childhood stress and family environment. *Current Anthropology, 36,* 854–866.

Gangestad, W. W., & Buss, D. M. (1993). Pathogen prevalence and human mate preferences. *Ethology and Sociobiology, 14,* 89–96.

Gangestad, W. W., & Simpson, J. A. (in press). The evolution of human mating: Trade offs and strategic pluralism. *Behavioral and Brain Sciences.*

Gangestad, W. W., & Thornhill, R. (1998). Menstrual cycle variation in women's preferences for the scent of symmetrical men. *Proceedings of the Royal Society of London, B,* 265, 927–933.

Goode, W. J. (1993). *World changes in divorce patterns.* New Haven, CT: Yale University Press.

Gottlieb, G. (1991). Experiential canalization of behavioral development: Theory. *Developmental Psychology,* 27, 4–13.

———. (1992). *Individual development and evolution: The genesis of novel behavior.* New York: Oxford University Press.

Grammar, K., & Thornhill, R. (1994). Human (*Homo sapiens*) facial attractiveness and sexual selection: The role of symmetry and averageness. *Journal of Comparative Psychology,* 108, 233–242.

Granger, D. A., Schwartz, E. B., Booth, A., & Arentz, M. (1999). Salivary testosterone determination in studies of child health and development. *Hormones and Behavior,* 36, 18–27.

Granger, D. A., Serbin, L. A., Schwartzman, A. E., Lehoux, P., Cooperman, J., & Ikeda, S. (1998). Children's salivary cortisol, internalizing behavior problems, and family environment: Results from the Concordia Longitudinal Risk Project. *International Journal of Behavioral Development,* 22, 707–728.

Granger, D. A., Weisz, J. R., & Kauneckis, D. (1996). Neuroendocrine reactivity, internalizing behavior problems, and control-related cognitions in clinic-referred children and adolescents. *Journal of Abnormal Psychology,* 103, 267–276.

Granger, D. A., Weisz, J. R., McCracken, J. T., Ikeda, S., & Douglas, P. (1996). Reciprocal influences among adrenocortical activation, psychosocial processes, and clinic-referred children's short-term behavioral adjustment. *Child Development,* 67, 3250–3262.

Gubernick, D., Worthman, C., & Stallings, J. (1991). *Hormonal correlates of fatherhood in man.* Unpublished manuscript.

Gunnar, M., Mangelsdorf, S., Larsen, M., & Herstgaard, L. (1998). Attachment, temperament, and adrenocortical activity in infancy: A study of psychoendocrine regulation. *Developmental Psychology,* 25, 355–363.

Halpern, C., Udry, J., & Suchindran, C. (1998). Monthly measures of salivary testosterone predict sexual activity in adolescent males. *Archives of Sexual Behavior,* 27, 445–465.

Hart, J., Gunnar, M., & Cicchetti, D. (1995). Salivary cortisol in maltreated children: Evidence of relations between neuroendocrine activity and social competence. *Development and Psychopathology,* 7, 11–26.

House, J. S., Landis, K. R., & Umberson, D. (1988). Social relationships and health. *Science,* 241, 540–545.

Jockin, V., McGue, M., & Lykken, D. T. (1996). Personality and divorce: A genetic analysis. *Journal of Personality and Social Psychology,* 71, 288–299.

Julian, T., & McKenry, P. (1989). Relationship of testosterone to men's family functioning at mid-life: A research note. *Aggressive Behavior,* 15, 281–289.

Julian, T., McKenry, P., & McKelvey, M. (1990). Mediators of relationships stress between middle-aged fathers and their adolescent children. *Journal of Genetic Psychology,* 152, 381–386.

Kendler, K., Kessler, R., Waiters, E., Maclean, C., Neale, M., Heath, A., & Eaves, L. (1995). Stressful life events, genetic liability, and onset of an episode of major depression in women. *American Journal of Psychiatry,* 154, 1398–1404.

Kiecolt-Glaser, J. K., Glaser, R., Cacioppo, J. T., & Malarkey, W. B. (1998). Marital stress: Immunological, neuroendocrine, and autonomic correlates. *Annals of the New York Academy of Sciences,* 840, 656–663.

Kirschbaum, C., Read, G. F., & Hellhammer, D. H. (1992). *Assessment of hormones and drugs in saliva in biobehavioral research.* Kirkland, WA: Hogrefe & Huber.

Lechman, J., & Mayes, L. (1998). Maladies of love—An evolutionary perspective on some forms of obsessive-compulsive disorder. In D. Hann, L. Huffman, I. Lederhendler, & D. Meinecke (Eds.), *Advancing research on developmental plasticity: Integrating the behavioral science and neuroscience of mental health* (publication 98, pp. 134–152). Washington, DC: National Institute of Mental Health.

Mazur, A., & Booth, A. (1998). Testosterone and dominance in men. *Behavioral and Brain Sciences,* 21, 353–363.

Mazur, A., & Michalek, J. (1998). Marriage, divorce, and male testosterone. *Social Forces,* 77, 315–330.

Mazur, A., Susman, E., & Edelbrock, S. (1997). Sex differences in testosterone response to a video game contest. *Evolution and Human Behavior, 18*, 317–326.

McClearn, G. (1993). Behavior genetics: The last century and the next. In R. Plomin & G. McClearn (Eds.), *Nature, nurture and psychology,* (pp. 27–51). Washington, DC: American Psychological Association.

McClintock, M., & Herdt, G. (1996). Rethinking puberty: The development of sexual attraction. *Current Directions in Psychological Science, 5,* 178–183.

McGue, M., & Lykken, D. T. (1992). Genetic influence on risk of divorce. *Psychological Science, 3,* 368–373.

Meyer, J. M., Eaves, L. J., Heath, A. C., & Martin, N. G. (1991). Estimating genetic influences on the age at menarche: A survival analysis approach. *American Journal of Medical Genetics, 39*, 148–154.

Mitton, J. B. (1993). Enzyme heterozygosity, metabolism, and developmental stability. *Genetica, 89*, 47–66.

Moffitt, T. (1993). Adolescence-limited and life-course-persistent antisocial behavior: A developmental taxonomy. *Psychological Review, 100*, 674–701.

Neale, M. C., & Cardon, L. R. (1992). *Methodology for genetic studies of twins and families.* The Netherlands: Kluwer Academic.

Nelson, R. J. (1999). *An introduction to behavioral endocrinology.* New York: Sinauer.

Ober, C., Simpson, J. L., Ward, M., Radvany, R. M., Andersen, R., Elias, S., Sabbagha, R., & The DIEP Study Group. (1987). Prenatal effects of maternal-retal HLA compatibility. *American Journal of Reproductive Immunology and Microbiology, 15*, 141–149.

Penton-Voak, I. S., Perrett, D. I., Castles, D. L., Kobayashi, T., Burt, D. M., Murray, L. K., & Minamisawa, R. (1999). Menstrual cycle alters face preference. *Nature, 399*, 741–742.

Pike, A., McGuire, S., Hetherington, E., Reiss, D., & Plomin, D. (1996). Family environment and adolescent depressive symptoms and antisocial behavior: A multivariate genetic analysis. *Developmental Psychology, 32*, 590–603.

Plomin, R. (1994). *Genetics and experience: The interplay between nature and nurture.* Thousand Oaks, CA: Sage.

——. (1995). Genetics and children's experiences in the family. *Journal of Child Psychology and Psychiatry, 36*, 33–68.

Plomin, R., McClearn, G., Pedersen, G., Nesselroade, J., & Bergeman, C. (1988). Genetic influence on adults' ratings of their current family environment. *Journal of Marriage and the Family, 51*, 791–803.

Plomin, R., Reiss, D., Hetherington, E., & Howe, G. (1994). Nature and nurture: Genetic influence on measures of family environment. *Developmental Psychology, 30*, 32–43.

Potts, W. K., Manning, C. J., & Wakeland, E. K. (1994). The role of infectious disease, inbreeding and mating preferences in maintaining MHC genetic diversity: An experimental test. *Philosophical Transactions of the Royal Society of London, Series B: Biological Sciences, B, 346,* 369–378.

Reiss, D. (1995). Genetic influence on family systems: Implications for development. *Journal of Marriage and the Family, 57*, 543–560.

Rodgers, J. L., & Doughty, D. (in press). Genetic and environmental influences on fertility expectations and outcomes using NLSY kinship data. In J. L. Rodgers, D. C. Rowe, & W. B. Miller (Eds.), *Genetic influences on fertility and sexuality.* Boston: Kluwer Academic.

Rowe, D. C. (1981). Environmental and genetic influences on dimensions of perceived parenting: A twin study. *Developmental Psychology, 17*, 203–208.

——. (1983). A biometrical analysis of perceptions of family environment: A study of twin and singleton sibling kinships. *Child Development, 54*, 416–423.

——. (1994). *The limits of family influence: Genes, experience, and behavior.* New York: Guilford Press.

Sanders, S., & Reinisch, J. (1990). Biological and social influences on the endocrinology of puberty: Some additional considerations. In J. Bancroft & J. Reinisch (Eds.), *Adolescence and puberty* (pp. 50–62). New York: Oxford University Press.

Scarr, S., & McCartney, K. (1983). How people make their own environments: A theory of genotype–environment effects. *Child Development, 54*, 424–435.

Shepher, J. (1971). Mate selection among second generation Kibbutz adolescents and adults: Incest avoidance and negative imprinting. *Archives of Sexual Behavior, 1,* 293–307.

Stansbury, K., & Gunnar, R. (1994). Adrenocortical activity and emotion regulation. In N. Fox (Ed.), The development of emotion regulation: Biological and behavioral considerations. *Monographs of the Society for Research in Child Development, 59,* 108–134.

Storey, A. E., Walsh, C. J., Quinton, R. L., & Wynne-Edwards, K. E. (in press). Hormonal correlates of paternal responsiveness in new and expectant fathers. *Evolution and Human Behavior.*

Susman, E. (1998). Biobehavioral development: An integrative perspective. *International Journal of Behavioral Development, 22,* 671–679.

Thomas, M. L., Harger, J. H., Wagener, D. K., Rabin, B. S., & Gill, T. J. (1985). HLA sharing and spontaneous abortion in humans. *American Journal of Obstetrics and Gynecology, 151,* 1053–1058.

Thornhill, R., & Gangestad, S. W. (1993). Human facial beauty: Averageness, symmetry and parasite resistance. *Human Nature, 4,* 237–269.

Tremblay, R., Schaal, B., Boulerice, B., Arseneault, L., Soussignan, R., Paquette, D., & Lauret, D. (1998). Testosterone, physical aggression, dominance and physical development in early adolescence. *International Journal of Behavioral Development, 22,* 753–777.

Turkheimer, E., Lovett, G., Robinette, C. D., & Gottesman, I. I. (1992). The heritability of divorce: New data and theoretical implications [abstract]. *Behavior Genetics, 22,* 757.

Turner, R. A., Altemus, M., Enos, T., Cooper, B., & McGuinness, T. (1999). Preliminary research on plasma oxytocin in normal cycling women: Investigating emotion and interpersonal distress. *Psychiatry: Interpersonal & Biological Processes, 62,* 97–113.

Udry, J. R. (1964). Complementarity in mate selection: A perceptual approach. *Marriage and Family Living, 25,* 281–289.

——. (1988). Biological predispositions and social control in adolescent sexual behavior. *American Sociological Review, 53,* 709–722.

——. (2000). Biological limits of gender construction. *American Sociological Review,* 65 (3), 443–457.

Udry, J. R., Morris, N., & Kovenock, J. (1995). Androgen effects on women's gendered behavior. *Journal of Biosocial Science, 27,* 359–369.

Uvnas-Moberg, K. (1997). Physiological and endocrine effects of social contact. In C. Carter, I.

Lederhendler, & B. Kirkpatrick (Eds.), *The integrative neurobiology of affiliation* (pp. 146–163). New York: New York Academy of Sciences.

Uvnas-Moberg, K., Widstrom, A., Nissen, E., & Bjorvell, H. (1990). Personality traits in women 4 days postpartum and their correlation with plasma levels of oxytocin and prolactin. *Journal of Psychosomatic Obstetrics and Gynaecology, 11,* 261–273.

Van Goozen, S., Weigant, V., Endert, E., Helmond, F., & Van de Poll, N. (1997). Psychoendocrinological assessment of the menstrual cycle: The relationship between hormones, sexuality, and mood. *Archives of Sexual Behavior, 26,* 359–382.

Wedekind, C., Seebeck, T., Bettens, F., & Paepke, A. J. (1995). MHC-dependent mate preferences in humans. *Proceedings of the Royal Society of London, B, 260,* 245–249.

White, L., & Booth, A. (1985). The quality and stability of remarriages: The role of stepchildren. *American Sociological Review, 50,* 689–698.

Widstrom, A., Wahlbert, V., Matthiesen, A., Eneroth, P., Unvas-Moberg, K., Werner, S., & Winberg, J. (1990). Short-term effects of early sucking on maternal behavior and breast-feeding performance. *Early Human Development, 21,* 153–163.

Wilson, E. O. (1998). *Consilience: The unity of knowledge.* New York: Knopf.

Winch, R. F., Ktsanes, T., & Ktsanes, V. (1954). The theory of complementary needs in mate-selection. *American Sociological Review, 19,* 241–249.

Wolf, A. (1995). *Sexual attraction and childhood association.* Stanford, CA: Stanford University Press.

Yamazaki, K., Beauchamp, G. K., Kupniewski, D., Bard, J., Thomas, L., & Boyse, E. A. (1988). Familial imprinting determines H-2 selective mating preferences. *Science, 240,* 1331–1332.

Epilogue

In the Introduction to this text we asked you to consider some fundamental questions about how individuals and families functioned—"Why do families do that?" and "Why do they behave that way?" In this book we have explored nine different ways in which family scholars have explained family functioning. Each theory provides a unique way to focus on family functioning and provides different answers to why families behave the way they do.

Figure 1 provides a basic comparison between the nine family theories that have been covered in this text. We have covered how families may be seen from both a broad, "macro" perspective as social institutions that function to maintain society and from an individual level to the specific "micro" perspective of individual analysis within the family system.

The purpose of social science is not to suggest there is only one truth about individuals and families but rather to discover the many layers of their complex lives. Thus, depending on the question, the situation, and the outcome needed, the theoretical perspective that is most useful will vary. In addition, knowing many theories gives us a multitude of options to choose from in order to assess, analyze, and understand a family better. Theories evolve over time, and these theories will continue to change and develop as research continues to challenge our understanding about families, increasing our knowledge of family issues, confronting our assumptions about how we define families, and expanding our perceptions of the complexities of family life.

The importance of knowing multiple theories can be seen in this example. Let's say that you are investigating the factors individuals consider when choosing an intimate partner, with a specific focus on the importance of social practice. As a result, structural functionalism or biosocial theory provides a sufficient framework for your research questions. However, if you want to look at how particular couples make their decisions about becoming life partners, or how individuals choose one person over another, then you can probably get a better understanding by using the theory of social exchange. Conflict theory or even feminism would also help you decide why individuals choose the person they do. Each theory would provide you with different ways to focus your questions, which would in turn reshape your answers to those questions.

Let's say that instead you want to know not just why people pick the partners they do but why they choose them at that particular time. In other words, if you had met this same person two years ago, would you still have fallen in love? The previously mentioned theories will not be as useful in answering this new question. Instead, you might turn to developmental, symbolic interaction, or even family systems theory to guide your research. Finally, you now decide that the most interesting questions have to do with the disagreements or tensions in relationships once they form. This results in turning to conflict, feminist, or stress theory to best answer your new questions.

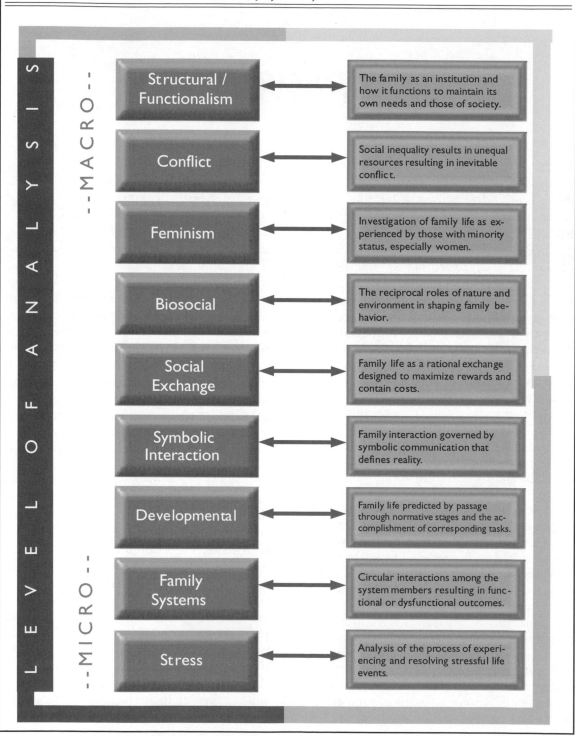

Epilogue Figure 1
Summary of Family Theories

Knowing which theory to use is often a matter of preference, can be dictated by the situation, and sometimes is simply based on guessing. Theories speak to us because they resonate with what we believe to be important. Because of this, you may have found, as you read these chapters, that you preferred some theories over others. That is a fairly typical experience. If you continue to work in this field, you will find that your colleagues will reflect theoretical orientations, either by training or by preference, in their work. The important thing is to remember that each theory has its usefulness. You may find, for example, that one theory explains 85 percent of the families that you work with. However, there will inevitably be situations when that one theory will not explain a family as well as another theory might, and when you are faced with that family, in your office or in your life, it is always useful to have other theories in your repertoire.

Because a theory can change the way we view and understand the world—and families—theories can also help us know how to intervene. When we approach families in a systematic way, we can be certain that we have considered all possible avenues of understanding families and therefore the most effective ways of helping families achieve their best selves.

Using the Theories

You have had the chance, in this book thus far, to consider each theory in its own historical context. It is important to practice using the theories in a more comprehensive way, to determine how each theory provides a focus for family issues. These theoretical lenses will give you a different perspective about a family's strengths, weaknesses, struggles, issues, challenges, and potentials.

Below is a complex case study of a three-generation family. Imagine that you are a helping professional, perhaps a family life educator or counselor, assigned to work with the family described below. Try to understand their situation and dynamics using each of the theoretical frameworks explained in this text.

Using each theory in the book, outline the major issues or crises facing the family from that perspective. Consider the strengths and weaknesses from that perspective. Find examples of basic assumptions and examples from the case study. What roles do the family members play, if any? How do they enact their roles? How are the societal or individual issues played out in the family?

After having considered each theory separately, consider them as a group. Which theories seem to be most useful to you in understanding the Maldonado family? Why did you prefer one over another? What is it about their perspective that you find more reasonable or useful for the kind of work that you would eventually like to do with families? Thus, use this application experience to illustrate not just the context of the theories but their applicability to your future career.

The Maldonado Family

Juan and Maria Maldonado have been married for fifteen years. They were both born in Mexico and immigrated to the United Stated five years ago. Life was difficult for them in Mexico. Juan worked very long, labor-intensive days in the factory for little pay, which was barely enough to support his four children and wife. Maria worked as a nurse in the local village hospital. Despite all their hard work, they were still poor and did not see much hope for their future. Because they could not see a way out of their economic situation, they decided to move to the United States in hopes of finding a better life for themselves and, in particular, for their children. Maria's aunt, who was already living in the United States, offered to help Juan find a job in there. With much sadness in leaving their extended family behind, but hopeful for the future, the Maldonados moved their family to the United States.

Since they have come to the United States, things have improved a little. Their children have learned English very well, although Juan and Maria still struggle with the language, which makes them depend a great deal on Marco, their eldest, for translation. Because Juan found a good job at a factory, their economic lives have improved. Maria cannot work as a nurse because she cannot speak English. As a result, she cleans houses to make some extra money. Granted, they will probably never be able to buy Nikes and fancy cars, but the children have clothes, shoes, medical care, and a dental plan.

Once Juan and Maria settled in the United States, both of their mothers came to live with them. The townhouse they rent is cramped with eight people living in it, but the two youngest children don't mind sleeping on the floor, and life is easier on Maria now that the older women are there, since they do all the cooking and cleaning for the family. She is free to do more housecleaning and to take English classes at the community college. Juan and Maria felt that bringing the grandparents to live with them was important. They missed the closeness of the family in Mexico, and they wanted their children to know their grandparents. They felt very sad that both of their fathers had died since they had left Mexico and they could not afford to go to their funerals. Having their mothers nearby meant they could also ensure that they had the best child care. And Maria's mother could now be nearer to her own sister, who had been so instrumental in getting the Maldonado family to move to the United States in the first place.

Despite an improved living situation, the Maldonado family still has many problems. Both Juan and Maria worry about what will happen if Juan loses his job. They know that their inability to speak English puts them both at risk with employment. Maria really wants a job at a hospital, but it costs money to take the special "English for Nurses" classes required to work at the hospital. Besides, the classes are taught at night, when she needs to be at home with the boys helping them with their homework. Marco, who is now 14, and his brother, Phillip, 12, are very little help around the house and seem to be getting into trouble more and

more in the neighborhood. They used to come straight home from school, but now they hang out with friends Maria doesn' t know and seem to defy her authority. Juan, who is working the night shift, is either sleeping or at work and sees his sons only on the weekends. Katrina, who is 10, is a very quiet girl and is very pleasing to everyone. She quietly does her homework, and stays with her grandmothers when Maria must go out. Everyone thinks Katrina is a wonderful little girl, but secretly Maria worries that perhaps Katrina is a little too withdrawn.

Recently, Juan and Maria were called in for a parent-teacher conference to discuss Rosina, their 8-year-old daughter. They had to take Marco to be their translator. The school offered to provide one, but they felt more secure with Marco. But they were embarrassed by Marco's attitude when they got to the school, because he was rude to the teacher instead of being respectful. He said it was because the teacher "talked bad" about Rosina. According to her teacher, Rosina's grades, which have never been great, were getting even worse. They found out that Rosina had also been talking a lot in class and was frequently disruptive. They also discovered that other children in class teased her because of her clothes and her accent. When this happened, she yelled at them and once even attempted to hit another child, which is ultimately what prompted this conference. The teacher suggested that perhaps Rosina needed to see the school counselor for some help. That apparently is what made Marco angry, causing him to be rude to the teacher, since he believed that Rosina was provoked and therefore did not need any help from a school counselor. The teacher suggested that perhaps Marco needed some help as well. Juan and Maria went home from the conference very upset and didn't really know what to think.

In addition, Juan and Maria have been fighting more than usual since their parents came to live with them. When Juan and Maria first invited their mothers to live with them, they imagined the extended family in only positive ways—the larger family festivities, the holidays with grandmothers present, the traditional foods being taught to their daughters, the sense of honor to women that the older women would instill in their sons. Both Maria and Juan know that their mothers are happy to be with them, but they also know that they miss Mexico. Although Maria appreciates their help around the house, she still feels overwhelmed with having to take care of four children while also working and going to school. She has to do all of this while under the watchful eyes of her elders and never seems to do anything up to their level of standards. She feels that they do not see the value of the sacrifices that she and Juan make for the sake of their children. For example, Juan works the night shift so he can earn more money. In fact, he wishes that Maria didn't have to work at all. He feels that he should earn enough money to care for her and the family. But his mother says that he should work while his children are in school, like his father did, so he can be *un papa verdadero*—a real father—to them in the evenings and set *un buen ejemplo*—a good example—to them. Maria and Juan never seem to have any time alone together.

Trying to meet the expectations of their parents while establishing new goals for their own family is difficult for Juan and Maria. Even though they see each other only between shifts or on weekends, those times are often spent arguing about the children or which bills to pay this month and which things can wait a little longer. Occasionally Maria thinks about the times in Mexico when she was poorer but had more family to support her, had more social status in the village, and fought less with Juan. She wants her children to have every opportunity, but she also wants her family to be happy. Perhaps they should consider moving back to Mexico and give it another try there? ✦

Author Index

Subject Index